Falangist and National Catholic Women in the Spanish Civil War

Although there is an established historiography on women's roles during the Spanish Civil War (1936–1939), little has been written on Nationalist women in the Republican-held zones. Such women were the anti-Republican resisters of the first hour in the capital, but they have been largely overlooked in the historical record. During the bitter civil conflict, a sector of dissidents helped to create a subversive and clandestine national Catholic space in the heart of Republican Madrid. By examining the vital and invisible role played by women within Madrid's 'fifth column' this monograph offers a new contribution to the gender historiography of the Spanish Civil War and re-evaluates the significance of women in the Nationalist war effort. It explores how and why a sector of Falangist and Catholic women decided to mobilise against the legally constituted Popular Front government in support of an undemocratic military coup. While women's subversive activities often involved the transgression of traditional gender norms, their social and political agency arose within the conditions and precepts of Catholicism and was conceptualised and imagined within new national Catholic discourses of 'holy Crusade.'

Angela Flynn is a historian at Oxford University, UK, who completed a DPhil under the supervision of Dame Frances Lannon. She co-teaches a third-year undergraduate Special Subject on "France from the Popular Front to the Liberation, 1936–1939" and co-convenes an inter-disciplinary seminar series sponsored by TORCH Oxford/Stanford University in Oxford entitled "Conversations on Identity, Ethnicity and Nationhood."

Routledge/Cañada Blanch Studies on Contemporary Spain

Edited by Paul Preston and Sebastian Balfour, Cañada Blanch Centre for Contemporary Spanish Studies, London School of Economics, UK

Mass Killings and Violence in Spain, 1936–1952
Grappling with the Past
Edited by Peter Anderson and Miguel Ángel del Arco Blanco

Claiming the City and Contesting the State
Squatting, Community Formation and Democratization in Spain (1955–1986)
Inbal Ofer

Guns, Culture and Moors
Racial Perceptions, Cultural Impact and the Moroccan Participation in the Spanish Civil War (1936–1939)
Ali Al-Tuma

Revolution and the State
Anarchism in the Spanish Civil War, 1936–1939
Danny Evans

Medicine and Conflict
The Spanish Civil War and its Traumatic Legacy
Sebastian Browne

Nineteenth Century Spain
A New History
Mark Lawrence

Also published in association with the Cañada Blanch Centre:

Spain and the Great Powers in the Twentieth Century
Edited by Sebastian Balfour and Paul Preston

The Politics of Contemporary Spain
Edited by Sebastian Balfour

Falangist and National Catholic Women in the Spanish Civil War (1936–1939)

Angela Flynn

Routledge
Taylor & Francis Group
LONDON AND NEW YORK

First published 2020 by Routledge

2 Park Square, Milton Park, Abingdon, Oxon OX14 4RN
605 Third Avenue, New York, NY 10017

Routledge is an imprint of the Taylor & Francis Group, an informa business

First issued in paperback 2021

Publisher's Note

The publisher has gone to great lengths to ensure the quality of this reprint but points out that some imperfections in the original copies may be apparent.

British Library Cataloguing-in-Publication Data
A catalogue record for this book is available from the British Library

Library of Congress Cataloging-in-Publication Data
A catalog record has been requested for this book

ISBN: 978-0-367-14674-0 (hbk)
ISBN: 978-1-03-217331-3 (pbk)
DOI: 10.4324/9780429053030

Typeset in Garamond
by Deanta Global Publishing Services, Chennai, India

Contents

Acknowledgements

I am greatly indebted to my supervisor Dame Frances Lannon without whose wisdom and patience this work would never have been completed. I also thank the members of the Oxford History and Modern Languages Faculty for their unfailing kindness and support, in particular, Robert Gildea, Martin Conway, Tom Buchanan, Christine Jackson and Ann Jefferson. I am also greatly indebted to Professors Paul Preston, Julius Ruiz and Mary Vincent for their great encouragement and immensely helpful insights and suggestions at various draft stages. I also thank Professors José Núñez Seixas and Aurora Morcillo for their kind encouragement. Also, Elisabeth Bolorinos Allard, Kathryne Crossley, Carlos Píris, Raúl Moreno Almendral and Suan Sheridan Breakwell .

I also thank Alex Vickers, Andrea Hopkins and Isabelle Moriceau at the History Faculty and Freyja Madsen and Felicity Reeves at New College. Many thanks also to the staff at New College and Lady Margaret Hall. A huge thanks to the librarians at the Portal de Archivos Españoles (PARES), and to Ana Huete Caballo and Ángeles Sánchez at the Universidad Pontificia de Salamanca (UPSA) for their warm welcome and unfailing patience. Also, Asunción Miralles de Imperial y Pasqual de Póbil and Oscar Torre at the Real Academia de la Historia (Madrid) (RAH) and the librarians at the Archivo General Militar de Ávila (AGMA). A huge thanks also to Jayanthi Chander at Deanta Global for her invaluable assistance.

Finally, the most sincere and heartfelt thanks to my husband, children, family and friends for all their loving support and kindness without which this work could never have been completed.

Abbreviations

AP Acción Popular (Popular Action). A right-wing Catholic and Alfonsine monarchist party which was called Acción Nacional (National Action) until 1932.

AR Acción Republicana (Republican Action). Manuel Azaña's progressive Republican party.

CEDA Confederación Española de Derechas Autónomas (Spanish Confederation of Autonomous Right-Wing Parties). A coalition of right-wing Catholic and monarchist groups founded in 1933 by José María Gil Robles.

CNT Confederación Nacional del Trabajo. The anarcho-syndicalist trade union founded in 1910.

CT Communión Traditionalista (Traditionalist Communion). A Catholic traditionalist and legitimist party that sought to establish a separate line of the Bourbon dynasty on the Spanish throne. This 'Carlist' line descended from Don Carlos Count of Molina (1788–1855). The party was formed during the early 1930s following the fusion of three Traditionalist groups (*Jaimista*, *Mellista* and *Integrista*).

CPIP Comité Provincial de Investigación Publica (Provincial Public Investigation Committee). A security organisation formed in October 1936 under the aegis of the DGS and led by the former IR politician Manuel Muñoz.

DEDIDE Departamento Especial de Información del Estado (Special Department of Public Information).

DGS Dirección General de Seguridad (General Directorate of Security). The Republican police force.

FAI	Federación Anarquista Ibérica (The Iberian Anarchist Federation). An anarchist group created in 1927 as a break-away from the CNT.
FE	Falange Española (The Spanish Falange Party). A fascist party formed by José Primo de Rivera in 1933.
FET Y DE LAS JONS	Falange Española Tradicionalista y de las Jons (The Traditionalist Falange and Jonsist Party). Also known as the "National Movement." Created after the 'Unification' of the rebel factions in April 1937.
FNTT	Federación Nacional de Trabajadores de la Tierra (The National Federation of Landworkers). The agricultural labourer's section of the UGT.
FUE	Federación Universitaria Escolar (University Student Federation). A pro-Republican university student union established during the Primo de Rivera era.
IR	Izquierda Republicana (Left Republicans). A coalition of AR, the Left of the PRRS, Santiago Casares Quiroga's party and other small Republican parties.
JAP	Juventudes de Acción Popular (Popular Action Youth). The youth section of the AP and CEDA.
JDM	Junta de Defensa de Madrid (Madrid's Defense Committee). An emergency military defence committee established on 6 November 1936 and led by General Miaja following the departure of the Largo Caballero government to Valencia. The head of security was the Communist Santiago Carillo.
JONS	Juntas de Ofensiva Nacional-Sindicalista (National Syndicalist Offense Juntas).
JSU	Juventudes Socialistas Unificadas (United Socialist Youth group). Created in Spring 1936 through the fusion of the Communist and Socialist youth groups and controlled by the Communists.
MVR	Milicias de Vigilancia de la Retaguardia (Rearguard Security Militias).
NIA	Non-Intervention Agreement, an international agreement ratified by twenty-seven nation

	states in September 1936 with the aim of ensuring the isolation and arms blockade of the Spanish Civil War.
NKVD	Narodnyi Komisssariat Vnutrennikh Del (People's Commissariat for Internal Affairs). The Soviet secret police and intelligence service led by Alexander Orlov in Madrid.
PCE	Partido Comunista de España (Spanish Communist Party) which arose from the merger of two small Spanish Communist parties in November 1921.
PNV	Partido Nacionalista Vasco (Basque Nationalist Party). The leading Nationalist Basque party founded by Sabino Arana in 1895.
PRRS	Partido Republicano Radical Socialista (Radical Socialist Republican Party). The Jacobin and anticlerical party which formed part of the governmental coalitions of 1931–3. Divided in 1933, the left of this party joined Manuel Azaña to form IR and the right joined Diego Martínez Barrios to set up UR.
PSOE	Partido Socialista Obrero Español (Spanish Socialist Worker's Party) founded in 1879.
RE	Renovación Española (The Spanish Renewal Party). An Alfonsine monarchist party led by José Calvo Sotelo after 1934.
SEU	Sindicato Español Universitario (Spanish University Syndicate). The Falangist student union formed in November 1933 by Manuel Valdés Larrañaga, David Jato and others. Valdés became the leader of the Clandestine Falange in 1937.
SIFNE	Servicios de Información del Frente Noreste. Bertrán i Musitu's intelligence organisation which was based in France and created with funding from Juan March and Francesc Cambó.
SIM NACIONAL	Servicio de investigación Militar (Nationalist Military Intelligence Service). Established in July 1937 in co-operation with Axis (German and Italian) intelligence services. It merged with other rebel intelligence services such as the SIFNE into a centralised intelligence service the SIPM in November 1937.

SIM REPUBLICANA (MADRID)	Servicio de Investigación Militar (Republican Military Intelligence Service). Created in August 1937 and led by Ángel Pedrero, former second-in-command of the García Atadell Brigade.
SIPM	Servicios de Información Política y Militar (Political and Military Information Services). A centralised Nationalist intelligence service formed in November 1937 through the merger of the intelligence services of the military, Traditionalist and Falangist rebel factions.
TYRE	Tradicionalistas y Renovación Española (Traditionalist Communion and Spanish Renewal Party). A fusion of members of the CT and RE.
UGT	Unión General de Trabajadores (The United General Workers Union). The main socialist trade union created in 1889.
UME	Union Militar Española (Spanish Military Union). An anti-Republican military association that included former members of the UP.
UP	Unión Patriótica (Patriotic Union). The political movement that supported the dictatorship of General Primo de Rivera in 1923.
UR	Unión Republicana (Republican Union). A political party founded in September 1934 by former members of Radical Party and the PRRS. The leader was Diego Martínez Barrios.[1]

Note

1 Romero Salvadó, Francisco (2005) *The Spanish Civil War, Origins, Course and Outcomes* (Hampshire: Palgrave) and Romero Salvadó (2013) *Historical Dictionary of the Spanish Civil War* (Plymouth: Scarecrow).

Introduction

A "fifth column" in Madrid

The devastating Spanish Civil War (1936–9) represents a defining moment of catastrophic rupture in contemporary Spanish history that shaped the nation's social and political inheritance for decades to come.[1] The bitter conflict also facilitated a temporary shift in perceptions of gender and women's prescribed social roles.[2] After the failed mainland coup of 18 July 1936 around 1,000 women rallied to the Republican cause and joined the front-lines as militia women; thousands more performed vital auxiliary roles in the rear-guard.[3] Similarly in the rebel-held zones women were encouraged to transcend the domestic sphere in order to 'join the struggle to save the Fatherland.'[4] The experience of total war meant that women were afforded new possibilities for agency.[5]

This work explores how and why a significant sector of formerly law-abiding Roman Catholic women were mobilised to commit acts of treason in support of an undemocratic military coup against the legally constituted Popular Front government in the Republican-held zones. While these women were just as politically committed as men, they remain invisible in the record. This is primarily because a false distinction has been drawn between 'authentic' fifth-column activities (predominantly male) and the merely supportive and auxiliary activities where women were crucial and in the majority.[6] This work demonstrates that the fifth-column resistance of the first hour was performed by women.[7] It arose in part as a survivalist response to the violent extra-judicial repression that occurred during the first five months of the conflict,[8] but also because an underground Sección Femenina network was organised before the war (see Chapter 1). This explains how a small group of Falangist and Catholic women were the first to organise effective liaison, welfare-aid, safe-housing and embassy escape-lines for fugitives and members of the religious community from the outset of the hostilities.[9] Although Madrid's female fifth-columnists were the earliest and, arguably, the most effective resisters, they have been largely ignored in the historical record. This is because women's resistance involved auxiliary and welfare-aid roles that were perceived to form an integral part of women's routine domestic duties, chores and social obligations.[10] Consequently, the serious risks and dangers associated with women's gender-specific resistance have been routinely underestimated and overlooked.[11] In circumstances of violent conflict and severe social dislocation during the first months of the war, the ordinary and everyday became fraught with danger and the 'feminine' domestic space was politicised and transformed into a clandestine and subversive political space. These women were able to construct new political identities during the bitter civil conflict, and this work examines the real and symbolic meanings ascribed to their subversive practices and motivations for resistance.

Origins of the "fifth column"

Soon after the coup, "the term 'fifth columnist' came to denote any rebel supporter, whether real or potential, active or imprisoned."[12] It is generally believed that General Emilio Mola first coined this expression during an international press conference on the eve of the rebel offensive against Madrid in early October 1936.[13] When journalists enquired as to which of General Varela's four columns might be the first to reach the capital, Mola replied that the attack was sure to commence with a fifth column which was already in Madrid. Mola's threat formed part of a concerted campaign of psychological warfare aimed at lowering civilian morale prior to the rebel offensive, despite the fact that in October 1936 there was nothing like an organised fifth column in the capital.[14] More recently, it has been suggested that the rumours of a dangerous 'enemy within' were instigated by undercover Russian agents in Spain in a bid to rally popular resistance prior to the rebel assault on Madrid in autumn 1936.[15] The communist leader Dolores Ibárruri was the first to refer to a 'fifth column' in the Republican press in order to generate fear and rally resistance.[16] The term was rapidly popularised on the international stage by Ernest Hemingway and a small group of foreign correspondents who thronged to the capital during the siege of Madrid.[17] News of the real and imagined exploits of the fifth column was circulated in the popular press and radio, generating fear among Republicans and stimulating violent forms of extra-judicial and legal repression (see Part 2).

The fifth column rumours, when combined with press reports of the bloody repression which was being perpetrated in the rebel-held zones, generated a powerful collective paranoia in the capital.[18] This mass obsession with spies and hidden enemies was shared by Madrid's security leaders.[19] The perceived need to 'cleanse the enemy within' to ensure the survival of the Republic fanned the flames of a violent extra-judicial repression.[20] On 28 October 1936 Prime Minister Largo Caballero informed Willie Forrest, the London *Daily Express* correspondent, that the lives of around 100,000 anti-Republicans might be jeopardised during the Battle for Madrid.[21] These figures indicate the extent of the perceived threat of a terrifying 'other' in the popular imaginary at this time.[22] Around 11,000 individuals were obliged to seek diplomatic asylum within Madrid's foreign embassies and consulates during the first six months of the war.[23] Hundreds more went into hiding in safe-houses and boarding-houses in order to avoid the extra-judicial reprisals or military conscription.[24]

This work is divided into two parts. Part 1 explores the role of women within a series of organised political groups and networks which fell under the banner of the Clandestine Falange. These engaged in co-ordinated saboteur, intelligence gathering and espionage practices. They also cached arms and, under the directions of the Nationalist Intelligence and Military Police Services (SIPM), devised plans for a take-over of key Republican nerve-centres during a Francoist occupation of the capital. However, the Clandestine Falange did not have the expertise, organisational skills, funding or indeed the backing from Franco to mount any significant armed civilian resistance or large-scale sabotage in the capital. Part 2 examines forms of 'autonomous,' uncoordinated and spontaneous civilian resistance involving small groups and individuals. Both types of resistance imbricated survivalist practices, particularly the autonomous resistance. In the eyes of the Republican government all fifth-column activity represented a significant threat to public security and the integrity of the war effort, and new legislation was implemented in order to combat the 'enemy within' via new legal and judicial channels as discussed below.

The war waged in the rear-guard by the Republic's hidden enemies (*emboscados*) was in the main a psychological war aimed at lowering civilian morale and disrupting the war effort.[25] The fifth column engaged in espionage and intelligence-gathering, defeatist and saboteur practices including illegal hoarding (*acaparamiento*), rationing infractions, disseminating defeatist news and spreading false rumours (*bulas*) via word of mouth or via crudely printed tracts that denounced the Republican war effort and the dire material conditions. Defeatist information was obtained from the broadcasts of censored Nationalist radio stations such as Radio Seville and Radio Burgos. The radio constituted a powerful weapon in the resistance arsenal, not least because hidden transistors regularly delivered encoded intelligence across the lines to the Nationalist SIPM.[26] In contrast to the resistance movements in German-occupied Europe, there were no notable clandestine newspapers, and this may attest to the closed and close-knit nature of Madrid's dissident community. There was little need to preach to the converted. It was only in the early weeks when it was believed that the Nationalists would quickly occupy the capital, and then again during the final months, when the Republican cause seemed lost and a generalised war-weariness took hold of the rear-guard, that there was any noticeable increase in the circulation of clandestine pamphlets denouncing the semi-starvation conditions in the rear-guard and encouraging popular demonstrations to end to the conflict.

Women chose to join the fifth column pursuant to their politico-religious convictions, class interests and intimate familial obligations and loyalties. Many mobilised in response to the violent extra-judicial repression that took place in Madrid's rear-guard at the start of the war. As indicated, women's rescue and aid initiatives constituted the earliest, most extensive and effective form of resistance in the capital. Anti-Republican women saved hundreds of lives, and their efforts were crucial to the survival of Clandestine Madrid. In the absence of fathers and husbands, women became heads of household charged with the material and moral well-being of the family. Meanwhile, during the early months, anti-Republican men were literally and symbolically excluded from the public space as fugitives, prisoners, embassy asylees and draft-dodgers. Formerly law-abiding citizens came to operate within a new and dangerous counter-culture that helped to establish a flourishing black-market in false documentation and supplies. Women used networks of intimacy and influence within the Republican regime in order to establish a web of mutual-aid and assistance that frequently cut across ideological divides.[27] Clandestine networks of solidarity were created in order to raise funds for food, clothing, medicine and false documentation in aid of political prisoners, fugitives and their families. In collaboration with a network of underground priests, nuns and devout Catholics, Auxilio Azul helped to ensure the spiritual and material survival of Madrid's beleaguered anti-Republican community. A new collective Catholic resistance identity was forged within the crucible of a bloody and violent civil conflict.

The fifth column served an important cultural and symbolic function within a secret anti-Republican community known as 'Clandestine Madrid.' It was composed of a minority of active fifth-columnist spies and saboteurs, a wider community of defeatists (*derrotistas*) and disaffected persons (*desafectos*), alongside a base of passive *attentistes* who hoped for a swift rebel occupation.[28] The fifth column also fostered solidarity among a wider dissident community and facilitated 'safe spaces' within which to imagine a national Catholic nationhood.[29] This Catholic, patriotic and authoritarian imaginary had much earlier origins, but the circumstances of war lent it a new relevance and urgency.[30] The fifth column also provided social and military intelligence to the Nationalist General Staff in Burgos. These activities constituted forms of accusatory practice that assisted in the consolidation of the Francoist regime 'from below' both during and after the war.[31] However, "selective and intimate violence" is a feature of irregular warfare and was also used by the Republican authorities in their efforts to ensure the survival of the Republic (see Part 2).[32]

Accurate figures in relation to the periodisation and size of the fifth column groups and networks in the capital and in other Republican-held towns and cities are not available on account of a lack of written records.[33] However, the general consensus is that an organised fifth column arose in December 1936, in the wake of earlier organisations like Auxilio Azul, in response to repression in the rear-guard.[34] Around twenty Falangist groups were loosely coordinated within a single network over the course of 1937 by the leader of the 'Clandestine Falange' Manuel Valdés Larrañaga at the orders of Lt. Colonel Bonel Huici whose Nationalist Intelligence section was stationed near the Madrid front-lines at Torre de Esteban Hambrán (Toledo).[35] The capital's close proximity to the front-lines provided ample opportunities for early contact with the rebel intelligence services stationed along the fronts. A more recent investigation has focussed on the existence of a series of Falangist and Traditionalist Communion (Traditionalist) cells prior to December 1936.[36] The operations of Auxilio Azul in early August 1936 also constituted forms of organised political resistance. After the outlawing of the Falange Party on 14 March 1936, the party went underground and Falangist women developed a series of underground liaison and relief networks. Despite the imprisonment of the party's most senior male cadres, the hierarchy of the Sección Femenina was left relatively intact prior to the coup.

By the end of the conflict Madrid harboured the largest and most well-organised fifth column in Republican-held Spain. "It had an estimated 3,000 active members and around 30,000 collaborators including the 6,000 women of Auxilio Azul."[37] Barcelona had some 2,000 active members and another 20,000 collaborators. Valencia had only 500 activists and 5,000 collaborators.[38] Estimates for Murcia, Cartagena, Bilbao, Santander and other Republican-held cities are not known, but it is believed that resistance in these cities was more limited. It is impossible to accurately periodise or assess the true size and extent of the resistance because no records were kept for obvious reasons of confidentiality and anonymity.[39] However, the ranks of the fifth-column were modestly inflated during the final months by those who may have decided to join from motives of personal expediency or to avoid the post-war reprisals.[40] Immediately after the war, those who had 'fought for Franco,' whether on the front-lines or in the rear-guard as fifth columnists, were afforded important symbolic and material rewards including war pensions and public employment pursuant to their 'ex-combatant' status.[41] However, despite the initial prestige and recognition afforded to members of the fifth column, membership came to possess shameful connotations and associations, especially during the Transition and Post-Transition periods.[42] The intelligence sent to Burgos by fifth columnists was used for the purposes of repression both during and after the war and was significant in the construction of Francoism from below.[43] Consequently, former participants were reluctant to discuss their war-time activities, even to close family members years after the events.[44] The social stigma surrounding denunciation "drives even people who have denounced for 'legitimate' political and ideological reasons to keep it concealed."[45]

Conceptualisation and interpretative frames

The work is situated within a growing historiography on European women's lives, identities and representations and, more specifically, within a strand of Spanish gender history relating to Catholic and authoritarian right-wing women's identity and agency.[46] Although there is a growing scholarship on Nationalist women during the war, there remains a significant historiographical gap in relation to the role played by anti-Republican women in the

Republican-held zones.[47] The importance of these women's contribution to the Nationalist war effort has been underestimated and a re-evaluation is overdue.[48] This work is not conceived as a commemorative narrative of women's fifth-column resistance actions; rather it represents a contribution to the most recent Spanish gender historiography. While the primary aim is to offer a balanced and scholarly historical account, the work may also assist in the construction of a shared, nuanced and consensual collective memory space.[49] The primary and secondary sources are discussed in Appendix A.

While women were the first, most numerous and most effective fifth-columnists, their subversive actions have largely been ignored in the record.[50] This is because gender is a primary way of signifying relationships of power.[51] Consequently, women's perceived 'passive and auxiliary' resistance efforts have been routinely overlooked in mainstream histories that tend to prioritise 'active' armed political or military resistance.[52] To an extent, these women did what was expected of them in accordance with traditional gender norms and their own personal loyalties and social obligations. However, during a moment of severe social dislocation the private was politicised and domestic spaces were transformed into clandestine resistance spaces. Women also experienced a shift in gender-power in the absence of male kin.[53]

Women's auxiliary and escape-line initiatives constituted the earliest and most important forms of fifth-column 'resistance.' From a sociological perspective, the subversive practices performed by fifth-column women during the Spanish conflict were very similar to the resistance actions performed in German-occupied Europe between 1940 and 1944 by a good number of women of all ages who came from bourgeois Catholic, patriotic and military backgrounds.[54] However, the ideological mainsprings and conditions of enactment of the fifth-column resistance were different from those of the subsequent anti-fascist resistance in Europe during World War II. Fratricidal civil wars have their own dynamic and logic of intimate violence when compared with inter-state conflicts and situations of foreign occupation.[55] "A key difference between most of the European resistance groups and the fifth column was that the latter was in conflict with compatriots and neighbours rather than with a hated foreign enemy occupier."[56] However, in sociological terms, the intelligence gathering, saboteur and defeatist practices deployed by civilian groups in favour of the rebel insurgents in the capital and in other Republican-held cities may be classified as forms of 'civilian resistance.'[57] This category of resistance has been theorised in social histories of German-occupied Europe in World War II by German, Italian, English and French historians.[58] Most notably, German *Alltagsgeschichte* (everyday-life) historians conceptualised civilian resistance to the Nazi regime in its widest possible sense within two different resistance strands: *widerstand* to describe organised political resistance movements and networks and *resistenz* denoting small, routine dissident and subversive practices performed by ordinary individuals and groups that serve to weaken and destabilise authority from below.[59]

Consequently, civilian resistance was not confined to "fundamental, principled, and total resistance…Rather it embraced all forms of partial and limited rejection, whatever the motives…Instead of dealing in images of black and white, resistance was portrayed in shades of grey."[60] Frequently compliance and accommodation was practiced alongside dissident actions or symbolic resistance gestures. Social anthropologists have also categorised types of invisible, subaltern 'everyday resistance' that stop short of outright collective defiance and constitute the ordinary weapons of powerless groups including foot-dragging, dissimulation, desertion and sabotage.[61] More recently, these concepts have been appropriated by Spanish historians who draw continuities between resistance in Europe during World War II and the resistance against the Francoist regime.[62] These frames are useful because they envisage resistance within the context of ordinary daily routines and activities and include social groups such as women which are usually excluded from mainstream narratives of armed military and organised political resistance practices.[63] Part 1 examines fifth-column *widerstand* groups co-ordinated around the Clandestine Falange, and Part 2 examines *resistenz* practices among 'autonomous' groups and individuals.

The work also offers new perspectives on national Catholic and Falangist women's material and symbolic roles in the Francoist war effort with reference to post-structural theories on gender and habitus.[64] Pierre Bourdieu's sociological theories on the reproduction of cultural and social power retain their currency in the social sciences and are framed within key concepts of 'capital' and 'habitus' and 'field.'[65] The field of power is

> the space of relations between different kinds of capital (cultural, religious, economic, social and symbolic) or, more precisely, between agents who possess different kinds of capital and who struggle to occupy dominant positions within a specific field(s).[66]

Habitus is consciously and unconsciously instilled into members of a social group, class, gender or religion from birth through culturally specific and repeated group practices, values and dispositions which mould individual subjectivities and inform their conscious and unconscious tastes, ideals, values and beliefs. The 'embodied subject' is experienced as 'a social body' made up of meanings which are inculcated through repeated and specific gestures, postures, physical bearing, speech and language.[67] 'Habitus' has been re-framed within embodiment theories that examine the material and social dimensions of sexual identity as well as the symbolic and discursive construction of gender norms.[68] It is not a determining principle but rather a generative structure which permits the emergence of a concept of agency understood through the idea of regulated liberties.[69] Habitus is a 'structuring structure' that enables the individual to understand and negotiate the spoken and unspoken game-rules, expectations and proscriptions of a particular social group or field.[70] It operates within specific and overlapping fields of power and the discourses and structures that create the conditions of its enactment.[71] Habitus provides powerful explanatory framework for conceptualising Catholic and Falangist women's agency as 'docile agency.'[72]

While the civil war represented a period of catastrophic discontinuity and rupture, Catholic women imagined the conflict within pre-established Catholic religious and apocalyptic discursive frames.[73] During the 1920s the Church encouraged a new Catholic women's militancy as part of its 'Crusade to re-Christianize Spain.'[74] This new female political engagement has been conceptualised as a form of non-transgressive and socially acceptable 'Catholic feminism,' where religious and class interests took precedence over revindications for gender equality and conservative women actively supported the patriarchal 'dominant culture.'[75] After the enfranchisement of Spanish women in 1931, the authoritarian and anti-liberal Right developed new political discourses which encouraged the creation of a collective civic female identity that was constructed along ultra-Catholic, anti-democratic and patriotic axes. Catholic women were mobilised as bulwarks of the family and morality and as defenders of the faith. They were encouraged to participate in the public space in order to resolve the imagined problem of the 'Two Spains' and avert the perceived threat of communism.[76] Following the seismic power-shift which took place in Madrid's rear-guard after 18 July, anti-Republican women were obliged to 'play new games' within a clandestine political space. They devised strategies of survival and resistance and negotiated valuable forms of symbolic capital in order to maintain "their place and the place of others within the social space."[77] A new female Catholic resistance identity was constructed during the conflict and the pre-existing discourses of 'Catholic Crusade' were lent a new relevance and immediacy in circumstances of violent extra-judicial repression and social dislocation. This new politico-religious mobilisation was sacralised within traditional Catholic discourses of martyrdom and self-sacrifice.[78] Anti-Republican women helped to sustain imaginings of a new national Catholic nationhood and in so doing were agents of social change.[79]

Bourdieu's reflexive methodologies also require the researcher to situate themselves as an embodied historical subject.[80] The study of fascist and traditional Catholic women posed significant challenges to my own secular-liberal values, preconceptions and assumptions. It was difficult to understand why a sector of recently enfranchised women might want to risk their lives in order to mobilise behind an anti-democratic, authoritarian, patriarchal and nationalist movement that sought to 'turn back the clock,' ultimately depriving women of the hard-won civil and political citizenship rights granted under the progressive Republican regime.[81] More recently, gender historians have recognised

> a positivist bias in scholarly analyses of women's agency within authoritarian and religious traditions in the tendency to represent a cultural progression towards feminist consciousness and women's emancipation over time.[82]

Consequently, academics in the humanities and social sciences have recognised the need for "new analytical frameworks for the interpretation of modalities of agency among groups of women who eschew liberatory projects (whether feminist, leftist or liberal)."[83] This work does not seek to demonstrate Catholic women's feminism or their non-feminism or their efforts towards emancipation. It also avoids assumptions and conceptualisations of the subject as an autonomous individual.[84] Instead, anti-Republican women's agency is interpreted within the conditions determined by their culturally and historically situated Catholic and class 'habitus.'

Background and context

Madrid was Spain's most densely populated city with some 980,000 inhabitants in 1936.[85] It was the civil and administrative capital and, while it did not have a heavy industrial sector, it had a well-developed building, construction and services sector that was rocked by mass strikes and industrial unrest during the months leading up to the military coup.[86] It was one of only a few cities to witness a socialist victory in 1933 and was widely regarded as the capital of socialism in Spain.[87] After the failure of the rebels to take the city in winter 1936, Madrid became the pre-eminent and enduring symbol of Republican anti-fascist resistance 'against all odds.' Nonetheless, a significant and hidden sector of the civilian community sided with the rebels and these Republican *desafectos* (disaffected persons) suddenly found themselves trapped within a volatile and hostile 'enemy rearguard.'

The failed coup originated in Morocco on 17 July and spread to the Spanish mainland on the following day. It immediately divided Spain into two distinct warring zones. The coup was instigated by a dozen or so disaffected army generals and junior officers under the leadership of General Emilio Mola (the "Director"). The conspiracy arose soon after the Popular Front coalition victory of 16 February 1936. The insurgents (rebels) aimed to restore a hierarchical, centralist and authoritarian regime which was anti-democratic, anti-communist, Catholic and patriarchal. The rebels justified their illegal insurrection by claiming that the coup was unleashed in order to 'save the Fatherland' from regional separatism and the threat of communist revolution following the Asturian Revolt of 1934 and episodes of civil and industrial unrest after the February general elections. The prompt intervention of Germany and Italy on behalf of the rebels and then of Russia on behalf of the Republic, when combined with the policy of non-intervention of the UK and France ensured that the failed coup would evolve into a protracted, modern and mechanised 'total war.'[88]

The war arose from a complex combination of long-standing regional, structural and economic problems alongside more recent political, class-based, religious and cultural conflicts within the context of severe socio-economic crisis across the whole of Europe during the inter-war period.[89] Religion played a significant role in the social and political polarisation that occurred during the Second Republic.[90] Secularism and anticlericalism were basic components of the ideology of a majority of the Left. There was a long tradition of violent popular protest against the Catholic Church, and a pronounced anti-clerical discourse was disseminated by the popular Republican press during the first third of the twentieth century.[91] In particular, the alienated industrial workers in Madrid, Barcelona and other large cities, and the landless agricultural workers (*braceros*), believed that the interests of the Catholic Church were historically aligned with those of the propertied classes, the industrialists and the land-owners. The secularising measures implemented between 1931 and 1933 were among the most conflictive and divisive of all the Republican constitutional reforms and were greeted by a vocal opposition from a powerful Catholic constituency.[92] The measures included the separation of the Church from the state, the introduction of civil alternatives to baptism, civil marriage and divorce, the secularisation of burials, the dissolution of the Society of Jesus, the prohibition of Catholic teaching orders, the closure of Catholic schools and day-care nurseries and the banning of traditional forms of public confessional and devotional practice. The reforms were perceived by both the devout and many ordinary Catholics as a "direct assault on the rights of the Church and its members."[93] They provoked widespread protest and mobilised a mass resistance within Catholic society. Anticlerical violence flared up during the May 1931 church burnings and again during the Asturian Revolt in October 1934. However, it was only after 18 July 1936 and amid the shattering conditions of the civil war that "a full-scale and iconoclastic religious violence erupted which was among the most murderous ever seen in Europe."[94] Although the coup was not initially motivated by religion, the rebellion was promptly instrumentalised and sacralised by the Right as a religious crusade.[95] While the Catholic Church was not involved in the military conspiracy, its hierarchy immediately rallied to the rebel cause and the notion of 'Holy War' constituted the foundational myth of the post-war Franco state.[96] Of course not all Catholics were anti-Republican,[97] but many ordinary and sincere Catholics came to understand the war in culturally specific terms as a religious war: *una guerra civil de la espiritualidad.*[98]

The rebel coup instigated a partial breakdown of the mechanisms of state and administrative power in villages, towns and cities such as Madrid, Barcelona, Valencia, Málaga and Alicante which remained under the nominal control of the Second Republic. The fragmentation of power caused by the coup resulted in the government's loss of its monopoly of violence and unleashed a period of violent extra-judicial repression that lasted until January 1937.[99] The Republican government was obliged to compete for power alongside a host of local powers, socialist, communist and anarchist committees, unions and syndicates.[100] These competing political forces mistrusted the Republican authorities because in many regions the local administration and security forces had immediately sided with the rebels. The unlawful coup unleashed a violent and widespread "highly endogenous process whereby collective and individual preferences, strategies, values and identities were continuously shaped during the course of the war."[101]

The failure of the insurrection in the capital was due to indecision and inaction of rebel Generals Fanjul and Villegas and to the effective defensive action of loyal Republican assault guards and armed popular militias. The soldiers remained stationed in the garrisons following government orders of 13 July and "a great confusion ensued, the rebel liaison agents received no clear orders and lacked morale."[102] After the fall of the Montaña barracks on 20 July the coup was successfully suppressed in the capital and hundreds of insurgents were arrested and summarily tried for treason in Madrid's overflowing prisons. The Falangist and Traditionalist underground networks which were created before the war were momentarily paralysed, although a few men managed to escape across the front-lines in order to fight on the rebel side.[103] Falangist leaders such as Joaquín Romero-Marchant and David Jato went into hiding, the latter seeking the protection of a socialist cousin.[104] After the suppression of the barracks, there were isolated episodes of rebel sniper fire (*pacoteo*) but, despite the popular and governmental fears, there was no significant, armed and organised fifth-column resistance in Madrid at the start of the war. In August 1936, there was an abortive plot involving a handful of Falangists, including Fernando and Pilar Primo de Rivera, to occupy the Telefónica building and the Home Office, but no decisive action was taken and the plot was quickly dismantled.[105] This episode testifies to the existence of a series of fractured Falangist and Traditionalist cells at the outset of the hostilities which were in early contact with rebel intelligence posts on the front-lines.[106] However, during the first months of the war the fifth column lacked access to the necessary weapons and, in any event, armed resistance was deemed futile and unnecessary because a rebel occupation of the capital was anticipated within a matter of weeks.[107] Therefore, despite the existence of fifth-column activity at the start of the war, most notably that of Auxilio Azul, it was only after the failure of Franco's troops to occupy the capital in December 1936, when a protracted conflict seemed most likely, that concerted steps were taken to co-ordinate a series of armed resistance networks in the capital.[108]

Consequently, the earliest and most significant forms of fifth-column resistance in 1936 involved women's rescue and aid initiatives during a moment of violent social upheaval across the whole of Spain when the rebels were rapidly advancing towards the capital and news of the bloody extra-judicial 'cleansing' perpetrated in the rebel-held zones reached the ears of Madrid's terrified civilians.[109] The endogenous violence and social dislocation in the capital after 18 July was aggravated by severe food and fuel shortages and repeated aerial and artillery bombardments after 27 August 1936 which continued for the duration of the war. In addition, the influx of some 250,000 Republican refugees from the rebel-occupied zones placed an acute strain on infrastructure and resources.[110] Madrid's supply-lines were compromised for the duration of the war, and the near-starving capital was besieged by Franco's forces until its eventual occupation on 28 March 1939.

In circumstances of country-wide violence and administrative collapse, the capital witnessed a severe and bloody extra-judicial repression. Around twenty-five principal checas and dozens of 'health and defence' committees and squads led by socialist, anarchist and communist groups sprang into action after 18 July.[111] The victims were the religious, right-wing politicians and military personnel, aristocrats and land-owners, industrialists, journalists, academics, lawyers and those involved in the repression of October 1934. The extra-judicial repression mainly occurred between 18 July until late December 1936, and it took the form of *paseos* (illegal summary executions) and *sacas* (extra-judicial prison removals). A mass prison evacuation took place between October and December 1936 at the instigation of public order officials within the Dirección de Seguridad (DGS) and Madrid's Defence Junta (JDM). The *sacas* resulted in the execution of around 2,400 military, political and religious prisoners in wasteland areas outside Paracuellos del Jarama and Torrejón de Ardoz.[112] There were no recorded *sacas* from Madrid's women's prisons.[113] The mass extra-judicial execution of political prisoners occurred within the context of a country-wide and bloody civilian conflict when the rebels occupied positions in the Casa de Campo which was less than a kilometre away from the Model Prison. An estimated 8,815 persons were killed,[114] including some 617 women[115] (approximately 4.4% of the total victims).[116] The killings took place across the whole of Madrid but were concentrated in the Western Zone (21%), the Carretera de Andalucía (11%), the Pradera de San Isidro (8%) or near municipal burial grounds such as the Eastern Cemetery (18%).[117] Around 33% of the deaths occurred in August 1936, and the repression reached its height in the autumn of 1936.[118] December witnessed 4.4% of the total number of deaths.[119] By January 1937 the violence had almost completely subsided, and in April the government regained full control of the levers of power in the capital.[120] However, it was only in June 1937, when the battle fronts around Madrid were finally stabilised, that any semblance of 'normality' returned to the capital's rear-guard.[121]

The religious were the first and the most visible targets of the Republican extra-judicial repression in the capital and in other Republican-held cities.[122] The religious represented some 18.11% of the total deaths in Madrid.[123] Catholicism was deemed *prima facie* disloyal to the Republican regime.[124] Anticlerical violence throughout the whole Republican zone, with the exception of the Basque region, resulted in the deaths of 6,832 religious including 4,184 diocesan priests and seminarians, 13 bishops, 2,365 male religious and 296 nuns.[125] Around 90% of all anticlerical murders in the Republican-held zone occurred by 30 November 1936.[126] In the Madrid-Alcalá diocese 435 diocesan priests were killed.[127] It was believed that churches safe-housed arms and rebels. Some fifty churches were sacked and/or burned and many were re-purposed as warehouses or dance halls. These figures evidence the "determination of some political groups, especially the anarchists, to wipe out the church completely."[128] The churches remained closed and public acts of worship were outlawed for the duration of the war despite the efforts of Manuel Irujo the Basque Justice Minister to reinstate public worship in June 1937. His efforts met with little support from the Catholic hierarchy in Burgos or Rome.[129] The religious persecution caused grave and lasting damage to the Republic's international reputation.

A new Republican justice

The violence of the first weeks culminated in the events of the Model Prison on 22–23 August 1936 and the extra-judicial execution of some thirty political and military prisoners which unleashed an international outcry. The government sought to limit the political damage and to curb the violence while at the same time satisfying the popular demand for an expedited 'revolutionary justice' or 'People's justice' (*justicia del pueblo*). This resulted in the creation by emergency decree on 23 August 1936 of special emergency civil and military courts to expedite crimes of rebellion, sedition and crimes committed against the security of the state.[130] These tribunals were created to identify and suppress enemies and put an end to the extra-judicial summary justice of the early months.[131] They were initially established in the prisons in order to expedite hundreds of cases of military rebellion, espionage and high treason, and they operated around the clock during the first months. By November 1936 around 10,000 persons including around 1,500 women were imprisoned as enemies of the state by the Republican authorities in Madrid.[132] The sudden and dramatic increase in the prison community meant that ordinary prison institutions were overflowing and requisitioned religious buildings were re-purposed as prisons. On 26 December 1936 the Justice Minister García Oliver decreed the opening of new labour camps for political prisoners.[133]

An impressive 14,862 cases were heard in Madrid's popular tribunals over the course of the war.[134] This figure evidences the importance attributed to the perceived need to 'cleanse the enemy within.' As indicated above, 'special emergency courts' were created on 23 August, and on 25 August these popular tribunals were rolled out throughout the whole Republican zone. Due legal and evidential procedures were not observed. The emergency tribunals were presided over by three court-appointed judges (who determined the law) and fourteen jurors who determined the facts and were the appointed representatives of Madrid's Popular Front parties. The lay judges had considerable control over the legal process including the admission of evidence, sentencing and appeals.[135] A 'tribunal of civil responsibilities' was created by decree on 23 September, and 6 October 1936 that imposed economic penalties on 'enemies of the state' and a War Reparations Bank was opened.[136] Anti-Republicans were purged from the military, civil service and the professions and denied employment, pensions, ration-books and other important civil and citizenship rights. This raft of legislation was implemented in order to protect the Republic from spies and 'dangerous fascists.'[137] A new crime of 'disaffection' was created by emergency decree on 10 October 1936 which sought to repress all actions, beliefs and behaviours that, "while legal under the pre-existing legislation, constituted acts of hostility against the Republican regime."[138] This legislation was retroactive and attracted substantial fines and/or terms of imprisonment of between one and three years (later increased to five) together with the suspension of civil and political rights. Around 73% of the popular tribunal trials related to 'disaffection.'[139]

In addition to the popular tribunals, new military tribunals (*jurados de guardia*) were created to prosecute public order crimes including the dissemination of anti-Republican propaganda, illegal hoarding (*acaparamiento*), price-tampering and acts of sabotage or terrorism. On 17 October 1936 three emergency military courts (*Jurados de Guardia*) were established in Madrid. They were presided over by a professional judge and six lay jurors and created in order to 'maintain collective security.' These military courts expedited public order crimes including rebellion, espionage and the illegal possession of arms and explosives for terrorist activities.[140] New 'special military tribunals' (*tribunales especiales de guardia*) were established in November 1937 and March 1938. However, after 24 March 1938, a sharp increase in cases of treason, rebellion and espionage led to the use of the 'special military tribunals' which were created before the war but were now used in a new and more repressive capacity.[141]

Following the arrest of Barcelona's POUM leaders on charges of treason, on 22 June 1937 the Republican ministry of justice created a new emergency tribunal of 'espionage and high treason' in Valencia that operated separately from the emergency popular and military tribunals (*jurados de urgencia y de guardia*). It was presided over by three ordinary judges or magistrates and two military or naval lawyers.[142] In addition, a new crime of 'defeatism' was created to suppress the increasing instances of defeatism, disloyalty and low civilian morale. In the most serious cases, defeatism attracted sentences of life imprisonment, and in rare instances capital punishment. Addressing 'the problem of the enemy within' involved surveillance, interrogation and judicial processes that violated fundamental Republican constitutional guarantees including the equality of all citizens before the law.[143] The new emergency courts represented a decisive break with the civil and criminal safe-guards enshrined in the Republican Constitution of 1931.[144] However, as a safe-guarding measure, death penalties imposed by the emergency courts had to be reviewed and ratified by the cabinet.[145]

The conservation of public order and civilian morale became more pressing over the course of 1938, in step with a succession of serious Republican military defeats and political reverses. Treason and defeatism came to attract severer penalties at this time. Nonetheless, the number of death and life sentences delivered in Madrid's new 'courts of espionage and high treason' and the 'special military courts' were relatively low in comparison with those of other Republican-held cities. Of the 566 treason trials heard in Madrid only

8.48% resulted in the death penalty, 30.50% resulted in imprisonment and a further 24.20% in absolution or suspension. These figures should be compared with the death penalty statistics for treason in Valencia (43.82% out of a total 89 trials) Barcelona (32.79% out of 427) and Bilbao (31.76% of 403).[146] The majority of the cases discussed in this work relate to crimes of treason, espionage or defeatism which were heard in the emergency tribunals, the new high courts of treason and espionage and the special military tribunals. The most serious cases were referred up from the Madrid high courts to 'the high courts of treason and espionage' in Valencia and later Barcelona.

Chapter outline

Part 1 – The Clandestine Falange

Chapter 1 explores the origins and operations of Auxilio Azul which provided vital material, economic and spiritual aid to the anti-Republican community. It also explores how and why women were the first and most effective at mobilising the fifth column resistance in Madrid. Chapter 2 examines the organisational structure of Auxilio Azul and its different service divisions. The chapter explores the meanings ascribed by women to their gender-specific welfare-aid resistance and demonstrates how the agents of resistance were also sometimes its beneficiaries. The Clandestine Falange was as much preoccupied with survival as with resistance, and women attended to the well-being of 'Clandestine Madrid' and saved the lives of hundreds of fugitives. Chapter 3 provides a brief overview of the structure and aims of the mixed-gender Falange groups before examining the role played by individual women who acted as liaison and recruitment agents, spies and escape-line operators. The Clandestine Falange was a closely inter-connected resistance community. During a moment of violence and social dislocation, anti-Republican women held the threads of this community together.

Part 2 – Madrid's autonomous fifth-column resistance

Part 2 examines Madrid's 'autonomous resistance' community. It was composed of dozens of small associational or professional groups and hundreds of individuals who performed acts of dissidence and subversion in the rearguard. Chapter 4 examines the autonomous resistance from the Republican legal and retributive matrices. It explores women's involvement in capital crimes of treason and rebellion and also the lesser crimes of defeatism and disaffection. Women were subjected to less severe punishments than men because they were seldom perceived as political agents in their own right and, therefore, their treasonous crimes were conceived as arising from the effects of undue (male) influence, mental instability or gender-specific medico-legal pathologies and illnesses. Chapter 5 examines female spies and demonstrates how few women, aside from those in the Clandestine Falange, practised high-level espionage in the rear-guard. It also reveals how social class was an important vector for the signification of relationships of power despite circumstances of social revolution. Middle-class women used their social, cultural and symbolic power and their networks of influence in order to navigate the disciplinary regimes of the prison and the court-room. They often escaped the severest sanctions of the tribunals, while their poor, working-class counterparts lacked the necessary social and cultural capital (powerful contacts and education) to deflect the rigours and injustices of the popular tribunals. Despite Republican aspirations for a new and egalitarian social order, poor and uneducated women were routinely treated more unfairly at the hands of the new Republican people's justice.

The following chapter explains how women came to be the resisters of the first hour. They played the most important resistance roles through their provision of urgent and life-saving welfare-aid for fugitive anti-Republicans. These women were active in the public space, meanwhile, their formerly powerful male counterparts were forced into the private sphere. This significant but temporary shift in gender-power began several months before the war, in particular after the outlawing of the Falange Party in March 1936, when Falangist women began to create a series of underground welfare-aid and liaison networks for Falangist prisoners and their families.

Notes

1 Ealham, Chris, Richards Michael (eds) (2005) *The Splintering of Spain, A Cultural History and the Spanish Civil War* (Cambridge: CUP), p. 2.
2 Prada Rodríguez, Julio " 'Mujeres contra la revolución.' La movilización femenina conservadora durante la Segunda República española y la Guerra Civil," *Femmes et Militantisme,* (2008) Volume 8, at para. 20. Last accessed on 6 January 2020 on *Amnis* [on line] http://journals.openedition.org/amnis/599; DOI: 10.4000/amnis.599. See also, Cenarro, Ángela "Movilización femenina para la guerra total (1936–9)," *Historia y política: Ideas, procesos y movimientos sociales*, 16 (2006), pp. 159–182.
3 Nash, Mary (1995) *Defying Male Civilisation: Women in the Spanish Civil War* (Denver: Arden), pp. 105–117. By as early as September 1936 Prime Minister Largo Caballero endorsed military ordinances ordering women to withdraw from the militias. See also, Lines, Lisa, (2011) *Milicianas Women in Combat in the Spanish Civil War* (Lanham: Lexington).
4 Prada Rodríguez, Julio "'Mujeres contra la revolución.' La movilización femenina conservadora durante la Segunda República española y la Guerra Civil," in *Femmes et Militantisme* (2008), Volume 8 at para. 20. Last accessed on 6 January 2020 on *Amnis* [on line] http://journals.openedition.org/amnis/599; DOI: 10.4000/amnis.599
5 Romero Salvadó, Francisco (2005) *The Spanish Civil War, Origins, Course and Outcomes* (Basingstoke: Palgrave Macmillan), p. 103.
6 Rodríguez López, Sofía and Cazorla Sánchez, Antonio "Blue Angels: Female Fascist Resisters, Spies and Intelligence Officials in the Spanish Civil War, 1936–9," *Journal of Contemporary History*, 53 (4) (2016), pp. 692–713 at p. 692.
7 Chapter 9 "Las primeras las mujeres," in Cervera, Javier (1998) *Madrid en Guerra, La Ciudad Clandestina, 1936–9* (Madrid: Alianza), pp. 263–282. The use of the term "resistance" with regard to fifth-column practices has been interrogated by Carlos Píris who argues that the term was also used in Francoist discourses in order to associate the fifth column with resistance movements in German-occupied Europe between 1940

and 1944; see Píris, Carlos "Los servicios de información Franquistas en la capital," in Gómez Bravo, Gutmaro (ed) (2018) *Asedio. Historia de Madrid en la guerra civil (1936–9)* (Madrid: UCM), pp. 139–168 at p. 141. However, from a sociological perspective fifth-column practices constituted forms of civilian resistance, see the section on "Conceptualisation" below.

8 Ruiz, Julius (2012) *El Terror Rojo, Madrid, 1936* (Barcelona: Espasa), p. 218.

9 Primo de Rivera, Pilar (1983) *Recuerdos de una vida* (Madrid: Dyrsa), p. 76.

10 The concept of women's rescue and aid efforts as types of political resistance is well-established in gender histories of resistance in German-occupied Europe. See, for example, Schwartz, Paula "Redefining Resistance: Women's activisim in Wartime France" in Higgonet, Margaret and Collins Weitz, Margaret et al. (ed) (1987) *Behind the Lines, Gender and the Two World Wars* (Yale: YUP) at pp. 141–153. Also, Collins Weitz, Margaret (1995) *Sisters in the Resistance, How Women Fought to Free France, 1940–45* (Canada: John Wiley). In relation to anti-Francoist resistance, see Mercedes Yusta Rodrigo, "Las mujeres en la resistencia antifranquista, un estado de la cuestión," *Arenal, Revista de historia de las mujeres*,12:1 January–June, 2005, pp. 5–34. ⟨hal-01493607⟩. Submitted to HAL open access archives in 2017. Last viewed 6 January 2020. Also Douzou, Laurent and Yusta, Mercedes (eds) (2018) *La Résistance à l'épreuve du genre. Hommes et Femmes dans la Résistance antifasciste en Europe du Sud (1936–1949)* (Rennes: Pur).

11 Rodríguez López, Sofía, and Cazorla Sánchez, Antonio. "Blue Angels: Female Fascist Resisters, Spies and Intelligence Officials in the Spanish Civil War, 1936–9." *Journal of Contemporary History* 53 (4) (2016), pp. 692–713 at p. 692. A similar "historigraphical silence" surrounds women resisters in mainstream histories of German-occupied Europe, see explanations in Andrieu, Claire "Women in the French Resistance: Revisiting the Historical Record," *French Politics, Culture and Society*, 18 (1) (Spring, 2000), pp. 13–27.

12 Preston, Paul (2012) *The Spanish Holocaust, Inquisition and Extermination in Twentieth Century Spain* (London: Harper Press), pp. 293–294.

13 Cervera, Javier (1998) *Madrid en Guerra, La Ciudad Clandestina 1936–1939* (Madrid: Alianza), pp. 139–140. Also, Thomas, Hugh (2003) *The Spanish Civil War* (London: Penguin), p. 456. According to Thomas, the expression was used much earlier to describe the Russian supporters inside the fortress of Ismail which was besieged by Alexander Suvorov in 1790.

14 Heiberg, Morten, and Ros Agudo, Manuel (2006) *La trama oculta de la guerra civil. Los servicios secretos de Franco* (Barcelona: Crítica). pp. 186–187 at p.186.

15 Ruiz (2012) *El Terror*, p. 25 and pp. 215–218.

16 Ibárruri, Dolores *El Mundo Obrero*, dated 3 October 1936. Cited in Preston (2012) *The Spanish Holocaust*, at p. 293.

17 Hemingway, Ernest (1966) *The Fifth Column* (London: Penguin). See also Chapter 2, "The Capital of the World: The Correspondents and the Siege of Madrid," in Preston, Paul (2008) *We Saw Spain Die, Foreign Correspondents in the Spanish Civil War* (London: Constable).

18 Ruiz (2012), p. 26. See also, Píris, Carlos "Miedo: Reflexiones téoricas y metodológicas sobre la quinta columna en la ciudad de Madrid," in Oviedo Silva, Daniel, Pérez-Olivares García, Alejandro (eds) (2016) *Madrid, una ciudad en guerra (1936–48)* (Madrid: Catarata), at pp. 73–96.

19 Aróstegui, Julio, Martínez, Jesus (1984) *La Junta de Defensa de Madrid* (Madrid: Comunidad de Madrid), pp. 226–234 at p. 234.

20 For an analysis of the political uses of violence see Chapter 2 "Violence as Politics" in Tilly, Charles (2003) *The Politics of Collective Violence* (Cambridge: CUP), pp. 26–54, Sémelin, Jacques (2013) *Purify and Destroy, The political uses of massacre and genocide* (London: Hurst & Co) and Kalyvas, Stathis (2006) *The Logic of Violence in Civil War* (New York, NY: CUP).

21 Source: Ruiz (2012), p. 235.

22 For an analysis of constructions of identity based on the stigmatisation of difference and "othering" discourses based on the perceived "need to destroy 'them' in order to save 'us'," see Chapter 1 "The imaginary constructs of social destructiveness," in Sémelin (2013) *Purify and Destroy*, pp. 9–51 at pp. 48–51.

23 Source: Moral Roncal, Antonio Manuel "An analysis of Foreign Diplomatic Aid to the Catholic Clergy during the Spanish Civil War (1936–1939)," *Religions*, 4 (1) (2013), pp. 96–115 at p. 96. See also, Moral Roncal (2008) *Diplomacia, humanitarismo y espionaje en la Guerra Civil Española* (Madrid: Biblioteca Nueva).

24 Alcocer, Santos (1976) *La Quinta Columna* (Madrid: G. del Toro). This memory text details the experiences of the author, a Catholic *El Debate* journalist, who was obliged to go into hiding during the war for fear of extra-judicial reprisals.

25 Heiberg and Ros Agudo, p. 195.

26 Scott, James C. (1985) *Weapons of the Weak, Everyday Forms of Peasant Resistance* (New Haven: Yale University Press), at p. xvi

27 The strength of intimate and familial ties has also been observed in relation to "maquis" resistance after the war when right-wing "persons of order" willingly safe-housed "maquis," see Yusta Rodrigo, Mercedes (2005) *La Guerra de los vencidos, El maquis en el Maestrazgo turolense, 1940–1950* (Zaragoza: CSIC), p. 125.

28 Cervera (2006) *Madrid*, p. 136.

29 Anderson, Benedict (1983) *Imagined Communities, Reflections on the Spread and Origin of Nationalism* (London: Verso). According to the author nations are social constructs. "Nation" is defined as "an imagined political community … imagined as both inherently limited and sovereign," and nations are "imagined because the members of even the smallest nation will never know most of their fellow-members, meet them, or even hear of them, yet in the minds of each lives the image of their communion" (p. 6).

30 See for example Chapter 7, "The 'Two Spains'," in Álvarez Junco, José (2011) *Spanish Identity in the Age of Nations* (Manchester: MUP), pp. 246–289. This author analyses the failures of nationalism in the nineteenth century and argues that the Spanish state failed to cultivate the myths, symbols and rituals of nationhood. Consequently, the Right continued to identify with traditional Catholic religious, symbols, images and discourses of the "Cross" and the "Reconquest." In relation to national Catholic identity and women's Catholic movements in the early twentieth century, see Arce Pinedo, Rebeca (2008) *Dios, Patria y Hogar. La construcción social de la "mujer Española" por el catolicismo y las derechas en el primer tercio del siglo XX* (Santander: Universidad de Cantabria), at pp. 31–148.

31 Anderson, Peter (2017) *Friend or Foe? Occupation, Collaboration and Selective Violence in the Spanish Civil War* (Sussex: Sussex/Cañada Blanch).

32 The author argues that civil wars are unconventional or irregular wars which alter the nature of sovereignty in a fundamental way because in this type of conflict sovereignty varies by zone between rival actors and the boundaries between the zones are fluid. The objective of the warring rivals is to establish control over contested areas, and this often involves two co-ercive options: (1) selective violence which personalises targeting and requires civilian collaboration or (2) indiscriminate or collective targeting. For the use of denunciation in civilian conflict and its conceptualisation as a form of "selective violence," see Chapter 7, "A Theory of Selective Violence," in Kalyvas (2006), pp. 176–181. "The 'shame' surrounding the social phenomenon of private and anonymous [rather than public] denunciation … is reflected in the pejorative terms used to refer to denouncers: rats, snitches, touts, *soplones*, *chivitos*, *sapos*, *orejas*, *mouchards* and the like … This stigma drives even people who have denounced for 'legitimate' political and ideological reasons to keep it concealed. During my field work in Greece, I was unable to find anyone who openly acknowledged having denounced, even though I found several people willing to acknowledge participation in all kinds of unsavoury activities and acts of violence … Thus denunciation is not easily observable, even *ex post*" (p. 177). See also the seminal work by Fitzpatrick, Sheila and Gellately, Robert (eds) (1996) *Accusatory Practices, Denunciation in Modern European History, 1789–1989* (Chicago: UCP).

33 Heiberg and Ros Agudo (2006), p. 194. Similar observations are made in relation to Málaga's fifth column in "Vivir La Cruzada en el infierno. La quinta columna" in Rodríguez Barreira, Óscar (2013) *Miserias del poder, Los poderes locales y el nuevo estado franquista, 1936–51* (Valencia: PUV).

34 See Heiberg and Ros Agudo (2006), p. 188, Auxilio Azul's auxiliary activities are distinguished from the subsequent "fifth-column" political resistance in 1937. See also, Ruiz (2012) "Supervivencia no resistencia," pp. 218–231, Alía Miranda, Francisco (2015) *La agonía de la República, el final de la Guerra Civil española (1938–9)* (Barcelona: Crítica), p. 187.

35 Cervera (2006) *Madrid en guerra, La ciudad clandestina, 1936–9* (Madrid: Alianza), p. 243.

36 Píris, Carlos "Los servicios de información franquistas en la capital," in Gómez Bravo, Gutmaro (ed), at pp. 139–168.

37 Heiberg and Ros Agudo (2006), p. 189. Auxilio Azul women are classified as "collaborators."

38 Source: Heiberg and Ros Agudo (2006) *La Trama*, at p. 194.

39 Bertrán í Musitu, Josep (1940) *Experiencias de los Servicios de Información del Nordeste de España (SIFNE) durante la guerra* (Madrid: Espasa-Calpe). The extreme paucity of records is lamented in Ros Agudo, Manuel "El espionaje en España en la guerra civil y la segunda guerra mundial: una vision general," *Diacronie, Studi di Storia Contemporanea*, 28 (4) (2016), at p. 3. The author notes that while there is an abundance of records relating to espionage and the intelligence services in the Anglo-Saxon archives, which archives increase year upon year with new de-classifications. In contrast, the Spanish archives contain scant information relating to espionage and intelligence during the civil war, either because such documents did not survive the conflict or because they were destroyed under the Franco regime or because they continue to exist in classified archives. This article describes in summary the operations of intelligence and security services in both the Nationalist and the Republican held territories immediately prior to, during and after the civil war.

40 Paniagua, Javier, Lajo Cosido, Benjamín (2002) *Sombras en la retaguardia testimonios sobre la 5a columna en la retaguardia en Valencia* (Valencia: Centro Francisco Tomás y Valiente). The phenomenon of membership inflation towards the end of conflicts also features in histories of resistance in German-occupied Europe during WW2, see Introduction in Moore, Bob (ed) (2000) *Resistance in Western Europe* (Oxford: Berg), at pp. 1–27.

41 Chapter 3 "Repression and remembrance: the victor's liturgy of memory," in Richards, Michael (2013) *After the Civil War, Making Memory and Re-Making Spain since 1936* (New York, NY: CUP), at pp. 87–115 and pp. 91–94. The widows and children of those who fought on the Francoist side were also eligible to receive compensation and war pensions.

42 Pastor Petit, Domenèc (1978) *Los dossiers secretos de la guerra civil* (Barcelona: Argos), p. 271.

43 See in particular Part III in Anderson, Peter (2010) *The Francoist Military Trials, Terror and Complicity, 1939–45* (Oxford: Routledge/Cañada Blanch), pp. 60–107 at p. 89.

44 Rodríguez Barreira, Óscar (2013) *Miserias del poder, Los poderes locales y el nuevo estado franquista, 1936–51* (Valencia: PUV).

45 Kalyvas (2006), pp. 176–181.

46 See Koonz, Claudia (1987) *Mothers in the Fatherland: Women, the Family and Nazi Politics* (New York: St Martin's Press) and De Grazia, Victoria (1992) *How Fascism ruled women in, Italy, 1922–1945* (Berkeley: California University Press). See also, Richmond, Kathleen (2003) *Las mujeres en el facismo Español, La Sección Femenina de la Falange 1934–59* (Madrid: Alianza), Cenarro, Ángela (2006) *La sonrisa de Falange, Auxilio Social en la Guerra Civil y en la posguerra* (Madrid: Crítica), Ofel, Inbar (2010) *Señoritas in Blue, The Making of a Female Political Elite in Franco's Spain* (Brighton: Sussex Academic Press) and Blasco, Inmaculada (2003) *Paradojas de la ortodoxia. Política de masas y militancia Católica femenina en España (1919–39)* (Zaragoza: Prensas Universitarias de Zaragoza), p. 13.

47 Martínez Rus, Ana María "Mujeres y guerra civil: Un balance historiográfico," in *Studio Histórico de la Historia Contemporánea*, 32 (2014), pp. 333–343 at p. 343.

48 Rodríguez López, Sofía and Cazorla Sánchez, Antonio "Blue Angels: Female Fascist Resisters, Spies and Intelligence Officials in the Spanish Civil War, 1936–9," *Journal of Contemporary History*, 53 (4) (2016), pp. 692–713 at p. 692.

49 See also Rodríguez López, Sofía (2008) *Quintacolumnistas, Las mujeres del 36 en la clandestinidad almeriense* (Almería: IEA).

50 Cevera (2006), p. 269.

51 Scott, Joan W "Gender a Useful Category of Historical Analysis," *The American Historical Review*, 91 (5) (1986), pp. 1053–1075 at p. 1067.

52 These observations have also been made with regard to women in the French Resistance. See Collins Weitz, Margaret (1995) *Sisters in the Resistance, How Women Fought to Free France, 1940–45* (Canada: John Wiley), p. 11 and Von List, Corinna (French ed) (2012) *Résistantes* (Paris: Alma), Kindle ed. Loc. 2723.

53 The archives provide countless examples of this temporary power-shift. See for example, *Expte. 486 instruido contra Teofila Abad Benito y Mercedes Rivero Calvo por el delito/s de Desafección al Regimen*, AHN, FC-CAUSA_GENERAL, 116, Exp. 9. Imagen no. 8/66. In this case two domestic-workers were accused of espionage but tried for disaffection on account of passing letters between homes and embassies. The temporary shift in gender-power is illustrated in one of these letters dated July 1937 from Don César Coro to his wife. Coro was a former conservative councillor who was obliged to seek asylum at the Norwegian Embassy. While in asylum, his wife and children fled Madrid for reasons of personal safety. In the letter, Don Coro explicitly entrusted his wife "with the important task of recovering the family property and possessions" and with responsibility for his economic affairs. She was also charged with the discipline and religious education of the children in his absence. The letter reflected Catholic discourses relating to "the need for reserves of courage, self-abnegation, fortitude and acquiescence to suffering." Coro also believed that his lack of piety, alongside that of other ordinary Catholics, was responsible for the calamity of war which was conceptualised as a form of divine punishment. The language of the letter also reflected more recent Falangist discourses relating to the need for a new and "joyful" militancy.

54 See, for example, Marie-Pierre d'Udekem d'Acoz (2016) *Andrée de Jongh, Une vie de résistante* (Paris: Racine). The Catholic Andrée de Jongh was the leader of the famous Belgian Comète escape network.

55 Kalyvas (2006) *The Logic of Violence*, the author differentiates civil war from inter-state war and defines it as "armed combat within the boundaries of a recognised sovereign entity between parties subject to a common authority at the outset of the hostilities" (p. 17). The author argues that local dynamics are of fundamental importance in civil conflicts and that violence appears to be "less the result of powerful political identities and divisions and more their cause" (pp. 14–15). The author proposes a theory of selective violence which involves the "privatisation" of the politics of civil war through the role of denunciation motivated by personal "intimate" conflicts.

56 Heiberg and Ros Agudo, p. 190.

57 Sémelin, Jacques (2013) *Sans armes face à Hitler: La résistance civile en Europe, 1939–1943* (Paris: Les arènes), pp. 78–86. Here the author provides his own definition of "*résistance civile*" as a form of collective and unarmed rejection of foreign aggression. Resistance refers to actions that evidence a collective rejection (*refus*). To resist is primarily to find the will to say "no" (*dire non*) without necessarily having any clear idea of one's aims: "*Le terme de résistance renvoie à des actes par lesquels un volonté de refus s'exprime collectivement. Résister, c'est d'abord trouver la force de dire non sans nécessairement avoir une idée très clair de ce à quoi l'on aspire*" (p. 79).

58 An easily accessible overview of theories of Resistance in German-occupied Europe is provided in Chapter I "Introduction: Defining Resistance" in Moore, Bob (ed) (2000) *Resistance in Western Europe* (Oxford: Berg), at pp. 1–27. For sociological frames see Marcot, François "Pour une sociologie de la Résistance: intentionnalité et fonctionnalité," in Prost, Antoine (ed) (1997) *La Résistance, une histoire sociale* (Paris: Atélier/Ouvrières) pp. 21–41.

59 Broszat, Martin "Resistenz und Widerstand," in Broszat, Fröhlich, Eike et al. (ed) (1981) *Bayern in der NS-Zeit* (Munich: Oldenbourg), Vol. 4, pp. 691–709. Lüdkte, Alf, "De los heroes de la resistencia a los coautores. 'Alltagsgeschichte' en Alemania," *Ayer*,

Historia de la vida cotidiana, 19 (1995), pp. 46–69. These frames have been appropriated by Mercedes Yusta in her conceptualisation of civilian resistance to the Franco regime: see Yusta Rodrigo, Mercedes, "Las mujeres en la resistencia antifranquista, un estado de la cuestión," *Arenal*, 12:1, enero -junio, 2005, pp. 5–34 at p. 11. Last accessed 6 January 2020 on <hal-01493607>,

60 Kershaw, Ian (2015) (4th ed) *The Nazi Dictatorship Problems and Perspectives of Interpretation* (London: Bloomsbury Revelations) Ebook, p.224.

61 Scott (1985) *Weapons of the Weak*, p. xvi. Both Scott and the German "Everyday" historians were influenced by earlier theories on subaltern peasant and working-class resistance developed by the English eighteenth- and nineteenth-century social historian E.P. Thompson. Thompson's ideas informed German theories of "history from below" during the 1970s Bavarian Project. See, for example, Thompson, Edward P. (1979) *Tradición, reveulta y consciencia de clase, Estudios sobre la crisis de la sociedad preindustrial* (Barcelona: Crítica).

62 Yusta Rodrigo, Mercedes, Las mujeres en la resistencia antifranquista, un estado de la cuestión. *Arenal*, 2005. <hal-01493607>, Yusta Rodrigo, Mercedes "The Early Years of Franco's Regime As 'Seen from the Bottom,' Armed Resistance and Everyday Resistances (1939–1952)," *Vingtième Siécle, Revue d'Histoire*, 27 (3) (2015), pp. 231–224 [Full text in French]. Yusta Rodrigo, Mercedes "Rebeldía familiar, compromiso individual, acción colectiva. Las mujeres en la resistencia al franquismo durante los años cuarenta," *Historia del Presente*, 4 (2004), pp. 31–46. Yusta, Rodrigo, Mercedes (2003) *Guerrilla y resistencia campesina, La resistencia armada contra el franquismo en Aragón (1939–1952)* (Zaragoza: PUZ).

63 The historical invisibility of women within resistance narratives of German-occupied Europe has been explored in Bravo, Anna and Bruzonne, Anna María (1995) *In guerra senza armi. Storie di donne, 1940–45* (Rome: Laterza), Andrieu Claire in Prost, Antoine (ed) (1997) *La Résistance, une histoire sociale* (Paris: Atélier/Ouvrières), Schwartz, Paula "Redefining Resistance: Women's Activism in Wartime France," in Higgonet, Margaret et al. (ed) (1987) *Behind the Lines, Gender and the Two World Wars* (London: YUP), pp. 141–154.

64 See, for example, feminist conceptualisations of gender as "performance" and "practice" in Butler, Judith (1990) *Gender Trouble, Feminism and the Subversion of Identity* (London: Routledge), at p. viii. Butler examines "the signifying gestures through which gender itself is established" and queries whether "being female constitutes a 'natural fact' or a cultural performance." Also, the classic and seminal conceptualisation of gender as a primary way of signifying relationships of power in Scott, Joan "Gender: A Useful Category of Historical Analysis?," *American Historical Review*, 91 (5) (1986) at pp. 1053–1075 and Scott, Joan "Gender: Still a Useful Category of Analysis?," *Diogenes*, 57 (225) (2010). Scott acknowledged her indebtedness to Bourdieu's theories on habitus in her 1986 article. See also, Adkins, Lisa, Skeggs, Beverley (2006) *Feminism after Bourdieu* (Oxford: Blackwell).

65 Savage, Mike (2016) *Social Class in the 21st Century* (London: Pelican), p. 5. Also, Thatcher, Jenny, Ingram, Nicola, Burke, Ciaran, Abrahams, Jessie (eds) (2016) *Bourdieu – The Next Generation: The development of Bourdieu's intellectual heritage in contemporary UK sociology* (Abingdon: Routledge).

66 Bourdieu, Pierre (2003) *Practical Reason, On the Theory of Action* (Oxford: Polity), at p. 34. These fields include the government, police, judiciary, civil institutions, associations and local political and neighbourhood groups.

67 Adkins, Lisa, Skeggs, Beverley (2006) *Feminism after Bourdieu* (Oxford: Blackwell), p. 21.

68 McNay, Lois (2000) *Gender and Agency, Reconfiguring the Subject in Feminist and Social Theory* (Oxford: Polity Press), p. 25.

69 McNay (2000) *Gender and Agency*, p. 26.

70 Bourdieu, Pierre (2013) *Outline of a Theory of Practice* (Cambridge: CUP), p. 72.

71 Mahmood, Saba (2005) *The Politics of Piety: The Islamic Revival and the Feminist Subject* (Princeton, NJ: PUP), pp. 47–50.

72 The concept of "docile agency" is developed in Saba Mahmood's sociological analysis of the twenty-first century Muslim women's *da'wa* (piety) movement. See Mahmood (2005) *The Politics of Piety…*

73 "In the early 1900's the Catholic Church, for the first time in its history, appealed directly to women for help in defending Catholic values in society. As a result, various Catholic women's associations came into being, with the aim of assisting the Church in its mission by disseminating religious propaganda and alleviating serious social problems." See Dawes, Helena (2014) *Catholic Women's Movements in Liberal and Fascist Italy* (Basingstoke: Palgrave Macmillan), at p. 10.

74 Sources: Universidad Pontificia de Salamanca (UPSA), Acción Católica de España (ACE), Mujeres de Acción Católica, MAC, Inventario (1934–68), Memorias Diocesanas and Las Jóvenes de Acción Católica, (JFAC), Inventario (1926–1961), Memorias Diocesanas, 1–7. Estadísticas Diocesanas (1936–45), pp. 8–9. See also, Blasco Herranz "Citizenship and Female Catholic Militancy," pp. 441–466, Blasco Herranz, Inmaculada, (1997) *Armas femeninas para la contrarevolución: La Sección Femenina en Aragón (1936–50)* (Málaga: IAM), Blasco, Inmaculada (2003) *Paradojas de la ortodoxia, Política de masas y militancia católica femenina en España (1919–1939)* (Zaragoza: PUZ) and Arce Pinedo, Rebeca (2008) *Dios, Patria y Hogar. La construcción social de la "mujer española" por el catolicismo y las derechas en el primer tercio del siglo XX* (Santander: Universidad de Cantabria) and Blasco, Inmaculada "Las Ramas femeninas de la AC durante la II República," in Montero, Feliciano (ed) *La Acción Católica en la II República* (Alcalá: UAH), pp. 43–73.

75 Pinedo (2008), *Dios, Patria y Hogar*, p. 22. This author argues that masculine domination is culturally reproduced through the exercise of "symbolic violence" in combination with "symbolic compensations" such as the practice of gallantry towards the *naturally* weaker sex, gifting the fairer sex in recognition of their beauty and exalting mothers as queens of the hearth (p. 20). The author cites Bourdieu, Pierre (2006) *La dominación masculina* (Barcelona: Anagrama), pp. 49–50.

76 Ortega López, Teresa María "¡Cosa de coser…y cantar! La derecha antiberal," in Ana Aguado and Teresa Ma. Ortega (eds) (2011) *Feminismos y antifeminismos, culturas, políticas e identitdades de genero en las España del Siglo XX* (Valencia: PUV), pp. 173–206 at p. 176.

77 Bourdieu, Pierre "Social Space and Symbolic Power," *Sociological Theory*, 7 (1) (Spring, 1989), pp. 14–25 at p. 19

78 Mother María Luisa Fernández and Mother María Leturia (1939) *Catorce meses de aventuras bajo el dominio rojo* (Rome: ACI), at p. 30.

79 Blasco (2003) *Paradojas*, p. 43.

80 Adkins and Skeggs (ed) (2004) *Feminism After Bourdieu*, p. 21.

81 For an overview of constructions of womanhood during the Republican and Francoist periods see Morcillo, Aurora Chapter 11 "Gender," in Shubert, Adrian, Álvarez Junco, José (2018) *The History of Modern Spain, Chronologies, Themes, Individuals* (London: Bloomsbury), pp. 171–175. The seminal work on the role of women in the Republican war effort is Nash, Mary (1995) *Defying Male Civilization, Women in the Spanish Civil War* (Denver: Arden). For an analysis of the conflicts and ambiguities of the new Francoist national Catholic gender constructions, the "nationalising" of women and their involvement as producers and consumers in an expanding market economy see Morcillo, Aurora (2008) *True Catholic Womanhood, Gender Ideology in Franco's Spain* (Illinois: Northern Illinois University Press). For memories of women's hard-won civil rights and political activism see Martínez Sierra, María (1989) *Una mujer por campos de España* (Madrid: Castalia). Also, Campoamor, Clara (2007) *La revolución Española vista por una Republicana* (Madrid: Espuela de Plata) and Fagoaga, Concha y Saavedra, Paloma (1981) *Clara Campoamor, La sufragista Española* (Madrid: Gráficas Oggi).

82 De Groot, Joanna and Morgan Sue "Beyond the 'Religious Turn'? Past, Present and Future Perspectives in Gender History," *Gender and History*, 25 (Nov, 2013), pp. 395–442 at p. 398. Blasco Herranz, Inmaculada (translated from Spanish by Jeremy Roe)

"Citizenship and Female Catholic Militancy in 1920's Spain," *Gender and History*, 19 (3), (November, 2007), pp. 441–466 at p. 443

83 Mahmood, Saba (2005) *The Politics of Piety: The Islamic Revival and the Feminist Subject* (Princeton: PUP), p. 12 and at p. 63. These frames are controversial because they have been interpreted as ploys to "restore agency" to women who operate within the Muslim piety (*da'wa*) movement.

84 Blasco "Citizenship and female Catholic Militancy," p. 442.

85 Source: Romero Salvadó, Francisco (2013) *Historical Dictionary of the Spanish Civil War* (Plymouth: Scarecrow Press), p. 198.

86 See Juliá, Santos (1984) *Madrid 1931–34, De la fiesta popular a la lucha de clases* (Madrid: Siglo Veintiuno).

87 Source: Ruiz (2012), p. 32.

88 Preston, Paul "The Great Civil War: European Politics, 1914–45," in Blanning, Tim (ed) (1996) *The Oxford Illustrated History of Modern Europe* (Oxford: OUP), pp. 169–173.

89 Moradiellos, Enrique "Ni gesta heroica, ni locura trágica: Nuevas perspectivas sobre la guerra civil," *Ayer*, 50 (2003), pp. 11–39, at p. 26, Juliá, Santos (1999) *Un Siglo de España. Política y Sociedad* (Madrid: Marcial Pons), p. 118, Graham, Helen (2005) *The Spanish Civil War* (Oxford: OUP), p. 2.

90 Vincent, Mary "The Spanish Civil War as a War of Religion," in Baumeister and Schuler-Springorum (eds), pp. 74–89 at p. 75.

91 Salomón Chéliz, María Pilar "El anticlericalismo en la calle. Republicanismo, populismo, radicalismo y protesta popular (1898–1913)," in de la Cueva, Julio, Montero, Feliciano (eds) (2007) *La secularización conflictiva, España (1898–1931)* (Madrid: Biliotecа Nueva), pp. 121–139.

92 De la Cueva, Montero (eds) (2007), p. 21.

93 Lannon, Frances "The Church's Crusade against the Republic," in Preston, Paul (ed) (1984) *Revolution and War in Spain 1931–1939* (London: Methuen), pp. 35–48 at p. 36.

94 Vincent, Mary "Made Flesh? Gender and Doctrine in Religious Violence in Twentieth Century Spain," *Gender and History*, 25 (3) (November, 2013), pp. 668–680 at p. 668. See also Thomàs, María "The Civilisation that Is Being Forged Amid the Thunder of the Cannons," in Anderson, Peter and del Arco Blanco, Miguel Ángel (eds) (2015) *Mass Killings and Violence in Spain, 1936–1952: Grappling with the Past* (New York, NY: Routledge), pp. 112–132. These authors investigate the cultural semiotics and the rationale behind the religious violence. See also Montero García, Cantano Moreno, Tezanos Gandarillas, Marisa (eds) (2014) *Otra Iglesia. Clero disidente durante la Segunda República y la guerra civil* (Gijón: Trea).

95 Rodríguez Barreira, Óscar (2013) *Miserias del poder, Los poderes locales y el nuevo estado franquista, 1936–51* (Valencia: PUV), pp. 83–98 at p. 83.

96 Richards, Michael (2013) *After the Civil War, Making Memory and Re-Making Spain since 1936* (New York, NY: CUP), pp. 103–105.

97 Including the Catholic Basques and and also certain members of the Catholic hierarchy, see Lannon, Frances (1987) *Privilege, Persecution, and Prophecy: The Catholic Church in Spain, 1875–1975* (Oxford: Clarendon Press), pp. 182–183. Marco Sola, Luisa "El factor Cristiano. Católicos y sacerdotes antifranquistas en los medios republicanos," *El Argonauta español, Janvier, La presse espagnole et la guerre civile. Entre rupture et propaganda (1936–1939)*, 7 (2010), https://journals.openedition.org/argonauta/421, pp. 1–24. Last accessed 11 July 2019. Also Montero, García, Feliciano, Moreno Cantano, Antonio, Tezanos Gandarillas, Marisa (eds) (2014) *Otra Iglesia, Clero disidente durante la Segunda República y la guerra civil* (Gijón: Trea).

98 González Cuevas, Pedro Carlos "La guerra civil de la espiritualidad: el catolicismo español y sus enemigos (1898–1936)," in de la Cueva, Montero (ed) (2007) *La secularización*, at p. 68.

99 Cervera, Javier (2015) *Contra el enemigo de la República…Desde la Ley. Detener, juzgar y encarcelar en Guerra* (Madrid: Biblioteca Nueva), p. 14.

100 Ledesma, José Luis "Total War behind the Front-lines? An Enquiry into Violence on the Republican side in the Spanish Civil War," in Baumeister and Schuler-Springorum (eds) (2008) *'If you tolerate this…'*, pp. 154–170 at p. 165.
101 Kalyvas (2006), p. 389.
102 Jato, David (1953) *La rebelión de los estudiantes* (Madrid: Cies), pp. 234–238 at p. 234.
103 [Fal Conde, undated] *Gesto Glorioso del Requeté en Madrid* (Julio 1936–Marzo 1939), *Archivo General Militar de Ávila*, C2505, Cp.4/43 and C.2498.20, Legajo no. 285, Carpeta 20, Armario 5. at pp. 6–8.
104 Ruiz, Julius (2012) *El Terror*, p. 73.
105 Pieza separada…no 27 derivada del sumario por rebellion militar del Jusgado Especial del Tribunal Supremo contra Fernando y Federico Primo de Rivera y Cobo de Guzmán, Rafael Aznar Gerner, Constantino Palcios López, José Cubero Mateo, José María de Arriaga y Cobo de Guzmán, Amaro Márquez Alcaide y Fermín Sánchez Mateo, AHN, FC-CAUSA_GENERAL, 1525, Exp. 18, Imágenes 1–40. See also, Cervera (2006), p. 56.
106 Píris "Los servicios de información franquistas en la capital," at pp. 139–168.
107 Ruiz (2012), pp. 73 and 219.
108 Ruiz (2012), pp. 218–228.
109 See, for example, the newspaper article entitled "The horrors committed by the Fascists in Badajoz, Thousands shot in the Bull Ring," *ABC*, Madrid, 24 September 1936, p. 9. The article reported that "thousands and thousands of militias, communists and social ists were put to death for the sole crime of having attempted to defend the legitimate government of the Republic." Such terrifying reports created popular panic and stimulated an already heightened climate of political violence in the capital.
110 For an account of the violent repression in the rebel-held zones where a state of war was immediately declared by the insurgents, see Chapter 5 "Queipo's Terror: The Purging of the South" and Chapter 9 "The Column of Death's March on Madrid," in Preston (2012) *The Spanish Holocaust*, at pp. 131–179 and 303–340.
111 Preston (2012), p. 260. See also, AHN, ES.28079.AHN/2.1.2.28.4, CAUSA_GENERAL, D. *Pieza Cuarta de Madrid. Checas.* Preston observes that there were "nearly two hundred squads, if those set up by recently freed common criminals are included" (p. 260).
112 Gibson, Ian (1983) *Paracuellos, Como fué* (Barcelona: Argos), p. 191. See also Ruiz, Julius (2015) *Paracuellos, Una verdad incómoda* (Madrid: Espasa).
113 See "La cárcel de mujeres en el antiguo convento," in Schlayer, Félix (2008) *Diplomático en el Madrid Rojo* (Madrid: Espuela de Plata), pp.155–164. Schlayer's intervention on the night of 4 November 1936 in the Conde de Toreno women's prison is also related in the testimony of Dr. Amelia Azarola Echevarría (widow of the Falangist leader Julio Ruiz de Alda) in FC-CAUSA_GENERAL, 1526, Exp. 6.
114 Source: Preston (2012) *The Spanish Holocaust*, Appendix, p. 667.
115 Source: Casas de la Vega, Rafael (1994) *El Terror: Madrid 1936: Investigación histórica y catálogo de víctimas identificadas* (Madrid: Fénix), pp. 399–407.
116 Source: Cervera (2006), p. 80.
117 Source: Cervera (1998), p. 77.
118 Juliá Díaz, Santos (ed) (1999) *Víctimas de la Guerra Civil* (Madrid: Planeta de Agostini), p. 121.
119 Cervera (1998), pp. 69–73.
120 Cervera, Javier "Violencia en el Madrid de la Guerra Civil: Los 'paseos' (julio a diciembre de 1936)," *Studia Histórica. Historia Contemporanea*, 13014 (1995–1996), pp. 63–82. Ruiz (2012), pp. 173–198. Esparza Torres, José Javier (2007) *El Terror Rojo en España: Epílogo el Terror Blanco* (Madrid: Altera).
121 Montoliú, Pedro (2000) *Madrid en la guerra civil, Vol. 1* (Madrid: Silex), p. 147.
122 Juliá (ed) (1999) *Víctimas*, p. 121.
123 Source: Cervera (2006), p. 80.
124 Rodríguez López, Sofía and Oscar Rodríguez Barreira "La Quinta Columna y la Guerra Civil en Andalucía," *Andalucía en la Historia*, 46 (October–December 2014), p. 73.

125 Source: Oviedo Silva, Daniel, Pérez-Olivares García, Alejandro (eds) (2016) *Madrid, una ciudad en guerra (1936–48)* (Madrid: Catarata), p. 60. See also, Montero Moreno, Antonio (1961) *Historia de la persecución religiosa en España 1936–9* (Madrid).

126 de La Cueva Merino, Julio "Si los frailes supieran…la violencia anticlerical," in Santos Juliá (ed) (2000) *Violencia Política en la España del Siglo XX* (Madrid: Taurus), pp. 191–233 at p. 223.

127 Source: Alfaya, José Luis (1998) *Como un río de fuego, Madrid, 1936* (Barcelona: EIU), p. 103.

128 Lannon "The Church's Crusade Against the Republic," in Preston, Paul (ed) (1984) *Revolution and War in Spain, 1931–1939* (London: Methuen), pp. 35–58 at p. 53.

129 Marqués, Pierre (2000) *La Croix-Rouge pendant la guerre d'Espagne (1936–9)* (Paris: L'Harmattan), p. 242.

130 *Gaceta de la República, No. 237*, 24 August 1936. See also, "1.3 Los nuevos organos de la justicia popular," in Cancio Fernández, Raúl (2007), pp. 55–95 at p. 55.

131 Graham, Helen (2002) *The Spanish Republic at War, 1936–9* (Cambridge: CUP), pp. 160–161.

132 Source: Ruiz (2012), p. 239

133 Ruiz, Julius "'Work and Don't Lose Hope': Republican Forced Labour Camps during the Spanish Civil War," *Contemporary European History*, 18 (4) (2009), pp. 419–441.

134 Source: CDMH, Fondos Contemporáneos, Causa General, Tribunales Populares y Jurados de Urgencia y de Guardia de Madrid, ES.28079.AHN/2.2.6

135 Canció Fernández, Raúl (2007) *Guerra Civil y Tribunales: De los jurados populares a la justicia Franquista (1936–9)* (Cáceres: Universidad de Extremadura), p. 56.

136 *Gaceta de la República*, 25 September and 7 October 1936. See also, Sánchez Recio, Glicerio (1991) *Justicia y Guerra en España. Los Tribunales Populares (1936–1939)* (Alicante: Instituto de Cultura Juan Gil-Albert), p. 64.

137 *Sumario 81/1938 contra varions (including Carmen Torres Pino) por espionaje y otros delitos contra la seguridad del Estado.* The proceedings commenced in *Expte. 3700,* AHN, FC-CAUSA-GENERAL_110. EXP.29.

138 *Gaceta de Madrid*, Núm.285, 11 October 1936, p. 289, www.boe.es/datos/pdfs/BOE/1936/285/B00289-00289.pdf

139 Disaffection is examined in Flynn, Angela (2013) *Las Desafectas al Régimen, Anti-Republican Women and Republican Justice in Madrid (1936–9)* (Oxford: Unpublished Mphil). Chapter 2, "Republican Justice" examines the legislative measures implemented by the Republican government in order to combat anti-Republicanism in the rearguard, pp. 32–52.

140 *Gaceta de la República*, 18 October 1936. See also, Sánchez Recio (1991) *Justicia en Guerra*, pp. 61–62.

141 Sánchez Recio (1991), pp. 66–67.

142 *Gaceta de la República*, 23 June 1937.

143 Graham, Helen (2005) *The Spanish Civil War* (Oxford: OUP), p. 108.

144 Sánchez Recio, Glicerio "El control político de la retaguardia republicana durante la Guerra Civil. Los tribunales populares de justicia," *Espacio, Tiempo y Forma*, Serie V, Historia Contemporanea, 7 (1994), pp. 585–598 at pp. 591–592. Sánchez Recio, Glicerio (1991) *La República contra los Rebeldes y los Desafectos, La Represión Económica durante la Guerra Civil* (Madrid: Universidad de Alicante).

145 Graham, Helen (2002) *The Spanish Republic at War, 1936–1939* (Cambridge: CUP), p. 347. Here, the author argues that Republican government's infringement of the independence of the judiciary must be assessed in the "extraordinarily fraught" context of war and social upheaval.

146 Source: Sánchez "El control político…," p. 596.

Part 1

The role of women in the Clandestine Falange

1 The origins of Auxilio Azul

Auxilio Azul was the earliest, most extensive and most effective fifth column resistance network in Madrid.[1] It was formed soon after 18 July 1936 in order to provide safe-housing and escape-lines for fugitives. Its origins lay in the underground networks of the pre-war Sección Femenina. The paucity of original source materials, the self-censorship of the protagonists and the gender-specific and 'everyday' nature of women's resistance practices meant that their dangerous resistance exploits have been overlooked. Many who self-identified as dutiful and submissive handmaidens of the 'national Catholic Cause' were in fact highly politicised activists who consciously and willingly engaged in treason and illegality. Women's routine domestic and affective labour was politicised within a subversive anti-Republican resistance space.[2] Falangist women were political agents in their own right and the 'invisibility' conferred by their gender became a useful asset which was consciously exploited by those who "concealed guns in their coats and inside their boots."[3]

The network was officially named 'María Paz Martínez Unciti's Blue-Aid Sisterhood' (*La Hermandad Auxilio Azul – María Paz Martínez Unciti*) after its founder who was an eighteen-year-old Falangist student-union activist. The cumbersome official name was abbreviated to "Auxilio Azul" (Blue Aid) after the blue-shirted uniforms of the Falange. Its resistance activities commenced soon after 18 July 1936 and continued throughout the war until it was demobilised by Pilar Primo de Rivera in April 1939. Socorro Blanco (White Aid) was a Traditionalist women's relief network established circa 1932.[4] During the war it was operated by the "Margaritas" (the Traditionalist Women's Section) who rallied to join Auxilio Azul in the months after 18 July.[5] The organisation was also known as Socorro Azul (Blue Aid) and was conceived as the clandestine counterpart to the Republican Socorro Rojo (Red Aid). The names 'Auxilio Azul' and 'Socorro Blanco' were frequently used interchangeably by the members.[6] The organisation was never infiltrated or dismantled by the Republican security forces on account of its effective recruitment and security methods and despite the dismantlement of some fourteen mixed-gender Falangist groups.[7] By the end of the war it is said to have mobilised around 6,000 women.[8] "Enough to ensure that Madrid's streets were festooned with 10,000 Nationalist flags at 8 a.m. on 27 March [sic] 1939."[9]

The organisation operated off-shoots in Valencia, Murcia and Alicante. Carmen Tronchoni was one of the leaders of Valencia's Socorro Blanco. She frequented the city's bars, theatres and cafés, in particular *Bar Vodka* where members of the International Brigades congregated. She was also a liaison and escape-line agent who arranged false-documentation and accompanied fugitives into the Nationalist zone. She was arrested in Barcelona in November 1937 and executed for treason in March of the following year.[10] The Falangist Carmen Calvo Alonso founded a group in Alicante.[11] A Socorro Blanco network was also established in Almería by the Sindicato Católica de la Aguja in 1937 and led by Carmen Góngora López. It included nuns, carabineers, civil servants, especially doctors and magistrates, CAMPSA, the local Home Office Department and the Port Works Commission. This network was incorporated into the Clandestine Falange in 1937 and by mid-1938 it had around 500 women and men.[12] María Gómez del Olmo led a small group in Linares.[13] The organisation was in contact with the Nationalist security services in Burgos and with various Sección Femenina groups in the rebel-held zones.[14]

During the earliest months of the conflict, Catholic habitus experienced '*hysteresis*' which is defined by sociologists as a sudden and catastrophic mismatch between the aspirations of habitus within a particular social field.[15] The coup immediately unleashed an endogenous and violent extra-judicial repression that lasted until the beginning of January 1937 in the capital. Some 46 churches were burned within the first seventy-two hours of the failed insurrection. After 19 July public worship ceased and churches remained closed for the duration of the war.[16] Many were re-purposed as storage facilities and warehouses. The religious were evacuated, and Catholicism went underground. In the city and province of Madrid some 1,000 priests died violently during the first six months of the conflict when the power of the Republican state was at its weakest.[17] Many were killed, not in their capacity as individuals, but as the living symbols and embodiments of hated Catholic institutions; others died pursuant to forms of 'intimate violence' that constitute a feature of most civil conflicts. Anti-clerical violence has been linked to the symbolic destruction of the cultural power of the Church.[18] The groups on the left may also have used violence to re-affirm their masculinity over priests who were perceived to have too much power and political influence over women.[19] This religious persecution animated a pre-existing disposition for Catholic crusade among ordinary Catholics.[20]

Anti-Republicans also experienced forms of legal repression during the hostilities. They were arrested for treason or disaffection, their property and businesses were impounded and their belongings confiscated pursuant to a new 'financial reparations' legislation as compensation for the illegal coup and in aid of the war-effort.[21] These war-time confiscations and requisitions engendered powerful resentments and the desire for revenge and restitution after the war.[22] Formerly legal activities such as regular church attendance, membership of CEDA and subscriptions to right-wing newspapers or the

Catholic periodical *El Debate* came to constitute evidence of 'disaffection' pursuant to the new emergency legislation implemented in October 1936. Many lost their jobs during the professional purges at the start of the war and suffered economic hardship, and those who went into hiding were unable to claim state benefits including pensions or rations. Private homes were converted into safe-houses for fugitives and religious personnel.[23] In the absence of the male heads of household, many of whom were in hiding, in prison or victims of the extra-judicial repression, anti-Republican women were able to construct new war-time resistance identities. In circumstances where 'new and stable field structures had yet to emerge new opportunities and possibilities for agency arose.'[24] However, narratives of *hysteresis* and repression during the earliest months must be balanced alongside civilian practices of tolerance, compromise and accommodation despite the bitter ideological divisions, especially after the fronts were stabilised in June 1937.[25]

In August 1936 a small group of Falangist, Catholic and monarchist women began to form an extensive 'Sisterhood' based on close family, friendship and religious connections. The women were committed to the difficult and dangerous task of ensuring the physical, moral and spiritual survival of Madrid's clandestine anti-Republican community. Auxilio Azul provided a wide variety of auxiliary services including safe-housing and escape-line networks, distributing food, assisting conscription evasion, providing political prisoners with food, clothing and contraband (including Nationalist war reports), providing nursing and welfare-aid services for orphans and anti-Republican families, collecting and distributing money, circulating censored war reports from Burgos in the food queues, over the telephone, in Republican offices and within the military barracks, safe-guarding valuables including Falangist flags, incriminating documents, jewellery and compromising photographs, procuring favourable sentences from 'sympathetic' popular tribunal judges, by means of bribery or by infiltrating the police and the judiciary and 'providing consolation and continual aid' including smuggling communion hosts into the prisons.[26] This exhaustive list of represented 'menial' tasks was traditionally assigned to women pursuant to the symbolic division of labour.[27] However, in the context of extreme violence and social upheaval these actions represented acts of political subversion that attracted severe sanctions and reprisals. Those members who were politically inactive before the war represented their politico-religious actions as those of dutiful and abnegated Catholic women. They interiorised a religious vocabulary and discourse that was very similar to that of the lay Catholic association Mujeres de Acción Católica (MAC) and its youth section which mobilised alongside Auxilio Azul soon after the start of the war.[28] Such women experienced a political awakening and assumed the material and affective burden of 'preserving Clandestine Madrid alive in both body and soul':

> Auxilio Azul ... provided spiritual aid, sustained the Spanish spirit (*la tensión española*)... prayed and, united together in God's will, provided Christian

> burials for the assassinated … organized clandestine and make-shift Chapels, organised safe spaces for the performance of mass, baptism, marriage, communion … raised funds and worked tirelessly … and provided examples of fortitude, courage and trust in God and love of Spain.[29]

This distinctive national Catholic discourse of suffering, self-sacrifice and redemption reflected Nationalist efforts to unite the rebel factions during the war. It also evidences the construction of new war-time anti-Republican resistance identities. This new 'community of suffering' came to form part of a post-war shared culture of civil war victors.[30]

The origins of Auxilio Azul within the pre-war Sección Femenina

Until 18 July 1936, the Falange was a small and insignificant fascist party inspired by Italian and German models of fascism and influenced by "a European culture of violent politics during the inter-war period."[31] It promoted forms of authoritarian, ultra nationalist and corporatist governance in response to the perceived ills of regional separatism, party-political divisions and class-based conflicts. In February 1936 it had 1,040 male members and 63 Sección Femenina members in Madrid and some 9,000 supporters throughout Spain.[32] During the Popular Front elections of 16 February 1936 it garnered a mere 0.7% of the popular vote in all Spain (i.e. 44,000 votes) and 1.2% of the total votes in Madrid (i.e. 4,995 votes).[33] However, after the Popular Front victory its membership grew significantly and new members were drawn from the ranks of Renovación Española (RE), the Catholic Confederación Española de Derechas Autonomas (CEDA) and Juventudes de Acción Popular (JAP).[34] The Falange's violent rhetoric and its utopian fascism appealed to the young, students, poor white-collar workers and to a small constituency of blue-collar workers.[35] At least half of the total following in Madrid came from university or secondary-level students.[36] The Falange also appealed to young middle-class and lower-middle-class women who gained a measure of political visibility within this youth-orientated movement. These women were all Catholics of varying degrees of confessionalism and piety, and fascism was readily interiorised and willingly reproduced by them "because fascist gender ideals resonated with traditional authoritarian Catholic values and gender norms."[37] The party experienced a significant increase in membership after the February 1936 general elections and again after 18 July.

The female members were committed activists who willingly embraced the undemocratic rhetoric and the culture of violence of the Falange. This may explain how the seemingly demure and self-effacing Pilar Primo de Rivera, who was depicted by close associates as being "modest and agreeably timid, with a child-like voice,"[38] came to be implicated in the assassination of the Socialist Youth member Juanita Rico in June 1934.[39] It was rumoured that she and another woman were in Antonio Ansaldo's car at the time of the attack.[40] During a meeting in May 1935 hosted by the upper-middle-class socialite

Marichu de la Mora, José Antonio made it clear that violent action was necessary in order to further the party's political aims.[41] After the February 1936 general elections, the Falange stepped up its campaign to destabilise the government through an increased participation in violent clashes with members of the Federación Universitaria Escolar (FUE), Juventudes Socialistas (Socialist Youth) and communist and anarchist militias on the university campus, in working-class areas and in the Casa de Campo.[42] The sectarian violence was frequently instigated by Falangists who entered working-class spaces such as Cuatro Caminos or the Casa de Campo in order to distribute their periodicals which were entitled *¡Arriba!* and *¡No importa!* There were at least 444 political killings across Spain including some sixty-nine mortalities in Madrid between 16 February and 17 July 1936.[43] The sectarian violence and tit-for-tat reprisals hastened the military rising on 17 July.[44]

Paradoxically, despite the Falange's neo-traditional gender ideology the cadres accommodated and encouraged female activism. "Women were a good medium through which to promote National-Syndicalist ideas, as women did not arouse as much police suspicion as men at this time."[45] According to a former female activist, José Antonio welcomed female involvement in SEU militancy and actively appointed women into leadership roles.[46] Falangist women were political agents in their own right. Carmen Díaz Roca distributed Falangist propaganda and dared to put up a monarchist flag in a local Casa de Pueblo.[47] Marcelina Mateos was arrested on 22 July 1936 and accused of "complicity in the death of [Republican Assault Guard] Lieutenant Castillo." After her release she "continued to work even harder than before on behalf of the glorious National Syndicalist Movement."[48] Dolores Amador went into hiding for five months after 18 July 1936 because she was involved in the publication and dissemination of Falangist propaganda prior to the 16 February 1936 general elections.[49] Ana María Rizzo y Goñi was a committed activist who worked closely with José Antonio during the 1936 general election campaign.[50] While the party ideology sought to impose domestic exile upon women,[51] in practice Falangist women were visible in the public space prior to March 1936, and thereafter they formed a series of underground networks after the male leaders were imprisoned. Falangist women achieved a visibility within the party which was denied to their CEDA and Traditionalist counterparts; they not only sewed the blue shirts of their male comrades but they also wore them.[52]

Although women were debarred from official party membership because of its commitment to the use of paramilitary violence, this stance was not adopted with regard to membership of its student union (SEU) "because in professional terms it made no sense to deny university women membership."[53] Prominent activists were able to participate in party politics via union membership. The SEU was formed soon after the Falange's inaugural meeting on 29 October 1933, and it was "dedicated to the mobilisation of civilian 'services' and violent street confrontations."[54] The leaders were David Jato Miranda, Matías Montero, Alejandro Allánegui and Manuel Valdés Larrañaga, who subsequently became the head of the Clandestine Falange in Madrid in

1937.[55] Pilar Primo de Rivera (aged twenty-nine years and training to be a nurse at this time) together with a small group of non-university women who had been vocal in their desire to join the party from the outset were instead obliged to join the SEU in early 1934 in order to enrol as "official and active militants within the ranks of the Falange."[56] In addition, a few women were allowed to join the paramilitary 'shock troops' led by Agustín Aznar Gerner.[57]

The activism of women like Pilar Primo de Rivera was influenced by the self-identifications of a generation of middle-class, well-educated Spanish women from conservative and Catholic backgrounds who grew up against the background of the Rif War in the early 1920s and came into maturity during the Second Republic. The experience of the colonial war

> fostered in them a desire for national regeneration, and while the Republic offered them new professional, legal and political opportunities and fashioned their aspirations and ambitions in the public space, it also challenged their moral and religious convictions and their socio-political beliefs.[58]

Years after the events, Pilar Primo de Rivera continued to represent her political convictions as 'a way of being' (*una manera de ser*) or 'culture and formation' (*cultura y formación*) arising from family habitus, as determined by the political beliefs of her father General Primo de Rivera and the religious beliefs of her aunt 'Tia Ma,' in combination with a self-directed and heart-felt political commitment: "I didn't immediately join the Falange on account of my brother José Primo de Rivera, but because I was completely convinced that the Falange represented the salvation of Spain *at a given moment in time*."[59] It has been observed that her memories, including those in her official biography, are rather static and immutable,[60] although the phrase 'at a given moment in time' indicates a desire to contextualise personal motivations and actions within a specific historical and socio-political context. Pilar's 'epic' and immutable group memory script is also reflected in the memory texts of other prominent female Falangists, and such rigid narratives may derive from motives of self-censorship and a desire to vindicate and justify past actions.[61] Mercedes Fórmica joined the SEU in 1935 while she was a law student at Madrid University and was rapidly promoted into a senior delegate position. She and other students were motivated to join "because José Antonio offered the possibility of devising new solutions for Spain's grave social problems and provided an alternative to Marxism."[62] According to Fórmica, despite the Falange's ideological opposition to women's suffrage and its desire to confine women to the home, José Antonio "counted on female university students and nominated them for responsible roles." In her official biography, penned years after the events, she condoned Falangist sectarian violence as a form of 'self-defence':

> The 'dialectic of pistols' pre-supposed a previous dialogue, one initiated by those who had first used these [violent] means. It wasn't based on the

> medieval dialectic of 'an eye for an eye', rather on the logical response of a person who knows themselves to be under attack.[63]

Falangist women not only raised funds and disseminated propaganda but they were also willing accessories to illegal and violent political practices. In June 1934 women's student activism was re-directed into a new auxiliary Women's Section (Sección Femenina) which was assigned welfare-aid roles in response to an increasing number of police arrests and political prisoners. Pilar Primo de Rivera's accounts of women's activism before the war[64] contest the prevailing Falangist discourses that consigned women to a subaltern and secondary role.[65] While Pilar emphasised women's "natural acceptance of a life of submission, service, self-abnegation to a task,"[66] Falangist women self-identified as 'militants' who participated in political protests and 'joyfully' undertook dangerous subversive activities.[67] "During the heady days between February and July 1936 women aided and abetted male violence."[68] They smuggled weapons by concealing guns in their coats and inside their boots and provided *alibis* for the gunmen.[69] A significant minority "provoked riots that evoked the surprise and admiration of comrades."[70]

While women were officially discouraged from participation in the violent street clashes, they were involved in the planning and logistics and a few learned how to handle fire-arms during illicit target practices in the Casa de Campo. The party's ideals and values were reflected in its austere military-style clothing and bodily comportment which was appropriated by women.[71] The SEU activist María Laura Colmeiro was mortally 'wounded in action' during a sectarian street battle and her dying wish was for a "blue shirt from Pilar Primo de Rivera so that she might die wearing the Falangist uniform."[72] The sisters Carmen, Matilde and Ángela Soria Viejo were devout members of Acción Católica who later became shirt-wearing members of the Sección Femenina in 1935 and were "involved in the political upheavals and attended various meetings … from which they always returned with unkempt hair and torn clothing."[73] These three sisters and their father, a military officer, were extra-judicially killed in October 1936. The youngest, Carmencita, was sixteen years old.[74]

The female activists tirelessly published and disseminated propaganda across the capital on a shoe-string budget. The eighteen-year-old student María Paz Martínez Unciti sold membership stamps and soaps, edited newspapers, composed songs (*octavillas*) and disseminated copies of *La Conquista del Estado*, *¡Arriba!* and *FE* (Falange Española).[75] In defiance of the orders of the Dirección General de Seguridad (DGS) and the frequent raids on the party offices,[76] 'women spread propaganda everywhere on trams, in the metro, on shop displays, in cafés and cinemas':

> Women were also useful vehicles for the dissemination of national-syndicalist ideas, given that at this time they still aroused less suspicion than the men of the Movement. And so, with that characteristic joyfulness (*alegría*) with which everything was done in the Falange, extra membership stamps

> and propaganda were ordered from the girls (*chicas*) so that they could distribute them absolutely everywhere … Sometimes we marked the walls with red lipstick, so that the message showed up bright and red, at other times clandestine propaganda leaflets and membership stamps (*sellos de cotización)* suddenly appeared under the plates in some bar where the girls had had a drink, or they posted leaflets into the post-boxes so that the post men would find and read them, and one day the national syndicalist women even pasted membership stamps in the Home Office.[77]

Lipstick graffiti represented a new and subversive gendered cultural practice. Sexual difference may be interpreted as a series of culturally and historically constructed meanings expressed through specific embodied acts or performances.[78] Lipstick as a gender-signifier channelled new constructions of the 'modern woman' and Falangist women broke with traditional conventions by daring to wear lipstick and using it to leave distinctively feminine traces in the public space. The red slogans were a type of visual pun which both 'made-up the feminine' and 'marked' the Republican space with a new female political presence. Such was 'the enthusiasm for this type of street sport' that, instead of getting together after work for tea or to go to the cinema, 'our comrades' (*camaradas*) would meet in the city centre and split off into pairs in order to distribute membership stamps on every street corner.'

> The police threats were absolutely useless, as were the constant house-searches ordered by the DGS in order to stop Falangist women from hiding Falangist propaganda.[79]

An idealised 'film-noir' visual representation of Falangist women's transgressive political effervescence in the pre-war public space is provided in the post-war film *Rojo y Negro* (1942) which was based on the political life of María Paz Unciti and scripted and directed by the Falangist fifth-columnist, Carlos Arévalo, who was also a close friend of Carmen Timmermans (a senior leader of Auxilio Azul).[80] Women's high visibility in the immediate pre-war period would seem to indicate that female activism was taken much less seriously by the authorities than that of their male counterparts. After 16 February 1936 only sixteen Falangist women were imprisoned throughout Spain, and this figure is low in comparison with the male detentions.[81] In reality these women were no less threatening than men, and while women were tasked with making blue shirts, bracelets, banners, flags and other Falangist regalia, they also cached weapons and performed gun-running operations.[82] The Falange consciously exploited the traditional gender stereotypes surrounding women's conformist and apolitical nature and entrusted women with dangerous and illegal 'masculine' activities. Both before and after 18 July 1936 Falangist women hid guns and safe-housed fugitives.[83]

> The most tragic aspect of the political meetings from the point of view of the Sección Femenina was the fact that, because [initially] the police

> only performed body searches on the men, women carried the pistols and truncheons into and out of the meetings so that these wouldn't be confiscated.[84]

During the war the threat posed by these committed women became evident to the Republican authorities and the checa leaders. The women smuggled arms into the embassies including the Finnish and Turkish Embassies, and risked their lives in order to safe-house Falangists, weapons and documents.[85] María Luisa Lagunés was a prominent (*destacada*) liaison agent who visited the Falangist leaders in the Model Prison and co-ordinated intensive propaganda campaigns before the war. After 18 July 1936, she was arrested by the Republican Security Services, the Servicios de Información Militar (SIM), on several occasions. After obtaining asylum at the Paraguayan Embassy she continued to perform resistance activities including smuggling weapons into the Turkish Embassy and physically assaulting a Republican lieutenant in order to steal his identification documents.[86] These young Falangist women were committed and fearless activists who smuggled guns in their '*Katiusa*' boots.[87] Despite the traditional and patriarchal constructions of women in the official Falangist discourses of the time, in practice women were accepted as an integral part of liaison, fund-raising and propaganda activities.

On 14 March 1936 José Antonio Primo de Rivera and other Supreme Junta leaders were arrested and accused of the attempted assassination of the Republican politician Luis Jiménez de Asua. The Falangist leadership was beheaded, and the only sector that was left relatively intact was the Sección Femenina, although, according to Pilar, at this stage 'even the women were hunted by the police and menaced by communist death threats.'[88] This situation created a new space for women to perform important roles within the organisation. Elena Rodríguez was tasked with safe-guarding the Falange's membership records and 'in doing so she was able to save many lives.'[89] Pilar Primo de Rivera conducted clandestine meetings in the Prado Museum's Velázquez room from where orders were issued and a series of underground liaison and welfare-aid networks were mobilised.

The Sección Femenina also provided vital links between the male Junta leaders in the prisons and the members on the ground. After José Antonio's transfer from the Model Prison in Madrid to Alicante on 5 June 1936, his aunt "Tia Ma, Carmen and Margot Primo de Rivera served as liaison agents (*enlaces*) and one day they were chased under gun fire while taking a message from José Antonio to a nearby village."[90] Margarita Larios (Margot), the wife of Miguel Primo de Rivera, visited her husband and José Antonio twice daily in Alicante prison. Margot was accused of military rebellion for passing messages and contraband into the prison and "for organising secret Falangist meetings at her home where orders and instructions would be given to the leaders."[91] Contact with the prisoners was facilitated by a prison guard who had been ordered by the director of Alicante prison to turn a blind-eye on the illegal activities of Margot, Agustín Aznar and other leaders who regularly visited José Antonio in the Alicante prison. With the collusion of the prison guards and officials it was possible to smuggle messages, wine and even a gun into Alicante prison. The popular balladist 'La Goya,' (wife of Tomás Borrás) was also a go-between (*enlace y recadera*) for José Antonio while he was imprisoned in Alicante during the war.[92] Prior to 18 July 1936 Falangist women also played key liaison roles between José Antonio and the other Falangist leaders in relation to the rebel conspiracy. Sección Femenina women allegedly passed coded letters from José Antonio to Franco and the other generals. The letters passed the censorship controls "because they looked innocuous as they were handwritten by women in different coloured inks."[93]

Auxilio Azul

According to Pilar Primo de Rivera a small number of committed Sección Femenina members formed Auxilio Azul between July and August of 1936.[94] These members included María Paz Martínez Unciti and her older sister Pilar who was also a Falangist. María Paz was a former SEU student activist and a personal friend of José Antonio. The organisation initially provided safe-houses for political fugitives.[95] It also provided child-care, cooking, laundering, medication and food for fugitives, prisoners and their families. These 'services' represented a continuation of the clandestine welfare-aid services performed by the Sección Femenina after the outlawing of the party. However, Auxilio Azul is almost exclusively remembered for its role in arranging escape-lines and obtaining asylum for anti-Republicans within Madrid's foreign embassies during the first months of the war.[96] In addition to providing welfare-aid to 'needy persons' the members were also involved in treasonous and illegal activities. They acted as prison liaison agents,[97] smuggled arms[98] and cached weapons[99] and explosives. They also hid fugitives and military deserters,[100] devised escape-lines and obtained false ration cards and identity documentation.[101] Others helped conscripts to evade their front-line duties and "ensured that disaffected soldiers were assigned military posts where they could perform acts of sabotage against the reds."[102] Some infiltrated military hospitals as nurses in order to aid the escape of patients and "save them from the firing squad."[103] These women disseminated defeatist anti-Republican propaganda including Nationalist war reports[104] and communiqués.[105] A few managed to infiltrate Republican civil and military institutions and received their orders directly from the SIPM. Others liaised with the Red Cross in order to obtain food, condensed-milk and other supplies using false food coupons (*vales falsos*).[106] They infiltrated the SIM and other Republican organisations and institutions as administrative assistants, secretaries, office workers and nurses.

The founder members were 'old shirts' or the relatives and intimates of male Falangist activists. Rafaela de Castro Gutiérrez became the Secretary General in 1937. She had joined the Falange in June 1936, and efforts to re-establish contact with Falangists after the coup resulted in her imprisonment in the Checa de Fomento in September 1936. De Castro's brother was imprisoned in Porlier and killed during an illegal prison *saca* in Paracuellos del

Jarama.[107] María González Tablas y Mendizábal had been a Falangist activist since March 1934; she was imprisoned in the Checa de Bellas Artes in late 1936 because her name appeared in a centralised register of anti-Republicans (Control de Nóminas) held at the DGS head office.[108] Melchora Gutiérrez Monje was arrested by a CPIP brigade on 4 September 1936 and held in Fomento on account of her activism in the Falange.[109]

After 18 July 1936, the general public and the authorities became more aware of the specific threat posed by Falangist women; around fifty-nine female activists were killed in the Republican- held zones.[110] A further 1,500 anti-Republican women were imprisoned in Madrid. Pilar was surprised by the coup in the capital and immediately went into hiding with Marichu de la Mora, Inés and Dolores Primo de Rivera and her friend Dora Maqueda. She made efforts to disguise herself by dyeing her hair blonde,[111] and hid in a succession of safe-houses until María Paz Martínez Unciti organised her asylum at the Argentinian Embassy in late July 1936.[112] José María Jardón managed to obtain a false Argentine passport for Pilar in early August that enabled safe passage to Alicante with her cousin Dolores, the girlfriend of Augustín Aznar, and her sister-in-law Rosario, the wife of Fernando Primo de Rivera. Once in Alicante the women boarded the *Graf Spee* (a German patrol ship) bound for Seville in late August 1936 where they laundered the crew's clothing in 'recompense for their salvation.' Upon arrival, Pilar contacted the leaders of Seville's Sección Femenina: Carmen Azancot, Syra Manteola, Amelia Medina and Mercedes Fórmica. After a short stay in Seville, Pilar established a Head Office in Salamanca, and by January 1937 she claimed that the organisation had already recruited as many as 60,000 women in the rebel-held zone.[113]

After Pilar's dramatic escape, María Paz became the leader until she was arrested by communist militias during a failed attempt to smuggle Emilio Franco (an eighteen-year-old SEU activist) into the Finnish Embassy on 31 October 1936.[114] María Paz was taken to the Checa de Fomento from where she was removed and extra-judicially executed during the early hours of 1 November in a wasteland area outside Vallecas.[115] Thereafter, her elder sister Carina Martínez Unciti aged twenty-four years became leader for the duration of the war. Carina claimed that the organisation had helped to save the lives of many prominent anti-Republicans including General Millan Astray's mother, the Catholic Action leader Teresa Luzzati and several Falangist leaders including Raimundo Fernández Cuesta and Manuel Valdés Larrañaga.[116] Carina was a devout Catholic with no prior political affiliations or background in activism. She renamed the organisation "La Hermandad de Auxilio Azul – María Paz Martínez Unciti" in memory of her younger sister. This name change brought with it a shift in the organisation's ideology which moved from the fascist Falangist model to a more traditionalist Catholic framework of core-ideas, values and beliefs. This new 'Sisterhood' began to attract a larger following. After November 1936 membership rose dramatically from within a wider constituency of anti-Republican women that included members of Catholic Action, CEDA, Alfonsine monarchist and Traditionalist members. However, the vast majority had no prior associational or political affiliations before the war.

This secret organisation was the most efficient and well-organised of all the fifth column networks in Madrid during the war.[117] At some time soon after the conflict María del Carmen López Mancisidor helped to compile a comprehensive membership list under the direction of her leader Emilia Martí Melguizo.[118] However, I was unable to locate these records, and they may still be preserved in a private family archive.[119] In early 1937 the leaders of the 'Castilla Group,' Helen Garrigues Walker and her husband Antonio Garrigues y Díaz-Cañabete, introduced Carina to their contacts at the International Red Cross and to Manuel Valdés Larrañaga, the leader of the Clandestine Falange. Auxilio Azul fell under the nominal control of Valdés, maintaining regular contact with the Clandestine Falange.[120] In January 1937 Carina and a few trusted senior members also came to form part of the 'Galicia' intelligence network which was in contact with the SIPM in Burgos.[121]

Auxilio Azul grew rapidly over the course of 1937. It was organised into thirty-seven separate divisions called 'Connections' that came to incorporate around 165 members each.[122] It mainly operated in the upper-middle-class districts of Buenavista and Salamanca (where the embassies were located) but also in Congreso, Universidad, Hospital, Hospicio, Inclusa and Chamberí.[123] Support grew steadily within familial, confessional, professional and friendship networks. Members were united by their Catholic faith and their anti-Republicanism. By February 1937 Auxilio Azul had grown into an extensive clandestine community which was made up of hundreds of members who came from a variety of Catholic, political and social backgrounds including nurses, house-wives, domestic and factory workers and actresses.[124] The members were proactive and successful in their recruitment efforts. In 1938 a member who was resident in the Buenavista district claimed to have "recruited as many as seventy new members."[125] Dolores Núñez provided food for members and medicines for 'needy' anti-Republicans on a regular basis.[126] Membership bestowed a sense of mission, higher purpose and belonging during moments of extreme danger and uncertainty. When this danger passed in around mid-1937 after the battle-lines were stabilised the network expanded into a secret Catholic social enterprise network (discussed in Chapter 2 below).

In order to ensure the utmost security a careful selection and vetting procedure was developed. Membership was strictly by invitation only: "in February 1938, I was asked by my good friend Rafaela de Castro [the General Secretary] who was an 'old shirt,' to work alongside her for the good of the National Movement."[127]

The members described their resistance as part of a divine and redemptive mission or "*Magna obra*" (Magnum Opus).[128] Most of the collaborators were unaware that they formed part of an extensive and illegal network. The strict membership rules ensured secrecy and security. The members were only allowed to recruit trustworthy friends, relatives or close acquaintances (*'personas de confianza'*). Prospective members were required to demonstrate evidence of devout Catholicism and a genuine religious conviction. Strangers were treated with suspicion as potential informants, and unsolicited membership requests were rejected as a matter of course.

As the network rapidly expanded over the course of 1937 the selection process became more formal. A sub-group leader might invite a friend to collaborate on a specific project, for example, by making clothes for prisoners, visiting them and giving them parcels. The candidates were then invited to an informal initiation meeting (*tertulia*) at the leader's home where the essential aims and ideals of the Work (*el espíritu de la Obra*) were explained. The candidate's reactions and responses were closely monitored. The political convictions and the loyalty of prospective members would be established during this meeting. The principal criterion for selection and the chief guarantee of loyalty was whether the candidate was a practising Catholic. Suitable candidates were subjected to a period of surveillance. Auxilio Azul managed to successfully infiltrate two women within the Republican SIM who were able to perform background security checks on prospective candidates using information which was held in the Control de Nóminas. This may explain why the network was never dismantled, although individual members were sometimes arrested for disaffection. It was also able to warn members of the Clandestine Falange (see Chapter 3) of forthcoming house searches and arrests. One woman was embedded in the SIM's 'arrest and detentions department' and the other within the records department. Both were Group Leaders codenamed "J" and "L" respectively. "L" was María Felisa Parés.[129] The main task of these two agents was to expose Republican informants who were infiltrated within the fifth column. Agent J (Emilia Martín Melguizo) was also the Group leader of AA[130] (a detailed description of the structure of the group and the use of alphabetical code names is provided in Chapter 2 below). Agent J also received intelligence from a communist named Enriqueta López Moncade.[131] López (aged twenty-four years) was a committed and influential card-carrying member of the Spanish Communist Party (PCE) who lived in calle Cadarso behind a former Carmelite building which was ransacked during the terror. López was also a former work colleague and friend of Carina. She was able to use her communist contacts to discover where María Paz was being held after her arrest on 31 October. With López's aid Carina obtained the release of several anti-Republicans including an infantry commander (who was also an old family friend) from a Checa known as the *Troika* that was operated by communist and UGT members. López's networks of influence contributed significantly to Carina's reputation as a reliable safe-house and escape-line coordinator. In September 1936 López informed Agent J that the Siam Embassy which was situated in calle Juan Bravo, 12 was a sham operation that had been established by unscrupulous profiteers who merely wanted to exploit wealthy asylum seekers. Group AA issued warnings that this embassy should be avoided at all costs. Following a tip-off from López, Agent J was able to warn the Clandestine Falange that the SIM was planning to raid the fake embassy in December 1936. According to Manuel Valdés Larrañaga (the leader of the Clandestine Falange) these women regularly provided vital intelligence to the Clandestine Falange groups: "One of the girls who was infiltrated within the SIM provided us with the card index (*fichero*) of the [Republican] agents who were infiltrated in Burgos."[132]

In order to ensure safety and anonymity only the seven Junta leaders and thirty-seven network leaders (described below) knew of the true size and extent of the operations. The grass-roots 'militants' were only ever informed of the identity of their immediate leader (*Jefa*). New members were assigned a code-name which was known only to the most senior members. Most members were led to believe by their sub-group leaders that they were merely helping friends and relatives as part of a spontaneous and *ad hoc* welfare-aid initiative. Carina's 'cardinal rule' was that assistance should only be given to close friends or family. Even Carina's sister Pilar (who was a Falangist) was allegedly unaware of the true size and nature of the organisation.[133] It was only after the war that friends and acquaintances discovered that they had been involved in the organisation.

Auxilio Azul – Motivations for mobilisation

While the organisation provided practical and economic assistance, it also offered religious, spiritual and emotional support. Auxilio Azul provided an emotional refuge for anti-Republicans.[134] Like-minded individuals were able to "unite with other victims and do something to avenge their dead."[135] The resistance was conceived as a form of spiritual resistance that provided moral as well as material support.[136]

The earliest women were mobilised into resistance because of their politico-religious convictions or personal experiences of repression. They wanted to avenge perceived Republican injustices and 'do something' for the rebel cause. The nurse Trinidad Palacios Gónzalo lost her husband and a brother during the repression.[137] Her husband, Teófilo Peña Franco, was also a nurse and president of the civil guard committee of calle Gúzman el Bueno. He was executed by POUM militias in September 1936. Her brother, Brother Rufino Palacios Gonzalo, was a member of an Augustinian order who voluntarily gave himself up to the DGS in September 1936. He was imprisoned in Porlier from where he was removed during a *saca* on 18 November 1936 and killed in Paracuellos. Ana María Rizzo Goñi was the daughter of a retired army general who had served in the Philippines. She was also a Falangist activist and propagandist who had organised clandestine meetings at her house after March 1936. On the eve of the rebel coup she safe-housed "five Falangists with guns and truncheons who were being hunted by the reds."[138] She was sought by Republican security services because she was listed as a member of the Falange in the Control de Nóminas.[139] On the night of 17 July 1936, militias came to her home and fired several shots through the door. She and her 'comrades' were forced to flee the house. Her father was imprisoned as a *desafecto* at the start of the war, and her mother, two aunts and her sister Dolores were arrested and interrogated at the Checa de Fomento (the notorious CPIP headquarters). The women, together with several other female friends, were mistreated, deprived of food and sanitation and forced to sleep on the floor of an over-crowded cell. They were threatened during interrogation because they refused to reveal the identity or whereabouts of anti-Republican relatives and friends. Doña Dolores Rizzo Goñi (mother of Ana and Dolores) was found guilty of disaffection and incarcerated in Conde de Toreno prison. Meanwhile, Ana María managed to avoid arrest. After the deaths of several male members of the immediate family, Ana and her sister Lolita (Dolores) were involved in "raising funds, sewing, hiding fugitives and organising clandestine masses."[140] Ana María also "recruited a considerable number of comrades into the Falange, especially during the time of the communist revolution."[141]

Denunciations, house searches and citizen's arrests became a feature of everyday life during the first six months of the war. María Emilia Azas Trigueras' family resorted to burning incriminating religious artefacts, monarchist memorabilia or right-wing propaganda because they were fearful of the regular militia searches.[142] By late October 1936 around 1,500 women were imprisoned in Madrid.[143] Approximately 29% of a total 1,171 female political prisoners who were interviewed by the International Red Cross in December 1936 claimed that they had been the victims of denunciation.[144] For women like Rafaela Castro Gutiérrez and Andrea Pariente Suárez, denunciations, repeated house searches, arbitrary arrests and the wave of *paseos* and prison *sacas* mobilised them into resistance.[145] Caridad Muñoz del Valle's son was 'taken for a ride' in November 1936.[146] Carmen García Vallejo was arrested because she 'belonged to a fascist family' and was in possession of two military uniforms. García's father was a first infantry commander, and her brother was 'a dangerous element' who was killed on 31 October, 1936.[147] Many victims of the repression came to collaborate with Auxilio Azul. Dolores Amador López testified that she was forced to "remain in hiding for five months because she was fearful of arrest as it was widely known that she had distributed anti-Republican propaganda alongside her brother during the 1936 elections."[148] Consuelo Pérez de Barradas safe-housed a female cousin for a period of twelve months after her release from prison. She was subsequently arrested for aiding a priest. Her mother and grandmother died during the war because of the "many upsets and privations suffered at this time."[149] The Republican militias had searched the family property on four separate occasions.

The violent anticlerical repression which occurred at the start of the war posed an unprecedented threat to Spanish Catholic habitus. Madrid's religious establishments were amongst the first targets of the popular anger.[150] The speed with which religious persons and establishments came under assault reflected a deep-rooted popular anticlericalism.[151] This extra-judicial repression was accompanied by forms of legal repression. Defence militias entered religious buildings in order to perform searches and confiscations. On 11 August 1936 the government implemented an emergency decree that provided for:

> the immediate closure of all Religious orders and Congregations, now existing in Spain, that in some manner or other participated in the present insurrectional movement, whether directly or indirectly participating in it, or providing aid or assistance of whatever nature to seditious and rebellious persons.[152]

While the Church was not involved in the military conspiracy, the authorities believed that it actively supported the rebellion, harboured dangerous fugitives and held illegal weapons. Hundreds of religious personnel were forced to abandon their homes and seek refuge within the Catholic community. Amparo Fernández Ceballos belonged to the Adoratrices of Guadalajara; she was transferred to a safe-house in Madrid soon after 18 July but was arrested on 15 October 1936 'because of her religious antecedents.' She was eventually absolved and released from prison on 3 May 1937.[153] Public confessional practice was banned, and the Catholic religion was forced underground. This continued for the duration of the war, despite the efforts the Basque Minister of Justice Manuel Irujo[154] to re-open the churches and to restore public confession in the Republican-held zones after May 1937.

During the early months of the war evidence of confessional practice constituted *a priori* evidence of disaffection and hostility towards the Republican regime. Auxilio Azul members felt a moral compulsion to 'do something' in aid of religion and the beleaguered anti-Republican community. The Republican government was held accountable for the revolutionary unrest and the violent killings. Resistance was couched in spiritual and religious terms. Personal experiences of physical and emotional suffering were conceptualised and afforded meaning within specifically Catholic frames of suffering and redemption. The repression was conceived within new Catholic discourses as a 'providential'[155] and potentially redemptive "*Via Crucis* of suffering in Madrid-Golgotha."[156] Resistance was viewed as an imperative Catholic duty. The confessional aspects of this resistance are reflected in the testimonies of former members and in memory texts. Carina recalled that she was unable to remain passive in the face of injustice after the death of her sister. She was 'emboldened to continue María Paz's resistance efforts despite the grave risks and dangers because inaction was a form of suicide and because her sister's death could only be avenged by good works.'[157] The 'hot' repression of the early months mobilised hundreds of Catholics into resistance and strengthened religious convictions. A few openly confessed to the authorities that they had been mobilised into resistance "because they were Catholics and because they [the Republican authorities] would not let me practice the Catholic rites."[158] Group Leader Elvira Martínez Ostendi was a devout Catholic and a former member of Acción Popular. She was arrested in August 1937 and interrogated about her "social and religious ideology." She responded: "I am a Catholic and I am willing to die shouting *Viva Cristo Rey* (Long live Christ the King)."[159] Such politico-religious performances constituted powerful forms of contestation. When performed in the context of the prison or the court-room these emotive utterances and gestures constituted a symbolic occupation of the Republican space. Only the most brave and defiant individuals openly declaimed the traditional Carlist call to arms.

Women were motivated to join Auxilio Azul for reasons which combined personal, political and religious motivations. Some had been politically active within the Falange or Catholic or Monarchist parties such as Acción Popular and Renovación Española.[160] María Baeza Torrecilla de Picatoste (who safe-housed the Martínez Unciti family in November 1936) was a former member of Juventudes Católicas (Catholic Youth) and Acción Popular.[161] On 28 October 1936, the Falangist Carlota Narcisa González (who later became the Treasurer of Auxilio Azul) was arrested during a failed attempt to smuggle arms into the Finnish Legation.[162] Communist militias took her to the Checa de la calle Españoleto where she was allegedly "subjected to all manner of ill treatment and humiliations … and beaten with a whip and a belt." She claimed that she had refused to betray other members of her group or to divulge the final destination of the weapons. Despite 'threats of execution by firing squad' she was subsequently released. González joined Auxilio Azul in January 1937 in order to fight back against her experiences of repression. María del Carmen Díaz Aguado was motivated to join Auxilio Azul after five of her brothers, one of whom was a Falangist First Centurion, were imprisoned. Her father died shortly afterwards "on account of the suffering and upset caused by these persecutions."[163] A significant proportion of members joined after their release on charges of disaffection.[164] Andrea Pariente Suárez claimed that her brother was killed by Republican militias on 21 August 1936.[165] Dolores Amador López was a former Falangist activist who was forced into hiding after her brother, who was a Falangist squad leader, was arrested and shot. She joined Auxilo Azul "in August 1938 at great personal risk despite being a well-known Falangist."[166] Juana Sánchez Aguado testified that nine members of her family were "taken for a ride (*paseados*) by the reds."[167] The deputy leader of one group decided to join the organisation after five of her brothers were arrested.[168] María Ugaldezubiaur worked as a liaison agent at the Panamanian Embassy. She sought asylum at the embassy at the start of the war because her family was 'very persecuted.' She made no pretence of her motivation for joining in 1937: "Two sons were killed while fighting on the Nationalist front-lines. My family was forced into hiding for several months in Madrid and we all experienced extreme hardship."[169] She wanted retribution for the deaths of her sons and the 'persecution' of her family. Most members, including Carina, were devout Catholics who had no political affiliations before the war. Their lived experiences of personal suffering, bereavement and repression mobilised them into resistance and prompted them to forge new political identities.[170] Resistance was driven by powerful emotions including feelings of persecution and the desire for revenge. Maria del Carmen Aguado's brother was a leader of a First Centurion in the Nationalist zone, as a result of which all her family was 'very persecuted' including five brothers who were arrested in the Republican zone. She became the sub-group leader of AP-3.[171] The testimonies also revealed resentment and moral outrage at the repression of Catholics, and forms of calling to account may have been perceived by some as a function of their Christian duty.[172] In particular, Falangist women and those with Catholic and conservative military backgrounds often harboured a desire to avenge the death of intimates following the illegal *paseos* and *sacas* of 1936. Revenge was realised in the denunciatory social intelligence gathering practices described in Chapters 2 and 3 below, and such accusatory practices became a feature of the post-war judicial repression.[173] Rather than just politicising private life, civil war also has the effect of privatising politics by allowing personal desires, motivations and loyalties to inform political action.[174]

El Espiritu de Auxilio Azul – core values

The organisation's core values and beliefs were reflected in its membership 'Regulations' and 'Action Points' created in February 1937 by the General Secretary Rafaela de Castro Gutiérrez in collaboration with Carina Unciti.[175] They incorporated traditional Catholic discourses and the emotive politico-religious discourses of José Antonio who sought to mobilise a "revolutionary army of Angels with swords."[176] After his execution on 20 November 1936, Pilar Primo de Rivera incorporated her brother's discourses in her writings and speeches in order to perpetuate his memory and disseminate his political beliefs.[177] The Sección Femenina's 'Codes of Conduct' which were re-drafted in 1937 stipulated in Item 2: "Be Disciplined, disciplined, disciplined." Auxilio Azul's Rules of Governance and Regulations (set out below) also adhered to this austere and disciplinarian regime. Former members were expected to "obey and blindly complete all the orders issued by their leaders at great personal risk."[178] Most of the testimonies were prefaced with: "I performed everything as commanded"[179] and ended with: "I completed all my orders with great enthusiasm."[180]

The testimonies evidence the creation of a new and distinctive discursive gender identity that collapsed traditional gender binaries by conflating 'feminine' attributes (meekness and self-abnegation) with 'masculine' attributes such as bravery and military discipline. Similar forms of emotional intensity and mystical idealism were reflected in the emotional regimes of other European fascist groups at this time.[181] The Falange emphasised organic unity and the replacement of parliament by an authoritarian system, while invoking the Catholic religion. An early Falangist manifesto, the "Puntos Iniciales," stated that "All reconstruction of Spain must have a Catholic character."[182] The Falange's brand of fascism was specific and unique to Spain; it was corporatist but it also embraced Catholic, traditionalist and monarchist elements. Falangist women were also Catholic women and "very few ideological features *a priori* distinguished them from the followers of Acción Catolica."[183] This interpretation nuances historical representations that portray the Falange as a predominantly secular political movement which was inspired by laicising Italian and German fascism.[184] The party's ideology shifted over time and in order to accommodate Franco's National Movement and the Catholic Church.[185] The leaders encouraged 'virile' and self-sacrificial forms of militancy in both men and women, and the party's mobilising and militarising discourses provided fertile sites for cross-gender identification and the performance of new forms of female political agency:

> See women, how we have made a capital virtue of 'abnegation', which is above all a woman's virtue … hopefully we will reach such levels of virtue that through this virtue we shall be so feminine that one day we may also be regarded as being truly like men![186]

Auxilio Azul's rules of governance

The organisation's rules of governance were never written down for fear of reprisals. The rules were memorised by the sub-group leaders and communicated to the new members who were required to memorise the Action Points (set out below) as part of their initiation. The regulations reflected the core values of the Falange and its politico-religious and militaristic 'emotional regime.'[187] This regime incorporated strands of Catholic mysticism, ardour, self-abnegation and ascetic military discipline, discourses that reflected José Antonio's martial and quasi-mystical pre-war political writings.[188] The affiliates were encouraged to operate within rigid codes of piety, courage, discipline and self-abnegation. After the death of María Paz in November 1936 the network was led by Carina who was a devout Catholic and Catholic values also pervaded the organisation's core values, ideals and beliefs:

> Daily and upon rising, offer up your heart to God and entrust your soul to Him and to Spain.
>
> Your security rests entirely upon Him on this difficult path that you have chosen.
>
> During all your daily activities remember that our Fallen Ones look upon all that you do.
>
> No one can give what they do not have, pray that you may recruit into this charitable endeavour new recruits who have a genuine Christian and Spanish spirit.
>
> Our brothers are falling '*cara al sol*' (heads raised to the sun). Take care that your home is never clouded by the darkness of necessity![189]

Once the organisation grew beyond a small circle of founder members, the leaders ('*Jefes*') devised a set of 'Action Points' which reflected the fierce loyalty and discipline required from all members of the Falange:

> Never speak of this organisation except with your immediate liaison agents (*enlaces*), and only when necessary.
>
> Never ask to know more than that which is required for your purposes, never divulge more information than you have to.
>
> You must become accustomed to immediately obeying instructions, in this way you will achieve the greatest of all satisfactions: That of a duty duly performed.
>
> When in doubt as to the necessary course of action, chose that course which involves the most personal sacrifice.
>
> May your actions speak louder than your words *¡Arriba España!*[190]

Sub-group leader Inés Martín Monjas testified as follows:

> I performed my duty with great zeal and enthusiasm because of the terrible times that we were going through … it was my duty as a good comrade to sacrifice myself on behalf of our brothers [in arms] who were also honourably suffering … above all, I obediently and unquestioningly (*ciegamente*) followed every single order and instruction given to me by my leaders at great personal risk because, on several occasions, I was the subject of several denunciations but these never came to anything concrete against me … I was simply a militant who performed many duties and when I came to have the honour of being promoted to the position of Sub Group Leader these duties only increased.[191]

Auxilio Azul's emotional regime accommodated traditional Catholic discourses and 'modern and revolutionary' Falangist discourses. Members self-identified as 'obedient and disciplined militants' who dutifully fought in aid of Franco's 'Glorious Nationalist Movement.' The formulaic testimonies often ended on an exalted note similar to that of a sub-group leader who proudly declared:

> I completed everything that my leaders ordered with great enthusiasm on account of the great elation of my spirit.[192]

Catholicism constituted a key component of this ideology and Auxilio Azul's discourses incorporated the language of the Catholic liturgy and of lay Catholic associations like Acción Católica which required 'the faithful to offer up their hearts to God and to entrust their souls to him and to Spain.' While a majority of the leaders were activists in the Falange before the war, most of those who mobilised after 18 July conceptualised resistance within traditional

Catholic paradigms of suffering, self-sacrifice, martyrdom and redemption and interiorised new national Catholic discourses of 'Holy Crusade against anti-Spain.' Rosario Queipo de Llano (the sister of Seville's notorious rebel general) was tried for treason in 1937. She fashioned herself as a devout Catholic and recalled having defiantly stated during trial:

> Yes, we are all Catholics. My sister was a nun ... our mother taught us to pray and to believe in God, and these beliefs, when implanted from childhood, are difficult to forget. I cannot speak for individual beliefs. But, undoubtedly, during times like these the Faith is exalted. For my own part, I can say that my own faith in God and my belief in His protection have provided me with the courage to bear my situation with patience. I am prepared to resignedly suffer whatever the Good Lord requires of me![193]

The extract illustrates how interiorised Catholicism contributed towards constructions of new and subversive female resistance identities. Such discourses evidence the 'politicisation of martyrdom and afforded sanctity to those who otherwise would be vilified as rebels and traitors.'[194]

After the outlawing of the Falange on 14 March 1936 women became key liaison agents between the imprisoned leaders and the members on the ground. This explains how women were best-positioned to mobilise an early resistance after 18 July. While the base of the organisation was composed of Catholics with no prior political convictions, many of the most senior leaders (with the notable exception of Carina) were Falangist activists. In November 1936 membership rapidly increased and the organisation came to appeal to a wider constituency of disaffected Catholics including members of the outlawed monarchist, CEDA and Traditionalist Communion parties. Auxilio Azul's core values and its distinctive emotional regime reflected the ideology of the Falange and its military and disciplinarian ethos while incorporating traditional national Catholic discourses of 'crusade and martyrdom.' These discourses of suffering, persecution and redemption also came to form part of a new national Catholic cultural currency. After 1 April 1939, Falangist and Catholic women were rewarded for their loyalty to the 'Glorious Movement' by achieving senior positions within the Sección Femenina hierarchy which became the official transmission belt of Falangist ideology after the war.[195] The next chapter examines Auxilio Azul's leadership, structure and operations and explores how women were often the agents and beneficiaries of their vital welfare-aid resistance.

Notes

1 Cervera (1998), p. 282.

2 Bourdieu, Pierre (2003) *Practical Reason, On the theory of Action* (London: Polity), p. 68. The burden of affective labour in order to generate 'family and community feeling' mainly falls upon women.

3 *Historia de la Sección Femenina, "Capitulo II-La Propaganda,"* p. 29.

4 Píris, "Los servicios de información franquistas en la capital," at p. 143. Very little is known about the Traditionalist groups in Madrid, but see Fal Conde's [undated] *Gesta Gloriosa del Requete en Madrid* (Julio 1936–Marzo 1939), *Archivo General Militar de Ávila,* C2505, Cp.4/43 and C.2498.20, Legajo no. 285, Carpeta 20, Armario 5. Also, a country-wide study of the mobilisation of the Carlist militias after 1931 is contained in Gonzalez Calleja, Eduardo and Julio Arosteguí "La tradición recuperada. El requeté carlista y la insurrección," *Historia Contemporánea*, 11, pp. 29–53.

5 [Fal Conde] [undated] *Gesta Gloriosa del Requeté en Madrid* (Julio 1936–Marzo 1939), *Archivo General Militar de Ávila,* C2505, Cp.4/43 and C.2498.20, Legajo no. 285, Carpeta 20, Armario 5.

6 Paz, Armando (1976) *Los Servicios de Espionaje en la Guerra Civil de España, 1936–9* (Madrid: Editorial San Martín), p. 141.

7 Cervera (1998) *Madrid*, p. 271.

8 Borrás (1965) *Seis Mil*, p. 10. Cervera (1998), p. 270. Heiberg and Agudo (2006), p. 194.

9 Carina Unciti, ABC, Madrid, 18 July 1961.

10 *Asesoría Jurídica,* Report on Carmen Tronchoni (b. 23 April 1915–d. 29 March 1938), Document 7, ANA, Carpeta B 18, RAH, Madrid. Carmen Tronchoni was born in Picassent, Valencia. She was employed as a telephone-exchange operator and typist. She was arrested in Barcelona on 28 November 1937 during a failed escape-line operation alongside three male fugitives who had earlier fled Madrid and obtained asylum at the Panamanian Embassy in Valencia pending escape into the Nationalist zone. The men were a former general staff officer, an officer of the *Regulares* and an eighteen-year-old Falangist. The group was arrested while hiding-out in an abandoned building in calle de Monestril. They were entrapped by Republican SIM counter-espionage agents including a female agent named Inés Jiménez Lumbrera who gained the confidence of Carmen, infiltrated the group and gave evidence at trial. Tronchoni was accused of 'organising fascist activities' including providing intelligence relating to the position of Republican troops. She was found guilty by the 'Barcelona High Court of Treason and Espionage, No. 1' in February 1938, sentenced to death and executed on 29 March 1938 following the failure of Red Cross prisoner-exchange negotiations. See Soria Sánchez Blanco, Laura (2016) *Rosas y Margaritas, Mujeres falangistas, tradicionalistas y de Acción Católica asesinadas en la Guerra Civil* (Madrid: Actas), pp. 117–127.

11 Borrás (1965), p. 159.

12 Rodríguez López, Sofía (2008) *Quinta Columnistas. Las mujeres del 36 en la clandestinidad almeriense* (Almería: IEA). See also, Rodríguez López, Sofía and Oscar Rodríguez Barreira "La Quinta Columna y la Guerra Civil en Andalucía," *Andalucía en la Historia*, 46 (October–December 2014), pp. 72–77.

13 Borrás (1965), p. 152.

14 *Asesoría Jurídica* Testimony of Ángela Ibáñez Calvo dated 9 October, Document 225, ANA, Carpeta B 12, RAH, Madrid. She also recruited seventy new members and established contact with María Lemus's Sección Femenina Group in Linares (Jaén).

15 Hardy, Cheryl "Chapter Eight: Hysteresis," in Grenfell Michael (ed) (2012) *Pierre Bourdieu: Key Concepts* (London: Routledge), pp. 126–148 at p. 126.

16 Alfaya, José Luis (1998) *Como un río de fuego, Madrid 1936* (Madrid: EIU), p. 57.

17 See de la Cueva Merino, Julio Chapter 18 "Religion," in Shubert, Adrian, Álvarez Junco, José (2018) *The History of Modern Spain, Chronologies, Themes, Individuals* (London: Bloomsbury), pp. 276–291 at p. 284–285.

18 De la Cueva, Julio "Religious persecution, Anti-clerical Tradition and Revolution: on atrocities against the clergy during the Spanish Civil War," *Journal of Contemporary History*, 33 (3) (1998), pp. 355–369.

19 Thomàs, María (2013) *The Faith and the Fury: Popular anticlerical violence and iconoclasm in Spain, 1931–36* (Brighton: Sussex Academic Press), pp. 100–120.

20 Vincent "The Spanish Civil War as a War of Religion," in Baumeister, Martin and Schuler-Springorum, Stefanie (eds) (2008) *'If you tolerate this…' The Spanish Civil War in the Age of Total War* (Frankfurt: Campus), pp. 74–89 at p. 83.

21 Sánchez Recio, Glicerio (1991) *La República contra los Rebeldes y los Desafectos, La Represión Económica durante la Guerra Civil* (Madrid: Universidad de Alicante). Cervera Gil, Javier (2015) *Contra el enemigo de la República…desde la Ley, Detener, juzgar y encarcelar en guerra* (Madrid: Biblioteca Nueva).

22 Anderson, Peter (2017) *Friend or Foe? Occupation, Collaboration and Selective Violence in the Spanish Civil War* (Sussex: Sussex/Cañada Blanch), p. 167.

23 *Asesoría Jurídica*, Testimony of María Asunción Escondrillas Gil dated 22 September 1939, Document 187, ANA, Carpeta B 12, RAH, Madrid. This former Bachiller student testified to having hidden at least five prominent anti-Republican families, together with other individuals wanted by the police. Her group leaders were Isabel Lacasa and the lawyer Dolores Muñoz Tuero.

24 Hardy, Cheryl "Chapter Eight: Hysteresis," in Adkins, Lisa and Skeggs, Beverley (ed) (2006) *Feminism after Bourdieu* (Oxford: Blackwell) pp. 126–148 at p. 126.

25 See Appendix A (Sources) and Montoliú, Pedro (1999) *Madrid en la guerra civil, Volumenes I and II* (Madrid: Silex).

26 Borrás (1965) *Seis Mil*, pp. 73–74.

27 Bourdieu (2007) *Masculine Domination*, p. 24.

28 See "Actuación durante el dominion en zona Roja" in UPSA, JFAC, 1.4.3. Historia de la asociación de las Jovenes de Acción Católica de la diocesis de Madrid-Alcalá 1926–1948, pp. 4–6. "The female youth section was not terrified by the religious persecution … against certain members of Acción Católica. From the outset, our young women worked tirelessly to help priests and nuns and risked their lives bringing into checas, prisons and safe-houses all the spiritual comforts and consolations afforded by our holy religion" at p. 4. See also, Alfaya (1998) *Como un río de fuego*, p 53. This author notes that the Catholic youth also mobilised to save the contents of burned and vandalised churches.

29 Borrás (1965) *Seis Mil*, pp. 73–74.

30 Ortega López, Teresa María, Cobo Romero, Francisco, del Arco Blanco, Miguel Ángel "The Stability and Consolidation of the Francoist Regime. The Case of Eastern Andalusia, 1936–1950," *Contemporary European History*, 20 (1) (2011), pp. 37–59 at p. 37.

31 Bloxham, Donald and Gerwarth, Robert (eds) (2001) *Political Violence in Twentieth Century Europe* (Oxford: OUP), pp. 154–155.

32 Payne, Stanley (1999) *Fascism in Spain, 1923–1977* (Wisconsin: WUP), p. 164.

33 Payne (1999) *Fascism in Spain*, p. 183.

34 See for example, Expte. 205, *contra* María Dolores Mazón Sanz *por delito/s de Desafección*, AHN, FC-CAUSA_GENERAL, 112, Exp. 16, Imágen 15/35. Trial relating to seventeen-year-old student who had been a member of Renovación Española (RE) and also the Falange which resulted in her arrest on 6 August 1936. She was sentenced to one year in a work camp together with a suspension of all civil and political rights for a period of three years. The monarchists and Catholic parties shared members; see for example, *Expte 11 contra Josefa Sánchez Sánchez por delito/s de Desafección*, AHN, FC-CAUSA_GENERAL, 163, Exp 4 and Expte. 510, AHN, FC-CAUSA_GENERAL, 221, Exp. 7. A thirty-eight-year-old single woman was found to have been a former member of Acción Popular and Renovación Española but had joined the Falange de las JONS party. She was imprisoned during the war in a labour camp for four years for illegal possession of weapons, namely an Astra 6,35 mm pistol and a Saqueta rifle.

35 Victoria López Jimeno Expte. 263, FC-CAUSA_GENERAL, 237, EXP.22, a factory worker, aged seventeen years, was arrested in February 1937 having been denounced by a co-worker for having 'Falangist friends' and owning a signed photograph of José Antonio Primo de Rivera.

36 Payne (1999) *Fascism in Spain*, p. 164.

37 Gallego (1983) *Mujer*, p. 188. See also Sánchez López, Rosario, *Mujer española: Una sombra de destino en lo Universal (trayectoria histórica de Sección Femenina de Falange, 1934–1977)* and Cenarro, Ángela "Trabajo, maternidad y feminidad en las mujeres del fascismo español," in Ana Aguado and Teresa Ma. Ortega (eds) (2011) *Feminismos y antifeminismos, culturas, políticas e dentitdades de genero en la España del Siglo XX* (Valencia: PUV), pp. 229–252 at p. 229.

38 Author's description of Pilar Primo de Rivera upon their first meeting in 1935, see Ridruejo, Dionisio (1976) *Casí unas memorias* (Barcelona: Planeta), p. 52.

39 Primo de Rivera, Pilar (1983) *Recuerdos*, pp. 70–71.

40 Despite the rumours, the newspaper reports do not appear to have identified the Falangist perpetrators by name; see, for example, Melchor Rodríguez in *La Tierra*, 22 June 1934, see also *Mundo Gráfico*, 27 June 1934 and *Heraldo de Madrid*, dated 25 June 1934 which refers to "*Señoritos desconocidos*." Source: anonymous article in www.agenteprovocador.es [La Felguera Editores: Madrid] [last accessed 27 November 2017.]

41 Ridruejo (1976) *Casí unas memorias*, p. 51.

42 A Republican student union. Founded in 1926 as a rival secular body to the Association of Catholic Students (*Asociación de Estudiantes Católicos*). It was a protest group against the Primo de Rivera dictatorship and during the Second Republic against Alfonso XIII's monarchy.

43 Ruiz (2012) *El Terror*, p. 38.

44 Lannon, Frances (2014) *The Spanish Civil War: 1936–1939* (London: Osprey) ebook, Loc 387 of 1536.

45 *Historia de la Sección Femenina*, "*La Ante Guerra*," p. 18.

46 Fórmica (2013) *Memorias*, p. 151.

47 *Asesoría Jurídica*, Testimony of Carmen Díaz Roca, Document 261, ANA, Carpeta B 12, RAH, Madrid. During this war she was imprisoned in the Checa Marqués de Riscal and was transferred to Conde Toreno, San Rafael, Ventas, Alacuas, Muchamiel (Alicante) and finally the Provincial Prison (Alicante) until 29 March 1939.

48 *Asesoría Jurídica*, Testimony of Marcelina Mateos Mateos, Document 179, ANA, Carpeta B 12, RAH, Madrid.

49 *Asesoría Jurídica*, Testimony of Dolores Amador López, Document 189, ANA, Carpeta B 12, RAH, Madrid.

50 *Asesoría Jurídica*, Testimony of Ana María Rizzo y Goñi dated 29 September 1939, Document 248, ANA, Serie Azul, Carpeta B 12, RAH, Madrid.

51 Tavera García "Las mujeres de la Sección Falange," pp. 207–228 at p. 211.

52 Vincent, Mary "Chapter 12, Spain" in Kevin Passmore (ed) (2003) *Women Gender and Fascism in Europe 1919–1945* (Manchester: MUP), pp. 189–213 at p. 209.

53 *Sindicato Español Universitario*, the first Falangist student syndicate whose leader was Manuel Valdés Larrañaga (an architecture student and national Spanish 100 metres swimmer).

54 Gil Pecharromán (2003) *José Antonio Primo de Rivera. Retrato de un visionario* (Madrid: Temas de Hoy), p. 217.

55 Jato, David (1953) *La Rebelión de los estudiantes* (*Apuntes para una historia alegre del S.E.U*) (Madrid: Talleres Gráficos Cíes), p. 11.

56 Jato (1953), *La Rebelión*, p. 94.

57 See Tavera García, Susanna (2011) "Las mujeres de la Sección Falange: Una afirmación entre el activismo político y la sumisión patriarcal, 1934–1939," in Ana Aguado and Teresa Ma. Ortega (eds) (2011) *Feminismos y antifeminismos, culturas, políticas e identitdades de genero en las España del Siglo XX* (Valencia: PUV), pp. 207–228 at p. 217.

58 Ofer, Inbal "Pilar Primo de Rivera," in Adrian Shubert and José Álvarez Junco (ed) (2018) *The History of Modern Spain, Chronologies, Themes, Individuals* (London: Bloomsbury), pp. 465–472 at p. 465.

59 Pilar Primo de Rivera filmed interview excerpt [1980s] televised in documentary "La Sección Femenina" Paisajes de la historia. RTVE. La 2. First broadcast 8 October 2006 and released on internet on 7 September 2012. www.rtve.es/alacarta/videos/paisajes-de-la-historia/paisajes-historia-seccion-femenina/642193. See also Box, Zira "Presentación:

Más que un programa, un modo de ser," *Historia y Política: Ideas Procesos y Movimientos Sociales*, 27 (2012), pp 13–25. The author argues that the Falange was inspired by the doctrines of Mussolini and believed that political programmes which lacked content and ideas were far more effective because it was perceived that pluralism had played a key role in the downfall of liberal democracy. Over and above any detailed political programme, Spanish fascism was 'a way of being,' and its simplistic, binary and Manichean doctrine was based on affirmations of Fatherland (*Patria*).

60 Primo de Rivera, Pilar (1983) *Recuerdos de una vida* (Dyrsa: Madrid). See also Ofer, Inbal "Fragmented autobiographies: a style of writing or self-perception? The case of Pilar Primo de Rivera," *Iberoamericana*, III, 9 (2003), pp. 37–51.

61 In relation to 'epic' memory scripts, see: Portelli, Alessandro "On the peculiarities of oral history," *History Workshop Journal*, 12 (1981), pp. 96–107 at p. 101. The author distinguishes between 'ironic' and 'epic' narratives and observes that in the case of epic memory scripts "the narrator's consciousness appears to have been arrested at climactic moments of their personal experience." He offers examples such as the memories of resistance fighters, war veterans and militant students of the 1960s. In the case of the Falangist women discussed here, such rigid scripts might also evidence motivations of self-vindication and self-justification.

62 Fórmica, Mercedes (2013) *Memorias, visto y vivido, escucho el silencio (1931–1947)* (Seville: Renacimiento), p. 151.

63 Fórmica (2013) *Memorias*, p. 180.

64 *Historia de la Sección Femenina por Pilar Primo de Rivera, Libro Primero, Primera Parte – "Capitulo II-La Propaganda,"* (typescript), ANA, Carpeta 1-B, RAH, Madrid, p. 29.

65 Monica Orduña Prada (1996) *El Auxilio Social, (1936–40) La etapa fundacional y los primeros años* (Madrid: Escuela Libre Editorial), p. 33.

66 *Historia de la Sección Femenina por Pilar Primo de Rivera, Libro Primero, Primera Parte – "Las Visitas a la cárcel de Madrid,"* (typescript), ANA, Carpeta 1-B, RAH, Madrid, p. 27.

67 The adjective 'joyful' (*alegre*) used in conjunction with Falangist activities/duties is a key feature of José Antonio's militant rhetoric (Oxford: Berg), pp. 167–188.

68 Vincent (2002) "*Camisas Nuevas*," p. 172.

69 *Historia de la Sección Femenina por Pilar Primo de Rivera, Libro Primero, Primera Parte – "Capitulo II-La Propaganda,"* (typescript), ANA, Carpeta 1-B, RAH, Madrid, p. 29.

70 Gallego (1983) *Mujer*, p. 41.

71 See Vincent, Mary "*Camisas Nuevas*: Style and Uniformity in the Falange Española 1933–43," in Wendy Parkins (ed) (2002) *Fashioning the Body Politic, Dress, Gender, Citizenship* (Oxford: Berg), pp. 167–188. For an idealised visual representation of this austere and martial bodily 'hexis' see the film by Carlos Arévalo "*Rojo y Negro*" (Cepisca: 1942) as restored by Filmoteca Española. This film is of historic value because it is the first film to depict the idea of a Clandestine Falangist resistance in the capital. It is rich in visual symbolism and was inspired by American film noir and also employed 'modernist, Italian neo-realist, Russian avant-garde and surrealist techniques.' The scenes depicting an open cross-section of the Checa de Fomento building are particularly innovative. See article by Arturo Pérez-Reverte "La Película Maldita," in *XL Semanal* dated 19 April 2010.

72 Jato (1953) *La Rebelión*, p. 289.

73 SF report re Carmen, Matilde, Ángela Soria Viejo, Doc. 21, *Recompensas (Asesoría Juridica), Historiales de Camaradas Caidas*, ANA, Carpeta B-18, RAH, Madrid.

74 ANA, Carpeta B-18 Doc 21 "Carmen, Matilde y Angelita Soria" and B-18, 40 and 41. Their lives and deaths are memorialised in Sánchez Blanco, Laura (2016) *Rosas y Margaritas. Mujeres falangistas, tradicionalistas y de Acción Católica asesinadas en la Guerra Civil* (Madrid: Actas), pp. 45–49.

75 Borrás (1965) *Seis Mil*, p. 5.

76 Jato, David (1953) *La Rebelión de los Estudiantes (Apuntes para una historia alegre del SEU)* (Madrid: Talleres Gráficos Cíes), p. 68. The SEU student Francisco de Paula Sampol was killed while reading the second edition of *F.E.* in calle de Álcala.

77 *Historia de la Sección Femenina por Pilar Primo de Rivera, Libro Primero, Primera Parte – "La Ante Guerra,"* (typescript), ANA, Carpeta 1-B, RAH, Madrid, pp. 18–19.

78 Butler, Judith (2010) *Gender Trouble: Feminism and the Subversion of Identity* (Oxford: Routledge). 'Normative gender presumptions delimit the field of description that we have for the human' at p. xxiii.

79 *Historia de la Sección Femenina, "La Ante Guerra,"* pp. 18–19.

80 *Rojo y Negro* (Cepisca: 1942), by Falangist film director/scriptwriter Carlos Arévalo. Produced by CEPISCA and starring Conchita Montnegro as 'Luisa' (a young Falangist activist based on María Paz) and Ismael Merlo as 'Miguel' (a committed socialist) whose friendship and lives are destroyed by the conflict. The film was funded by a Francoist production company but was censored soon after its release on account of its complex and potentially subversive themes. The unorthodox and nuanced plot considers the motivations of the Republican militias in human terms. Meanwhile, the 'old Falange' is depicted as an 'idealistic and revolutionary party' that identified with the plight of the working-classes as evidenced in the friendship between the protagonists. The film depicted the devastating 'fratricidal' war as a source of pointless suffering and loss 'on both sides' rather than as a heroic and victorious crusade. In these respects, the film contested the prevailing Francoist propaganda, and its message of shared responsibility was years ahead of its time. For it was only during the late 1950s/early 1960s that the regime adopted narratives of 'we were all to blame.'

81 Cervera (1998), p. 266.

82 *Asesoría Jurídica*, Testimony of María Luisa Lagunés Torres, Document 253, ANA, Carpeta B-12, RAH, Madrid. See also, Testimony of Carlota Narcisa González de Usqueta, Document 196, ANA, Carpeta B-12, RAH, Madrid.

83 *Asesoría Jurídica*, Testimony of María Asunción Escondrillas Gil, Document 187, ANA, Carpeta B 12, RAH. María hid Corporal Emeterio de la Fuente after the fall of the Montaña Barracks on 20 July. See also, *Asesoría Jurídica*, Testimony of María Josefa Fernández [Florales], Document 191, ANA, Carpeta B 12, RAH, Madrid, who also safe-housed an artillery captain who had deserted the Republican army.

84 *Historia de la Sección Femenina por Pilar Primo de Rivera, Libro Primero, Primera Parte – "Capitulo II-La Propaganda,"* (typescript), ANA, Carpeta 1-B, RAH, Madrid, p. 28.

85 *Asesoría Jurídica*, Testimony of María Luisa Lagunés Torres dated 16 August 1939, Document 253, ANA, Carpeta B 12, RAH, Madrid and *Asesoría Jurídica*, Testimony of Ana Rizzo y Goñi, Document 248, ANA, Carpeta B 12, RAH, Madrid, p. 21.

86 *Asesoría Jurídica*, Testimony of María Luisa Lagunés Torres dated 16 August 1939, Document 253, ANA, Carpeta B 12, RAH, Madrid

87 *Historia de la Sección Femenina, "Capitulo II – La Propaganda,"* p. 29.

88 *Historia de la Sección Femenina, "Capitulo V – Ultimos Tiempos,"* p. 79.

89 *Asesoría Jurídica*, Testimony of Elena Rodríguez Mazaira, Document 263, ANA, Carpeta B 12, RAH, Madrid.

90 Primo de Rivera (1983) *Recuerdos*, p. 70. These three women were later arrested and incarcerated in Alicante's Adult Reformatory on 1 August 1936, p. 77.

91 Testimonios de fé del Fiscal Secretario relativos a las declaraciones, propuestas de pruebas, acusación de Fiscal y defensa de José Antonio Primo de Rivera en el juicio instruido por el Tribunal Popular de Alicante contra José Antonio y Miguel Primo de Rivera y Margarita Larios Fernández por Rebelión militar, AHN, FC-CAUSA_GENERAL, 1501, Exp 14. See Testimony of Margarita Larios [undated] Imágenes 34-35/195.

92 See article "Ha Muerto Tomás Borrás," *El Pais* dated 28 August 1976 http://elpais.com [last accessed on 17 May 2017]. See also article "La Cupletista Bilbaina Aurora Jauffret (1891–1950)," dated 9 December 2014 on http://elcorreo.com [last accessed on 17 May 2017].

93 *Historia de la Sección Femenina, "Capitulo II – La Propaganda,"* p. 20.

94 Primo de Rivera (1983) *Recuerdos*, p. 76.

95 *Asesoría Jurídica*, Testimony of María Asunción Escondrillas Gil, Document 187, ANA, Carpeta B 12, RAH, Madrid. See also, *Asesoría Jurídica*, Testimony of María Josefa Fernández Forarez, Document 191, ANA, Carpeta B 12, RAH, Madrid, who also safe-housed an artillery captain who had deserted the Republican army.

96 Vincent, Mary, Chapter 12, "Spain" in Passmore, Kevin (ed) (2003) *Women, Gender and Fascism in Europe, 1919–1945* (Manchester: MUP), pp. 189–214 at p. 201.

97 See for example, *Expte. 1697 instruido contra varias personas por el delito/s de Adhesión y Auxilio a la Rebelión*, Imágenes 1/1733. This case relates to twenty-two individuals (including two prison guards and eight women) who were arrested in August 1937 for illegal activities including passing information and contraband into and out of Porlier prison.

98 *Asesoría Jurídica*, Testimony of Carlota Narcisa González (1939), Document 196, ANA, Carpeta B 12, RAH, Madrid. This woman was arrested when she attempted to smuggle fire-arms into the Finnish Embassy. See also, *Asesoría Jurídica*, Testimony of María Luisa Lagunés Torres, Document 253, ANA, Carpeta B 12, RAH, Madrid.

99 *Expte. 510 instruida contra* Josefa Sánchez Sánchez *por tenencia ilicita de armas*, AHN, FC-CAUSA_GENERAL,221, Exp. 7. A former member of AP, RE and JONS aged thirty-eight years, sales woman, sentenced on 1 June 1937 to four years in a labour camp for illegal possession of an Astra Pistol 6,35 mm and a Sarasqueta Rifle.

100 *Asesoría Jurídica*, Testimony of María Lemus González Campusano dated 27 October 1939, Document 254, ANA, Carpeta B 12, RAH, Madrid. Also see, Testimonies of Ángelita Blanco de Castro dated 2 October 1939, Document 144, ANA, Carpeta B 12 and Rosalia Manrique Núñez dated 23 September 1939, Document 145, ANA, Carpeta B 12.

101 *Asesoría Jurídica*, Testimony of Milagros Encuentros Buisan dated 27 September 1939, Document 287, ANA, Carpeta B 12, RAH, Madrid and *Asesoría Jurídica*, Testimony of María Lemus González Campusano dated 27 October 1939, Document 254, ANA, Carpeta B 12, RAH, Madrid and *Asesoría Jurídica*, Testimony of Teresa González de la Puente dated 15 September 1939, Document 166, ANA, Carpeta B 12, RAH, Madrid.

102 *Asesoría Jurídica*, Testimony of Rosa Sainz de los Terreros Llavador dated 20 September 1939, Document 185, ANA, Carpeta B 12, RAH, Madrid.

103 *Asesoría Jurídica*, Testimony of Rosalia Manriquez Núñez dated 23 September 1939, Document 145, ANA, Carpeta B 12, RAH, Madrid.

104 *See Expte. 23 instruida contra María Redondo Piquenque por el delito de Desafección al Régimen*, AHN, FC-CAUSA_GENERAL, 235, Exp.4. *imágenes* 10-21/73.

105 *Asesoría Jurídica*, Testimony of Palmira Miguel Marco dated 20 September 1939, Document 148, ANA, Carpeta B 12, RAH, Madrid.

106 *Asesoría Jurídica*, Testimony of María del Carmen Carnicero Espino dated September 1939, Document 239, ANA, Carpeta B 12, RAH, Madrid. See also María Eulalia Gómez del Valle Testimony dated 1939, Document 180, ANA, Carpeta B 12.

107 *Asesoría Jurídica*, Testimony of Rafaela de Castro Gutiérrez dated 6 November 1939, Document 143, ANA, Carpeta B 12, RAH, Madrid.

108 *Asesoría Jurídica*, Testimony of María Teresa González Tablas y Mendizábal dated 6 October 1939, Document 233, ANA, Carpeta B 12, RAH, Madrid. Sub-leader of Group AY2.

109 Expte. 364, FC-CAUSA-GENERAL, 115, Exp.29, *por delito/s de Espionaje.*

110 Primo de Rivera, Pilar (1951) "Relación oficial de afiliadas de la *Sección Femenina de la FET y de las JONS caídas en acto de servicio*," *FET y de las JONS: La Sección Femenina –Historia y organización* (Madrid: n.p.), pp. 21–22; copy held in ANA, Carpeta 1-B, RAH, Madrid.

111 The choice of blonde (Hollywood film star) hair may have drawn more attention to the fugitive Pilar. Instead of highlighting the pious, subaltern and meek character traits for which she subsequently became known, this 'high femme' blonde transformation underscores an element of risk-taking and transgressive gender performativity which is seldom revealed in Pilar Primo de Rivera's memory texts or those of friends and acquaintances like Dionisio de Ridruejo.

112 Ruiz (2012) *El Terror*, p. 231.
113 Primo de Rivera, Pilar [c. 1942] "Principales obligaciones que la jefes deben inculcar en las camaradas," in *Discursos, Circulares, Escritos* (Madrid: Gráficas Afrodísio S.A.), p. 102.
114 Jato (1953) *La Rebelión*, p. 283.
115 *Sección Femenina* internal report on María Paz Martínez Unciti, Doc. 20, *Recompensas (Asesoría Jurídica), Historiales de camaradas caídas*, ANA, Carpeta B-18, RAH, Madrid.
116 Carina Martínez Unciti *ABC* (Madrid) 18 July 1961, p. 56.
117 Cervera (1998) *Madrid*, p. 287.
118 *Asesoría Jurídica*, Testimony of María del Carmen López Mancisidor Solano dated 6 October 1939, Document 201, ANA, Carpeta B 12, RAH, Madrid.
119 Barrachina, Marie Aline "La section féminine et ses paradoxes (1934–1977)," in Marie Aline Barrachina, Danièle Bussy Genevois and Mercedes Yusta (eds) (2007) *Femmes et Democratie, les Espagnoles dans l'éspace public (1868–1978)* (Nantes: Éditions du Temps) at p. 147.
120 Cervera (1998) *Madrid*, p. 265.
121 AGMAV, C. 2851, 14, Expediente SIPM personal de Martínez Unciti, Carina, 16408, dated 31 March 1942. I am extremely grateful to Carlos Píris for bringing this recently released source to my attention.
122 Borrás (1965) *Seis Mil*, p. 67.
123 These upper-middle- and middle-class districts were spared the Nationalist bombings throughout the war. They also accommodated the foreign embassies and experienced a huge increase in the number of inhabitants at this time due to the influx of refugees and evacuees whose homes had been destroyed during air-raids.
124 Including Anita Marcos de la Escosura, Tarsila Criado, Fifi Morano, Juliá Delgado Caro and Paso Andrés. Marcos was involved in the Checa Services. Source: Borrás (1965) *Seis Mil*, p. 154. We should recall that Borrás' wife was a liaison agent and a popular ballad singer.
125 *Asesoría Jurídica*, Testimony of Ángela Ibáñez Calvo dated 9 October, Document 225, ANA, Carpeta B 12, RAH, Madrid.
126 *Asesoría Jurídica*, Testimony of Dolores Núñez Fagoago dated 9 September 1939, Document 156, ANA, Carpeta B 12, RAH, Madrid.
127 See *Asesoría Jurídica*, Testimony of María Pilar Ortega Iturria, Document 160 dated 8 September 1939, ANA, Carpeta B 12, RAH, Madrid.
128 Borrás (1965) *Seis Mil*, p. 70.
129 Cervera (1998) *Madrid*, p. 277.
130 Cervera (1998) *Madrid*, pp. 131 and 157.
131 "*Ficha de recomendado, prestar servicio en el Negociado de Trabajos Hídraulicos.*" CDMH/10.8.10.14.1728.4.7/PS – Madrid, 1825,3,9,7.
132 Cervera (1998) *Madrid*, p. 277. Interview between the author and Manual Valdés on 14 November 1994.
133 Borrás (1965) *Seis Mil*, p. 69.
134 Reddy, William (2001) *The Navigation of Feeling, A Framework for the History of Emotions* (Cambridge: CUP). See also Stearns, C. and Stearns, P. "Emotionology: Clarifying the history of emotions and emotional standards," *The American Historical Review*, 90 (1985), pp. 813–836.
135 *Asesoría Jurídica*, Testimony of Juana Sánchez Aguado dated 9 October 1939, Document 234, ANA, Carpeta B 12, RAH, Madrid. She claimed that nine members of her family had been 'killed by the reds.'
136 *Asesoría Jurídica*, Testimony of Dolores Núñez Fagoago dated 9 September 1939, Document 156, ANA, Carpeta B 12, RAH, Madrid.
137 *Pieza décima de Madrid. Persecución Religiosa, AHN, FC-CAUSA_GENERAL, 1557, Exp. Imágenes 363-4/364.*
138 See *Asesoría Jurídica*, Testimony of Ana María Rizzo Goñi dated 29 September 1939, Document 248, ANA, Carpeta B 12, RAH, Madrid. Leader Sub-Group 1-A-P. This testimony is largely corroborated by information provided during an [undated] interview

between Tomás Borrás, Ana María and Dolores Rizzo Goñi: see Borrás (1965) *Seis Mil*, pp. 178–183.

139 The Control de Nóminas was a centralised DGS register that contained the card-indexed names and addresses of members of the outlawed CEDA, Falangist, Traditionalist and Renovación Española parties. The Falange had managed to destroy its official membership files before the war.

140 Interview (undated) between author and Ana and Lolita Rizzo Goñi recorded in Borrás (1965), pp. 178–183 at p. 182.

141 See *Asesoría Jurídica*, Testimony of Ana María Rizzo Goñi dated 29 September 1939 Document 248, ANA, Carpeta B 12, RAH, Madrid.

142 Expte. 562 contra *María Emilia Ázas Trigueras por delito/s de Desafección al Régimen*, FC-CAUSA_GENERAL,227, EXP.40, Imagen 5/24. Also see CDMH, Comité Internacional Cruz Roja, ACICR, C_ESCI, 186, pp. 79–101, *Liste 224 de détenues á la Prison de Femmes de Madrid* dated 24 December 1936: María Josefa Jiménez Crozat was imprisoned for being in possession of a scapulary and García San Miguel was found in possession of an 'old nun's habit.' Unsurprisingly, the vast majority of the female political prisoners interviewed by the International Red Cross in December 1936 claimed to be ignorant of the reasons for their arrest.

143 Ruiz (2012) *El Terror*, p. 237.

144 CDMH, ACICR, C_ESCI, 186, pp. 79–101, *Liste 224 de détenues á la Prison de Femmes de Madrid* dated 24 December 1936.

145 *Asesoría Jurídica*, Testimony of Rafaela Castro Gutiérrez dated 6 November 1939, Document 143, ANA, Carpeta B 12, RAH, Madrid. *Asesoría Jurídica*, Testimony of Andrea Pariente Suárez dated 9 October 1939, Document 169, ANA, Carpeta B 12, RAH, Madrid.

146 Expte. 352, *contra varias personas* (including Muñoz del Valle, Caridad), *por delito/s de desafección* AHN, FC-CAUSA_GENERAL, 113, Exp.38

147 Expte. 151, contra Carmen García Vallejo por delito/s de Desafección AHN, FC-CAUSA_GENERAL, 12, EXP 13.

148 *Asesoría Jurídica*, Testimony of Dolores Amador López dated 6 October 1939, Document 189, ANA, Carpeta B 12, RAH, Madrid.

149 *Asesoría Jurídica*, Testimony of Consuelo Pérez de Barradas y García Ochoa dated 1 October 1939, Document 232, ANA, Carpeta B 12, RAH, Madrid.

150 Religious buildings were ransacked as early as 19 July 1936, see Rodríguez Fernández (2006) *El Hábito y la Cruz, Religiosas asesinadas en la guerra civil Española* (Madrid: Edibesa), p. 22.

151 de la Cueva, Julio "Si los Frailes Supieran…la violencia anticlerical," in Santos Juliá (ed) (2000) *Violencia política en la España del Siglo XX* (Madrid: Taurus), pp. 191–234.

152 *Gaceta de Madrid*, Núm. 226, 13 August, 1936, Article 1. www.boe.es/datos/pdfs/BOE /1936/226/B01222-3.pdf.

153 Expte,1870, *contra* Amparo Fernández Ceballos, *por delito/s de Desafección*, AHN FC-CAUSA_GENERAL, 14, Exp.111,38/44.

154 Manuel de Irujo Ollo was a Catholic and a Basque Nationalist Party leader. He was appointed Minister of Justice in Juan Negrín's government in May 1937, prior to which he was a 'minister without portfolio' between September 1936 and May 1937 in Francisco Largo Caballero's government.

155 See Chapter 6 Benoit Pellistrandi "La historia y la idea de España en las pastorales de los obispos españoles," in Botti, Alfonso, Montero Feliciano and Qurioga, Alejandro (ed) (2013) *Cátolicos y Patriotas, Iglesia y Nación en la Europa de Entreguerras* (Madrid: Silex), pp. 141–160 at p. 155. "the Bishops of the inter-war period … had a providential vision of history (History in general and Spanish History) … Christ himself, during his sermons, had predicted the sufferings of the Catholic church … during future centuries of struggle." The conflict was viewed as a difficult 'trial' or test of faith for Spanish Catholics who were required to mobilise and resist against the Republican government.

156 Borrás (1965) *Seis Mil*, pp. 178–183 at p. 179.
157 Borrás (1965), p. 57.
158 *Causa No. 2 instruida contra varias personas por el delito/s de Espionaje y derrotismo,* AHN, FC-CAUSA_GENERAL, 148, Exp. 40, Imagen 34/240.
159 *Expte. no. 609 contra* Elvira Martínez Ostendi *por el delito/s de Desafección al Régimen*, AHN, FC_CAUSA_GENERAL, 270, Exp. 10. Imagen 4/84. Witness statement dated August 1937. The defendant was initially charged with 'Adhesion to rebellion and disaffection,' but the charges were reduced to disaffection.
160 *Asesoría Jurídica*, Testimony of Consuelo Rocha dated 16 August 1939, Document 181, ANA, Carpeta B 12, RAH, Madrid. Rocha was affiliated to Renovación Española since its foundation.
161 *Expte. contra María Baeza Torrecilla por delitos de Desafección al Régimen por pertenencia a Acción Popular,* AHN, FC-CAUSA_GENERAL, 184, Exp. 14, Imagen 2-3/46.
162 *Asesoría Jurídica*, Testimony of Carlota Narcisa González de Uzqueta y Cerrillo dated 20 September 1939, Document 196, ANA, Carpeta B 12, RAH, Madrid.
163 *Asesoría Jurídica*, Testimony of María del Carmen Díaz Aguado Arteaga dated 1 September? 1939, Document 158, ANA, Carpeta B 12, RAH, Madrid. Aguado joined the *Sección Femenina* in March 1936 and was also a defendant in the famous Golfín-Corujo espionage trial discussed in Chapter 3.
164 e.g. *Asesoría Jurídica*, Testimony of Consuelo Rocha Muñoz dated 2 October 1939, Document 224, ANA, Carpeta B 12, RAH, Madrid. Also, Testimony of Matilde Mercader Ximénez dated 5 October 1939, Document 228, ANA, Carpeta B 12, RAH, Madrid.
165 *Asesoría Jurídica*, Testimony of Andrea Pariente Suárez dated 9 October 1939, Document 169, ANA, Carpeta B 12, RAH, Madrid.
166 *Asesoría Jurídica*, Testimony of Dolores Amador López dated 6 October 1939, Document 189, ANA, Carpeta B 12, RAH, Madrid.
167 *Asesoría Jurídica*, Testimony of Juana Sánchez Aguado dated 9 October 1939, Document 234, ANA, Carpeta B 12, RAH, Madrid.
168 See *Asesoría Jurídica*, Testimony of María del Carmen Aguado Arteaga dated 1 September 1936, Document 158, ANA, Carpeta B 12, RAH, Madrid.
169 *Asesoría Jurídica*, Testimony of María Ugaldezubiaur dated 12 October 1939, Document 218, ANA, Carpeta B 12, RAH, Madrid.
170 *Asesoría Jurídica*, Testimony of Teresa Pérez Aznar dated 28 September 1939, Document 199, ANA, Carpeta B 12, RAH, Madrid.
171 *Asesoría Jurídica*, Testimony of María del Carmen Aguado Arteaga [undated] Document 158, ANA, Carpeta B 12, RAH, Madrid. See also, *Asesoría Jurídica*, Testimony of Andrea Pariente Suárez dated 9 October 1939, Document 169, ANA, Carpeta B 12, RAH, Madrid.
Asesoría Jurídica, Testimony of Rafaela de Castro Gutiérrez dated 6 November 1939, Document 143, ANA, Carpeta B 12, RAH, Madrid.
172 See Lease, Gary "Denunciation as a tool of Ecclesiastical Control," in Fitzpatrick, Sheila and Gellately, Robert (eds) (1996) *Accusatory Practices, Denunciation in Modern European History, 1789–1989* (Chicago: UCP), pp. 73–84 at p. 73.
173 Anderson, Peter "Singling Out Victims: Denunciation and Collusion in the Post-Civil War Francoist Repression in Spain, 1939–45," *European History Quarterly*, 39 (1) (2009), pp. 7–26.
174 Kalyvas, Stathis (2006), p. 389.
175 *Asesoría Jurídica*, Testimony of Rafaela de Castro Gutiérrez (General Secretary) dated 6 November 1939, Document 143, ANA, Carpeta B 12, RAH, Madrid.
176 See José Antonio Primo de Rivera, *Discurso sobre la revolución Española, Discurso pronunciado en el Ciné de Madrid,* 19 May 1935, cited in del Río Císneros, Agustín (ed) (1971) *José Antonio Primo de Rivera, Textos de Doctrina Política* (Madrid: Delegación Nacional de la Sección Femenina), pp. 557–570 at p. 570.
177 See Primo de Rivera, Pilar (1942) *Discursos, Circulares, Escritos, Sección Femenina de FET y de las JONS* (Madrid: Graficas Afrodisio Aguado).

178 *Asesoría Jurídica*, Testimony of Inés Martín Monjas dated 28 October 1939, Document 183, ANA, Carpeta B 12, RAH, Madrid.

179 e.g. *Asesoría Jurídica*, Testimony of Ángelita Blanco de Castro dated 2 October 1939, Document 144, ANA, Carpeta B 12, RAH, Madrid. Blanco de Castro stated "I belonged from the very first months of the Movement in ... Group AY2 no.4, always doing everything within the organisation as ordered by the Group Leader."

180 *Asesoría Jurídica*, Testimony of Isabel Arroyo Pertasse dated 4 October 1939, Document 202, ANA, Carpeta B 12, RAH, Madrid

181 Eksteins, Modris (1989) *Rights of Spring: The Great War and the Birth of the Modern Age* (Boston: Houghton Mifflin), cited in Reddy, W. "Historical Research on Self and Emotions," *Emotions Review*, 1 (4) (2009), pp. 302–315, at p. 310.

182 Payne, Stanley (1999) *Fascism in Spain*, pp. 92–93.

183 Rodríguez López, Sofia "La Sección Femenina, La imagen del poder y el discurso de la diferencia," *Feminismo/s 16*, (Deciembre 2010), pp. 233–257, at p. 238. See also, Arce Pinedo, Rebeca (2008) *Dios, Patria y Hogar. La construcción social de la mujer española por el catolicismo y las derechas en el primer tercio del siglo XX* (Santander: Universidad de Cantabria).

184 Morant, Toni "'Para influir en la vida de del estado futuro': Discurso Y Practica Falangista sobre el papel de la mujer y la feminidad, 1933–45," *Historia y Política*, 27 (enero-junio 2012), pp. 113–141, at p. 124. See also Maestre, Gonzalo "El tema religioso-católico en Falange Española durante la Segunda República," *Aportes*, 90 (XXXI) (2016/1), pp. 65–100, which explores Spanish Catholic fascism through its publications.

185 For arguments that the Falange was a form of political religion see Box, Zira, Saz, Ismael "Spanish Fascism as a Political Religion (1931–1941)," *Politics, Religion and Ideology*, 12 (4) (2011), pp. 371–389. These authors chart the diachronic shifts in the ideology of the Falange and argue that the Falange Española de las JONS "can be interpreted as a form of political religion, understood in the sense of Emilio Gentile. The central thesis is that Spanish Fascism was a political religion during the Republican period ... and, this is the main analytical challenge – it was also one after July 1936, in spite of the fact that the formation of Franco's *Movimiento Nacional* imposed no small changes upon it" at p. 371. Nonetheless, when viewed from gendered frames, it is more difficult to interpret the fascism of women such as Pilar Primo de Rivera as 'forms of political or secular religion' based on ultra-nationalism and the sacralisation of *Patria.*

186 *Historia de la Sección Femenina por Pilar Primo de Rivera, Libro Primero, Primera Parte – "La Ante Guerra"*, (typescript), ANA, Carpeta 1-B, RAH, Madrid, p. 27.

187 "Emotional regimes" and "emotives" are conceptualised in Reddy, William (2001) *The Navigation of Feeling, A Framework for the History of Emotions* (Cambridge: CUP). In particular, see Chapter 3 "Emotional Expression as a Type of Speech Act" at pp. 63–111.

188 Primo de Rivera, José Antonio (1971) *Textos de doctrina política*, Augustín del Río Císneros (ed) (Madrid: Delegación Nacional de la Sección Femenina).

189 Borrás (1965), p. 61.

190 Borrás (1965), p. 62.

191 *Asesoría Jurídica*, Testimony of Inés Martín Monjas dated 28 October 1939, Document 183, ANA, Carpeta B 12, RAH, Madrid.

192 *Asesoría Jurídica*, Testimony of Josefina García Folez de Velador dated 27 September 1939, Document 203, ANA, Carpeta B 12, RAH, Madrid.

193 Queipo de Llano, Rosario (1939) *De la cheka de Atadell a la prisión de Alacuas* (Madrid: Imprenta Castellana), p. 111.

194 Freeman, Thomas "The Politicisation of Martyrdom," in Freeman, Thomas, Mayer, Thomas (ed) (2007) *Martyrs and Martyrdom in England c.1400–1700* (New York: Boydell), pp. 35–69 at p. 69.

195 Gallego, María Teresa (1982) *Mujer, Falange, Franquismo* (Madrid: Taurus), p. 200–201.

2 The structure and organisation of Auxilio Azul

Auxilio Azul's earliest activities involved rescue and aid operations for fugitives. However, it quickly infiltrated Republican institutions including the police, the judiciary and civil and administrative nerve centres. The predominantly middle-class members used their social capital and networks of influence in order to provide safe-housing, raise funds and obtain false documentation. Significant sums were raised to pay for food, clothing and medicines. Fund-raising networks were developed within the local anti-Republican community. The organisation also established a series of informal business networks that helped to ensure the survival of individual members as well as the recipients of their welfare-aid. These commercial networks evidence these women's visibility in a semi-public space and the creation of networks of solidarity and mutual co-operation and assistance.

The majority of the members were middle-class Catholic women who before 18 July 1936 had "never belonged to any political party or organisation whatsoever."[1] These women forged their political identities in the crucible of war.[2] By autumn 1936 the group was structured along the hierarchical and triangular lines of the pre-war underground Sección Femenina. Affiliates were allocated a number and every three new affiliates would form a new 'triangle.' In theory, the identity of each member was only ever known to the two other members who formed part of the relevant triangle. Initially, the senior leaders knew the identity of all the leaders (*Jefas*) within the succession of triangles below them. A Directory (*Jefatura*) issued instructions which were passed down through each successive triangle. In this way the arrest of any individual might only result in the detection of three women or, at worst, five women in cases where the arrestee was the leader of a triangle.[3] During autumn 1936 the network began to rapidly expand, and in November 1936 Carina joined forces with María Baeza Torrecilla de Picatoste in order to enlist new recruits.[4] The organisation was officially 'baptised' as 'La Hermandad de Auxilio Azul – María Paz Martínez Unciti' in February 1937 when its Rules of Governance (Reglamentos) were also implemented (these were discussed in Chapter 1).[5] As the group expanded, its triangular structure became impractical, and in May 1937 a new 'cellular network' was devised which would allow for the sub-division of groups into separate and autonomous nuclei or 'cells' which operated independently and generally had no connection with each other.[6]

Rosa Sainz recalled joining in June 1937 but believed that Auxilio Azul was formally established much later in August 1938. She was promoted to Sub-Group Leader K1 (Clothing Section) under Fe Santos Giraldo in November 1938. The discrepancy in dates may be an error of memory or may evidence how members were only ever informed of the true nature and extent of the organisation after their admission into senior leadership positions.[7]

Clandestine meetings with the senior Group Leaders were held weekly in public spaces such as the Paseo de la Castellana because large home gatherings attracted suspicion. The members identified themselves by wearing pre-agreed coloured ribbons, a specific item of clothing or by carrying a distinctive object. In November 1936 Auxilio Azul began to attract former members of the recently outlawed Catholic parties including Elvira Martínez Ostendi who was a propagandist for Acción Popular,[8] and Mercedes Folch Fou who was a member of the Traditionalist Communion (Traditionalists).[9] The translator Consuelo Rocha (aged forty-four) was a former member of Renovación Española who was arrested and imprisoned on charges of disaffection in January 1937.[10] Consuelo joined Auxilio Azul in September 1937.[11]

Auxilio Azul continued to grow over the course of 1937 and came to be organised into a series of separate 'Networks' (Conexiones) which were divided into Groups and Sub-Groups. According to the Secretary Rafaela de Castro Gutiérrez, a new Directory (Jefatura) was created in February 1937. Carina was appointed as President of a new Leadership Committee (Junta Directora) composed of six persons including María de los Ángeles Forníes Cantó (General Secretary), Rafaela de Castro Gutiérrez (General Secretary *bis*), Maruja Sainz (Treasurer) and Father Tomás Ortega (Religious Counsellor) and Vicente Busso (General Accountant).[12] Each Network had its own sub-treasurer, and detailed accounts were submitted to Maruja Sainz in respect of all sales and donations.[13] The Leadership Committee was subsequently increased to seven leaders and included Carlota Narcisa González de Urqueta y Cerillo (Treasurer), Cristina Moreno Fernández, Carmen Palacios, Nena Sanz Benito and Asunción Petit.

An accurate periodisation is not possible on account of the lack of written records. An estimated 200 Margaritas (the Traditionalist Women's auxiliary section) joined forces with Auxilio Azul at some time after 18 July.[14] The ANA testimonies indicate that admissions spiked in January 1937 and then again in May/June 1938. However, these testimonies are not statistically significant in terms of sample size. Also, those who showed membership potential worked 'on probation' without knowledge of the wider organisation for a period of months before formal admission. The increased membership in January 1937 probably reflects the fact that December 1936 witnessed a sharp decline in the extra-judicial repression. Certainly, by February 1937 rumours of the rise of a Socorro Azul circulated within the anti-Republican community.[15] The subsequent spike in mid-1938 was most probably prompted by the series of Republican political and military reversals over the course of 1938 culminating in the Nationalist occupation of Viñaroz on 15 April and Prime Minister Negrín's publication of the "Thirteen Points" on 30 April which signalled to all that a negotiated peace settlement was envisaged by the Republican government.

By the end of the war in April 1939, it is believed that there were thirty-seven Network Leaders who supervised some 165 Network 'affiliates.' The Network Leaders managed the activities of 111 Group Leaders who, in turn, oversaw the activities of 333 Sub-Group Leaders. Each Sub-Group was comprised of fifteen affiliates. Three Sub-Groups constituted a Group. Every three Groups were organised into a Network (Conexión). The Directory (Jefatura) and the leaders of each of the Networks, Groups and Sub-Groups were obliged to devise contingency plans in the event of their arrest, and this was not an uncommon occurrence. Carina was arrested and released without charge on two separate occasions. Therefore, leaders were required to nominate deputy leaders who would replace the relevant Group Leader or Sub-Group Leader in the event of that person's arrest. When any Group was led by a deputy leader, the name of that group would be pre-fixed with a '*bis*.'

After November 1936 a complex system of alphabetical and numerical code-names was devised by Carina and Rafaela de Castro. The code names for the thirty-seven Networks were as follows: the first nine Networks were code named with three letters between A and Z (e.g. ABC, DEF, GHI … XYZ), Networks 10–18 used the same code-names but were pre-fixed with an "A" (e.g. AABC, ADEF, AGHI … AXYZ); Networks 19–27 used the same code-names but were pre-fixed with a "B" (e.g. BABC, BDEF, BGHI … BXYZ). The remaining Networks were prefixed with a "C" or a "D" and the last Network (the thirty-seventh) was code-named DABC.[16] This complex organisational structure probably existed more in theory than in practice, not least because after January 1937 Carina lost direct communication with many of the Sub-Group Leaders and with the rapidly expanding number of new affiliates. Further, only the most trustworthy recruits who demonstrated a genuine leadership potential were ever informed of the true nature, size and extent of the organisation. Most of the affiliates were unaware that they had been assigned code names. The identity of their Sub-Group Leader was only known to them in a personal capacity, i.e. as a friend who had asked them to complete a specific task, as a favour, or out of loyalty or for personal and familial reasons, rather than in their capacity as the leader of a clandestine network. The need for utmost secrecy and discretion meant that the Leadership Committee only gathered formally on three occasions in May, July and November of 1937. The Directory was in charge of the Network Leaders (Jefas de conexión) and the Networks were divided into nine 'Service Divisions' or 'Groups' discussed below.

Auxilio Azul's service divisions

Embassies, safe-houses and escape lines (the 'Embassy Group')

This section provided safe-houses, false documentation and temporary embassy asylum with the aim of organising escape-lines into the Nationalist zone. After the fall of the Montaña Barracks on 20 July 1936 hundreds of disaffected officers and soldiers went into hiding together with a sector of civil guards. They wanted to avoid the extra-judicial reprisals, imprisonment or conscription with the Popular Front militias. Aristocrats, professionals, businessmen, politicians and religious personnel also required safe hiding places.[17] Madrid's foreign diplomatic corps, the Basque PNV and the Catholic Church collaborated in efforts to obtain asylum for hundreds of anti-Republicans.[18] Auxilio Azul also provided safe-housing.[19] Fugitives would pass through a succession of safe-houses until the necessary asylum documentation was obtained. While in asylum, escape-lines were organised into the Nationalist zone or abroad, often using embassy vehicles. The women also acted as liaison agents between the Clandestine Falange groups on the ground and the leaders in the embassies. They "smuggled weapons into and passed intelligence out of the embassies."[20] The members were only authorised to help those who were personally known to them.[21] Carolina Illescas worked as an embassy liaison agent; she managed to recruit some twenty friends who helped her to obtain asylum for fugitives.[22]

During the war around twenty-nine nation states continued to operate embassies and consulates in Madrid.[23] The diplomatic buildings were mainly situated in the affluent Buenavista and Salamanca districts and a few embassy properties were located in Chamberí. The Republican authorities and the press, including Julián Zugazagoitia,[24] suspected that the vast majority of the embassies were pro-Nationalist and therefore hot-beds of fifth-column subversion. Negative press reports fuelled the "popular desire to lay siege to the embassies and to hundreds of private embassy buildings which were believed to have provided refuge to thousands of fascists."[25] Negative press campaigns occurred periodically in 1936, 1937 and 1938 and posed a serious threat to embassy security because they encouraged illegal incursions against diplomatic buildings.[26] The press campaigns fuelled the general resentment against the asylees who were perceived as dangerous (and well-provisioned) fifth columnists.[27] Indeed, members of the foreign diplomatic corps such as Félix Schlayer maintained contact with Burgos and actively worked for the Nationalists.[28]

Relations between the government and the embassies reached various crisis points. The German Embassy was closed by the government on 20 November 1936. The German and Italian governments recognised the belligerent status of the rebels on 18 November 1936 and Madrid's Defence Junta suspected that the German embassy housed a 'nest of fifth columnists.' The German diplomatic corps was given twenty-four hours to evacuate the embassy buildings. Santiago Carillo, the leader of public order with the Madrid Defence Committee, authorised the militias to shoot at the tyres of one of the German embassy vehicles in order to impede the escape of fugitives. The incident did not infringe the extra-territorial status of the embassy and the vehicle contained fire-arms.[29] There were also several security raids on embassy buildings of which the most notable were those on the Finnish and Turkish Embassies which openly violated political asylum rights. On 4 December 1936 government security forces raided the Finnish Embassy and a cache of firearms and bombs was discovered and several illegal asylees were detained. The raid on the Turkish Embassy on 28 January 1938 led to the arrest of the Falangists Antonio Rodríguez Aguado and Joaquín Jiménez de Anta who were in contact with three Falangist *banderas* and with Lt. Colonel Bonel Huici's Nationalist intelligence services in La Torre de Esteban Hambrán (Toledo).[30] These men also cached weapons, made use of an illegal radio transmitter which was hidden at the embassy in order to send encoded messages and also passed intelligence via diplomatic dispatches.[31] They were assisted by Roseda Blanco Martínez.[32] Ángel Pedrero raided the Turkish Embassy under orders of the SIM Headquarters in Barcelona.[33] The raid had been carefully planned for over a year and led to the arrest of over one hundred individuals.[34]

Despite the government raids, the embassies were perceived to be the safest place for anti-Republicans.[35] Diplomatic extraterritoriality was officially recognised by the Republican government, and Madrid's embassies and consulates provided asylum for around 6,000 individuals in early 1937.[36] There were around 11,000 legal asylees over the course of the war.[37] These asylees enjoyed embassy protection because of their status as foreign nationals and often wore an official embassy arm-band as identification. Most often they continued to live in their own private residences while enjoying a range of much envied diplomatic privileges which included extra food rations and special vehicle parking discs. These privileges were a source of popular resentment because the civilian population in Madrid began to experience hunger and material deprivation in early 1937.

Most of the illegal asylees were anti-Republican men from military, religious, political or professional backgrounds. They lived in cramped and overcrowded conditions and slept on the floor or on camp-beds. Although food was limited, the embassy rations were greater than those allocated to the general public and this fuelled popular resentment. During the first months of war the asylees were not allowed to leave the embassy buildings, all curtains and blinds were drawn and there was no access to the gardens for security reasons. All extra-territorial communications were banned, and it was difficult to communicate with family members.[38] However, in 1937 it became possible to resume normal contact with the outside world. Nonetheless, life within the embassy was stressful, overcrowded, uncomfortable and monotonous. Embassy living generated feelings of anxiety and cabin fever. Joaquín Calvo Sotelo's play '*La Vida Inmovil*'[39] was based on his personal experiences of the depression and frustration of "life on hold" in an overcrowded embassy. One of the few highlights was listening to the war reports on banned Nationalist radio stations such as Radio Burgos or Radio Sevilla. This defeatist news was circulated via Auxilio Azul into the wider anti-Republican community. Embassy officials also provided other types of assistance, including facilitating escape lines into the enemy zones[40] or negotiating with the Republican authorities in relation to political prisoners. The Norwegian consul Félix Schlayer was involved in various Red Cross prisoner-exchange negotiations, prisoner-welfare initiatives and in the prevention of a *Saca* in the women's Conde de Toreno prison on 4 November 1936.[41] He estimated that there were around 10,000–12,000 asylees in Madrid in November 1936, 1,000 of whom were under his responsibility.[42] In around July 1937 the government in Valencia approved the evacuation of around 8,000 embassy refugees from the capital, of which some 2,400 were men aged between eighteen and forty-five years who were to be exchanged against the same number of political prisoners in the Nationalist zone.[43]

Asylees were required to pay for expensive asylum accommodation and administrative fees. Auxilio Azul raised around 512,225 pesetas towards these expenses.[44] The Chilean Embassy accommodated over 1,200 persons at its official residence in Paseo de la Castellana, 29, and another 1,000 persons in various diplomatic properties, the Cuban Embassy housed 539 refugees, the Finnish Embassy took in between 400 and 600 persons, the French Embassy accommodated around 2,420 persons, the Mexican Embassy housed 3,733, the Norwegian Consulate housed 524 refugees, the Panamanian Embassy took in 847 and the Turkish Embassy provided asylum for 808 refugees.[45] Auxilio Azul placed most refugees at the Chilean, Panamanian, Cuban, Mexican, French, Polish, Norwegian, Finnish and Turkish Embassies. However, it also had links with embassy personnel at the Argentinian, Columbian, Peruvian, Bolivian, Uruguayan, Haitian and Swiss Embassies. Other hiding places were located in small hotels and in individual homes. Embassy vehicles were used to transport refugees to the embassies and, later, to transfer them to the Nationalist zone or to Getafe airport and into foreign exile.

Women arranged hundreds of asylums through embassy contacts like Félix Schlayer or Luis Serrano Novo and through Republican administrative and associational networks. Concepción Fortis Benedicto[46] testified that she "helped relatives and close friends to avoid the arrests and *paseos* or military service." Her husband was imprisoned throughout most of the war, and a warrant had been issued for her son's arrest following a denunciation by their concierge. "With great effort, suffering and personal danger to us both, I managed to obtain a place for my son at the Swiss embassy." The living expenses at the embassies were often prohibitive. The reference to great 'effort and suffering' relates, in part, to her efforts to raise the money to cover her son's embassy fees and her husband's 5,000 peseta criminal fine. She also contributed 25 pesetas monthly to Auxilio Azul and raised an extra 35–40 pesetas monthly in third-party donations. The son remained at the embassy for the duration of the war until March 1939 when he joined the Falange.

Auxilio Azul also brought money, clothing and medicines to the asylees on a weekly basis. Cecilia Antón Medina regularly brought food and other items to the refugees in the Norwegian and Chilean Embassies along with documents that might assist their escape into the Nationalist zone. She also "hid asylum seekers prior to their transfer into the embassies and on one occasion safe-housed their weapons and munitions before these were smuggled into the embassies."[47] This operative initially worked for Father Tomás

Ortega (see Spiritual Services below) before formally joining Auxilio Azul in February 1938 as a liaison and recruitment agent. She was arrested by the DGS in November 1936 but managed to get out of prison by making a false declaration, although, thereafter, her name was listed in the Control de Nóminas and she was unable to escape into the Nationalist Zone. Her mother was also arrested, and other members of her family were placed under surveillance. Carlota González de Uzqueta y Cerillo procured asylum for several Falangists at the Finnish Embassy and was arrested while attempting to transfer arms into this embassy.[48] Inés Martín Monjas joined Auxilio Azul in August 1937 after which she quickly became a Sub-Group Leader and "collected money and clothing and … regularly visited an embassy where a male religious had taken refuge."[49] As in the case of María Ugaldezubiaur, the asylees were sometimes also Auxilio Azul operatives. As indicated in Chapter 1, this woman had lost two sons on the Nationalist front-lines and, in consequence, her family had been sorely persecuted. She sought asylum at the Panamanian Legation during the first months of the war, but when the 'terror' of the first months abated, she was able to move relatively freely around the city, in her capacity as official seamstress for the Legation, selling scarves and lighter flints 'in aid of Auxilio Azul' and passing false documentation into the embassy.[50] This is testimony to the relative ease and freedom with which the operatives circulated around the capital.

The Group that liaised between the Norwegian and Panamanian embassies was called Group Y. The Group Leader was Elvira Martínez Ostendi who was the widow of an officer named Martín de Pozuelo. She was aged forty-eight years at the time of her arrest in 1937 and a resident of Avenida Eduardo Dato, 29. She had been active within Acción Popular before the war.[51] Elvira's son (an infantry lieutenant) and her brother (a factory owner) were arrested on 24 August 1936, 'interrogated and badly treated' by communist militias for several days. However, they were fortunate enough to be released following the intercession of her brother's former employees who provided good-character references (*avales*). On 30 August 1936 Elvira was arrested for being a 'fascist' and detained for three hours. She was interrogated and threatened with execution by militias of the socialist García Atadell Brigade. From July until 23 October 1936 the family underwent various house searches "and all manner of injuries and persecutions."[52] Finally, with the help of Father Recaredo Ventosa, she found refuge for her son and for Santiago Pineiro (the son of the Count of Canillas) at the Norwegian Embassy. Personal experiences of repression motivated her to join Auxilio Azul. Thereafter, she 'dedicated herself to the service' and became the principal liaison agent between the Y Group and the Norwegian and Panamanian Embassies. In 1937 she was able to organise safe-housing and asylum at various embassies for as many as fifty-seven individuals, mostly military personnel, religious, Falangists and their relatives. On 10 August 1937 Elvira was re-arrested and accused of 'Adhesion to the Rebellion' but the charges were eventually reduced to disaffection. The DGS accused her of the following crimes:

> having served the Nationalist cause with great success by procuring and having procured asylum for fugitive fascists at various embassies … she also obtained false passports in order to facilitate foreign travel for fascists, either using their own names or false names, with the assistance of her extensive knowledge and contacts.[53]

She was also accused of having compiled a list of asylum seekers at the Norwegian Embassy who were "willing to rise up one day and take up arms against the legitimate Government."[54] The list contained the names of seven men: two industrial workers, a medical assistant, a scaffolder, a draughtsman, an electrician and a mechanic. The embassies were filled with a cross-section of society including working classes and affluent middle classes, the religious and the military. Elvira also provided safe-housing for valuables (e.g. jewellery, money, shares, military insignia and religious artefacts) on behalf of friends and neighbours who had been forced into hiding or who had fled Madrid. "The militias made regular house searches and took everything of value that they found."[55] These confiscations were made pursuant to new emergency war confiscation and reparations legislation implemented in Autumn 1936. New legislation dated 23 September 1936 created a War Reparations Chest (Caja General de Reparaciones de daños derivados de la guerra civil),[56] Article 4 of which established a special tribunal to assess the damages arising from anti-Republican behaviour. According to Elvira, after her release from prison in 1937, Fernando Bustillo (the Marquis of Villanueva), one of the most senior leaders of the Clandestine Falange, ordered her and Elena Cano to form a same-gender Falangist group in Madrid. 'Group Y' was responsible for protecting hundreds of individuals including the Falangist sympathiser and academic Santiago Montero Díaz who was provided with false documentation and, together with some seventy other individuals, safe-housed at the Hotel Atlántico. Montero also came to work for the Y Group's false documentation section which created hundreds of false documents, and it is believed that he only decided to flee Madrid after Elvira's subsequent detention on 15 March 1938.[57]

Years after the events Elvira recalled that her Group had comprised some 850 affiliates who collectively received a Silver "Y" award after the war.[58] An *ABC* obituary dated May 1970 described her as:

> an exemplary woman of singular virtues who had consecrated her life to her home and to the immediate service of the Fatherland for which she sacrificed her liberty. On account of her activities during the Liberation Crusade she received those military honours due to an ex-combatant and an ex prisoner.[59]

The members of other Groups were also involved in the Embassy Networks. These included Ana María Rizzo Goñi,[60] and Elena Herzog (widow of Sevilla Bahamonde) who was involved in Group 4K and safe-housed Antonio Sainz de Heredia, an uncle of José Antonio Primo de Rivera. Herzog also testified to having worked for the Traditionalist Socorro Blanco organisation and to disseminating Nationalist war reports.[61] The sisters Pilar, Rosita and Lolita Merlo assisted in the safe-housing of nuns; one was a telephone exchange operator at the Telefónica 'who regularly intercepted phone calls.' Pilar Merlo entered the holy orders after the war, taking the name 'Sor Elvira.'[62]

Ana María Rizzo Goñi was the leader of Sub-Group 1-A-P. She and her sister Dolores lived near the San Antón Prison and provided safe-housing at their home in calle del Espejo for military deserters, politicians,[63] Falangist spies and various San Antón prisoners who managed to avoid the *sacas* with the aid of a prison guard named Baudilio Fernández Pérez. Ana María also safe-housed at least fifty fugitives and supplied them with false identification documents.[64] Both she and her sister Dolores maintained regular communications with the prisoners in San Antón. According to Jesus Laporta Girón, who was the prison director in 1938, these women:

> performed invaluable and courageous services by hiding fugitive prisoners in their own home in grave circumstances and at risk to their own lives … They helped me to save several other comrades who were in grave danger because they had been involved in espionage by providing them with hiding places, food and false ration cards and other documents and they acted as liaison agents between certain prisoners and myself and Commander González Abela. They also organised escape lines for comrades into the Nationalist zone and provided us with some clothing.[65]

The two sisters pulled strings within the Republican administration in order to obtain the release of their mother (Dolores Rizzo Goñi) from the Conde de Toreno Prison. They were assisted by a '*rabano*' (radish) named Manuel Acal Marín de las Barcenas who was a senior civil servant in the foreign office consular department charged with the appointment of new consuls.[66] This man was in contact with a senior militia leader named Rincón who guarded the Conde de Toreno Prison and organised the release of Dolores. In exchange for this favour Rincón asked de las Barcenas for a safe consular posting and, being unable or unwilling to comply, the latter promptly sought asylum in an embassy with the help of Group Y.

Mari-Nieves Villa García Gómez was the leader of Auxilio Azul's Group AY. Her group provided safe-housing for many individuals including the Traditionalist Rodrigo Ochoa y de Murga and the journalist Ignacio Catalán Alday who became editor of Seville's *ABC* newspaper after the war.[67] The brothers Martín and Francisco Parrilla were also safe-housed for a period of six months until they were arrested during a house search. Similarly, Andrea Pariente Suárez testified that her home was "packed with fugitives … who were being hunted down, including my brother, a politician, who was taken from the house and assassinated on 21 August 1936."[68] Pariente Suárez also safe-housed priests including Father Eugenio García Gúzman who regularly celebrated clandestine masses.

María Baeza **Torrecilla de Picatoste** was a founder member of Auxilio Azul. She safe-housed the Martínez Unciti family in November 1936 after the death of María Paz when the family was forced underground. Picatoste was aged thirty-nine years and a housewife (*sus labores*) on the date of her arrest on 1 May 1938. She lived with her three young sons, her father (aged seventy-six years), her mother-in-law (aged seventy-one years) and a bed-ridden aunt. Her husband and brother-in-law were military officers who were imprisoned in Duque de Sexto Prison. Her brother had found asylum within the Chilean Embassy, and her sister had fled Madrid. She maintained regular contact with her brother at the embassy. Following an anonymous denunciation, the DGS searched her home and confiscated two gold topped batons, items of ceremonial military uniform, service medals, a photograph of Gil Robles and a small amount of silver currency (two two-peseta pieces, two one-peseta pieces and eight hundred and fifty centimos) together with various un-incriminating letters from her brother at the embassy and an illegal "Orbe" radio set and five lamps.[69] Her defence counsel pleaded that the entire burden of affective labour had now fallen upon the defendant and that:

> these unfortunate circumstances had ... isolated her from all social activities and relationships and led to her seclusion within the home in circumstances where she was on less than cordial terms with her husband.[70]

She was found guilty of disaffection for being a former member of Acción Popular because her name appeared in the Control de Nóminas. The fact that she was a senior leader within Auxilio Azul and the co-ordinator of the 'Embassy Services' was never disclosed during the trial. Baeza was released from prison on 1 October 1938 and granted a suspended sentence (two years in a labour camp) because the tribunal believed that 'she did not pose any serious threat to the Republican regime.'

Labour Section (Trabajos)

This section (in combination with Clothing Services below) had the largest number of members and affiliates who collected and distributed charitable donations from sympathetic individuals and businesses. It also established several small workshops that manufactured and sold clothing, hats and shoes. Lighter flints and candles were sold in local cafés and bars.[71] It organised fund-raising initiatives, collected weekly donations and distributed financial aid and false documentation. In effect, it operated an extensive clandestine business network which was reliant on the black-market economy and provided a living income for members as well as charitable funds for fugitives, political prisoners, religious persons and their families. Both the Labour and Clothing Services Networks (discussed below) enabled the members to both help the needy and also achieve a measure of economic independence. The Labour and Clothing Services developed as a series of informal business networks that generated 'secret profits' within the wider black-market economy.

According to the 1930 census only 9.2% of Spain's female population worked outside the home, and the largest occupation for women was described as 'being a member of the family.' The census also recorded that 24% of single women worked, 14% of widows and 4% of married women formed part of the paid workforce.[72] At this time women in paid employment were mostly drawn from the working classes, and domestic service constituted the largest paid occupation for women. To a lesser extent, women found jobs in textile and paper manufacturing, shoe making, baking, food processing and the tobacco industries. A woman's identity and status were defined by reference to the household in which she lived, and to the occupation of her husband or father. However, these official figures do not reflect the real numbers of 'invisible' and informal female workers, and these increased during the war. Working-class and lower-middle-class women often undertook unofficial and poorly paid piece-work at home such as sewing or dress-making. Middle-class women were also trained in needle-work, gave private lessons or taught piano to family friends and formed part of the informal labour market.

The financial hardship experienced by anti-Republican families during the war meant that many middle-class women were obliged to enter the male-dominated workplace for the first time. In many instances women also became temporary heads of household who were responsible for the material, economic, emotional and religious welfare of the family.[73] The experience of paid work was a source of new financial independence and freedom for many of the members.[74] After the extra-judicial violence ended in January 1937, these anti-Republican women exerted influence and practiced forms of class-based 'symbolic violence' (gentle, invisible, pervasive violence exercised through the everyday practices of social life) in their efforts to survive and maintain their social positions within a conflictive and male-dominated Republican social field.[75]

The Head of this Network was Carina's sister María de los Ángeles Martínez Unciti. Labour Services were divided into three sections: Acquisitions, Manufacture and Sales.

One of the most senior Group Leaders was María Felisa Parés (codename "L") who worked closely with Group Leader María del Carmen Timmermans who distributed the false documentation. María Lemuz González Campuzano (Sub-Group Leader L-III) recruited around one hundred members and worked under Group Leader María Felisa Parés ("L").[76] Lemus also raised funds and distributed money among "needy persons of the Right" and obtained provisions from the SIM, the Red Cross and other governmental organisations with the aid of false documentation.[77] She stored food, clothing and shoes at her home and distributed these items within the prisons. She also acted as a liaison agent and provided fugitives with false identity documents so that they might enter embassies and hospitals or escape into the Nationalist zone. Her Group Leader, María Felisa Parés, also guarded money, jewels and other valuables that were 'entrusted to the organisation by fugitive anti-Republicans.' María Felisa Parés was also infiltrated as a secretary within the SIM records department. Josefina García Folez (K-2) "collected money, clothing, food, visited prisons, families in hiding and provided whatever was needed [including] ration cards."[78] Not all the women's testimonies were as forthcoming, many simply provided the following formulaic statement: "I gathered money, helped families in need and followed all the orders of my Group Leader."[79] Fund-raising was possible via neighbourhood, confessional and associational networks, many of which were established before the war because in June 1934 José Antonio created a separate gendered space within which to channel Falangist women's enthusiastic activism. The new Sección Femenina:

> was born from the urgent need to attend to Falangist prisoners and their families. It was a clandestine and rather dangerous social initiative which was performed by female affiliates who would raise funds from friends, organise raffles, sell memberships stamps … and soaps which bore a political message on a red and black label: "In aid of the National-Sindicalist Revolution, the Fatherland, Bread and Justice, *¡Arriba España!*"[80]

The majority of Auxilio Azul's members participated in the Labour Network whether through fund-raising, collecting clothing or distributing food and medicines to destitute anti-Republicans and prisoners. Magdalena Sánchez Velasco "sewed many clothes for the children of prisoners who had given birth in prison."[81] Donations were collected on a weekly basis from reliable businesses and trustworthy individuals (*personas de confianza*) who were secretly sympathetic to the Nationalist cause. Rosina Frutos Paris joined in January 1937 and operated in Buenavista where she "collected money, made items for sale and … took ration books to the Red Cross requesting foodstuffs which were then collected in calle de Goya and distributed among the sick and infirm."[82]

By late 1938 Madrid's civilians (especially infants and the elderly) suffered the ill-effects of prolonged malnutrition due to the severe restrictions on food rations. Items such as fuel, clothing, cigarettes and medicines were also extremely scarce. Those who had sufficient financial resources had regular recourse to the black-market. Women also travelled to the surrounding countryside in order to barter clothes, jewellery and money in exchange for eggs, potatoes and meat. Thanks to these strategies, "the majority of Madrid's population managed to survive the war, although, as is always the case, there were some who had no problems at all in obtaining provisions and others who starved to death."[83]In this context private charitable initiatives (whatever their political complexion) may have been cautiously accommodated by the Republican authorities.

Clothing Services

As the war progressed fabric, thread, wool and other basic items became scarce commodities. The members were involved in the recycling and re-distribution of clothing. The Clothing Services and Clothing Sales were a form of social enterprise. Women began to sell raffle tickets, Red Cross food stamps and even nylon tights in order to raise funds.[84] Almost all of the members were involved in some aspect of the collection, cleaning and recycling. According to Auxilio Azul's accounting records, 2,140 items of male clothing were distributed 'to prisoners and the needy, 2,950 female items and 4,630 children's clothes were distributed during the lifetime of the organisation."[85] These clandestine activities mirrored those which were openly undertaken by Auxilio Social which was established by Mercedes Sanz Bachiller in October 1936 in the Nationalist-held zone.[86]

Goods which had been requisitioned by the popular militias for the war effort were appropriated from official warehouses and storage depots were sold 'under the counter' via a series of retail networks. Making clothes was the only source of income for many of the women: "we had to make and sell embroidery in the shops in order to eat."[87] These workshops also ran fund-raising 'raffles' which were started by the Sección Femenina before the war. Between January and March 1939 raffle revenues generated 228,185.00 pesetas.[88]

Acquisitions

The 'Acquisitions Section' collected funds and donations from retailers and businesses that were 'sympathetic' to the anti-Republican cause. Prominent individuals, embassies and businesses donated money, medicines, clothing, milk, food, fabric and sewing materials. Regular benefactors were known as 'protectors,' and their aid extended to offering storage space in warehouses, providing transportation for food and fuel supplies and assisting in the collection and distribution of false documentation. The Red Cross supported the work of Auxilio Azul.[89] Similarly, operatives were embedded within Madrid's hospitals, including the Hospital Militar (4th Network). Large quantities of condensed milk and tobacco were acquired and then re-distributed via Clandestine Falangist networks.[90] The boundaries between 'legitimate' auxiliary activities and the illegal sabotage of Republican distribution operations were blurred, and the sanctions against those who crossed these boundaries were harsh, often involving a significant fine or a term in prison or a labour camp.

Ángelita Blanco de Castro (2-AY-4) was a member of Group AY4 and she dedicated herself to "collecting money and clothing for the persecuted."[91] The leader of her Sub-Group was code-named 2-AY, Rosa Mazarracín Lalanda.[92] Mazarracín was the leader of the Hospicio district Sub Group AY. The overall leader of Group AY was María de las Nieves Villa García Gómez who worked in Madrid's central food depot La Empresa Municipalizada del Mercado Central.[93] The members performed services which included gathering and distributing donations, food and medicines to the needy. Mazarracín Lalanda testified that she had regularly:

> collected money from all the right-wing persons that I knew. I gave the funds to my immediate superior, Manolita Villa García, in order to help numerous people who were under the yoke of the Reds, I also collected clothes for the same ends.[94]

María Dolores Núñez Fagoaga was employed as a Delegate in the Hospicio district from August 1937 until the 'Liberation' in April 1939. She was involved in the collection of money and clothing from various donors and collaborators which she then passed on to her immediate superior Mercedes Criado.[95] Her sister María Carlota Núñez Fagoaga also worked for the same group and "distributed food to the needy." She also circulated copies of Nationalist war reports "which came from the Generalissimo's Headquarters in Burgos," both at her office and in private houses, for a period of over twelve months until she was sacked for disaffection (see Security Services below).[96]

Financial donations from sympathetic businesses were vital. The most generous donors included the retailers Simeon, Encarnación Arias, Samaral, Álfaro, Cabezón and a specialist linen shop situated in calle del Barquillo. A few factories kept secret accounts relating to their illegal business dealings.[97] Other benefactors volunteered hundreds of assistants and donated large quantities of food, clothing and money. Helen Garrigues Walker was the daughter of the US International Trade (ITT) representative in Spain during the Second Republic. In 1931 she married the Catholic lawyer Antonio Garrigues y Díaz Cañabete who was a leader of the Falangist Castilla group which was infiltrated within the International Red Aid (Socorro Rojo) and the Catholic journalist Santos Alcocer was also a member of this group. Garrigues "collaborated with the Falange as one of the notorious fifth columnists in Madrid, devoted to sabotage and propaganda on behalf of Franco."[98] Helen was involved in the Castilla group and also became the leader of Auxilio Azul's Provisions Group (Víveres). She was a protestant but the rest of her family were devout Catholics and her daughter Elena took the veil in 1963.[99] She used her social capital and her influence within US business and diplomatic circles and the International Red Cross, the Swiss Red Cross and the Republican Red Cross in order to obtain food, milk and medical supplies. She also used her family's influence and US diplomatic back channels in order to obtain the release of Carina and several other leaders who were arrested while celebrating a clandestine mass at the dairy in calle Velázquez, 46 which operated as a secret chapel. Other benefactors included Helen's husband Antonio Garrigues, Juan Lillo Orzaes, Luis Serrano Novo (a Clandestine Falange Junta leader) and Vicente Busso who managed Auxilio Azul's secret accounts.

Operatives were embedded within the public administration and various municipal co-operatives. María Nieves Villa García was infiltrated in the Mercado Central and, in her capacity as the leader of Group AY, she siphoned off "as many items as possible in aid of the Nationalist Cause."[100] Such resistance strategies meant that these formerly law-abiding women now operated within an illegal counter-culture. The 'illegal stockpiling of rationed goods' was a treasonous activity.[101] The Group Leader Carmen Vera Aguilera distributed condensed milk and other rationed goods.[102] On 13 February 1939, Vera Aguilera, a Cuban National, was acquitted on charges of "Defeatism" and "infractions relating to subsistence materials."[103] A cache of twenty-five boxes of condensed milk was discovered at her home. However, she was released from prison because the 'controlled food items' had been legitimately obtained from the Cuban and Panamanian Embassies. These 'everyday' forms of resistance were similar to those performed by many ordinary Republican civilians at this time.[104] Madrid experienced severe material hardship during the conflict, and black-market practices were frequent and widespread during and after the war.[105] According to the organisation's accounting records which are dated between 1 August 1936 and 28 March 1939, the acquisition of materials for the Labour section amounted to 731,580 pesetas. The acquisition of clothing and other 'sewing items' amounted to 718,875 pesetas. Food acquisitions amounted to 2,303,660 pesetas. Finally, 57,272 pesetas were spent on the acquisition of children's toys as Christmas gifts during 1938 and 1939.[106] The total money spent on charitable acquisitions was 4,339,812 pesetas.[107]

Manufacturing

The 'Manufacturing Section' processed the fabrics and other raw materials which were collected by the Acquisitions Section. These materials were distributed among individuals or small groups who would make clothing and other items for the needy.[108] Women worked at home and organised small manufacturing networks based on associational and friendship groups.[109] They made fashionable clothing, slippers, socks, bags, belts, lace, embroideries.[110] Also, paper flowers and painted silk scarves were sold at the embassies.[111] In addition, they improvised clothes, toys and Moses baskets.[112] The baskets were made for prisoner's wives[113] and for Falangists women who had babies in prison.[114]

Women embroidered garments in order to augment the organisation's monthly revenues. They also engaged in dangerous symbolic resistance practices by sewing "flags, arm bands, pendants and bracelets in an anticipation of the day of our liberation."[115] This was an extremely risky activity which was directly organised by Carina. After 18 July 1936, the Sección Femenina supplied the Falangist militias with blue shirts and bracelets, and after the coup failed in Madrid these deeply incriminating items, along with religious artefacts and monarchist memorabilia, had to be hidden[116] or burned.[117] Soon after 18 July Rosina Frutos Paris "was obliged to flee from the militias under cover of darkness at great personal risk, with 10 large flags and 45 banners wrapped around my body and various parcels in my arms."[118] During the war this same activist

> donated a great quantity of fabric for arm bands and flags at a time when the streets were taken by the communists and machine-guns were positioned at every street corner. The shops that sold the fabrics were guarded by militias and there were body searches on entry and departure but [she] still managed to sequester large quantities of fabric, duping the militias on both on arrival and departure.[119]

In 1938 a Falangist in Barcelona named María Coll Codina was sentenced to six years in a labour camp in 1938 for 'defeatist practices and for making quantities of Falangist bracelets and banners.'[120]

Felisa Ruiz de Alda was the leader of a manufacturing group which operated from within Ventas Prison.[121] The prison group produced clothing and other items for distribution and sale to the local community in aid of Auxilio Azul. Felisa was the first cousin of Julio Ruiz de Alda (one of the three founders of the Falange). She became involved in Auxilio Azul after her imprisonment for disaffection along with Matilde Casáñ Pablo and María de los Ángeles Forníes Cantó during their time in Ventas.[122] Felisa claimed that the prison director "don Victor was sympathetic to the Cause and some great old-school prison guards acted as liaison agents (*enlaces*) on the outside (*la calle*)." The Falangist leader Luis Serrano Novo (code-named "Benigno") brought materials into the prison for members to make belts, woollen items, dresses and leather goods which they pretended were for their own families. Felisa set up a work-shop where "all worked secretly together … and contributed to the sacrifices that were being made by people on the outside … We did a great deal and with a great deal of joy."[123]

The Falangist spy and actress Matilde Casáñ Pablo joined Auxilio Azul while in Ventas. She was accused of espionage and imprisoned for high treason on account of her involvement in the Golfín-Corujo espionage network (discussed in Chapter 3).[124] She became the Group Leader of prison group H-1. She was an 'old shirt' who joined the Falange in 1934 as member no. 6-6-4. Before the war she was an activist in the Buenavista district under the orders of José Luis de Zaragoza for whom she "did all types of work in accordance with my orders." After 18 July and 'the outbreak of the 'Glorious movement' she was disconnected from her group but eventually entered an espionage organisation where she worked as a spy for nine months. She managed to infiltrate into the head office of the General Command of the Militias (Secretario General de la Comandancia de las Milicias) but was arrested on 4 May 1937 and imprisoned in the Checa de los Salesianos. From this Checa she was transferred to Ventas and thereafter to a Valencian prison, then to Alacuas labour camp (Valencia), on to Cehegín (Murcía) and then back to

Ventas where she "joined Auxilio Azul making products for sale and disseminating propaganda among the Republican prisoners and

> helping out our boys for whom, with the aid of my lawyer Gómez Arias, I could always get was needed in the form of false work certificates and I did everything that my leader in the prison Felisa Ruiz de Alda asked of me.[125]

Sales

The Sales Section supplied and distributed goods within a clandestine network of 'trusted' retail outlets. The leaders of the Group were Carmen Timmermans, María Luisa Rubio and Nena Toffé whose immediate subordinates were Josefina and María Ignacia Sánchez López Guerrero. In 1937 the distinctive *monos* (boiler suits) and informal worker's clothing of the earliest months were once again replaced by formal suits and middle-class attire, albeit without hats and ties.[126] Fashionable clothing was a scarce and highly desirable commodity in circumstances of food, fuel and clothing restrictions. Women sold 'coveted' hand-made items in private boutiques and market stalls. Lighter-flints and candles labelled "in aid of Auxilio Azul" were sold cafés, bars and restaurants.[127] Dolores Ochoa Malagón successfully sold her 'fashionable creations' at the Torrijas flea market. Florinda Aparicio Prieto sold clothes in aid of Auxilio Azul from her exclusive boutique in calle de Hortaleza which was named "Florinda. Latest Fashions."[128] Several other women also testified to having supplied clothing to Florinda's Boutique.[129]

Carmen Dávila and Carmen Timmermans ran various small workshops including one which reconditioned second-hand clothing and used fabrics which had been donated by shops and businesses. The women reconditioned summer frocks, *lingerie* and made pretty slippers with cardboard soles covered in black satin. They sometimes received the full retail price of the goods which were sold on their behalf by generous shop-keepers who kept secret accounts of these under-the-counter transactions. Women transported contraband clothing by wearing it in layers in order to conceal the illegal sales.[130] This section created a new 'fashion craze for an elegant white jacket (*perchera*)' made from hospital linen. The nurse Carmen Cueto Maroto stole sheets from the storage depots of several military hospitals. These women had few scruples or compunction in respect of the theft of items that had been requisitioned for the war effort for they believed that these had been stolen from anti-Republican families rather than requisitioned. The *percheras* sold for a profit at retailers such as "Cabezón" and "Florinda's Boutique." Nena Toffé was a Group Leader who worked as a seamstress "from dawn till dusk in cold, damp and dark conditions."[131] Nena's customers formed part of a new working-class social and economic elite; they included militia women and also the wives of politicians and military figures including General Líster and *El Campesino*.[132] Such clients were important, not least as sources of political, military and social intelligence. Despite the repression of the earliest months, anti-Republican women were able to assert their position in the social space through the exercise of forms of symbolic violence.[133] Their acculturated social and cultural capital ensured that despite the seismic power-shift, women like Nena retained status and distinction as the exclusive arbiters of "good taste and high fashion."[134]

Many found new opportunities and avenues to commercialise the valuable and expensive skills acquired via their middle-class habitus. The best measure of cultural capital is the amount of time devoted to acquiring it because the transformation of economic capital into cultural (social and symbolic) capital presupposes an expenditure of time made possible by possession of economic capital.[135] Some performed poetry recitals or sang during private recitals at home or in the embassies.[136] Others became tutors and music teachers. Most of the profits from such activities were donated to Auxilio Azul, but some was retained as personal income. The Rizzo Goñi sisters made a living from sewing fashionable bags and belts in suede and cloth: "We sold a huge amount. Most of the proceeds went to Auxilio Azul. We ate, when we could, from a small proportion of the proceeds."[137] They sold special lighter flints and candles which bore the label "*Para Auxilio Azul*" (In aid of Auxilio Azul).[138] This might suggest that certain types of charitable social enterprise may have been warily accommodated by the authorities. However, the risks were real and ever-present. A woman in Barcelona was arrested by militias and charged with espionage in October 1937 for selling Falangist soaps at 3 pesetas each; this woman was denounced as a spy because of her relationship with members of the Falange and others.[139]

Auxilio Azul offered opportunities to re-negotiate the notion of separate spheres of home and work. The organisation provided women with opportunities to exercise economic freedom, spread economic risk and allay the economic shocks produced by the civil conflict. Many became responsible for their own survival and economic well-being. The stronger the networks of support, the greater their chances of surviving the socio-economic impact of the conflict.[140] Paradoxically, circumstances of war and repression enabled many of these women to acquire a measure of personal independence and economic agency. In many cases the members were both the agents and beneficiaries of Auxilio Azul's welfare-aid initiatives.

Health Services

Around forty-three male doctors, and female nurses led by Carmen Cueto Maroto, together with pharmacists, nursing auxiliaries and administrative assistants, collaborated with Auxilio Azul in hospitals and clinics across Madrid. The Health Services formulated its own set of code-names using the 'College of Medicine's Directory' as a key. A list of medics was transcribed 'onto a small piece of thin onion paper which could be easily circulated and then swallowed in an emergency.'[141]

The Auxilio Azul doctors offered free medical assistance to fugitives. They also provided the organisation with false medical reports and sickness and disability certificates for the purposes of evading conscription. The networks organised the transfer of healthy inmates into prison hospitals with the aid of false medical reports. They fabricated evidence of bogus ailments including stomach ulcers, renal lesions, cardiac diseases, epilepsy and psychosis in order to avoid conscription among anti-Republican men aged between sixteen and fifty-five years of age. Medics coached their patients on how to fake symptoms during medical examinations. Doctors and nurses provided supplies of milk for infants, children and the infirm from hospital rations. Pharmacists, whenever possible, provided free medication and medical supplies which were distributed via the Auxilio Azul networks.

The leader of Auxilio Azul's medical operations was Dr. Emilio Franco Martín, who had been the Director of Radiography at the Carabanchel Military Hospital before the war. His deputy was Dr. Antonio Martín Calderín and the Group Secretary was Isidoro García. Father Tomás Revilla Franco was a qualified doctor who was also leader of Group VA-2 as well as being one of the organisation's spiritual advisors (see below).

Carmen Cueto Maroto (who took the veil after the war) was Group Leader of Health Services. She was in charge of fifteen Sub-Groups which incorporated around 289 female nurses of whom only a few knew about Auxilio Azul. The leader of each Sub-Group was in direct contact with one doctor. María Luisa Miret de Grassa worked for the Health Section from April 1937. She joined this section in her capacity as a member of Group E, whose leader was Mercedes Criado and, together with Carmen Perla, she worked under the direct orders of doctors Enrique Martí and José Moza.[142] These operatives "saved many from being shot"[143] by falsifying medical records. Pilar Allas López[144] was a nursing assistant who had worked in Buenavista's anti-Tuberculosis clinic. She was involved in the falsification of medical records and the distribution of false invalidity certificates for conscription evaders. Pilar claimed that her actions were taken with the full collaboration and knowledge of the medical staff. María Josefa Fernández Fournier was also involved in the production of "invalidity and medical certificates for wanted persons and safe-housing soldiers."[145] Other forms of sabotage included the illegal distribution of medicines and medical supplies from hospitals and clinics.

Nurses posed a significant security risk because they were easily able to infiltrate civilian and military hospitals, treatment centres and surgeries. They were especially feared in the popular Republican imaginary because it was believed that they had control over the lives and well-being of vulnerable soldiers and posed a real threat to the success of the war effort. They also operated as liaison agents between the Clandestine Falange and prisoners in the prison hospitals. In one case nurse Margarita Álvarez Santiago was arrested (but later acquitted) for organising 'fascist meetings' with other nurses in order to conspire against the Republic.[146] Auxilio Azul also infiltrated the nursing and laundry services at the battle fronts. Teresa Monge Dávila worked as a nursing assistant on the fronts and was imprisoned for seven months for the illegal distribution of army food rations.[147] These women courted grave risks because the legal sanctions against them for treason were potentially severe and there was also a real risk of extra-judicial reprisals, especially during the earliest months when the government lost control of the levers of power. Three trainee International Red Cross nurses who belonged to Acción Católica were extra-judicially executed alongside two Falangist women in Somiedo near the town of Astorga on 28 October 1936; the nurses were believed to have aided the escape of Nationalist prisoners and were abused and killed in reprisal.[148]

Emergency Aid (Socorros)

This section was involved in the distribution of false identification documents with the aid of the journalist and author José Silva de Ambaru who had been a civil servant in the documentation department of Madrid's Town Hall before the advent of the Second Republic in 1931. Luis Cebrían Goyanes and Hípolito Escrivá de Romani were also embedded in the Town Hall and falsified as many as 3,500 family ration cards in the space of twenty months in order to help 17,000 individuals.[149] Caridad Rapallo Comaje was involved in Group K activities which included the "distribution of false ration cards and other false documentation."[150] María Piedad Torres Montero was infiltrated in the Federal Republican Youth Organisation (Juventud Republicana Federal) where she generated false work certificates and good character references.[151]

Milk supplies were obtained from the International Red Cross with the aid of Lt. Barrios, the head of its Civilian Provisions Section, who personally supplied the organisation with around 100 kilos of dried milk together with 35 kilos daily of lentils and between 20 and 35 litres of cooking oil. Red Cross trucks were diverted from official storage depots and their contents were unloaded in secret warehouses. Auxilio Azul also distributed false milk coupons which were redeemed at the Red Cross. Provisions were also obtained with the aid of Group Leader Helen Garrigues Walker (discussed above) who worked with the International Red Cross, North American Aid and Swiss International Aid. Carina also obtained supplies from the Republican civilian evacuation committee which was organised by the JDM (Madrid's Defence Junta). The women also went on foraging expeditions into the surrounding provinces in order to barter for local produce.

Individual members were assigned the care and supervision of particular individuals and families for the duration of the war or until such persons were able to escape into the Nationalist zone. As indicated above, money was raised from revenues derived from work-shops, raffles, clothing sales and private donations from within the business and local community. Manolita Despierto Vázquez "never failed to collect less than 50 pesetas per month from families who supported the Movement."[152] Matilde Babé y Gómez (Agent 5E-3)[153] looked after the widow of a Civil Guard Commander who had been killed at the start of the war. Auxilio Azul entrusted Matilde with a monthly allowance for the care of the widow and her family. Matilde also gave the widow an additional 200 pesetas per month out of her own pocket and 'donated thousands of pesetas to Auxilio Azul.' At first, the sums allocated to the families of prisoners were between 75 and 200 pesetas. These were increased to 150 pesetas per adult and 60 for children with a minimum of 200 and a maximum of 1,000 per family. In total Auxilio Azul distributed 1,316.844 pesetas monthly to families of the fallen and prisoners. Around 418,300 pesetas were spent on bribes for Checa officials and prison wardens in order to obtain the release of condemned prisoners. 512,225 was spent on embassy asylum fees, and another 328,150 pesetas was spent in aid of the religious.[154] Matilde Babé y Gómez was in contact with the Nationalist SIPM and was able to transmit coded messages. She performed a variety of services that involved varying degrees of risk and illegality including:

> raising funds, making clothing and on several occasions providing false documents … [I] raised thousands of pesetas for Auxilio Azul … and broadcasted a special message in code over Radio Nacional that some money had arrived safely to its destination.[155]

María de los Ángeles Las Heras Sanz worked at the Junta de Compras de Material del Ministerio de la Guerra (the war ministry's procurement and acquisitions department); she also operated as a spy from January 1937 (see Security Services below). In December 1937 she joined Auxilio Azul 'as a sympathiser' before becoming a fully fledged member of Group A2 which later fused with HY-1. She raised around 100 pesetas monthly from colleagues, and all monies raised were passed on by her immediate superior, Esperanza Cañizares, to the Group Leader Carmen Víves. As indicated above, María initially joined the Work's Group A-2:

> but because I was unable to perform this group's specialism – general needle-work (*labores*) – I dedicated myself instead to raising funds which I gave to Esperanza Cañizares.[156]

Security Services

This division gathered intelligence which was then passed on to Burgos directly via Carina or via members of the mixed-gender Falange groups discussed in Chapter 3 below. Members were infiltrated within the DGS, the SIM, the Telefónica, the CNT and various Republican administrative offices. Unsurprisingly, the testimonies in the ANA archives contain little evidence of women's active collaboration in treasonous intelligence gathering and denunciatory practices. As indicated in Chapter 1, the group was never dismantled on account of its rigorous security and intelligence services. María Felisa Parés was a Group Leader "L" who was infiltrated within the SIM records department and could perform security-checks on potential new recruits and warn about imminent arrests.

Carina was also the leader of an intelligence gathering sub-group that belonged to the 'Grupo Galicia' which was led by the Falangist Ramón Arnal Moreno who was a member of the Servicio de Información Nacional Sindicalista de España (SINSE) which operated under the direct orders of the SIPM. After the war, Arnal testified in a certified letter to the war office dated 2 October 1939 that Carina was a senior intelligence operative within the Galicia Group between January 1937 and October 1938:

> on several occasions the quality and quantity of the intelligence gathered [by Carina] and forwarded to the 'National Cause' was congratulated and commended by the Military Command and recognised as being beneficial to the war.[157]

Only the most dedicated and trusted members were involved in the sensitive and high-risk intelligence-gathering operations. Rosina Frutos Paris joined Auxilio Azul in January 1937 and became one of Carina's principal liaison agents. In her capacity as "a key confidante" she

> safe-guarded intelligence memos, plans and all manner of information which was then sent on to the Nationalist zone … including the last will and testament of José Antonio, and the Auxilio Azul records together with all the money which was collected on behalf of the organisation.[158]

Cecilia Antón Medina safe-housed a nationalist intelligence officer named Ramón Arnal who was the leader of a SIMSE [sic] group together with his male assistant, these men operated a small intelligence bureau from within her home.[159] Auxilio Azul passed military and political intelligence to the Nationalist side "sometimes, with favourable results."[160] Its members gathered "vital intelligence … and performed acts of espionage."[161] They also smuggled guns into embassies and hid valuables and weapons on behalf of the Clandestine Falange.[162]

María Pilar Ortega Iturria disseminated the latest war reports from the rebel zone via a male contact who worked at the Telefónica and for which he (the contact) was sentenced to death but managed to obtain a reprieve.[163] Amalia Martín was a civil servant in the Home Office who also supplied intelligence to Auxilio Azul. She was arrested and imprisoned by the DGS on three separate occasions following denunciations because of her frequent prison visits and safe-housing of right-wing individuals.[164] María Luisa Laguna Torres allegedly physically assaulted a police office in order to steal his identification papers.[165] She made regular visits to dangerous houses that were under constant police and SIM surveillance because they housed prominent Falangists (*personas destacadas en Falange*) and sometimes had to flee the premises on account of Republican SIM and police raids. María de los Ángeles Las Heras

Sanz was involved in intelligence gathering alongside her brother who was a member of the 'Junta de las Compras Group' which formed part of the larger 'Grupo Antonio' (Antonio Luna and Julio Palacio's) network which was created in 1937 and operated under direct orders of the Nationalist SIPM.[166] By the end of 1937 this group reported directly to Colonel José Ungría Jiménez's SIPM intelligence services by means of encrypted radio transmissions. In April 1938 the group established contact with the Republican leader Julián Besteiro who sought to negotiate the terms of a mutually acceptable peace-settlement.[167] Between late 1938 and March 1939 Grupo Antonio liaised between Besteiro, Colonel Casado, the SIPM and Franco in relation to the 'Casado Coup' which occurred in early March 1939. Grupo Antonio also had links with Elena and Antonio Garrigues' 'Castilla Group' which operated from within the Socorro Rojo offices situated in calle Alcalá, 6 and which included a cell led by the journalist Santos Alcocer.[168] María joined Auxilio Azul in December 1937.[169]

The 'old shirt' María del Carmen Díaz Aguado y Arteaga (Sub-Group Leader A-P-3) joined the Sección Femenina on 14 March 1936 and worked for Antonio Rodríguez Aguado and Joaquín Jiménez de Anta's organisation. She joined Auxilio Azul at some time in 1937 and between August 1937 and September 1938, together with María Carlota Núñez y Fagoaga (head of Group AY), disseminated defeatist war reports received from Franco's General Staff in Burgos within various offices situated in the Hospicio district until both women were dismissed for disaffection.[170]

Many women were involved in the organised and co-ordinated dissemination of defeatist anti-Republican propaganda and Nationalist war reports. Secret messages were passed to female operatives in cafés and in food queues; correspondence was also hidden in the cisterns of public lavatories.[171] Intelligence gathered by women who were infiltrated within the Republican civil and military administration was routinely passed on to members of the Clandestine Falange who operated hidden radio-transmitters or liaised directly with Lt Colonel Bonel Huici's SIPM services in La Torre de Esteban Hambrán (Toledo).

Finally, intelligence was routinely gathered by the SIPM from those who managed to escape into the Nationalist zones. These fugitives were routinely interviewed upon first arrival in the Nationalist zone. Elisa Pardo Ibáñez and her two daughters worked for 'Mil Raguette a Socorro Blanco leader.' In August 1938 they escaped from Madrid to Ceuta where they provided the Moroccan SIPM with detailed social and military information relating to the dire rationing situation ('even pencils were rationed'), the location of secret artillery emplacements and munitions factories, Casado's movements, the location of General Miaja's secret headquarters and vital intelligence on the extremely low levels of civilian morale in the capital at this time. This information was immediately forwarded to the General Staff in Burgos.[172] At the start of the war the Nationalists had no organised intelligence services and lacked access to the SIM archives in Madrid; consequently in 1936 they were reliant on the civilian intelligence provided by the Falange and the Traditionalists and encouraged and supported civilian intelligence gathering throughout the war. The SIPM maintained a rigorous division between the interrogation techniques used on genuine fugitives (*evadidos*) who provided valuable intelligence and were well-treated, and Republican prisoners of war who were swiftly subjected to the rigours of the military courts; in this way the Francoist apparatus was able to encourage desertion in the Republican ranks and create the foundations of the apparatuses of repression in the post-war period.[173]

Prison and Checa Services

These services represented a continuation of the Sección Femenina's pre-war underground welfare-aid activities. According to Pilar Primo de Rivera, after the February 1936 general elections, the number of Falangist prisoners grew to around 2,000 in Madrid.[174] There were some 10,000 nationwide.[175] In particular, after the 16 February 1936 general elections Madrid's prisons "began to seem less like prisons and more like the headquarters of the Falange Española y de las JONS."[176] The escalation of sectarian violence after the 16 February general elections resulted in the outlawing of the Falange party on 14 March 1936. After the attempted assassination of Luis Jiménez de Asua, José Antonio was charged with illegal arms possession and imprisoned in the Model Prison together with most of the Falange's Executive Committee (Junta de Mando) including Julio Ruiz de Alda, Raimundo Fernández Cuesta (General Secretary of the Falange Party and original leader of the Clandestine Falange) and Agustín Aznar.[177] Many of the provincial leaders were also arrested at this time.[178] The party went underground and was immediately re-mobilised as a clandestine organisation. After 14 March 1936, around twenty to thirty Sección Femenina members began to visit Madrid's male prisons and DGS detention centres on a daily basis in order to bring provisions and perform liaison functions. Despite the inconvenient visiting times, "there were a multitude of volunteer visitors, indeed, so many that the prison authorities declared that only family members were allowed to visit prisoners."[179]

As the Falangist prisoner population steadily increased during the lead up to the 17 July coup, the women were each assigned a prisoner who would receive a weekly food parcel. Women's fund-raising initiatives both before and during the war provided money for hundreds of packets of cigarettes, boiler suits (*monos*) and the sum of 100 pesetas per prison gallery in order to purchase coffees from the local café. Prisoners requested books, footballs and slippers. Before 18 July the Model Prison patio became the scene of many renditions of the Falange's anthem, *Cara al Sol,* and "an atmosphere of gaiety and *fiesta* filled the prison so much that even certain prison officials came to become Falangists, raising their arms in the Falangist salute."[180]

Passing items through visitor's window-grills was strictly prohibited and all food parcels and packages were subject to routine searches. However, 'special visits' were sometimes authorised at 11 a.m. in a room that had only one bar between the visitors and the prisoners. During the immediate pre-war period this enabled women to smuggle contraband and copies of *¡No importa!* which had replaced the censored *¡Arriba!*, a single copy of which would make its way around the galleries.

> Sometimes we even smuggled in bottles of wine, which were prohibited, but because women were not initially subjected to body searches we could hide them in our coats. This is how we were able to smuggle in everything that came into our imagination.[181]

During the war these women continued to visit the prisoners and brought food parcels and updates of Nationalist war reports and on the latest arrests. Auxilio Azul relied on 'sympathetic' prison guards to turn a blind-eye on their illicit prison visits given that, as indicated above, only family members were allowed to visit prisoners.

Women also became prisoners. Felisa Ruiz de Alda Mendivi[182] was widowed after the events of the Model Prison in August 1936. She became a fugitive and was safe-housed together with a male friend. She was arrested on or around 28 February 1937 on account of her regular visits to Porlier Prison where she communicated with Federico Valenciano Osenalde and Carlos Serrano Martín. Felisa was imprisoned in checas (San Mateo and Fomento) and prisons; Conde de Toreno, San Rafael and Ventas from February 1937 until March 1939.[183] She was found guilty of disaffection on 17 March 1938 and, as indicated above, became the Group Leader of a 'works' section in Ventas. An incriminating factor which led to her imprisonment was that she had failed to notify the DGS of her changes of address in accordance with new emergency public order legislation. However, her relationship with the Falange and with Auxilio Azul was never disclosed, and she operated as an Auxilio Azul leader throughout the whole of her time in Ventas.

Judicial Services

Auxilio Azul established an important network within the popular tribunals, the Supreme Court and the judicial services departments. The network developed contacts among court administrators, lawyers and the judiciary. Dolores Muñoz Tuero became the leader upon Carina's personal request. She had only recently qualified as a lawyer when the war broke out.[184] She operated as a liaison agent in the prisons, the main ones being San Antón, Duque de Sesto, Porlier and Ventas. She also worked in the prison hospitals in Paseo del Cisne and calle de Hortaleza, (the French Hospital) and 'another one in Lagasca or Núñez de Balboa.' Her familial relationship with the General Miguel Núñez De Prado[185] served as a 'shield' which protected her from suspicion for some time. She acted as a defence lawyer in the Popular Tribunals and used false medical certificates to delay the trials of many 'comrades' and clients, thereby saving their lives.[186] However, after almost three years of clandestine activity within the court and prison services she was arrested on charges of treason which were reduced to disaffection. In 1965 Muñoz recalled that she "had the honour of being entrusted with the judicial mission of Auxilio Azul."[187] She was allowed access into the prisons in her legal capacity in order to conduct client meetings. She claimed that her status as the first and only female tribunal lawyer had generated positive publicity for the Republican regime, and her gender and professional status were used by the Republican government "in order to support its unassailable legitimacy" by highlighting the government's progressive stance on gender equality. Muñoz was critical of the "ignorance, incompetence and prejudices" of the lay tribunal members. She routinely advised her defendants to deny any involvement or plead that they had joined the Falange "only in order to get a job with the monarchists." She fabricated evidence of loyalty to the Regime through the use of false good-character references which were provided by associates who were infiltrated within the CNT or other left-wing parties. When there was no realistic possibility of hiding the defendant's ideology, she would request a suspension on medical grounds (using 'favourable medical certificates') whereupon the defendants would be transferred to a suitable prison hospital. According to Muñoz, the prison doctors were happy to extend the sick-notes of those who were destined for the firing lines. Dolores particularly recalled the bravery of a doctor named Sánchez, who didn't hesitate to falsify his diagnoses from any scientific or professional scruples:

> [Sánchez] was capable of saying that a man who had two legs didn't have any … and he could prove it. Also, with the use of good character vouchsafes from very influential people, I could get a provisional release order pending judgement, I could then delay the judgement in collusion with an official in the secretariat, under the pretext that the hearing that we wanted to delay clashed with other hearings, or as a special favour, when I wasn't sufficiently confident that I could get a stay in proceedings. In some secretariats (clerk's offices) I could ask for whatever suited my plans with complete freedom, because the court officials were all hidden '*rabanos*.'[188]

In 1986 Dolores Muñoz Tuero was interviewed by the British historian Sheelagh Ellwood for *Historia 16* magazine. She recalled that she was:

> very lucky, partly because I was a woman, and partly because of the benign nature of the popular tribunals. Whatever people say, I worked with those tribunals and they acted with great justice. Leaving aside the problems of the *paseos* and the *chekas*. We should forget about those and wipe them from our memory, like good Spaniards. That was deplorable, but I repeat that after [the war] I realised that one side had as many *chekas* as the other. As regards the justice, however, that was composed of people's tribunals, they were juries. Good people, noble people. If one defended a case, one could pull their heart-strings and get an absolution.

This subsequent interview was conducted years after the events and, just as with the earlier interview, it reflects the effects of 'inter-subjectivity,' i.e. the responses evinced from the interviewees often reflect the interests, concerns and motivations of the interviewer.[189] It also resonates with the Post-Transition discourses of 'we were all to blame' which underpinned the 'the pact of forgetting.'[190]It is markedly more even and conciliatory in tone than the earlier interview where the popular tribunal judges are disparagingly referred to as the 'tribunal rabble' (*tribunaleros*). The memory-shift between 1965 and 1986 demonstrates how personal memories reflect historical shifts in collective memory scripts and "how memories are recalled, emerge, resonate and react with collective myths and grand narratives."[191] Dolores' recollections are linked to processes of social change and the shifting ideological master narratives of the Franco regime. Her earlier recollections reflected post-war narratives of 'persecution' and 'crusade.' Meanwhile her later recollections reflected new ideological master narratives surrounding concepts of 'fratricidal struggle' and discourses of 'we were all to blame' which gained momentum during the 1960s and 1970s at a moment of rapid structural and economic change.[192]

Ángeles García López was arrested on 6 March 1937 for disaffection and may have been helped by a 'sympathetic' Republican tribunal. She was acquitted on charges of disaffection despite the strong evidence against her. García López was a member of Acción Popular; her name had appeared as such in the Control de Nóminas, and she had already been imprisoned in October 1936 'for hiding a Jonsist gunman from the police.'[193] Evidence was produced at her trial[194] which indicated that her brother was a communist who was executed in Seville and that she was also a card-carrying member of the CNT. It is likely that she joined the CNT after 18 July in order to disguise her former political allegiances; the CNT was known to be lax with its membership security. She joined Auxilio Azul in February 1938 and worked under the orders of Group Leader Enriqueta Bustos and later for the lawyer Dolores Muñoz Tuero. She was decorated with the Silver 'Y' on 30 May 1939 for her wartime services in Auxilio Azul.[195]

Evidence suggests that many members of the judiciary and the legal profession were sympathetic to the fifth columnists. For example, the popular tribunal magistrate Ricardo Guerra presided over Jurado de Urgencia No. 7 which was one of the two tribunals that adjudicated in the San Rafael women's prison. Ricardo Guerra resigned from his job in May 1938 on account of "severe nervous exhaustion and depression brought on by an excessive work load."[196] He was associated with Félix Schlayer, and it was alleged that he was a member of Socorro Blanco and that, in concert with Schlayer, he had organised asylum and escape-lines for defendants. Guerra's defence alleged that an underlying disease in combination with the stresses of tribunal work had precipitated his mental breakdown. His case was suspended, and he was released from prison into a private sanatorium from where he was quickly released into the exclusive care of his family. On 24 February 1943, following a detailed judicial investigation into his war-time activities by a post-war Francoist tribunal, Guerra was "readmitted into active judicial service on full pay without the imposition of any sanctions."[197]

Spiritual Aid

The provision of 'spiritual aid' was central to the 'Work' of the organisation. The Catholic faith was intrinsic to the collective identity and core beliefs of Auxilio Azul. The women of Auxilio Azul worked in collaboration with those of Acción Católica who "from the outbreak of the Glorious National Movement … worked tirelessly to help priests and nuns risking their lives by visiting prisons, checas, safe-houses and houses under police surveillance."[198] The public celebration of religious festivals and saint's days was banned in the Republican-held zones.[199] After the closure of religious buildings in August 1936, Auxilio Azul provided safe-housing for the Catholic religious which included clergy, priests, monks, nuns and members of lay Catholic associations such as Teresa Luzzati who was a leader of Acción Católica. Auxilio Azul women arranged for the performance of weddings and other religious rites in their own homes at great personal risk.[200] Both Auxilio Azul and Socorro Blanco provided material and economic aid to Madrid's religious community within a group known as "El Socorro Blanco Sacerdotal." As a result of the efforts of this organisation thousands of persons received holy communion and hundreds of secret chapels were maintained across the capital. "During the war around 1,815,000 communion hosts were secretly fabricated in various clandestine workshops."[201] Father Tomás Ortega Orgaz was the 'Spiritual Advisor and Leader of Auxilio Azul's Spiritual Services' (Consiliario y Jefe del Servicio Espiritual de Auxilio Azul) and Cecilia Antón Medina was one of his key liaison agents as early as August 1937. She also safe-housed prominent individuals including two priests who performed daily masses at home for a period of around four months.[202]

The continuation of Catholic confessional practice was central to Auxilio Azul's collective identity and purpose. The organisation provided safe spaces within which to practice the faith; it also safe-housed the religious and brought the sacraments into the checas and prisons. The organisation established clandestine chapels in private homes. One was set up at the residence of Ana María and Dolores Rizzo Goñi in calle Espejo, 14, in the Palacio district. The masses were officiated by a priest in plain clothing with the sisters in attendance.[203] Another chapel was established at the home of Margarita Cuevo LaPeña. Ángela Ibañez Calvo joined in early 1938 and, as well as raising money and hiding priests and fugitives, she "helped many individuals to receive communion and the sacraments at her home."[204] Meanwhile, her cousins Ángeles and Maria Pilar García Ochoa e Ibañez also joined in early 1938. These women managed to recruit seventy new affiliates and safe-housed many military widows and fugitives including a priest named Eugenio García Guzmán who performed daily masses at their home and became the Cantor of the Ciudad Real Cathedral after the war. The group had links with María Lemus' organisation and also with the Sección Femenina in Linares, Jaén.[205]

Auxilio Azul's main chapel was set up in the basement of a dairy shop situated in calle Velázquez 46, directly opposite the SIM headquarters wherein masses, communions, baptisms, weddings and confessions were regularly performed. This building also served as the Auxilio Azul 'bank' where money was concealed within a brick wall cavity. The chapel was raided by the SIM in 1938 while a mass was in progress which was officiated by Father Tomás Ortega Orgaz, who was arrested and taken to the Checa de San Lorenzo. Carina and three other women managed to burn a large amount of money (*díez mil duros*) and incriminating documentation in the dairy's furnace prior to their detention at San Lorenzo. The Catholic lawyer and socialite Antonio Garrigues y Díaz-Cañabate and his American protestant wife Helen Garrigues Walker established a secret chapel in calle Velázquez, 46 which came to be the organisation's principal place of worship.[206] Another religious centre was established by a small community of *María Reparadora* nuns who had been evacuated from their convent in calle Torrijas. This clandestine chapel was known as the 'Catedral de Hermosilla,' and it operated from a first floor flat in calle Hermosilla, 12 which belonged to Commander Ucelay and which was under the protection of the Cuban Embassy. One of the nuns was a Cuban national whose sister also lived in the building. Fathers Hermenegildo López, Verdasco and other priests worked with these nuns in order to provide hundreds of masses, confessions and other sacraments to the members of Madrid's 'clandestine diocese.' Other priests included José María de la Higuera, Mariano Villapun, Ernesto de Santa Teresa, Alejo Revillo and Canon Andres Trillo Marín. Another priest, Father Tomás Revilla Franco, was also a doctor and the spiritual advisor and the leader of Group VA-2.[207]

According to historians the Communist International's Red Aid (Socorro Rojo) "lent an immense and unexpected aid to Madrid's 'persecuted Clandestine diocese.'"[208] It supported the spiritual initiatives of Auxilio Azul and a clandestine church network known as the *iglesia de catacumbas*.[209] As indicated above, Auxilio Azul's chief Spiritual Advisor was Father Tomás Ortega Orgaz, who was infiltrated as a teacher within Socorro Rojo together with around seven or eight priests.[210] Father Ortega was able to join a communist radio in order to avoid the repression at the start of the war with the help of his communist brother who subsequently went on to join Socorro Rojo. Father Ortega also joined this latter organisation and organised a clandestine network of priests, nuns and lay devout persons that operated from the Socorro Rojo headquarters. We will recall that Elena Walker's 'Castilla' network also operated from within the Socorro Rojo headquarters, and it is unclear whether this communist organisation deliberately turned a blind-eye on these clandestine activities. The priests administered the sacraments in private homes, hospitals, prisons, checas and the DGS with the aid of Auxilio Azul. Father Ortega was able to obtain work permits and passes for the priests who included Fathers Hermenegildo López, Ildefonso Miguelánez, Enrique

Masso and Jesús Catalán García. These men operated their ministries from within four Socorro Rojo centres in calles Lagasca 88, Zúrbano, Francisco Giner, 31 and Orfila. The priests volunteered as teachers and were provided with Socorro Rojo or CNT union cards which meant that they could move around the City more easily:

> As with all the best detective stories, a secret code was devised so that the Faithful could communicate with the priests without raising the suspicion of the security services. One only had to make a single call to a Socorro Rojo office or another centre and 'request the services of a medical practitioner,' and then provide details of the address and the name of the infirm/dying person in order to obtain rapid assistance … the medicinal 'camphor oil' was in reality an extreme unction; the 'pills' were the Communion hosts and, if 'laxatives' were mentioned, then what was being asked for was the sacrament of Confession (a true spiritual laxative) … the hosts were made in different sizes and hidden in the medical briefcases … The extreme unction was stored in face cream jars … the practitioners also carried … a tiny missal, a host vessel and a crystal glass, the hosts and small flask of wine. In that way we managed to perform the Holy Mass … We were driven about … in a FAI vehicle accompanied by two militia men who were ignorant of our activities.[211]

Auxilio Azul was responsible for arranging the visits and obtaining the hosts and other liturgical objects and it "devised various ways to deliver the sacraments, in particular, confession and communion into our homes."[212] Women were instrumental to the survival of the clandestine Catholic ministry. They sheltered priests and nuns, set up secret chapels in their homes, raised money for the religious and made thousands of hosts from fine white flour which, when possible, was made from premium-grade flour donated by the wealthier families and then shaped into hosts with hot irons. The hosts were also made from ordinary white bread from the bakery which was carefully moulded into shape, wrapped in fine linen and stored in medicine boxes, rouge tins, jewellery boxes or biscuit tins. The women smuggled these items into the checas, prisons, hospitals and private homes at great personal risk. Canon Trillo Marín's niece was involved in this mission 'heart and soul' (*pertenecia con alma y vida*).[213] Rosina Frutos Paris

> held clandestine masses at her home where communion was taken by numerous individuals including military personnel. The extreme unction for the sick and dying was obtained from the Reparadoras convent. Rosina visited the convent regularly and on Christmas day [1937] she distributed toys to the children of the needy.[214]

During 1937 religious communities were able to clandestinely regroup in the capital.[215]

The provision of Spiritual Aid was made particularly difficult because of the scarcity of priests to administer the sacraments, in particular within the prisons. According to Mother María Luis Fernández, who spent four months in Conde de Toreno after her arrest in September 1936, confessional practice continued in the prisons despite its official prohibition and the manifest dangers involved.[216] The actress María Cristina Montes Muñoz sided with the Nationalist cause from the outset. From December 1936 until March 1937 she safe-housed a Bernarda de Clausura nun named Ester Lerones García "by pretending that she was a servant so that she could live without raising suspicion in Chamberí which was a predominantly red neighbourhood." She also safe-housed twenty-three Adoratrice nuns who were later killed on 10 November 1936 outside the Eastern Cemetery. This woman was a well-known actress before the war, and she regularly performed songs and poetry recitals at the embassies in order to raise morale and money with great secrecy and at great risk. Her last recital of the war was performed at Carina Unciti's house where she managed to raise 220 pesetas; "it was an unforgettable evening, not only because of the sum raised, but also for the trust demonstrated by allowing her to personally meet Father Tomás Ortega and receive his enthusiastic thanks."[217]

The testimonials reflect the Francoist discourses that compared Madrid's '*perseguidos*' (fugitives) with the early Christians who sought refuge in Rome's catacombs. Such discourses evidence of the sacralisation of the war within new national Catholic discourses. The Auxilio Azul testimonies refer to the war as the 'Crusade.' These women wanted to protect the religious and keep the faith in addition to preserving their class and property rights and their social status. Sometimes sacred rites including marriage and baptism were performed by the women themselves in circumstances where priests were unavailable. Andrea Pariente Suárez hid the Cantor of Ciudad Real's Cathedral at her home because he was "being hunted to death." The Cantor regularly performed clandestine masses in her home "despite the fact that the house was full of red refugees."[218] This indicates that the network also offered aid to Republican refugees who had newly arrived from the rebel-occupied zones. The provision of Spiritual Aid to the needy and the faithful provided a sense of purpose, meaning and identity. The aim was to preserve an eternal religious time during a moment of violent secularisation. From the perspective of the members, the organisation was crucial to the preservation of a Catholic habitus during a moment of severe social upheaval and religious persecution. While a semblance of normality was restored to the civilian rear-guard in June 1937, public mass was only reinstated after the arrival of Franco's troops on 27–28 March 1939.

Auxilio Azul offered 'safe-spaces' within which to imagine a new national Catholic nationhood, maintain religious identity and conserve morale. These women helped to preserve the anti-Republican community during a moment of severe political, material and spiritual crisis. Years after the events Elvira Martínez Ostendi recalled that she had "formed part of a clandestine group of 6,000 women in Madrid during the war."[219] The organisation was never dismantled by the Republican authorities although the legal archives evidence the dismantlement of several Socorro Blanco groups and the Falangist Francisca Martínez Ramírez confessed under interrogation to the existence of a clandestine Sección Femenina in the capital (see Chapter 3 below). It may have been less risky for defendants to confess to an involvement in Traditionalist groups given the severity of the repression against the Falange. We should also recall that the terms 'Auxilio Azul' and 'Socorro Blanco' were used interchangeably, even by the members, and this is evidenced in the ANA testimonies.[220] After the war, Manuel Uribarri (head of the Republican SIM in 1938) claimed to have deliberately overlooked women's resistance efforts. While he viewed women as the nerve-centre (*entronque*) of the fifth column and believed that "for every man we should have had to arrest ten women," he decided to leave the "feminine hydra well-alone since evil resided in the fair sex."[221] Misogyny and gender prejudice may have informed these opinions, but pressing practical considerations were also evident. In circumstances of severe material deprivation commencing as early as September 1936, Auxilio Azul's legitimate social enterprise and welfare-aid initiatives may have been warily accommodated by the authorities. Similarly, confessional practice in the private sphere was generally tolerated after 1936, not least because the Republican authorities were mindful of the extremely negative impact of the early and violent religious repression on public and international relations. In contrast, illegal and subversive activities were actively repressed and a good number of Auxilio Azul women appeared before the popular tribunals, mainly on charges of disaffection. In the next chapter we will see that some fourteen mixed-gender Clandestine Falange groups were successfully dismantled pursuant to police surveillance and counter-espionage operations.[222]

After the occupation of the capital by Nationalist troops on 28 March 1939, many Auxilio Azul members chose to fall back into the invisible domestic space in accordance with the values and durable dispositions of their gendered Catholic habitus. After the arrival of Auxilio Social in the capital, the organisation was promptly demobilised and an official Sección Femenina hierarchy was established. Carina, Rosina Frutos and other senior members were involved in the demobilisation "for a period of five months after Liberation."[223] In August 1939 Carina was elected as Regional Delegate of Madrid, but she did not play an active role and resigned soon after on grounds of ill health. Carina also received the military honours and decorations due to an ex-combatant including those of Honorary Army Captain, a Campaign medal (with white colours), a War Cross, two Red Crosses for Military Merit and an individual and collective Silver Y award.[224] The conflict forged the political identities of the post-war leaders of the Sección Femenina which was tasked by Franco with the provision of health, education and welfare services across Spain.[225] Women's political impulses were channelled into gender-specific social welfare activities.[226] In this way a new Falangist female 'elite' was able to carve out a political space within the new regime and defend its own social and political agendas.[227] After the war, prominent members of Auxilio Azul came to enjoy the respect, recognition, preferment and privileges afforded to ex-combatants including state-pensions and other material and economic rewards.[228]

Notes

1 *Asesoría Jurídica*, Testimony of Teresa Pérez Aznar dated 28 September 1939, Document 199, ANA, Carpeta B 12, RAH. She joined Auxilio Azul in May 1938.
2 This observation has also been made with regard to the women of the Sección Femenina in Almería; see Rodríguez López, Sofía (2010) *El patio de la cárcel, La Sección Femenina de FET-JONS en Almería (1937–77)* (Seville: Centro de Estudios Andaluces), p. 45.
3 Cervera (1998), p. 267.
4 *Asesoría Jurídica*, Testimony of Carina Martínez Unciti, ANA, Carpeta B 12, RAH.
5 *Asesoría Jurídica*, Testimony of Rafaela de Castro Gutiérrez dated 6 November 1939, Document 143, ANA, Carpeta B 12, RAH.
6 Cervera (1998), p. 267. The triangular structure was similar to that used by clandestine communist cells at this time.
7 *Asesoría Jurídica*, Testimony of Rosa Sainz de los Terreros Llavador dated 26 September 1939, Document 185, ANA, Carpeta B 12, RAH.
8 *Expte. no. 609 contra* Elvira Martínez Ostendi *por el delito/s de Desafección al Régimen*, AHN, FC_CAUSA_GENERAL, 270, Exp. 10. This defendant testified to having been a member of Acción Popular prior to the war.
9 *Asesoría Jurídica*, Testimony of Mercedes Folch Fou dated 26 September 1939, Document 207, ANA, Carpeta B 12, RAH. Involved in Soccorro Blanco from October 1936. She joined Auxilio Azul in June 1938.
10 Expte. 131, instruido contra Consuelo Muñoz Rocha por delito/s de Desafección al Régimen, AHN, FC-CAUSA_GENERAL, 110, Exp. 31, Imagen 8/14. This single woman lived on her father's military pension and had 'voted for the Right in the February elections and often attended Church being a Catholic, she was arrested on 3 September but released and put under surveillance for six months.'
11 *Asesoría Jurídica*, Testimony of Consuelo Rocha dated 13 August, 1939, Document 181, ANA, Carpeta B 12, RAH. This woman testified to having been a founder member of Renovación Española.
12 *Asesoría Jurídica*, Testimony of Rafaela de Castro Gutiérrez dated 6 November 1939, Document 143, ANA, Carpeta B 12, RAH.
13 *Asesoría Jurídica*, Testimony of Emilia García San Nicolás dated 5 October 1939, Document 163, ANA, Carpeta B 12, RAH.
14 [Fal Conde] *Gesta Gloriosa del Requete en Madrid* (Julio 1936–Marzo 1939), *Archivo General Militar de Ávila*, C2505, Cp.4/43 and C.2498.20, Legajo no. 285, Carpeta 20, Armario 5, at p. 5.
15 Alcocer, Santos (1976) *La Quinta Columna* (Madrid: G. del Toro), p. 44.
16 Cervera (1998) *Madrid*, pp. 269–270, Borrás (1965) *Seis Mil*, pp. 67–68 and p. 71. The code names for the 111 Groups were as follows: Groups 1–27 were designated from A to Z; the next twenty-seven Groups were designated from A to Z but prefixed with an "A"; thereafter, each successive set of twenty-seven Groups was preceded by a B, C or a D with a total of 108 Groups, the last three of which were designated EA, EB and EC. The code names for the 333 Sub-Groups involved pre-fixing a number before the code name for the relevant Group, for example Group A had three Sub-Group Leaders whose code names were 1-A, 2-A and 3-A and the last Group EC had three Sub-Group Leaders whose code names were 1-EC, 2-EC and 3-EC. The 'militants' within each Sub-Group would be code-named as follows: 1-A-1, 1-A-2, 1-A-3, 1-A-4 … and so forth.

17 *Asesoría Jurídica*, Testimony of Inés MartIn Monjas dated 28 October 1939, Document 183, ANA, Carpeta B 12, RAH.

18 In relation to the involvement of the Church see Chapter XI "Enclaves Diplomáticos," in Alfaya, José Luis (1998) *Como un río de fuego* (Barcelona: EIU), pp. 181–188. Regarding the embassies see Moral, Antonio (2001) *El asilo diplomático en la Guerra Civil Española* (Madrid: Actas), pp. 25–42. Regarding the actions of the PNV see Galíndez, Jesus de (2005) (first ed. 1945) *Los vascos en el Madrid sitiado; memorias del Partido Nacionalista Vasco y de la Delegación de Euzkadi en Madrid desde septiembre de 1936 a mayo de 1937* (Tafalla, Navarra: Txalaparta).

19 *Asesoría Jurídica*, Testimony of Andrea Pariente Suárez dated 9 October 1939, Document 169, ANA, Carpeta B 12, RAH.

20 *Asesoría Jurídica*, Testimony of Luisa Laguna Torres dated 16 August 1939, Document 253, ANA, Carpeta B 12, RAH.

21 *Asesoría Jurídica*, Testimony of Josefina García Folez de Velador dated 27 September 1939, Document 203, ANA, Carpeta B 12, RAH. Known as K-2, this operative found refuge at various embassies for "various wanted friends."

22 *Asesoría Jurídica*, Testimony of Carolina María Illescas Burgallo dated 1939, Document 205, ANA, Carpeta B 12, RAH.

23 Cervera (1998) *Madrid*, pp. 369–374.

24 Julián Zugazagoitia Mendiete (1899–1940) was the editor of El Socialista the PSOE's mouth piece until his appointment as Minister of the Interior in Juan Negrín's first cabinet in May 1937. He saved the lives of many Nationalists and tried to improve the treatment of war prisoners. He was arrested by the Gestapo in Paris in July 1940 and executed by the Spanish authorities in November 1940.

25 Moral, Antonio (2001) *El Asilo Diplomatico en la Guerra Civil Española* (Madrid: Actas), p. 44. See also Cervera (1998) *Madrid*, p. 360.

26 Moral (2001) *El Asilo*, p. 187.

27 Etchébehere, Mitcha (1987) *Mi Guerra de España: Las apasionantes vivencias de una mujer que llego a ser Capitán de fuerzas Republicanas* [POUM] (Madrid: Plaza y Janés), p. 170. Also cited in Moral (2001) *El Asilo*, at p. 45.

28 e.g. the Belgian diplomat Baron de Borchgrave who was accused of espionage and executed by anarchists on 20 December 1936, the Belgian diplomat Marc Spacy Engelen, the Romanian Henry Helfant and General Lucco a military attaché at the Chilean Embassy who was arrested in possession of plans relating to Republican military campaigns. Also, the Norwegian business attaché Félix Schlayer.

29 Cervera (1998) *Madrid*, p. 361.

30 The group was known as La organización Rodríguez Aguado. It was dismantled by Ángel Pedrero's Special Brigade Agents who infiltrated the network in October 1937. See *Sumario no. 81/1938* del *Juzgado Especial por espionaje y otros delitos contra la seguridad del Estado contra Antonio Rodríguez Aguado y otros*, AHN, FC-CAUSA_GENERAL,1540, Exp.1, Imágenes 1-1805. See also Cervera (1998) *Madrid*, pp. 316–319.

31 See most recent accounts in Píris "Los servicios de información franquista…," pp. 151–153. See also, "Antonio Rodríguez Aguado, el hombre mas buscado," in Laguna Reyes, Alberto and Vargas Márquez, Antonio (2019) *La Quinta Columna, La guerra clandestina tras las líneas republicanas 1936–1939* (Madrid: Laesfera), pp. 155–219.

32 *Asesoría Jurídica*, Testimony of Roseda Blanco Martínez, Document 277, ANA, Carpeta B 12, RAH. She was agent (1HA).

33 Ángel Pedrero García was the Head of Madrid's SIM after August 1937. The SIM was created after the dissolution of the Special Brigades in July 1937. Pedrero was also second-in-command of the García Atadell Brigade until its dissolution in late 1936. See *Testimonio del Fiscal Secretario de la pieza segunda del auto resumen del procedimiento sumarisimo de urgencia no. 1549 seguido por la Jurisdicción Militar Nacional contra Ángel Pedrero García, Jefe del Servicio Militar (SIM)*, AHN, FC-CAUSA _GENERAL, 1520, Exp. 3. Imágenes 1-18. Affidavit Ángel Pedrero dated 2 January 1942.

34 Good diplomatic relations with Turkey were vital because Turkey had signed the Non-Intervention Agreement in 1936 and it controlled the straits of Bosphorus and the Dardanelles which was a route for vital Russian material shipments. This may explain the delay in raiding the embassy despite SIM knowledge of fifth-column activities within it.

35 Cervera, Javier (1998) *Madrid*, p. 350.

36 Moral (2001) *El Asilo*, at p. 44. The author cites the figures in the DPhil Dissertation of María del Carmen Gómez Reollo (1985) *Madrid, 1936–9: El asilo diplomático en la guerra civil española* (Madrid: UCM). See also, Cervera (1998) *Madrid*, at p. 351.

37 Cervera (1998) *Madrid*, p. 351. The figure is an approximate because of the discrepancies between sources in relation to the number of legal and illegal asylees.

38 *Expte. 486 instruido contra Teofila Abad Benito y Mercedes Rivero Calvo por el delito/s de Desafección al Régimen*, AHN, FC-CAUSA_GENERAL, 116, Exp. 9. In this case two domestic workers were initially accused of espionage because they had carried messages to and from embassies and private homes.

39 Díaz-Plaja, Fernando (1995) *La vida cotidiana en la España de la Guerra Civil* (Madrid: Edaf), p. 75.

40 *Causa 25 instruida contra Ricardo Guerra Blanco por el delito/s de Alta Traición*, FC-CAUSA_GENERAL, 145, Exp. 44. Guerra Blanco was the magistrate who presided over popular Tribunal no. 7 which heard cases of disaffection. He was accused of treason in May 1938 for plotting with Félix Schlayer and Socorro Blanco to organise the escape of fugitives into the Nationalist zone.

41 See "La cárcel de mujeres en el antiguo convento," in Félix Schlayer (2008) *Diplomático en el Madrid Rojo* (Madrid: Espuela de Plata), pp. 155–164.

42 Post-war declaration of Félix Schlayer, AHN, FC-CAUSA_GENERAL, cited in Moral Roncal, Antonio (2001) *El Asilo*, p. 32.

43 Marqués, Pierre (2000) *La Croix-Rouge pendant la guerrre d'Espagne (1936–9)* (Paris: L'Harmattan), p. 241.

44 Auxilio Azul Demobilisation Documents, 'Final Accounts' dated 1939, copy documentation reproduced in Borrás, (1965), Appendix, at p.141.

45 Cervera (1998) *Madrid*, pp. 371–373. See also DPhil Dissertation of María del Carmen Gómez Reollo (1985) *Madrid, 1936–9: El asilo diplomático en la guerra civil española* (Madrid: UCM).

46 *Asesoría Jurídica*, Testimony of Concepción Pilar Fortis Benedicto dated 14 October 1939, Document 213, ANA, Carpeta B 12, RAH.

47 *Asesoría Jurídica*, Testimony of Cecilia Antón Medina dated 6 October 1939, Document 293, ANA, Carpeta B 12, RAH.

48 *Asesoría Jurídica*, Testimony of Carlota Narcisa González de Uzqueta y Cerillo dated 20 September 1939, Document 196, ANA, Carpeta B 12, RAH.

49 *Asesoría Jurídica*, Testimony of Inés Martín Monjas dated 28 October 1939, Document 183, ANA, Carpeta B 12, RAH.

50 *Asesoría Jurídica*, Testimony of María Ugaldezubiaur dated 12 October 1939, Document 218, ANA, Carpeta B 12, RAH, Madrid.

51 *Expte. 609 contra* Elvira Martínez Ostendi *por el delito/s de Desafección al Régimen*, AHN, FC_CAUSA_GENERAL, 270, Exp. 10. Image 13/84.

52 Oral testimony of Elvira Martínez Ostendi in undated interview with author, see Borrás (1965), at p. 172.

53 *Expte. 609*, Imagen 3/84.

54 *Expte. 609*, Imagen 3/84.

55 *Expte. 609,* Imagen 4/84.

56 See *Decreto del Ministerio de Hacienda* dated 23 September 1936, cited in *Gaceta de la República,* 25 September, 1936. See also Sánchez Recio, Glicerio (1991) *La República contra los Rebeldes y los Desafectos, La Represión Económica durante la Guerra Civil* (Madrid: Universidad de Alicante), pp. 19–23.

57 Borrás (1965), pp. 169–178. See "Sobrevivir en el Madrid rojo," in Núñez Seixas, José Manoel (2012) *La sombra del césar, Santiago Montero Díaz, una biografía entre la nación y la revolución* (Granada: Comares), pp. 113–120 at p. 119. Montero was not a signed-up member of the Falange, but his fascist sympathies meant that after 18 July he was obliged go underground in Madrid where he happened to be conducting archival research. He was promptly dismissed from his academic post at Murcia University and thereafter suffered acute financial hardship. The violence at the start of the war "radicalized his political stance" (p. 113). Initially, he lived in a guest-house and went out as little as possible but eventually obtained asylum at the El Salvador Legation. His initial aim was to escape to South America and then return to the Nationalist zone. He lived in a flat under the protection of the Legation and endured conditions of material deprivation and overcrowding much like other asylees. He eventually left the protection of the Legation, and lived under a false identity supplied by Group Y for whom he worked until March 1938 creating false documents alongside José Dorrell and Andrés Révész, a Hungarian national and former *ABC* correspondent. Montero testified after the war that he had managed to infiltrate the *Sindicato de Técnicos de la Confederación Nacional de Trabajos.*

58 Oral Testimony of Elvira Martínez Ostendi, Borrás (1965) *Seis Mil*, p. 173.

59 Obituary of Elvira Martínez Ostendi, *ABC* (Madrid) dated 26 May 1970 at p. 46.

60 *Asesoría Jurídica*, Testimony of Ana María Rizzo Goñi dated 29 September Document 248, ANA, Carpeta B 12, RAH.

61 *Asesoría Jurídica*, Testimony of Elena Herzog dated 28 September, Document 222, ANA, Carpeta B 12, RAH.

62 Borrás (1965), p. 178.

63 The politicians included José Cruz Conde Fustegueras, a military officer and former President of Renovación Española, who represented the 'canditatura anti-revolucionaria' during the 16 February 1936 general elections. This monarchist politician was a Director of the Ibero-American Seville Exposition (1929), mayor of Cordoba (1924–5), and civil governor of Seville (1926–31). During the war he lived as a fugitive in Madrid in a succession of safe-houses and embassies including those of Peru, Argentina and Santo Domingo. He died in Madrid aged sixty years of a cardiac arrest on 31 January 1939.

64 See *Asesoría Jurídica*, Testimony of Ana María Rizzo Goñi dated 29 September, Document 248, ANA, Carpeta B 12, RAH.

65 *Archivo General Auxilio Azul, Cárceles, Doc 29717.* Letter from Jesus Laporta Girón to the FET de las JONS, dated 18 March 1940, a photo-copy of which is reproduced in Borrás (1965), in Appendix at p. 257.

66 The colloquial term for someone who was 'red on the outside but white inside,' i.e. a secret Nationalist sympathiser.

67 *Asesoría Jurídica*, Testimony of Marí-Nieves Villa García Gómez dated 20 September 1939, Document 149, ANA, Carpeta B 12, RAH.

68 *Asesoría Jurídica*, Testimony of Andrea Pariente Súarez dated 9 October 1939, Document 169, ANA, Carpeta B 12, RAH.

69 *Expte. contra María Baeza Torrecilla por delitos de Desafección al Régimen por pertenencia a Acción Popular*, AHN, FC-CAUSA_GENERAL, 184, Exp. 14, Imagen 2-3/46.

70 *Expte. contra María Baeza Torrecilla*, Imagen 33/46.

71 *Asesoría Jurídica*, Testimony of Emilia García San Nicolás dated 5 October 1939, Document 163, ANA, Carpeta B 12, RAH.

72 Lannon, Frances "Gender and Change: Identity and Reform in the Second Republic," in Xon de Ros, Geraldine Hazbun (eds) (2011) *Companion to Spanish Women's Studies* (London: Boydell and Brewer/Tamesis), p. 275.

73 *Expte. 486 instruido contra Teófila Abad Benito y Mercedes Rivero Calvo por el delito/s de Desafección al Régimen*, AHN, FC-CAUSA_GENERAL, 116, Exp. 9. Imagen no. 8/66. In this case a former Catholic town councillor and member of Acción Popular who was an asylee in an

embassy wrote to his wife granting her full authority over family, property and business matters while he remained in asylum.

74 *Asesoría Jurídica*, Testimony of Manolita Despierto Vázquez dated 4 October 1939, Document 147, ANA, Carpeta B 12, RAH, Madrid.

75 'Masculine domination' is a form of 'cultural arbitrary' which is reproduced in religious and state institutions and in the educational and academic fields; see Bourdieu (2001) *Masculine Domination*, at pp. 1–2 and pp. 34–42.

76 This member was also involved in the clandestine fifth-column operations of the "195 Group" discussed in Chapter 3 below.

77 *Asesoría Jurídica*, Testimony of María Lemus González Campuzano dated 27 October 1939, Document 254, ANA, Carpeta B 12, RAH. She was also a liaison agent with the Clandestine Falange and safe-guarded valuables.

78 *Asesoría Jurídica*, Testimony of Josefina García Fólez de Velador dated 27 September 1939, Document 203, ANA, Carpeta B 12, RAH.

79 *Asesoría Jurídica*, Testimony of María Tejedor Escribano dated 3 October 1939, Document 266, ANA, Carpeta B 12, RAH. See also, *Asesoría Jurídica*, Testimony of Cecilia Antón Medina dated 6 October 1939, Document 293, ANA, Carpeta B 12, RAH. Medina distributed Red Cross food to prisoners and those in hiding or in embassies. Amongst many other services rendered she "collected money, distributed raffle tickets, sewed, sold items, and provided emergency aid (*socorros*)."

80 Suárez Fernández, Luís (1992) *Crónica de la Sección Femenina y su tiempo* (Madrid: Nueva Andadura), p. 37.

81 *Asesoría Jurídica*, Testimony of Magdalena Sánchez Velasco dated 26 October 1939, Document 194, ANA, Carpeta B 12, RAH.

82 *Asesoría Jurídica*, Testimony of Rosina Frutos Paris dated 20 September 1939, Document 246, ANA, Carpeta B 12, RAH.

83 Montoliú, Pedro (2000) *Madrid en la Guerra Civil, La Historia Vol. I* (Madrid: Silex), p. 257.

84 *Asesoría Jurídica*, Testimony of Pilar Morga Méndez dated 26 September 1939, Document 198, ANA, Carpeta B 12, RAH.

85 Borrás (1965) *Seis Mil*, p. 81.

86 For a detailed account of Mercedes Sanz Bachiller and the origins of Auxilio Social see Orduña Prada, Monica (1996) *El Auxilio Social (1936–40), La etapa fundacional y los primerso años* (Madrid: Escuela Libre Editorial). This work is cited in "Mercedes Sanz Bachiller – So Easy to Judge," in Preston, Paul (2002) *Doves of War, Four Women of Spain* (London: Harper Collins), at pp. 205–293.

87 *Asesoría Jurídica*, Testimony of María Teresa González Tablas y Mendizábal dated 6 October 1939, Document 233, ANA, Carpeta B 12, RAH.

88 Borrás (1965) *Seis Mil*, p. 140.

89 *Asesoría Jurídica*, Testimony of Isabel Martín Monjas dated 28 October 1939, Document 182, ANA, Carpeta B 12, RAH. This affiliate and others testified that they secretly obtained milk and other supplies from the Red Cross.

90 *Asesoría Jurídica*, Testimony of Ángelita Blanco de Castro dated 6 November 1939, Document 144, ANA, Carpeta B 12, RAH.

91 *Asesoría Jurídica*, Testimony of Ángelita Blanco de Castro dated 6 November 1939, Document 156, ANA, Carpeta B 12, RAH. She was the leader of '*Barrio 4*.'

92 Cervera (1998) *Madrid*, p. 270.

93 *Asesoría Jurídica*, Testimony of Nieves Villa García Gómez dated 20 September 1939, Document 149, ANA, Carpeta B 12, RAH.

94 *Asesoría Jurídica*, Testimony of Rosa Mazarracín Lalanda dated 21 September 1939, Document 153, ANA, Carpeta B 12, RAH.

95 *Asesoría Jurídica*, Testimony of María Dolores Núñez Fagoago dated 20 September 1939, Document 156, ANA, Carpeta B 12, RAH.

96 *Asesoría Jurídica*, Testimony of Cecilia Antón Medina dated 6 October 1939, Document 193, ANA, Carpeta B 12, RAH.

97 Borrás (1965) "*Folio de la contabilidad de Auxilio Azul de la compañía de cerillas*." An excerpt of the Madrid Match Company Accounts as set out in Appendix at p. 262.

98 Antonio Garrigues y Díaz Cañabete, Marqués de Garrigues, lawyer and public servant (9 Jan 1904–24 Feb 2004) "was a unique figure in Spanish politics holding high office under the Republic in the 1930's, the Francoist dictatorship in the 1960's and the restored monarchy of King Juan Carlos in the 1970's." Despite being a devout Catholic he married Helen Walker, a protestant from Des Moines, Iowa, in 1931. They had nine children. Helen died in 1944 aged thirty-five. He was most well-known as the close friend of Jacqueline Kennedy after her husband's assassination in 1963. He became Spanish ambassador to Washington in 1962 because of his professional links with North America, his distance from Franco and his friendship with the Kennedy family. See Antonio Garrigues, Obituary, *Guardian* dated 1 March 2004.

99 See *ABC, Madrid* dated 28 September 1963, p. 57. "The daughter of the US Ambassador will make her perpetual vows next Sunday at the convent of the Irish Mothers of Seville."

100 *Asesoría Jurídica*, Testimony of María Nieves Villa García Gómez dated 20 September 1939, Document 149, ANA, Carpeta B 12, RAH.

101 *Sumario instruido contra Carmen Vera Aguilera y Antonio Capdevilla Massip por el delito/s de Derrotismo e infracción en materia de substancias*, AHN, FC-CAUSA_GENERAL, 59, Exp. 39. Imágenes 1-6.

102 Borrás (1965), p. 159.

103 *Sumario instruido contra Carmen Vera Aguilera y Antonio Capdevilla Massip por el delito/s de Derrotismo e infracción en materia de substancias*, AHN, FC-CAUSA_GENERAL, 59, Exp. 39. Imágenes 1-6.

104 Rodríguez Barreira, Óscar "Cambalaches: hambre, moralidad popular y mercados negros de guerra y posguerra," *Historia Social*, 77 (2013), pp. 149–174.

105 See "De los vales al mercado negro," in Montoliú, Pedro (2000) *Madrid en la Guerra Civil, La Historia Vol. I* (Madrid: Silex), pp. 151–156.

106 *Asesoría Jurídica*, Testimony of María Lava Casla dated 20 September 1939, Document 159, ANA, Carpeta B 12, RAH. This member testified to having purchased toys and distributed them at Christmas to the children of fugitive anti-Republicans.

107 Borrás (1965), p. 76.

108 e.g. *Asesoría Jurídica*, Testimony of Mercedes Sotillo Sancho dated 11 October 1939, Document 161, ANA, Carpeta B 12, RAH. Also, *Asesoría Jurídica*, Testimony of Isabel Martín Monjas dated 1 August 1939, Document 182, ANA, Carpeta B 12, RAH. And *Asesoría Jurídica*, Testimony of Francisca Calero Ruiz de Valbuena dated 26 September 1939, Document 197, ANA, Carpeta B 12, RAH.

109 *Asesoría Jurídica*, Testimony of Dolores Núñez Fagoago dated 9 September 1939, Document 156, ANA, Carpeta B 12, RAH.

110 *Asesoría Jurídica*, Testimony of Carmen Temprano Vidal dated 25 September 1939, Document 206, ANA, Carpeta B 12, RAH. She also collected Red Cross ration-books.

111 *Asesoría Jurídica*, Testimony of Manolita Despierto Vázquez dated 4 September 1939, Document 147, ANA, Carpeta B 12, RAH.

112 *Asesoría Jurídica*, Testimony of Pastora Vázquez Moreno dated 28 September 1939, Document 152, ANA, Carpeta B 12, RAH. See also *Asesoría Jurídica*, Testimony of María Lava Casla dated 20 September 1939, Document 159, ANA, Carpeta B 12, RAH.

113 e.g. *Asesoría Jurídica*, Testimony of Lillie Arroyo del Real dated 20 September 1939, Document 150, ANA, Carpeta B 12, RAH. A member of Group AY.

114 *Asesoría Jurídica*, Testimony of Rosa Mazarracín Lalanda dated 21 September 1939, Document 153, ANA, Carpeta B 12, RAH.

115 *Asesoría Jurídica*, Testimony of Inés Martín Monjas dated 28 October 1939, Document 183, ANA, Carpeta B 12, RAH.

116 *Asesoría Jurídica*, Testimony of María Josefa Cerezo dated [September] 1939, Document 176, ANA, Carpeta B 12, RAH. Cerezo testified to having hidden Falangist flags and false

documentation; see also *Asesoría Jurídica*, Testimony of María Teresa González Tablas y Mendizábal dated 6 October 1939, Document 233, ANA, Carpeta B 12, RAH.

117 Primo de Rivera, Pilar (1983) *Recuerdos de Una Vida* (Ediciones Dyrsa: Madrid), p. 69.

118 *Asesoría Jurídica*, Testimony of Rosina Frutos Paris dated 20 September, Document 246, ANA, Carpeta B 12, RAH.

119 *Asesoría Jurídica*, Testimony of Rosina Frutos Paris dated 20 September 1939, Document 246, ANA, Carpeta B 12, RAH.

120 See case of the Falangist María Coll Codina in *Testimonios de Sentencias dictadas por el Tribunal especial de Espionaje y Alta Traición de Cataluña en cuasas procedentes del juzgado especial no 1*, AHN, FC-CAUSA GENERAL, 1637, Exp. 38 Imagen [16/161].

121 *Expte. contra Felisa Ruiz de Alda por desafección al Régimen,5145*, AHN, FC-CAUSA_GENERAL,19, Exp.47 and Expte. 266, FC-CAUSA_GENERAL, 235, Exp. 5. Felisa Ruiz de Alda was arrested in late February 1937. She served her sentence in Madrid's Conde de Toreno, San Rafael and Ventas prisons and later in Alacuas, Valencia.

122 Hernández Holgado, Fernando (2003) *Mujeres encarceladas: La prisión de Ventas, de la República al Franquismo, 1931–41* (Madrid: Marcial Pons) p. 172. Ruiz de Alda continued to visit Republican prisoners in Ventas after the war. There is a typo here: "Matilide Casampallo" is correctly spelt "Matilde Casáñ Pablo."

123 Oral testimony of Felisa Ruiz de Alda in an undated interview with the author in Borrás (1965), pp. 196–201 at p. 197.

124 *Sumario, No. 4/1937 del Juzgado Especial del Tribunal Central de Espionaje no.1 contra Javier Fernández Golfín y otros*, AHN, FC-CAUSA_GENERAL, 1539, Exp. 1. Imágenes 1134.

125 *Asesoría Jurídica*, Testimony of Matilde Casáñ Pablo dated 14 October 1939, ANA, *Carpeta* B 12 folder? Source: www.plataforma2003.org [last accessed 21 February 2017]. The full reference for this document was not provided on the website.

126 See "La ciudad recupera su ritmo," in Montoliú, Pedro (2000) *Madrid en la Guerra Civil, La Historia Vol. I* (Madrid: Silex), pp. 279–286.

127 *Asesoría Jurídica*, Testimony of Emilia García San Nicolás dated 5 October 1939, Document 163, ANA, Carpeta B 12, RAH.

128 Cervera (1998) *Madrid*, p. 273.

129 *Asesoría Jurídica*, Testimony of Ángela Ibáñez Calvo dated 9 October 1939, Document 225, ANA, Carpeta B 12, RAH. See also, *Asesoría Jurídica*, Testimony of Ángeles García Ochoa Ibáñez dated 9 October 1939, Document 226, ANA, Carpeta B 12, RAH and *Asesoría Jurídica*, Testimony of María Pilar García Ochoa Ibáñez dated 9 October 1939, Document 227, ANA, Carpeta B 12, RAH.

130 Oral testimony of Carmen Timmermans in an undated interview with the author Borrás (1965) *Seis Mil*, pp. 192–195.

131 Oral testimony of Nena Toffé in undated interview with the author Borrás (1965) *Seis Mil*, p. 188.

132 Borrás (1965) *Seis Mil*, p. 189.

133 Bourdieu's term for the imposition on subordinated groups by the dominant class of an ideology which legitimises and naturalises the status quo, such as, for example, the imposition of middle-class aesthetic tastes and values and the imposition of 'appropriate' fashion and dress codes on the working-classes. "After so much historical work on the symbolism of power, it would be naïve not to see that fashions in clothing and cosmetics are a basic element in the mode of domination": Bourdieu, Pierre (2010) *Distinction* (London: Routledge), at p. 312.

134 See the discussion on the use of 'symbolic violence,' 'bodily hexis' and 'the transformation of self through fashion' in order to acquire cultural and social capital in Angela Mc Robbie "Notes on 'What not to Wear' and post-feminist symbolic violence," in Adkins, Lisa and Skeggs, Beverley (eds) (2007) *Feminism After Bourdieu* (Oxford: Blackwell Publishing), pp. 99–109. Bourdieu rejects the Kantian 'sense of taste' and argues that there is no innate aesthetic or pure taste, only 'taste' inculcated by social groups over time.

135 Bourdieu, Pierre (2001) *Practical Reason* (Oxford: Polity).

136 *Asesoría Jurídica*, Testimony of María Cristina Montez Muñoz dated 7 September 1939, Document 244, ANA, Carpeta B 12, RAH.
137 Oral testimonies of Dolores and Ana Rizzo Goñi, in undated transcript interviews with the author in Borrás (1965), at p. 187.
138 *Asesoría Jurídica*, Testimony of Emilia García San Nicolás dated 5 October 1939, Document 163, ANA, Carpeta B 12, RAH.
139 *Causa 1753 instruida contra Gabrielle Dumont por el delito/s de Rebelión y Espionaje*, AHN, FC-CAUSA_GENERAL, 201, Exp. 5. Imagen 5/9. This case (nine pages) was referred to the popular courts, and the final judgement is unknown.
140 See Kay, Alison (2006) *Reconstructing the role of the household in businesswomen's networks of support, London 1851–1861*, Session Paper, "Women and business networks in industrializing Europe, 1700–1900." XIV International Economic History Congress, Helsinki, Finland 21–25 August 2006, p. 1.
141 Borrás (1965), p. 101.
142 *Asesoría Jurídica*, Testimony of María Luisa Miret de Grassa dated 1939, Document 252, ANA, Carpeta B 12, RAH.
143 *Asesoría Jurídica*, Testimony of Rosalia Manriquez Núñez dated 23 September 1939, Document 145, ANA, Carpeta B 12, RAH.
144 *Asesoría Jurídica*, Testimony of Pilar Allas López dated 9 October 1939, Document 255, ANA, Carpeta B 12, RAH.
145 *Asesoría Jurídica*, Testimony of María Josefa Fernández Fournier dated 23 September 1939, Document 191, ANA, Carpeta B 12, RAH.
146 Expte.115 *contra* Margarita Álvarez Santiago, *por delito/s de Desafección,* AHN, FC-CAUSA_GENERAL, 231, Exp.11.
147 *Asesoría Jurídica*, Testimony of Teresa Monge Dávila dated 9 October 1939, Document 255, ANA, Carpeta B 12, RAH.
148 Sánchez Blanco, Laura (2016) *Rosas y Margaritas, Mujeres falangistas, tradicionalistas y de Acción Católica asesinadas en la Guerra Civil* (Madrid: Actas), pp. 177–197.
149 Borrás (1965), p. 85.
150 *Asesoría Jurídica,* Testimony of Caridad Rapallo Comatje, dated 3 October 1939, Document 192, ANA, Carpeta B 12, RAH.
151 *Asesoría Jurídica*, Testimony of María Piedead Torres Montero dated 1939, Document 192, ANA, Carpeta B 12, RAH. She also raised funds.
152 *Asesoría Jurídica*, Testimony of Manolita Despierto Vázquez dated 4 September 1939 Document 147, ANA, Carpeta B 12, RAH.
153 *Asesoría Jurídica*, Testimony of Matilde Babé y Gómez dated 9 October 1939, Document 260, ANA, Carpeta B 12, RAH.
154 Borrás (1965), p. 89.
155 *Asesoría Jurídica*, Testimony of Matilde Babé y Gómez dated 9 October 1939, Document 260, ANA, Carpeta B 12, RAH.
156 *Asesoría Jurídica*, Testimony of María de los Ángeles Las Heras Sanz dated 9 October 1939, Document 212, ANA, Carpeta B 12, RAH.
157 AGMAV, C. 2851, 14, Expediente SIPM personal de Martínez Unciti, Carina, 16408, [dated 31 March 1942]. This file contains nine documents including signed letters certifying Carina's involvement as Sub-Group Leader of the Galicia Group from Ramón Arnal Moreno (leader of SINSE's 'Galicia Group'), Rafael Blanco y Caro (General Secretary of SINSE during its demobilisation), José Ungria Giménez (Colonel of the General Staff and Head of the SIMP) and others.
158 *Asesoría Jurídica*, Testimony of Rosina Frutos Paris dated 20 September 1939, Document 246, ANA, Carpeta B 12, RAH.
159 *Asesoría Jurídica*, Testimony of Cecilia Antón Medina dated 6 October 1939, Document 193, ANA, Carpeta B 12, RAH.
160 *Asesoría Jurídica*, Testimony of María García Díaz dated 28 September 1939, Document 193, ANA, Carpeta B 12, RAH.

161 *Asesoría Jurídica*, Testimony of Carlota Narcisa Gónzalez de Uzqueta y Cerillo dated 20 September 1939, Document 196, ANA, Carpeta B 12, RAH. See also, *Asesoría Jurídica*, Testimony of María García Díaz dated 28 September 1939, Document 193, ANA, Carpeta B 12, RAH.

162 *Asesoría Jurídica*, Testimony of Carlota Narcisa Gónzalez de Uzqueta y Cerillo dated 20 September 1939, Document 196, ANA, Carpeta B 12, RAH.
Asesoría Jurídica, Testimony of Ana María Rizzo Goñi dated 29 September Document 248, ANA, Carpeta B 12, RAH.

163 *Asesoría Jurídica*, Testimony of María Pilar Ortega Iturria dated 20 September 1939, Document 160, ANA, Carpeta B 12, RAH. After the war her name appeared in the Nationalist 'Delegación Nacional de Servicios Documentales' which was created in 1944. This is because the Republican DGS had kept records about her during the war: Source: CDMH, DNSD, *Secretaria Fichero*, 48,00033079 and 33080.

164 *Asesoría Jurídica*, Testimony of Amalia Martín García dated 4 October 1939, Document 210, ANA, Carpeta B 12, RAH.

165 *Asesoría Jurídica*, Testimony of María Luisa Laguna Torres dated 16 August 1939, Document 253, ANA, Carpeta B 12, RAH.

166 *Asesoría Jurídica*, Testimony of María de los Ángeles Las Heras Sanz dated 9 October 1939, Document 212, ANA, Carpeta B 12, RAH.

167 *Testimonio de Particulares del Fiscal Secretario de la pieza segunda sobre la causa no. 1,449/1939 instruida por el Juzgado Militar no. 12 de la Primera Region Militar, y los tramites del juicio sumarisimo de urgencia contra Julian Besteiro Fernández*, AHN, FC-CAUSA_GENERAL, 1524, Exp. 15. Imagen 10-11/64. See also, Cervera, Javier (1998), pp. 335–337. See also, Chapter 3 "The Power of Exhaustion," in Preston Paul (2016) *The Last Days of the Spanish Republic* (London: William Collins), [ebook] Loc. 664.

168 Alcocer, Santos (1976) *La "Quinta Columna"* (Madrid: G. del Toro), p. 44.

169 *Asesoría Jurídica*, Testimony of María de los Ángeles Las Heras Sanz dated 9 October 1939, Document 212, ANA, Carpeta B 12, RAH.

170 Sumario no 81/del Juzgado Especial por espionaje y otros delitos contra la seguridad exterior del Estado contra Antonio Rodríguez Aguado y otros AHN, FC-CAUSA_GENERAL, 1541, Exp 1, 1/1265. See also *Asesoría Jurídica*, Testimony of María del Carmen Diaz Aguado Arteaga dated 1939, Document 158 ANA, Carpeta B 12, RAH. See also *Asesoría Jurídica*, Testimony of María Carlota Núñez y Fagoaga, Document 157, ANA, Carpeta B 12, RAH.

171 Sumario no.4/1937 del Juzgado Especial del Tribunal Central de Espionaje no. 1 contra Javier Fernández Golfín y otros, AHN, FC-CAUSA_GENERAL, 1539, Exp. Imágenes 116/1134 Testimony of Matilde Casáñ Pablo dated 24 May 1937. See 216/1134.

172 *Archivo General Militar de Ávila,* C2505, Cp.4/43 and C.2498.20, Legajo no. 285, Carpeta 20, Armario 5, Imagen 2/20.

173 See "Informar, Interogar y Filtrar," in Gómez Bravo, Gutmaro (2017) *Geografía humana de la represión franquista, Del golpe a la guerra de ocupación (1936–1941)* (Madrid: Cátedra), at pp. 99–100.

174 Source: *Historia de la Sección Femenina por Pilar Primo de Rivera, Libro Primero, Primera Parte – "Las Visitas a la cárcel de Madrid"*, (undated typescript), ANA, Carpeta 1-B, RAH, p.13.

175 *Historia de la Sección Femenina, Libro Primero, Capitulo V – "Ultimos Tiempos"*, p. 79.

176 *Historia de la Sección Femenina, Libro Primero, Primera Parte – "Las Visitas a la cárcel de Madrid"*, p. 13.

177 Agustín Aznar Gerner was an SEU leader who was appointed as *Jefe Nacional* of the Falangist para-military squads.

178 *Historia de la Sección Femenina, "Ultimos Tiempos"*, p. 79.

179 *Historia de la Sección Femenina, Libro Primero, Primera Parte – "La Ante Guerra"*, p. 10.

180 *Historia de la Sección Femenina, Libro Primero, Primera Parte – "Las Visitas a la cárcel de Madrid"*, p. 13.

181 *Historia de la Sección Femenina, Libro Primero, Primera Parte – "Las Visitas a la cárcel de Madrid"*, (undated typescript), ANA, Carpeta 1-B, RAH, p. 13.

182 Expte. 5145, *contra Felisa Ruiz de Alda por desafección,* FC-CAUSA_GENERAL, 19, Exp.47 and Expte. 266, FC-CAUSA_GENERAL,235, Exp. 5.

183 Oral testimony of Felisa Ruiz de Alda in an undated interview with the author, in Borrás (1965), pp. 196–201 at p. 196.

184 Ellwood, Sheelagh "Entrevista con Dolores Muñoz Tuero "Los tribunales populares fueron buena gente," in *Guerra Civil de Historia 16, "Sociedad y Guerra" vol 14* (1986), pp. 125–129 at p. 126.

185 General Miguel Núñez de Prado was the Head of Republican Aviation (*Dirección General de Aeronauticas*). He was also affiliated to the *Union Militar Republicana Antifascista* (UMRA). On 18 July 1936 he flew to Zaragoza to negotiate a cease-fire with rebel General Cabanellas. He was immediately arrested and executed on 24 July 1936 in Pamplona under the orders of General Mola.

186 Sánchez López, Rosario (2007) *Entre la importancia y la irrelevancia, sección femenina: de la República a la Transición* (Murcia: Editora Regional), p. 42.

187 Oral testimony of Dolores Muñoz Tuero in Borrás (1965), pp. 201–208 at p. 202.

188 Oral testimony of Dolores Muñoz Tuero in Borrás (1965), pp. 201–208 at pp. 202–204.

189 "Oral historians have for some time been sensitive to the instabilities of language in their research. They have become attuned to the silences, conflations and omissions in oral testimony; and to the significance of body language in gauging the meaning of what they are told. They recognise that for cultural reasons women and men may encode their memories differently at different times; and the so called inter-subjective element of the interview (the relationship between those present at it) can shape what is said. In short, they do not read testimony straightforwardly as a transparent window onto an individual's lived experience" in Tumblety, Joan (ed) (2013) *Memory and History, Understanding Memory as Source and Subject* (London: Routledge), at p. 4.

190 See Águilar Fernández, Paloma (1996) *Memoria y olvido de la Guerra Civil Española* (Madrid: Alianza). See also Boyd, Carolyn P "The Politics of History and Memory in Democratic Spain," *Annals of the American Academy of Political and Social Science*, 617 (The Politics of History in Comparative Perspective) (2008), pp. 133–148.

191 Richards, Michael (ed) (2013) *After the Civil War, Making Memory and Re-Making Spain since 1936* (New York, NY: CUP), [ebook] pp. 41–42/413.

192 See also Aguilar Fernández, Paloma (1996) *Memoria y olvido de la Guerra Civil Española* (Madrid: Alianza) and Aguilar, Paloma and Ramírez-Barat, Clara "The Politics of Memory," in Shubert, Adrian, Álvarez Junco, José (ed) (2018) *The History of Modern Spain, Chronologies, Themes, Individuals* (London: Bloomsbury), pp. 343–355.

193 Expte. 572, *contra* Ángeles García López *por delito/s de Desafección,* AHN, FC-CAUSA_GENERAL, 234, Exp. 13, Imagen 14/37.

194 Expte. 572, Imagen 22/37.

195 *Asesoría Jurídica*, Testimony of Ángeles García López, Document 164, ANA, Carpeta B 12, RAH.

196 See *Causa instruida contra* Ricardo Guerra Blanco por el delito/s de Alta Traición, AHN, FC-CAUSA_GENERAL, 145, Exp. 44.

197 BOE, 8 March 1943, at p. 2156.

198 UPSA, JFAC, 1.4.3. Historia de la Asociación de las Jóvenes de Acción Católica de la diocesis de Madrid-Alcalá 1926–1948, "Actuación durante el dominio rojo," pp. 4–5 at p. 4. These official archives contain extremely little information on the 'difficult times' in the Republican-held zones during the conflict, only two pages on the operations of JFAC in Madrid-Alcalá.

199 Saint's days were more significant than birthdays, even within the Republican community, and Republicans also missed celebrating Christmas. See for example, the war-time diary entries of the fourteen-year-old Republican Duyagües, Pilar in Balló, Tania and Berger, Gonzalo (eds) (2003) *Querido Diario, Hoy ha empezado la guerra* (Barcelona: Espasa).

200 *Asesoría Jurídica*, Testimony of Amparo Sanz Fernández, dated 28 September 1939, Document [192 bis], ANA, Carpeta B 12, RAH. A resident of Hospicio, this woman facilitated the Catholic marriage of her 'maidservant' who also became her goddaughter.

201 Alfaya, José Luis (1998) *Como un río de fuego, Madrid 1936* (Barcelona: EIU), p. 147.
202 *Asesoría Jurídica*, Testimony of Cecilia Antón Medina dated 6 October 1939, Document 193, ANA, Carpeta B 12, RAH.
203 Borrás (1965), pp. 92–93.
204 *Asesoría Jurídica*, Testimony of Ángela Ibañez Calvo dated 9 October 1939, Document 225, ANA, Carpeta B 12, RAH.
205 *Asesoría Jurídica*, Testimony of Ángeles and Maria Pilar García Ochoa e Ibañez dated 9 October 1939, Documents 226 and 227, ANA, Carpeta B 12, RAH.
206 Undated oral testimony of Antonio Cañabetes in thesis of Cervera, Javier (1996) *Violencia política y acción clandestina: La retaguardia de Madrid en Guerra 1936–9* (Universidad Complutense de Madrid), pp. 368–398. http://eprints.ucm.es/2456/1/T21383.pdf [last accessed 16 May 2017], p. 397.
207 Borrás (1965), pp. 95–96.
208 Alfaya, José Luis (1998) *Como un río de fuego, Madrid, 1936* (Barcelona: EUI), pp. 158–180 at p. 158.
209 Alfaya, José Luis (1998) *Como un río*, pp. 160–161. See also Part II, "Madrid, una iglesia de catacumbas," pp. 119–188, and in particular Chapter X "Organización Cladestina," pp. 155–171.
210 Alfaya (1998), p. 158.
211 Oral testimony of Father Félix Verdasco recorded in Alfaya, José Luis (1998) *Como un rio de fuego, Madrid, 1936* (Barcelona: EUI), pp. 160–161. Alfaya cites Montero, Antonio (1961) *Historia de la persecución religiosa* (Madrid: BAC), at p. 105.
212 *Asesoría Jurídica*, Testimony of Ángela Ibáñez Calvo dated 9 October, Document 225, ANA, Carpeta B 12, RAH.
213 Borrás (1965), pp. 95–96.
214 *Asesoría Jurídica*, Testimony of Rosina Frutos Paris dated 20 September 1939, Document 246, ANA, Carpeta B 12, RAH.
215 UPSA, JFAC, 1.4.3. Historia de la Asociación de las Jóvenes de Acción Católica de la diocesis de Madrid-Alcalá 1926–1948, "Actuación durante el dominio rojo," pp. 4–5.
216 See Mother María Luisa Fernández and Mother María Leturia (1939) *Catorce meses de aventuras bajo el dominio rojo* (Rome: ACI), p. 49. Contraband hosts were regularly smuggled into this prison.
217 *Asesoría Jurídica*, Testimony of María Cristina Montes Muñoz dated 7 September 1939, Document 244, ANA, Carpeta B 12, RAH. See also Rodríguez Fernández, G. (2006) *El habito y la cruz* (Madrid: Edibesa), pp. 88–102.
218 See *Asesoría Jurídica*, Testimony of Andrea Pariente Suárez dated 9 October 1939, Document 169, ANA, Carpeta B 12, RAH.
219 *La Vanguardia*, 28 May 1970 at p. 6.
220 See also, Paz, Armando (1976) *Los Servicios de Espionaje en la Guerra Civil de España, 1936–9* (Madrid: Editorial San Martín), p. 141.
221 Uribarri, Manuel (1943) *La Quinta Columna Española. Verdad y Justicia* (La Habana: La Universal), pp. 118–124. See also comments in Rodríguez López, Sofía and Cazorla Sánchez, Antonio "Blue Angels: Female Fasist Resisters, Spies and Intelligence Officials in the Spanish Civil War, 1936–9," *Journal of Contemporary History*, 53 (4) (2016), pp. 692–713 at p. 705.
222 Cervera (1998) *Madrid*, p. 293.
223 *Asesoría Jurídica*, Testimony of Rosina Frutos Paris dated 20 September 1939, Document 246, ANA, Carpeta B 12, RAH.
224 Laguna Reyes, Alberto and Vargas Márquez, Antonio (2019) *La Quinta Columna, La guerra clandestina tras las líneas republicanas 1936–1939* (Madrid: Laesfera), pp. 59–61.
225 Rodríguez López, Sofia (2010) *El patio de la carcel, La Sección Femenina de FET–JONS en Almería* (Seville: CEA), pp. 27–46 at p. 45.

226 Ofer, Inbal (2010) *Señoritas in Blue, The making of a female political elite in Franco's Spain* (Padstow: Sussex Academic Press), pp. 55–103. C.f. Ángela Cenarro's critique of Auxilio Social's social welfare programmes in Cenarro, Ángela (2006) *La Sonrisa de La Falange, Auxilio Social en la guerra civil y en la posguerra* (Barcelona: Crítica).
227 Ofer, Inbal (2010) *Señoritas in Blue*, pp. 1–2.
228 Heiberg and Ros Agudo (2006) *La Trama*, p. 194. See also Alcalde, Ángel (2014) *Los excombatientes Franquistas (1936–1965)* (Zaragoza: PUZ), p. 354.

3 The role of women in the mixed-gender Clandestine Falange groups

The women who joined the mixed-gender groups were committed political dissidents who knowingly engaged in crimes of treason, rebellion and espionage. The most senior were 'old shirts'[1] or the wives and widows of military officers. Their homes were used as safe-houses and weapon stores and, because women were traditionally expected to provide food and entertainment, female spaces were transformed into clandestine political spaces where high-level meetings, secret masses and 'clandestine dinners' were conducted. Women comprised some 10–15% of the membership of these mixed-gender groups. They operated as senior recruitment and liaison agents, spies and escape-line co-ordinators. Some were infiltrated as voluntary nurses, auxiliaries and administrative assistants within civil and military institutions. Such women consciously ventured into the realms of treason and transgressed traditional and symbolic gender boundaries "wherein men perform all the public, official or dangerous and spectacular acts."[2] These women made use of a clandestine political space in order to acquire a measure of power and political visibility.

María Ángeles Orozco del Riego (aged fifty years) was a leader of a mixed -gender group.[3] She hosted lavish dinners and held subversive meetings at her home in calle Juan de Austria, 10 where senior Falangist leaders were regularly in attendance.[4] She was a devout Catholic and related by marriage to the famous Colonel Rafael del Riego y Florés (1784–1823) whose death inspired the anthem *El Himno de Riego*. She regularly exploited this valuable social capital and was accused of being a "high-living and ostentatious woman who dreadfully abused her association with the del Riego name for her own economic ends."[5] Her Republican husband, General Alfonso del Riego, was believed to have been killed in action and three of her sons were missing in action; the fourth was a novice priest who died in Madrid of an unspecified illness, possibly tuberculosis. The group was dismantled in late August 1937 and twenty-two individuals were arrested including seven women and a group of Falangist draft-dodgers and middle-aged professional men. The liaison agent Rosina Cornide was arrested while *en route* to Valencia. She was found in possession of sensitive military intelligence relating to Republican troop positions and made a full confession to the Valencian DGS, naming all the members of the group. Ángeles and her two daughters were apprehended before their planned escape to Seville. They were able to obtain the requisite passports from the anarchist leader Melchor Rodríguez García (the Red Angel) whose family Ángeles had safe-housed in 1936.[6] María Luisa was an 'old shirt' who was engaged to a prisoner named José Rodríguez de la Puente ("Tarduchi") who was "a well-known and extremely dangerous element, the son of a founding member of the Falange." Both daughters were dismissed from the Ministry of Agriculture in 1936 for disaffection. All three women were caught *in flagrante* preparing food parcels for Falangist and Acción Popular prisoners. After a search of the premises the DGS discovered documents and letters revealing:

> the existence of a significant Socorro Blanco organisation which was in active collaboration with a nucleus of Falangist leaders. Regular meetings were held at the home of the widow Ángeles Orozco in order to plot against the Republic, and Ángeles was the instigator and leader of these reunions.[7]

Anti-Republican women were obliged to devise novel rules of engagement and 'play new games' in their efforts to both resist and survive within a new and revolutionary social space that was perceived as "a deeply hostile environment, more dangerous and difficult than the trenches."[8] They developed networks of influence within the Republican regime and exploited their reserves of social capital. Ángeles managed to obtain a widow's pension and family passports with the aid of Melchor Rodríguez.[9] She also stock-piled contraband obtained from contacts in military and governmental depots. Friends and contacts in high (and low) places were key to the safe navigation of the disciplinary fields of the police and the judiciary. The charges against Ángeles and her daughters were reduced from rebellion to disaffection, and her case rumbled along incurring delays in the court system until the end of the war. Despite the initiative, organisational skills and resilience of women like Orozco, women's perceived lack of power and influence in the public space meant that less political and symbolic value was attributed to their subversive practices.

The persistence of traditional patriarchal gender norms meant that the police and the popular tribunals often "failed to entertain the possibility that women posed a serious threat to Republican security."[10] Concepción del Rosal was initially charged with treason and rebellion alongside her husband and her brother, Antonio.[11] Her case was remitted to the lower courts for disaffection. Although she shared the same roof with one of the most notorious leaders of the Clandestine Falange, Concepción successfully convinced the tribunal that she was a loyal Republican who had "never undertaken any political activities and had exclusively dedicated herself to domestic duties, and in particular, to looking after her son who was only eight months old at the time of her arrest."[12] Following a positive good-character vouchsafe from the concierge of her building in calle General Arranda, 42,[13] and after almost a year of imprisonment, she was absolved and released. Women were certainly punished for their political crimes, but much less severely than men. Concepción's husband, her brother Antonio and twelve other (male) members of the group were executed for treason in around September 1938. Only a small number of women were found guilty of capital crimes, and their sentences were almost invariably commuted to life-sentences, and the case of Carmen Tronchoni who was executed in Montjuich prison constitutes a notable exception. Most of the Falange's 'Fallen Women' (women killed in active service) were the victims of extra-judicial reprisals, not legal repression.

Aside from Auxilio Azul, the Clandestine Falange groups were remembered after their male leaders, and while the authorities often overlooked women, contemporaneous press reports frequently highlighted the important threat posed by female fifth-columnists.[14] The 'Círiza organisation' was led by a young Falangist conscription evader who spent his days confined to a secret room in his sister Candida's home which was situated behind her kitchen cupboard. Félix Círiza was reliant upon his sister for food and shelter, and it was the women in the group who were tasked with activities in the public space such as raising funds and disseminating propaganda. María García Herraíz de Amilibia, Félix's girlfriend, was general secretary of the 'organisation.' She contacted the members and distributed the propaganda pamphlets, relayed orders and instructions and warned members of their imminent arrest in April 1937. Ernestina Pagés Lorner was the second most senior liaison agent. Carmen Gabuccio Sánchez-Mármol (alias *Camisita*) was one of seven senior go-betweens.[15] María and three other women were acquitted and released while the male leaders received capital sentences and were executed some months after.[16] In fact, opportunities for male resistance were extremely limited at this time. "The truth was that very little could be done from within the confines of the prison."[17] Most of the senior cadres spent the war in prison, in hiding or in asylum at the embassies and Anti-Republican women experienced a temporary gender-power shift at this time. Anti-Republican women experienced a temporary gender-power shift at this time.

The chapter primarily examines the individual experiences of a few prominent female leaders as reflected in witness statements and trial transcripts in order to explore women's roles within the mixed-gender groups. However, first it is necessary to provide a brief overview of the structure and aims of the mixed-gender groups.

Overview of the mixed-gender Clandestine Falange

According to historians the Falange groups were created "in the wake of the earlier women's welfare-aid organisations which greatly facilitated their formation."[18] The symbolic division of labour is reflected in narratives that distinguish women's 'passive' welfare-aid and auxiliary resistance practices from 'active' masculine forms of organised resistance. Aside from the existence of the Auxilio Azul organisation, it is generally believed that those Falangist and Traditionalist underground cells which were in operation before the war only began to regroup at some stage in late December 1936 or early 1937, i.e. after the failure of the rebel siege when a protracted conflict seemed likely. However, more recently there is evidence to suggest that a small number of mixed-gender cells were able to contact Nationalist intelligence services after 18 July.[19] According to the Traditionalist leader Fal Conde, "Falangist and Traditionalists united forces in order to do something while awaiting the right moment to take violent action."[20] 'Doing something' involved the provision of safe-houses and escape-lines, intelligence gathering and acts of defeatism and minor sabotage. In the event 'violent action' was never taken by the fifth column because Franco conceived of the occupation of the capital in exclusively military terms and sought to limit the influence and actions of the Falangist and Traditionalist factions in the capital.

Aims and objectives

The mixed-gender groups gathered social, political and military intelligence which was forwarded to Burgos via liaison agents or hidden radio transmitters. This intelligence included reports on government activities, civilian morale and the size and location of Republican combat units, armament depots, anti-aircraft artillery or the status of supply lines and, most significantly for the post-war period, social intelligence relating to the identities and activities of prominent Republicans and Republican sympathisers. The activities of the fifth column demonstrate how ordinary individuals helped to consolidate the Francoist regime from below through acts of selective violence in the form of denunciatory practices.[21] The main function of the "Antonio Bouthelier y Antonio Ortega Group" was to provide political and military intelligence to Lt. Colonel Bonel Huici's Nationalist SIPM Services.[22] According to the General Staff in Burgos, the most important intelligence related to the levels of morale and attitudes of the senior Republican officers '*who might be counted on*' during an occupation of the capital.[23] The groups compiled detailed lists of Republican sympathisers. This activity generated alarm among certain sectors of the Republican community who believed that Falangists were embedded within the CNT and could "bump you off (*apiolar*) at any moment."[24] The evidence contained in the popular tribunal records indicates that fifth-columnists did indeed gather intelligence against prominent and ordinary Republicans which was forwarded to Burgos on a regular basis. Madrid's fifth column also collaborated in those "local and intimate denunciatory practices that provided a vital glue for the nascent Francoist regime and evidenced the construction of Francoism from below."[25] By November 1938, the Nationalist SIM had already compiled a detailed card-file index of over two million names gathered from across the nation and "catalogued with the proofs of their crimes."[26] This information was used for the purposes of repression both during and after the war.[27]

Defeatism was the most effective resistance activity practised by the fifth column.[28] However it is impossible to assess the impact of this subversive practice because by as early as mid-June 1937 low morale was widespread within the general civilian population (see Chapter 4). In any event, defeatist practices boosted morale and fostered a sense of community, solidarity and shared identity among the resisters. Benedicta Lobo rallied her group with comments like: "When the Fascists enter Madrid they [the Republicans] will cry tears of blood and our left-wing neighbours will have to perform the straight armed [Falangist] salute."[29] Towards the end of the war in February 1939 defeatist pamphlets were so widespread that an illiterate tram-worker was arrested because his salary had been wrapped in a clandestine pamphlet that called for the "Mothers of Madrid to rise up in protest against the government's murderous continuation of the war and the starvation rationing which is killing our children."[30]

Another key aim was to sabotage, impede or disrupt the Republican war effort in as many ways as possible. The Nationalists sent a series of undercover agents into the capital to provide training in the sabotage of military equipment, although the large-scale sabotage of military material was rare.[31] However, small scale civilian sabotage was rife and included the circulation of false identification documentation, passports and ration cards, defeatist graffiti and vandalism; "the aim was to produce a breakdown in the rearguard. We never ceased in our efforts."[32] Forms of economic sabotage included the deliberate disruption of food and fuel supply chains, black-market activities and the introduction of large amounts of Republican currency into the capital from the newly occupied rebel zones. Candida Círiza was found in possession of defeatist pamphlets which encouraged acts of sabotage and defeatism:

> Comrades: It is necessary to create the maximum amount of conflict for the reds, to sow discontent *(desaliento)* among all those who surround you and provoke discord amongst the various organisations of the Popular Front … also abstain from buying the Republican press, going to the theatre or entertainments, paying subscriptions or paying for light, water, telephone services and rent when these are controlled by reds. In a word, you must wage a passive war against the reds; Help our friends in battle and do what you can to reduce the length of our captivity. Signed: *Falange Española de las JONS Junta local.*[33]

Finally, as illustrated in the case studies below, the key aim was to ensure public order and the continued function of public administrative services through the co-ordinated take-over of the nerve-centres of power in the event of a Nationalist occupation, and weapons were cached to this end.

The structure of the Clandestine Falange

Madrid's Supreme Junta was originally composed of Raimundo Fernández Cuesta who was also the General Secretary of the Falange, Manuel Valdés Larrañaga and Leopoldo Panizo. Fernández Cuesta was imprisoned in March

1936, and his ability to co-ordinate an effective resistance was compromised by his notoriety. After the 18 July coup those Falangist and Traditionalist cells that remained on the ground soon joined forces.[34] In October 1937 Fernández Cuesta was prisoner-exchanged for the Republican Justino de Azcárate.[35] Thereafter, his second-in-command, Manuel Valdés Larrañaga, was appointed leader. Valdés was also arrested in March 1936 and was evacuated from the Model Prison to Porlier in November 1936. In early January 1937 he was transferred to the Duque de Sesto Prison and from there to the Prison Hospital from where he was approached by agents attached to Lt. Colonel Francisco Bonel Huici's Nationalist SIM services in spring 1937.[36] Valdés recruited Leopoldo Panizo, Félix Campos Guereta (until his escape into the Nationalist zone) and the Chilean doctor Juan Francisco Jiménez Martín as senior liaison for around half a dozen early groups including "Arques," "Veglisson," "Arenillas-Matilde-Álvares-Vega-García Lomas," "Fernández Golfín" and "Corujo-Gómez Acebo-Urgoiti." Auxilio Azul came under the Clandestine Falange's umbrella via the introduction of Elena Garrigues of the "Castilla Network." In late 1937 Valdés began to articulate Falangist and Traditionalist groups into a cohesive network with Luis Serrano Pérez as his principal liaison agent, Marcos Pérez as chief liaison within the legal administration and Clara Mass who supplied vital false documentation.[37]

Francisco Bonel's Nationalist SIM intelligence out-post was based in La Torre de Estebán Hambrán (Toledo), a small village situated close to Madrid's front-lines. Bonel employed around one hundred agents. In June 1937 another SIM group was stationed in the Sección Destacada C-2 on the Sepúlveda-Guadalajara front-lines under the command of colonel Justo Jiménez Ortoneda.[38] Ortoneda was involved in Acción Católica before the war and was able to liaise with José María Taboada Lago (ex-secretary of the *Junta Central de Acción Católica*) so that that in May/June 1938 a Servicio de Información Exterior (SIE) intelligence organisation was established in the city. In September 1938 José Ungria Jiménez (head of the SIPM) appointed Taboada as Supreme Head of all the clandestine intelligence groups in Madrid. Thereafter, the SIPM took control of the fifth column in the capital.[39]

Efforts were made to structure the groups into a series of Banderas, Tercios, Centurias, Falanges and Escuadras (Squads) in accordance with the structure of the pre-war Falangist Death Squads. A bandera notionally incorporated around 900 individuals, a Tercio 300, a Centuria 99 plus one Jefe, a Falange 33 and an Escuadra nine individuals plus one Jefe and a sub-Jefe. At the lower levels the organisation adopted the same triangular structure as that of the early Auxilio Azul organisation (described in Chapter 2 above). The leaders of every 'triangle' received their orders from their local squad leader (*jefe de escuadra*) who, in turn, received orders from a district leader (*jefe de centuria*). As with Auxilio Azul, the triangles formed part of a "clock-work system and each new member was obliged to recruit two additional members."[40] According to French intelligence reports, by late 1938 Madrid's Clandestine

Falange comprised "five banderas of around 800 men [sic]"[41] who were ready for action within the spheres of welfare-aid, provisioning and transportation, public security and the army and assault guards.[42]

Recruitment was based on military, professional, associational, kinship and friendship groups and on the functional and practical requirements of the relevant groups. The functionalist aspect of resistance recruitment may account for the over-representation of seamstresses who made clothes for the wives of senior military and Republican personnel, secretaries like Matilde Casáñ Pablo (discussed below), who volunteered as an administrative assistant at General Staff offices, and nurses who had access to wounded soldiers recently returned from the fronts.[43] Members referred to and identified each other as '*un amigo/a de confianza*' (a trustworthy friend) and, in the right circles, trusted friends were easy to contact.[44]

The individual groups

There were around eighteen or nineteen Clandestine Falange groups in Madrid, fourteen of which were dismantled by the Republican security services with the aid of informants like the former Falangist Alberto Castilla Olavarría.[45] Castilla was employed by Fernández Valentí's Special Brigade after his arrest in 1937, and implicated in the demise of the Antonio Rodríguez Aguado and Golfín-Corujo Groups.[46] Aside from Auxilio Azul, the largest group was El Grupo de los 195 which was dismantled in 1938. Others included España Una (Antonio del Rosal's organisation which infiltrated the CNT), El Grupo de la Iglesia de San Francisco el Grande, El Grupo de Carlos Viada, El Asunto Círiza, Las Hojas del Calendario, La 16 Bandera, La Bandera Diego Alonso, La Organización Rodríguez Aguado, El Asunto de la Telefónica, El Complot de los 163, El Grupo de Jesús Hernández Cid y 63 mas, El Grupo de Antonio Bouthelier Espasa, La Organización Antonio (Luna) and Grupo Galicia. Auxilio Azul and Socorro Blanco provided auxiliary support to these Clandestine groups.[47] Their structure and operation and the role played by men within them have been explored in detail in earlier histories.[48]

In early spring 1937 Manuel Valdés was ordered by Franco's General Staff in Burgos to co-ordinate all the groups, including Auxilio Azul which continued to operate relatively separately from the mixed groups. After the political unification of the rebel factions in late April 1937, the overall strategic leadership was transferred to Bonel, although Valdés remained in charge of the day-to-day organisation. While the groups were never fully coordinated, they adhered to the same general aims and objectives and followed standard codes of conduct and practice issued by Burgos, particularly in relation to the dissemination of defeatist news and security issues.[49]

After spring 1937 the Clandestine Falange infiltrated every corner of the Republican rear-guard.[50] It was embedded within the Telefónica,[51] the DGS,[52] the International Red Cross,[53] the law courts,[54] the War Office's purchases and acquisitions department[55] and public and administrative buildings including the Town Hall, hospitals, military barracks, government warehouses, supply depots and distribution centres including the central bread distribution centre. It even came to infiltrate the revolutionary militias and syndicates, in particular the CNT.[56] Sympathetic doctors and medical experts were important fifth-column collaborators.[57] The aim was to delay or suspend the trials on fabricated medical grounds in order to wait out the war in prison hospitals or avoid charges of conscription evasion. Defendants were coached in how to fake symptoms.[58] María Jesus Roman Escribano was charged with espionage for her involvement in the Iglesia de Francisco el Grande group which involved the Falangist Francisco Ordeig in collaboration with a small group of devout Catholics who looked after the artwork and the church buildings.[59] She was transferred from Ventas prison to an observation ward at the Madrid Provincial Hospital, and her defence argued that she was unfit to appear in court. A medical certificate (signed by two court psychiatrists) indicated that she was unfit for trial on account of "severe dystemic attacks within the affective sphere combined with acute amnesia," the aetiology of which was unspecified.[60] The hospitals were less secure and allowed more freedom and opportunities for prisoners to escape with the collusion of hospital staff.

By the end of the war the fifth column managed to thoroughly infiltrate the police and the security services. Around 15% of Madrid's public order forces (Assault Guards, Civil Guards and Carabineers) were in regular contact with the fifth column or had acted in favour of the enemies of the Republic at some stage during the conflict.[61] Around 10% of Madrid's *emboscados* were active fifth-columnists, many of whom were recognised as official SIPM agents in the post-war.[62] After the violent Casado coup of 5–13 March 1939, the widespread infiltration of the Clandestine Falange within the Republican civil, security and military institutions assisted in a peaceful hand-over of the levers of power in the capital to Franco's troops on 28 March 1939.[63] The Clandestine Falange played a crucial role in the occupation of key Republican administrative and military buildings. The SIPM ordered José María Taboada to inform the clandestine groups that "all who did not obey the orders of the Madrid FET-JONS would be treated as enemies … and would suffer the relevant consequences and penalties for disobedience."[64]

The key role played by fifth-column women at the end of the war was to supply the flags and bunting that festooned the newly occupied Republican buildings and lined the streets in welcome to Franco's troops. The bracelets and arm-bands that the women had taken such risks to fashion immediately served to identify "friends from foes."[65] Although the hostilities officially ended on 1 April 1939 the clandestine war against Republican enemies continued in the post-war period. From April onwards SIPM detachments in Madrid tasked fifth-column groups (and ordinary individuals including building concierges) with intelligence gathering for the purposes of house searches, detentions and interrogations. The Clandestine Falange also assisted in the requisition of archives, records and classified military documentation.[66] Such information would form part of the Causa General enquiry and Franco's post-war justice.[67] Former male and female members of the Clandestine

Falange were recognised as military ex-combatants and awarded the status, decorations, financial rewards and compensations associated with this distinction. The widows and families of deceased ex-combatants were also eligible for pensions and compensation. Men like Manuel Valdés Larrañaga and Luis Serrano Novo achieved positions of power in the new regime and, as indicated in the previous chapter, women like Carina and Elvira Martínez Ostendi were awarded military decorations and financial compensation for their contributions to the Nationalist war effort.

The roles played by women within the groups

As with Auxilio Azul, the women came from predominantly Catholic middle-class and upper-middle-class right-wing, monarchist, military and Falangist backgrounds. The leaders were mostly 'old' shirts or the relatives of disaffected military officers. The majority were related to senior anti-Republican military officers, civil and military doctors, architects, lawyers, attorneys, civil servants and members of private organisations including artists and a wide range of middle-class persons of comfortable means, the majority of whom were infiltrated within official organisations who performed sensitive and trusted roles which enabled them to transmit data and confidential information to the Nationalist side via a variety of different mediums.[68] Most women were engaged in unpaid domestic work in the household (*sus labores*), but, as indicated above, there is an over-representation of seamstresses, nurses and secretarial and administrative assistants who worked in the barracks and the civil administration. The women employed in these sectors had access to Republican personnel and were more easily able to glean sensitive intelligence.[69] Candida Círiza had Republican clients and was "a well-known seamstress who was connected with aristocrats."[70] She and fifty-six others (including thirteen women) were indicted on 27 April 1937 on charges of conspiracy and aiding rebellion.[71] These well-connected women were able to infiltrate Republican spaces such as military barracks, hospitals, civil and administrative offices in their capacity as voluntary and unpaid nurses, auxiliaries, secretaries and administrative assistants.

They performed the same roles as men in their capacity as recruitment and liaison agents, spies and escape-line co-ordinators while also undertaking welfare-aid roles. A small minority were senior leaders like Francisca Martínez Ramírez, who was third-in-command of the 195 Group, or the military widow Esperanza Ortega Cebrían who became the leader of an armed '*esquadra*' after the escape of the former leader, Félix Campos Guereta, into the Nationalist zone.[72] In the absence of men, women filled the gaps.

Recruitment and liaison agents

The main role played by women within the groups was as recruitment and liaison agents. Women were more easily able to initiate contact with potential new recruits in public spaces such as the bars and cafés of central Madrid. They were perceived as being less politicised and therefore less threatening than men. Their potentially unwelcome approaches might be more easily dismissed as "laughable and hare-brained ideas and notions."[73] Women also acted as go-betweens at the embassies where the leaders of the Supreme Junta were in asylum. They also liaised between the prisons, hospitals, barracks and embassies, and their homes were venue to clandestine meetings. Such women held the threads of Clandestine Falange communication networks in place.

As indicated in Chapter 1, after March 1936 women played key liaison roles between the main Falange leaders (Jefes) and the administrative heads (Mandos) who remained on the ground. Sympathetic prison guards and prison officials were complicit in the dissemination of Falangist news, war reports and other contraband into and out of the prisons despite the government's attempts to repress this activity by posting militias within the prisons after the Model Prison assault of 22–23 August 1936.[74] Women also recruited within the military barracks in their capacity as auxiliaries, nurses and administrative assistants. The sisters María Juana (typist) and Francisca (nurse) Escalonilla Peña worked as auxiliaries with the Etapas First Battalion situated in calle Juan Bravo. They were accused of high treason together with several soldiers who were attached to the Etapas Battalion and the Transmissions Group, Second Division. Francisca would show potential recruits a thermometer that when viewed at a certain angle revealed the Monarchist flag. She would then ask "What do you see here? And then respond: yes, that's correct, the only true Spanish flag, because the current one is false."[75] The women were denounced by a SIM informant and eventually acquitted of treason but charged with disaffection in January 1939 and exiled as Argentinian nationals.[76]

Francisca Martínez Ramírez and "the 195 Group"

This pre-war Falangist activist became the third-in-command of Madrid's largest mixed-gender network which was coordinated in early 1938. The SIM described the organisation as a "complex fascist-type organisation."[77] The name "Los 195" referred to the number defendants. Miguel Cortez Rubio, Jeronimo López Batanero, Francisca Martínez Ramírez and José Banús Masdeu and an additional 191 persons were arrested in April 1938 and charged with high treason, espionage and defeatism for their involvement in:

> an extensive clandestine network that was … dedicated to uncovering intelligence in relation to military positions, the movement of troops and supplies, the location of munitions factories and to obtaining plans in relation to military positions in order to offer them to the enemy. It also operated Socorro Blanco services, spread false rumours and there was conclusive evidence that it had actively cooperated with the rebels and it was prepared to use violence in the event of a victorious attack against the capital.[78]

By April 1938 the group had infiltrated various military, governmental, civil service, legal and commercial institutions including the Tenth Urban Transport Battalion, police stations, the DGS and the Telefónica. The organisation was composed of Falangists, Traditionalists and monarchists whose general aims were to pass military intelligence into the Nationalist zone, sabotage Republican supply lines and services and prepare for the take-over of government nerve-centres and public services in the event of a Nationalist occupation. The key objective was "to organise a bloodless military coup in favour of the Nationalists in the event of an imminent Nationalist occupation of the capital."[79]Prior to her arrest Martínez and her accomplice Miguel Cortés Rubio had been informing potential new recruits that the group was in the process of putting together an organisation whose aims were to effect a bloodless *coup d'etat* and that it could rely on some 40 or 50 thousand men including members of the police force, the Retiro Park security forces and military elements, in particular members of the rank and file. In addition, a secret radio transmitter was installed in the basement of the *ABC* newspaper building which ensured direct contact with Salamanca.[80]

The network was dismantled on 5 April 1938 following a lengthy and detailed SIM surveillance operation that culminated in a raid on the offices of Pablo Moreno Ciges at the Glorieta de San Bernardo. Moreno was caught in the process of recording sensitive military intelligence which was supplied by two officers from Miaja's General Staff. Martínez was also in attendance, and she was later discovered in possession of classified military maps and other incriminating documents (supplied by Manuel Villafranca) including "information relating to the sabotage of 63 projectile bombs."[81] On 18 June 1938 the sentencing judge of the *Tribunal Especial de Guardia No. 1* found that:

> within the various groups which exist in Madrid and which are collectively known as the 'fifth column' the 195 Group was established with the specific aim to co-ordinate elements of self-appointed 'people of order' so that, in the event of the legitimate government abandoning the Republican capital, the Group would replace these authorities in the service of the fascists and would maintain public order and ensure the continuation of all public services … in anticipation of a swift and successful Nationalist advance from both the Levant and the East, the group's mission, following examples provided in various other Nationalist occupied cities, was also to undermine morale by spreading defeatist information (*derrotismo*). They also intended to organise an uprising in the capital that would coincide with an external attack.[82]

Pursuant to the above aims, the group had infiltrated army barracks and security buildings, local police stations, the Town Hall, the artillery and automobile parks, the Telefónica and numerous other nerve-centres in order to "take-over the levers of power at any given moment." Martínez gathered

Republican military information and passed it to the enemy and disseminated defeatist information in order to enlist new recruits within the civil service. Finally, the group provided auxiliary relief services, sometimes using code names, in the form of money and provisions to those who, on account of their hostility towards the Republic had been dismissed from their jobs. The sentencing judge caused a public controversy because he found that "the fifth column's hostility towards the Republic was, in part, generated by the professional purges of the early months of the conflict." Repression and financial insecurity had resulted in the creation of secret mutual aid networks within the anti-Republican community.

Martínez was one of the four main leaders alongside Miguel Cortés Rubio, Jeronimo López Batanero and José Banús Masdeu. Her name appears in most of the witness testimonies. She was the key recruitment and liaison figure and was central to the high-level negotiations that took place during early 1938 in relation to the integration of all the groups into a single co-ordinated network. She was the main contact for several larger groups (between twenty-five and fifty persons) and was also in charge of the recruitment of new members and the distribution of money and welfare-aid. She also regularly liaised with two other groups led by Antonia Lario and Dolores López Mendizábal (discussed below) and was in contact with Enrique Saiz de la Torre's cell which was led by Manuel Villafranca and included Florentino López, Filomena Serrano and various others. Via this group Martínez was connected with Commander Carlos Alfonso Sanz who, in turn, introduced her to Muñoz Valcarcel's group. Finally, Martínez was in direct contact with the group lead by José Banús Masdeu and Carmen De Blas Aranteguí which was also linked to several other cells. Martínez played a key role in the co-ordination of these groups in early 1938, and she also commanded a chain of spies that gathered political and military intelligence, including the movement of troops and the placement of anti-aircraft artillery. Martínez collated the intelligence and forwarded it Cortés Rubio who conveyed it to the SIM in Salamanca via a short-wave radio transmitter that was hidden in the basement of the *ABC* newspaper offices.[83] Martínez was also involved in escape-line co-ordination.[84]

At the time of her arrest "Comrade Fanny" was thirty-five years old, single and a seamstress. She was known as "Fanny" although her secret code-name was 9-85. During her first interrogation on 5 April 1938 she revealed that she had been a member of Renovación Española and had taught pattern cutting for the Sección Femenina and made clothes for the poor. She joined the Falange in March 1936 either in response to the 16 February 1936 general election results or in protest at the arrest of José Antonio. The interrogation records and her trial testimony differ in their accounts of her motivations for joining. She was immediately appointed as the secretary to the Palacios District Sección Femenina. Her political activism prior to 18 July 1936 resulted in her arrest on four earlier occasions by the Buenavista, Palacio and Universidad police stations. During her trial testimony on 24 July 1936 she claimed that she had managed to avoid arrest several times and obtained her own release from prison on three separate occasions without anyone's help. These repeated arrests "mobilised her to work against the Popular Front Regime and the working classes." She also gave evidence that in March 1938 around twenty-four soldiers, two Civil Guards and two SIM agents arrived at her home and that she "feigned a heart attack during her arrest and, despite being subjected to threats and verbal abuse, she managed to avoid arrest at this time."[85] She self-identified as a brave, resourceful and ardent Falangist.

After the outlawing of the Falange Martínez formed her own underground resistance group which was composed of committed Falangists (*Falangistas de Corazón*) and began to recruit 'in earnest' after she was appointed as Secretary of the Palacios District. She was also appointed to a liaison role between Rafael Aznar and José Antonio Primo de Rivera while the latter languished in Alicante prison. She also liaised between José Antonio, Pilar Primo de Rivera and Aznar.[86] Martínez established these connections at some time in late July 1936. She became acquainted with Manuel Valdés Larrañaga whilst in prison.[87] After her release in early 1937 Martínez contacted Rafael Aznar who appointed her as the liaison agent for a Nationalist agent named Dr Barrado who was based in Burgos. In May 1937 Martínez was promoted as the leader of the now evacuated Palacios District by Marina Navarro, the outgoing leader. Navarro resigned because she was getting married and Martínez testified that Navarro had subsequently disappeared. It is unclear whether Navarro was extra-judicially killed or had escaped Madrid or severed links with the Falange after her marriage.

Martínez first approached Miguel Cortés Rubio in the weeks leading up to the coup because he was a committed Falangist. Cortés was also a Falangist and an ex-Civil Guard who was sacked during the professional purges of 1936. The pair quickly became close associates and their written communications reflected the distinctive Falangist emotional regime. They addressed each other as "Comrade" and communications were signed off with the words "*¡Arriba España!*" Cortés agreed to "unite forces in order to recruit individuals who would be willing to take up arms against the Republic."[88] The members were composed of security personnel from the 10th Urban Battalion, the Security Corps, the Pontejo Barracks, the Home Office, the Automobile Depot, the Orphans School and Madrid University's Literature and Philosophy Faculty. By March 1938 Martínez had also recruited within the Admiralty, the Airforce, the Telefónica in Gran Vía, the General Staff and officers at the Palacio del Pardo which was strategically situated near the Manzanares River. She confessed to having recruited over forty individuals including two captains who were embedded within Miaja's General Staff of the Central Zone (Paz Zamarra and Martínez Pérez) and several ex-Falangists who were posted with the Artillery, Aviation and Carabineer Divisions. She also confessed to having taken part in intelligence gathering against "enemy reds, Jews and Freemasons in order to take the requisite precautions in defence of the Nationalist cause."[89] The information was used for the purposes of the Francoist repression both during the war and "pursuant to the state sanctioned economic repression and social marginalization of non-Nationalists after the war."[90] She also compiled lists of sympathetic Republicans who might be given due recognition after the Nationalist victory.

Martínez was also involved in fund-raising for the organisation and she provided welfare-aid and financial assistance to members.[91] These included Rogelio Sánchez who was imprisoned in Quiñones Prison and Dolores López Mendizábal who was sacked from the Telefónica because she was a Falangist. Martínez had access to a secret bank account and was authorised to take out significant sums of money for distribution among members. She distributed between 2,000 and 4,000 pesetas to various groups and individuals for living expenses and the purchase of weapons. For example, Jeronimo López Batanero lost his job as accountant to the Count of Romanones at the start of the war and he regularly received between 300 and 500 pesetas from Martínez via Pablo Moreno.[92] In this way the agents of resistance were also its beneficiaries. Martínez recruited

> many women into a new Sección Femenina that employed needy factory workers who were paid a daily rate and whose products were sold in various shops. The excess profits were distributed in order to aid needy persons in particular the deceased, prisoners, fugitives and their families.[93]

Martínez recruited María Felisa Parés as a liaison agent and Parés was also a senior member of Auxilio Azul who worked at the Republican SIM offices. Felisa Parés denied all involvement in the group's activities and only confessed to having allowed Martínez the use her home telephone on several occasions. Parés was acquitted on charges of treason and espionage and her case was referred to the lower courts for disaffection but never came to trial, possibly as a result of helpful back-channels at the SIM.

Martínez was an ardent and committed activist. According to several (male) defendants she was "very important, young and attractive ... sympathetic and agreeable, making herself attractive in the way that a female attracts a male."[94] Commander Carlos Alfonzo Sanz claimed that she was talented at 'instigating dangerous and subversive conversations' which might not have been received in the same way if initiated by a man. She was affectionately known as *La rubia* (the 'Blonde') among her male peers. Her sexual capital and extroverted character meant that she was often the first to approach potential recruits in bars and cafés. Alfonzo Sanz testified that during their first meeting he had thought that that her proposals were insane and that she could not be taken seriously. He claimed in mitigation that he had been unduly influenced by this dynamic woman "who had persuaded him to embark upon treason," although he and several other defendants took pains to emphasise her ideological commitment, sexual propriety and untainted moral character. She was frequently described as an 'authentic Falangist' and a 'true idealist.' The sanity, moral probity and the sexual proclivities of the male defendants were seldom publicly interrogated in this way. The routine interrogation of women's private morality and mental health during trial constitute forms of public humiliation and symbolic punishment for transgressive and politically subversive behaviour in the public sphere.[95]

Martínez was also highly valued and esteemed by her female peers among whom she inspired a profound and unwavering loyalty and admiration. Dolores López Mendizábal testified that she owed her loyalty to Francisca Martínez, not just because she was her superior, but also because she had provided her with regular financial assistance after her dismissal from the Telefónica on grounds of disaffection. Others described her as an authentic "old shirt" and committed Falangist. During the last of several interrogations on 5 April 1938 Martínez was reported to have defiantly performed the raised armed Falangist salute and declared:

> I have done as much damage as possible to the legally constituted Regime and I deserve the death sentence … I request a great favour from said Regime, I beg that my punishment be administered as swiftly as possible in consideration of all my humanitarian and charitable works. *¡Arriba España!*[96]

The words and the gesture alone constituted the crime of disaffection and few defendants confessed in such an incriminating and outspoken way. Immediately after performing the illegal salute, Francisca requested a swift execution because she believed that she would be subjected to torture while in custody. This emotive political performance reflects the emotional intensity of the hard-core 'old shirts.' During trial her advocate claimed that her actions were uniquely inspired by "humanitarian and charitable motives" and that her original confession was made 'under duress and while in a confused state.' Martínez was:

> guided by a spirit of fraternity that had been heightened by her deep religious convictions, she had assisted and saved persons from a variety of ideological backgrounds, as she thought fit, without ever having collaborated with or associated with other persons … motivated by this same spirit she provided assistance, as requested by Pablo Moreno, in order to minimize the negative consequences of the conflict in the event of an entry of enemy troops.[97]

This plea in mitigation resonates with the abnegated and selfless discourses of the Sección Femenina and Auxilio Azul. While Martínez primarily self-identified as an authentic Falangist, she was also constructed as a Catholic whose piety and sincere faith were invoked as mitigating factors. Martínez was awarded the death penalty which was subsequently commuted to life-imprisonment. A total of sixty-four defendants were condemned to death, and the fifty-eight men were killed by firing squad. The Republican repression against Clandestine Madrid continued throughout the course of 1938.[98]

Antonia Lario Alonso

Antonia Lario Alonso also formed part of the 5 April 1938 police round-up. After twenty-four hours in custody and she confessed that "when she first became involved in the organisation she knew that she was playing with her life but that, nonetheless, she would happily lose it knowing that she had proudly served her son."[99] Lario was a Puerto Rican national and a military widow who was aged forty-nine years at the time of her arrest. She came from a military family and her son, Joaquín García Lario, was a Falangist who had gone into hiding after 18 July 1936. Antonia used her connections to obtain his asylum at the French Embassy and also procured a pistol 'which he refused to take' and which was subsequently found at her home. With the help of the embassy she organised his escape into France in 1936 together with several other asylees, and the records indicate that Joaquín may have been involved with the Nationalist intelligence services in Paris. After his departure, Lario became the leader of an important group and the Republican SIM believed that she was in regular contact with members of Madrid's Supreme Junta. Her home was venue to high-level clandestine meetings. She raised a bandera and recruited Jeronimo López Batanero into the organisation. Her group "formed part of a large organisation that was infiltrated everywhere."[100] In early 1938 Lario hosted a meeting in order to discuss "the fusion of various groups which had already been working closely together."[101] López first made the acquaintance of "Fanny" (Martínez) and "Don José," the code name for Miguel Cortés Rubio, at this meeting. Thereafter, Lario met regularly with Martínez, Pablo Moreno, Miguel Cortés, Paz Zamorra, Pedro Martín and several Assault Guards, security officers and officers within Miaja's General Staff. On 12 March 1938 Martínez and Cortés "informed Lario in the presence of the leader of the 22 Bandera that the Junta Nacional had given orders to recruit more personnel in anticipation of an imminent military coup."[102] López and Lario obtained a cache of pistols, a sub-machine gun, hunting rifles and ammunition which Lario hid in a wall-cavity at home. A second cache was hidden at López's office in calle Españoleto. Lario also supplied an Astra 9 mm pistol to Captain Paz Zamorra, who formed part of Miaja's General Staff. She also entered into negotiations for substantial munitions with a soldier based in Alcalá de Henares. By April 1938, Lario was so confident of an imminent Nationalist victory that she defiantly performed the Falangist salute in public and became much more careless and incautious in her recruitment methods.[103]

Lario was a devout Catholic whose home was regular venue to clandestine masses which were attended by members like Jeronimo López Batanero. These religious gatherings provided recruitment opportunities, and the priest who officiated mass at her house also performed Sunday mass at the house of a high-ranking member of the DGS. Lario also liaised with agents embedded within various civilian and military institutions and she regularly visited Falangist prisoners. She was also in contact with one of Franco's SIM agents in Madrid named Delgado, and she was in communication with a cousin at the Llorente Institute, a popular tribunal lawyer named Rumbau (probably Gregorio Rabago), a Health Officer named Botana, various General Staff officers, other security personnel and, finally, a nephew of General Sanjurjo who was in asylum at the French Embassy under the pretext of being a French national. This man "had acquired increasing influence within the DGS and had sometimes been supplied with the names of individuals who were about to be arrested."[104] Lario was found guilty of co-ordinating a large and diffuse network of operatives whose most senior leader was known as Rabago. Gregorio Rabago Rodríguez was a Supreme Tribunal prosecutor who obtained the acquittal of many fifth-columnists. He was detained after the dismantlement of the case of the "The Local Junta of the Falange de las JONS" aka the "Golfín-Corujo" group which was dismantled in 1937.[105]

Lario also performed auxiliary relief services at the orders of senior Falangists. She regularly visited a group of ex-Civil Guards imprisoned at the monastery of Santa María de la Cabeza and had access to funds which enabled her to assist prisoners' families in places outside Madrid such as Jaen. After a house search during the early months of the war she claimed that she had been left penniless and deprived of her widow's pension. She claimed to have relied on donations from friends, but it was discovered that she had access to a clandestine account made out in the name of another resistance member whose name she refused to divulge. Lario also raised funds for her auxiliary relief work from acquaintances. Lario claimed that she "had always provided assistance to the needy regardless of their class"[106] and denied that the friends and acquaintances were members of Socorro Blanco.

Lario was also a spy who had regular access to several clandestine radio sets, one of which may have been hidden within the offices of the General Staff. In addition, she was accused of having audaciously used the DGS's public telephone services to pass intelligence information into the enemy zone. She was also accused of exposing a female Republican double-agent who was a telephone operator who was smuggled over the Republican lines in Victoria Kent's car. Lario also communicated military intelligence including information in relation to the movement of a large concentration of Republican troops in Huesca and also the position of Republican tanks in Guadalajara in January 1938. The Tribunal of Espionage and High Treason found her guilty of having passed military information, obtained from the General Staff and the French Embassy in Madrid, to Salamanca. Finally, like Martínez and Dolores López Mendizábal (discussed below) Lario also compiled lists of 'friends and enemies' within the Republican General Staff (Estado Mayor) and Military Headquarters (Cuartel General). The group gathered this information on behalf of the Nationalist SIPM which relayed this intelligence to the General Staff and to Marcelino de Ulibarri y Eguilaz's Documental Recuperation Services department which was based in the General Staff offices and tasked with recovering documents related to Marxist activities.[107] Lario also provided information on individuals in the Nationalist zone:

> Samuel Luchsinge, Mining Engineer, a Jew, resident in Pamplona, he has relatives in Madrid. An intervention by Nationalist authorities is required in relation to communications between this person and Julia Centeno and Carmen Topete both resident in Biarritz.[108]

Lario received the death penalty for her involvement in the group, but this sentence was commuted to thirty years' life-imprisonment.

Dolores López Mendizábal

Martínez introduced Lario to Dolores López Mendizábal in early 1938. This woman was the leader of cell that was embedded within the Telefónica offices, and it included Juan Marticorena, Teresa Bayod, Modesta Ramírez, Manuela Vargas, Carmela Rosillo, José Romero, Antonio González Trashorras, Afred Ruíz Crespón, Carmen García and Tomás Bertolín and various military personnel. In March 1938 López Mendizábal supplied Larios with a list of potential recruits within the Telefónica which was discovered along with intelligence documents during a search of Larios' premises.

López was single and aged thirty-five years at the time of her arrest. She had first met Martínez through her involvement in the Sección Femenina before the war. She joined the Telefónica as a telephone operator in 1929 but was dismissed in or around March 1936 because of her Falangist credentials. She claimed never to have known Martínez by her real name, only by her code number "9-85." López's code number was "9-67." At a secret street meeting some months prior to her arrest Fanny had given López three days to create a list of collaborators at the Telefónica who would be prepared to take-over the building in the event of a Nationalist occupation of Madrid. López claimed that she always obeyed the orders of Fanny. "The Falange doesn't ever give explanations, only orders."[109] She made efforts to recruit trustworthy individuals in order to form a cell that would come into action "in the event of a Nationalist occupation or when the fifth column finally came out onto the streets and took over the public buildings." Fanny managed to persuade her that "the moment had come to take action and that it was vital that contact should be made with trustworthy elements."[110]

López immediately contacted ex-colleagues who were still working at the Telefónica. She went to visit them at their homes. A few flatly refused to collaborate in view of the risks involved. Her colleague José Romero argued that the plan was madness and refused to help. López threatened him: "watch out Romero, we will go ahead without you anyway and you will be punished."[111] Meanwhile, Carmen García Álvarez, Modesta Ramírez, Pepita Messeguer and Teresa Bayod agreed to join the conspiracy. One of Bayod's brothers was killed at the start of the war, another was a senior Falangist who was forced to seek asylum at the Norwegian Embassy. Bayod's father was the Head of the Toledo Post Office. Carmen Carmentia and Manuela Vargas refused to collaborate because that they had already been acquitted of disseminating intelligence received from San Sebastián (probably from SIFNE). Paulina Caballero did not want to lose her job and disagreed with the ideas of the Falange. Carmen Jiménez had already been imprisoned and didn't want to get involved. On 19 March López submitted her list to Fanny and held a meeting at her flat on 24 March 1938 in order to plan the take-over of the Telefónica. López was found guilty of treason and sentenced to death, but her sentence was commuted to life imprisonment. In March 1939 after the capital was occupied, Martínez, Larios and López were released from prison.

Carmen de Blas Arantegui

Carmen de Blas Arantegui was twenty-seven years old and married to an army commander who was invalided out of service, possibly on false medical pretexts. She had a young son and was pregnant with another child at the time of her arrest. Her husband now worked at the National History Museum. De Blas denied any association with "active military personnel because her husband belonged to the Invalid Corps."[112] In fact, de Blas was one of the most well-connected Nationalist SIPM agents in Madrid.[113] She was also in communication with senior officials at the Telefónica. De Blas used ciphers and 'code-breakers' supplied by the Nationalists to key agents. Three cases of "Danubio" meant three cases of Dynamite; 150 boxes of tomatoes mean hand grenades; 7 cases of red wine mean flammable liquids, 100 boxes of pineapples meant bombs; 160/m/c.g. means 160,000 cartridges and 150/m of olives means 150,000 bullets.[114] Captains were code-named "onions" and lieutenant officers were code-named "garlic."[115]

De Blas was linked to José Moreno Ciges, Horacio Echevarrieta and José Banús Masdeu who worked as a physiotherapist ('therapeutic masseur') in a private health clinic in calle Montes where clandestine meetings took place.[116] José Banús made an immediate confession to the SIM on 5 April 1938 which lead to the arrest of Carmen de Blas and the other members of his group. He confessed that he had earlier joined Antonio Rodríguez Aguado's organisation which had established direct links with Franco's headquarters in Salamanca. The group was "comprised of a large number of military and civilian personnel who were infiltrated within the Republican regime and who had been entrusted with significant and powerful roles."[117] Banús claimed that de Blas was only known as Carmen Marquina (her married name).

Banús was first arrested in August 1936 on account of his lack of identification documents but released soon after. He was called to the ranks in Autumn 1936 but managed to avoid active service by obtaining a post as a nursing auxiliary in Military Hospital no. 24 in calle Monte Esquinza. In February 1937, alongside José Luis Moreno Ciges and Manuel Carpio and several others, he established one of Madrid's earliest fifth-column networks known as the Grupo Banús which managed to infiltrate the Usera and the Casa de Campo front-lines, the Grupo de Tren Batallion and a dozen military hospitals. In April 1937 Banús was approached by Paco Llanas (real name Francisco Grañen), the former leader of the Falange in Guadalajara, who invited him to join the Rodríguez Aguado organisation[118] which received orders from Bonel Huici to organise escape-lines for military officers and gather intelligence. Banús managed to establish communications with Bonel Huici and with informants in the Republican 'Posición Jaca' (the secret bunker of the General Staff of the Army of the Centre). After a bounty was issued for the arrest of Antonio Rodríguez Aguado and Joaquín Jiménez de Anta, it was Banús who persuaded a diplomat at the French Embassy to safe-house these men until they finally obtained asylum at the Turkish Embassy in December 1937.

Carmen de Blas attended meetings at José Banús' clinic in the Monte Esquinza hospital, in calle Montes and also in Café Granja del Henar and the Café de Europa situated in the Glorieta de Bilbao. She first made his acquaintance in this last café and put him in contact with the Basque multimillionaire Horacio Echevarrieta (one of the most powerful impresarios of the Alfonso XIII period) who was a committed Republican and close friend of Indalecio Prieto, the Minister of War in 1938. De Blas, Banús and Echevarrieta met on at least two separate occasions at Echevarrieta's palace which was situated between calles Diego de León and Claudio Coello. According to Banús, Echevarrieta claimed that although he wasn't a fascist, he did not agree with the current regime and agreed to put 3,000 armed men at Banús' disposal in order to take Madrid within 24 hours. The conspirators agreed that the Union Radio building would be the first to be occupied.[119]

De Blas always denied any involvement in the fifth column. She confessed to meeting José Moreno Ciges in December 1937 at his hair salon in calle Alcalá no. 2. She had been informed that Moreno's brother was a Communist Party member and she wanted him to obtain a communist membership card for her brother (aged sixteen) who had recently received his call-up. De Blas telephoned Moreno a few days after their initial meeting and arranged to meet him at a park in calle de Lista where she took her young son to play. Eight days later Moreno informed her that he was unable to obtain the necessary documentation. De Blas then asked Moreno if he might organise, with the aid of the International Red Cross, the release of her cousin Jeronimo López Batanero together with another three military prisoners as part of a civilian exchange programme. The International Red Cross had already informed her that it was not possible to organise exchanges on an individual basis; instead, it was necessary to put forward a group of men, and the Republican government's prisoner-exchange ratio was two Republicans for every Nationalist.

De Blas claimed that she would never endanger her husband and her infant son by involving herself in political matters. However, Banús confessed that she was an important fifth-column recruitment and liaison agent who was in contact with the Nationalist SIPM. Moreno also testified that he had given military plans to de Blas and that she in turn had passed these on to Banús.[120] De Blas's defence argued that she had become addicted to prescription drugs including morphine because of severe back pain during pregnancy and had been hospitalised twice for drug intoxication. She was released and the treason charges against her were dropped because the court found that she had been forcibly removed from hospital (while pregnant with her second child) and taken to the SIM headquarters for interrogation while under extreme sedation. The confessions made during her interrogations in April 1938 were made under the influence of drugs and were inadmissible. She pleaded ignorance and disorientation arising from drug intoxication and denied knowledge of the reasons for her arrest. The medical evidence obtained from two medical experts ensured her release, and her case was suspended.[121] She was transferred to a psychiatric establishment for treatment for 'prescription drug addiction which was caused by the back pain experienced after the birth of her first child' and absolved on grounds of 'mental irresponsibility' on 2 August 1938.[122] She never forgave Banús for his betrayal.[123] Fortunately, she was a powerful woman in her own right, and an influencer who possessed social capital and an extensive network of powerful Republican friends. De Blas survived the war and lived in Madrid until her death on 17 November 1986. She was remembered as a devout Catholic widow[124] and devoted mother of four children.[125]

Pilar del Olmo Sánchez

Pilar del Olmo Sánchez (aged thirty years, unmarried) was arrested in Madrid's High Court (*Palacio de la Justicia*) on 23 July 1938 and imprisoned in Ventas on charges of espionage and defeatism.[126] Her boyfriend, Julio Infiesta, was a Falangist defendant in the 195 Group trial. He was found guilty of treason and sentenced to twenty-five years' hard labour. Pilar was arrested during one of the public hearings, which she attended in the company of her boyfriend's mother, for "wearing an ostentatious silver ring … used by the affiliates of the fascist auxiliary and relief organisation Socorro Blanco as a distinctive symbol of membership of this group."[127] Pilar was a self-employed dressmaker, her father had been a member of the UGT glove makers' union since October 1929. Her brother was also a member of this union and both provided good-character references (*avales*). The court established that she left the family home each morning only returning late at night. She visited clients near her home in calle Santa Engracia 55 'in order to take measurements and to perform dress-fittings.' The prosecution argued that these house visits were in reality clandestine meetings. Pilar denied any knowledge that the ring symbolised an affiliation to Socorro Blanco and claimed that it had been given to her as a keep-sake by a former colleague. She also denied that her boyfriend had persuaded her to become a member of this organisation. She was released indefinitely on conditional bail and Pilar's Republican kin may have negotiated her release. The ring had been made to order by an anti-Republican silversmith who also made rings for other members, and it was worn as an act of defiance and symbolic protest in court.

While 195 Group was Madrid's largest network, only eighteen women received custodial sentences on 18 June 1938. The women were Francisca Martínez Ramírez, Teresa Bayod Rueda, Carmen de Blas Arantegui, Paulina Caballero Verde, Mercedes Gónzalez del Valle, Carmen Jiménez Crespo, Antonia Jiménez Díaz, Juana Jiménez Prieto, Dolores López Mendizábal, Josefa Meseguer Soto, Pilar Merlo Núñez, Matilde Poza Sánchez, María Felisa Parés Pérez,[128] Modesta Ramírez Blasco, Carmela Rosillo Valdivia, Filomena Serrano Ramírez and Manuela Vargas Vergara. Sentencing occurred between 18 July and 2 August 1938. According to an ABC newspaper report dated 3 August the death penalty for high treason was awarded to twenty-three men and women including Miguel Cortés Rubio, Jeronimo López Batanero, Pablo Moreno, José Banús Masdeu, José Moreno Ciges, Luis Paz Zamarra, Manuel Villafranca Muñoz, Carlos Alfonso Sanz and three women Francisca Martínez Ramírez, Antonia Lario Alonso and Dolores López Mendizábal.[129] The women's death sentences were commuted to thirty years' imprisonment. Filomena Serrano Ramírez was sentenced to thirty years in a labour camp, Carmela Rosilla Valdívia to twenty years, Carmen García Álvarez to fifteen years, Teresa Bayod Rueda to twelve years and Modesta Ramírez Blasco and Manuela Vargas Vergara were sentenced to six years each. Mercedes González del Valle was sentenced to exile from Spain for having engaged in conduct that was dangerous to the Republic. Carmen de Blas Aranteguí was absolved on grounds of mental incapacity. Juana Jiménez Prieto, Antonia Jiménez Díaz and María Felisa Parés Pérez (also Group Leader of Auxilio Azul) and Carmen Jiménez Crespo were also absolved. The following women were also absolved of treason but their cases were remitted to the popular tribunals (Jurados de Urgencia) on charges of disaffection: Josefa Meseguer Soto, Matilde Pozas Sánchez and Paulina Caballero Verde. All these prisoners were released when Franco's troops occupied Madrid on 28 March 1939.

Josefa Martí Tortajada

The case of the liaison agent Josefa Martí Tortajada (aged thirty-five years) illustrates how negative gender stereotyping was used to women's advantage by the defence. Josefa was a military widow whose husband had taken early retirement under the Azaña Laws but had disappeared without trace (as acknowledged by the trial judges) during the Model Prison *sacas* in November 1936. Josefa was arrested for high treason along with five soldiers in early 1939. She was a Falangist recruitment and liaison agent who was in contact with a group of around one hundred soldiers and officers embedded within the War Office and in various barracks. Josefa and her sister had already been arrested for disaffection but were released in April 1938. The women had been in possession of an unlicensed camera and various items of fascist propaganda including pamphlets which stated "*Long live Mussolini*" and "*Long live Fascism*." Josefa had also penned a Falangist poem which was entitled "*Melancolia Sentimental*."[130] During trial in 1939, her defence claimed that she was incapable of forming the necessary *mens rea* for the crime of high treason. Her actions were ascribed to a form of 'automatism' which was the fruit of a 'pathological romantic infatuation.' Two court appointed medical experts testified that:

> Josefa … suffered from an inherited, idiopathic, hysterical condition that caused great alterations to her affect, she was also highly suggestible and showed signs of automatism, therefore, although her free-will was not entirely suppressed (*anulación total*) it was intensely modified in the sense that it was diminished.[131]

Nonetheless, a SIM surveillance operation provided evidence that she met regularly with soldiers and officers at pre-agreed meeting points on street corners and in park spaces. She also frequented the central bars and cafés late at night. This constituted a startling change in her formerly 'respectable' habits and a flagrant contravention of societal gender norms and expectations. Her moral probity was impugned by the prosecution, but she testified that she went out at night to "ease her heart ache and improve her mood after the disappearance of her husband." Josefa principally socialised with male acquaintances who were officers and soldiers and she testified that she "she had no control over the flow and direction of her conversations" (a standard female defence). However, her unusual routines and habits indicated that she was engaged in liaison and courier activities. Her romantic attachment to a younger disaffected officer enabled the court to determine that she had been unduly influenced by him to the extent that her actions constituted "a quasi-automaton response produced by a morbid and obsessive romantic attachment."[132] This case was heard in late January 1939, but it was indefinitely suspended, possibly with the knowledge and collusion of the court.

Spies

Female spies and informants were often employed in civil and administrative, military or nursing and auxiliary jobs. They provided the General Staff in Burgos with intelligence relating to civilian morale and the political, social and economic situation in the capital. The capital was close to the fronts, and the militias were billeted within the civilian community which greatly facilitated intelligence-gathering operations.

Despite the existence of spies in Madrid, most social intelligence was provided by individuals who managed to successfully escape from the Republican zones. In November 1937 Colonel José Ungria Jiménez became leader of a centralised Nationalist intelligence and security service named the Servicio de Información y Policia Militar (SIPM). Ungria regularly received communiqués compiled from the testimonies of escapees in relation to, for example, the location of the capital's key political and military centres or the fortification emplacements located in the main city access routes.[133]

Informants were also embedded in key civil, administrative and security posts. The DGS's Central Information Office was located in calle Alcalá, 88 above Café Pelayo and "a certain Mr Espina, an absolutely trustworthy man, was infiltrated there and was able to provide a great deal of intelligence."[134] The double-agent Alberto Castilla Olavarría had regularly provided information to the SIPM before falling under the control of Valentí's Special Brigade after his release from prison in 1937. This married assault-guard was safe-housed by his former music teacher (and possibly lover) Pilar Ovejas Overjas, and both were charged with espionage in September 1938, although Pilar's charges were reduced to disaffection.[135]

The fifth column also managed to establish limited contact with the Gestapo, the German military intelligence services (Abwehr) and the Italian Secret Police (OVRA),[136] particularly in Catalonia and North Africa[137] where the fifth column maintained links with Bertrán í Musitu's North Eastern intelligence organisation (SIFNE).[138] However, there is scant evidence of significant liaisons with foreign intelligence agencies, although the Golfín-Corujo network (discussed below) managed to establish contact with members of the French extreme right-wing *Cagoule* terror group immediately before the war.

Matilde Casáñ Pablo and the Golfín-Coruju network

The Golfín-Corujo network was dismantled in the early summer of 1937 following its infiltration by Alberto Castilla Olavarría who worked for Fernández Valentí's Special Brigade at this time.[139] The POUM leader Andreu Nin was falsely implicated in this network (possibly by the NKVD leader Alexander Orlov). Nin's mysterious disappearance while in police custody caused both a national and an international outcry.[140]

The Junta leaders were the architect Javier Fernández Golfín, the public prosecutor Ignació Corujo López Villamil, Manuel Rosado Gonzalo, Luis García de Padín and Juan Francisco Jiménez Martín. These men were in contact with the leaders of the Clandestine Falange who were hiding in the embassies including Vicente Busso and 'Teddy' Feltham. Corujo's agents infiltrated various Republican institutions including the Palace of Justice. Rosado was in charge of gathering intelligence information which was received from spies embedded within several Republican institutions and from members of the other three groups. This intelligence was forwarded to General Franco's Headquarters in Burgos. Luis García de Padín was an embassy go-between. Juan Francisco Franco Jiménez also directly channelled information to Burgos, organised embassy asylums and was the main contact between these groups and the Falangist Félix Campos Guereta who was in regular contact with the Falange leaders in the Nationalist zone. Miguel Lomas obtained asylum at a Swiss Embassy building located in calle Velázquez and acted as a liaison agent.

The network had four main groups which focussed on three areas: (1) gathering military and other intelligence and forwarding these to contacts in Burgos, (2) infiltrating key Republican political and civilian institutions and planning for a Nationalist occupation of Madrid and (3) finding asylum for fugitives within embassies and safe-houses and "attending to the prisoners, finding out where they were imprisoned and commencing judicial proceedings."[141] The Special Brigade alleged that leaders were also "fanatic Falangist militants and a spies who had stealthy and easily infiltrated Republican nerve centres and established contact with officials."[142] The group also planned to take over key government and communication buildings in the event of an occupation.[143] Juan Manuel de la Aldea's cell plotted to cut off Madrid's electricity supply using agents who were infiltrated within the Compañía Electrica.[144] The group leaders formulated detailed plans for the take-over of the capital's key nerve centres including the War Ministry, the Telefónica and Radio Madrid with the aid of fifth-columnists who were infiltrated within these institutions.

There were only four senior women within the group. Matilde Casáñ Pablo (aka "Mati") aged twenty-one years joined the Falange in 1934. She was an actress who used the stage name Matilde Llonellama because she had lived for some time in Japan. Mati was "prepared to commit all necessary acts of espionage with important elements."[145] Mati worked as a spy for the network for nine months prior to her arrest. She was also the girlfriend of Golfín whom she had known for a period of six years. Mati was arrested on 4 May 1937 and taken to the Special Brigade's headquarters in Ronda de Atocha, 21 where she was "brutally tortured in order to obtain a confession, something which they never managed to get from me."[146] Golfín believed that Mati would eventually turn evidence, and prison informants alerted the Special Brigade to his fears. The couple communicated through a small hole between their cells; their signal was a whistled refrain from the opera Manon.[147] Initially Mati claimed that Golfín had never discussed politics or asked for any information and that "favourable things were always said about the Government."[148] She insisted that she was ignorant of the reasons for her arrest and never betrayed the other members. Golfín was tortured and admitted that Mati had passed on to him a detailed millimetric map of Madrid which contained classified information on anti-aircraft artillery positions and munitions storage depots. Thereafter, Mati confessed to having worked from October 1936 at the General Secretariat of the Militias as the private secretary to the Secretary General, Enrique Pérez Bolín. Mati had been employed in an unpaid and honorary capacity which enabled her to "keep up her typing skills while she lived with her mother on her personal savings and that she had never received any compensation or salary for her work and neither did Pérez Bolín pay anything to her on his own account." She had befriended Pérez Bolín in Segovia before the war and subsequently met him again in Madrid after the 'Movement.' After Pérez Bolín took sick-leave due to a heart condition she "attended to him at home in order to save on expenses as he had done such a great deal for the Republican cause."[149] Although she denied ever having spoken to Golfín about Pérez or her job, Golfín was found in possession of an undated note in her handwriting which stated that "Tomorrow the forces of the International Brigade and the 39th Brigade which is stationed in Cuatro Caminos will be relieved and on this day the 3rd and the 94th will march to the fronts."[150]

María Teresa Abarzuza y Robles (the 'ex Marquise of Fuenrrubia') was "one of the most high ranking spies in the group."[151] Her husband was imprisoned in the Model Prison on 24 September 1936 and transferred to Porlier on 6 November but was subsequently extra-judicially removed (*sacado*) on 18 November "after which he disappeared and, despite having made formal enquiries, she still doesn't know whether he has died or disappeared."[152] Julia Redondo Heredia was an 'old shirt' and the girlfriend of Félix Campos Guereta who founded the network in 1937 but managed to escape into the Nationalist zone. Julia was a liaison agent between the Supreme Junta and a lawyer named Barrobo who had also managed to evade arrest. Sofía Luengo Aras (another widow aged thirty-eight years) was also "a very skilful spy who made use of her son Manuel Espeso Luengo (a minor aged 12 years) as a courier."[153] The prosecution claimed that María Teresa worked alongside her cousin Carmen Zuñiga and Sofía Luengo. Sofía, Manuel and his older brother "disseminated war reports and passed intelligence to Dr. José Luis Bono via his aunts who lived in the adjoining apartment."[154] It was also rumoured that Sofía had bought votes during the February 1936 general elections, and in autumn 1936 she had sought the advice of a lawyer named Torres and taken legal action in order to vindicate her reputation. During a Special Brigade interview, which took place at her home because she was too ill to leave her bed, Sofía denied knowing Fuenrrubia.[155] However, her youngest son Manuel confessed that he had "delivered packages to Mari-Tere (the Marquise of Fuenrrubia) from Emelina Caso [sic] a Cuban national who was housing the evacuated Espeso Luengo family at her home in calle Blasco Garay, 60."[156] Fuenrrubia, Benito Pérez Moreno and Florencio Martínez formed part of a 'triangle' within a chain of liaison that had access to a clandestine radio transmitter which was used to pass confidential information to the enemy.[157]

Matilde Álvarez González and Concepción Valdés Larrañaga (sister of the leader of the Clandestine Falange) were also involved.[158] Concepción first became involved after she contacted the Chilean liaison agent Jiménez Martín in order to obtain the release of her brother.[159] Matilde was the daughter of Melquiades Álvarez González Posada, the former leader of the Republican Union party who was killed during the assault on the Model Prison on 22 August 1936. She joined the group at the behest of her old friend Corujo, and she first met Golfín during a secret meeting at her home. She managed to escape to Valencia with her partner in April 1937 before the group was dismantled. A further sixty men were arrested and indicted as 'secondary participants' and another two women named Carmen Reyes Recacho and María Cabezuelo.

Escape-line organisers

The Falange organised escape-lines for certain individuals pursuant to direct instructions from the General Staff Headquarters in Burgos.[160] The fugitives were mostly prominent right-wing military and political leaders and officials for whom specific roles were envisaged within the Nationalist war effort: around ninety persons were evacuated in this way.[161] The escape-line organisers received travel passes, vehicles and fuel from Clandestine Falange members who were infiltrated within the Republican military. The local escape-line guides who facilitated safe-passage through the wild Castilian sierras (frequently via the river Tajo) in to the rebel zone generally charged between 500 and 1,000 *pesetas* for their services.[162]

Matilde Jiménez Bofill (Mati) was an escape-line coordinator for one of the most longstanding and successful escape-line organisations.[163] She "was 30 years old, single, attractive, blonde and accustomed to using pseudonyms like Sta. Gutiérrez, Sta. García Rey."[164] Mati lived in calle de Goya near the old bull-fighting ring. Her home was venue to clandestine meetings, and she sometimes accompanied the escape expeditions. Her main job was to initiate contact with potential escapees and organise suitable pick-up locations. According to the SIM, the initial contact with escapees was made by "young women who were somewhat gifted in the art of seduction and the liaison agents who moved between the front and rear guards were travelling salesmen and members of the civilian population who lived in villages close to the fronts."[165] The women's activities were dangerous because sometimes the wrong individuals were mistakenly approached, based on faulty intelligence, and denunciations and arrests ensued.

Mati was second-in-command after Gustavo Villapalos who was an SIPM agent who had been sent on a mission to Madrid to train in sabotage and organise escape-lines. Villapalos was described in the police records as a tall, strong, and corpulent man with an arrogant swagger and proud and insolent air (*de aire flamenco*).[166] He drove the escapees from pre-agreed locations in city to the Extemadura fronts where local guides would accompany them across the front-lines on foot. Other members were senior elements in the Republican army who were in positions of authority including lieutenants in the Assault Corps, the Train Corps, Commissars and permanent tribunal members. The economic means

> were provided by Republican officials and agents embedded within the motorized Assault Guard, S.T.E vehicles were also used, and military travel passes (*hojas de ruta militares*), petrol and lubricants were obtained from various military supply depots and secret private depots.[167]

Mati and Gregoria Marticorena Muguruza were the key female liaison agents. Most often the escapees were prominent military or political personnel whose services were specifically requested by the General Staff in Burgos. However, the organisation also helped individuals in the Nationalist zone to contact relatives in Madrid via a chain of agents based both in the Nationalist zone and in Madrid. Mati made the initial contact with the escapees in Madrid by producing a signed letter from a relative together with other forms of identification documentation or photographs as proof that her organisation acted in good faith. Prior to any contact, security checks were completed so as to ensure that the prospective escapees were genuine '*desafectos*' rather than Republican SIM agents.

On 20 January 1939 fifteen men and two women were arrested on charges of high treason after a group of young men failed in their efforts to cross the front-lines and were arrested by soldiers in the 185 Battalion of the 47th Brigade, 36th Division. Gustavo Villapalos, Fernando Fuentes Bustillo and José Villaplana and two others managed to escape. The original escape party had set off in two military vehicles in or around the evening of 16 January 1939. Villapalos' car managed to cross into the enemy zone, but the second vehicle ran out of fuel at the Extremadura front and its three passengers were obliged abandon it and cross the mountains on foot. However, the local guide lost his way, and the fugitives were obliged to shelter in an abandoned mountain hut to await the next morning when their guide promised to return. The evacuees waited without provisions for around seventy-two hours before leaving the hut and making their way back towards Madrid on foot. They were denounced to patrol soldiers by local villagers.

The escape-line operations were well-established by this time. 'Numerous and frequent' evasions were orchestrated via a series of routes along the *Extremadura* front which was chosen because of its length, its many approaches, the unpopulated territory and "possibly because of the collaboration of certain commanders and military leaders embedded within the large units in this area."[168] The SIM criticised the army in this section and claimed that the security on these fronts was "null or virtually null."[169] It was also believed that the group "may have been started by or, at the very least, had links with and obtained funding from Socorro Blanco." The trial was subject to numerous procedural delays. As many as one-third of the defendants allegedly suffered from a variety of serious illnesses which required immediate hospitalisation. Mati Bofill's mother was diagnosed as being clinically insane and a seventeen-year-old male defendant suffered from severe epilepsy. Another middle-aged male was diagnosed with tuberculosis. These illnesses might evidence the collusion of the court administration and judiciary. The ubiquitous defence attorney Rogelio Rufilanchas Periquet (discussed further in Chapter 5 below) was employed as a defence counsel and the case rumbled along ineffectually incurring procedural delays until 'Liberation' in March 1939.

Esperanza Ortega Cebrían and the "Grupo de Jesús Hernández Cid"

Esperanza Ortega Cebrían was the leader of a Falange of around thirty men that formed part of a larger group led by José de Frutos Rey. Sixty-four individuals were arrested; the majority were soldiers.[170] Ortega's group was composed of young conscripts whose units were based on the front-lines and who regularly returned to the capital with intelligence. The group organised escape-lines through unguarded sections of the Guadalajara fronts using maps which had been stolen from the Army of the Centre's topography department. It also stock-piled weapons. In July 1938 it began to actively recruit soldiers in anticipation of an imminent Nationalist occupation. José de Frutos Rey made "regular expeditions into the surrounding countryside to villages like Fuentidueña in order to enlist more recruits."[171] New members were informed that "the Nationalist signal to occupy the streets would be *Madrileños Alerta*."[172] In late summer 1938 Jesus Cid (the leader of another group) approached Ortega with a view to arranging the escape of two members of his group who were sought by the police.

Ortega was an outspoken woman who asserted her authority and used threats and intimidation in order to counter a "complete lack of activity and enthusiasm among the recruits."[173] She may also have been involved in the failed attempt to spring José Banús Masdeu from prison during his transfer to the High Court. The Falangist emotional regime demanded an ardent and unflinching loyalty from its comrades. Group leaders like Ortega not only rallied morale but also threatened to 'eliminate' foot-draggers and informants. Ortega was a military widow aged twenty-four years. Her disaffected officer husband was imprisoned in early August 1936 and executed during one of the Model Prison *sacas* in November 1936. She had a two-year-old son and lived with her husband's mother and a sister-in-law in calle Hermosilla, 84. Her neighbour (and lover) was a twenty-two-year-old Falangist law student named Emilio Gómez Amigo who was now a corporal in the Etapas Battalion situated in calle Juan Bravo 10. The group members were young and inexperienced, and Ramón Gasset Neira (a Socorro Blanco leader) "dismissed the group's activities as 'child's play' and refused have any dealings with it."[174]

José de Frutos Rey was the main leader and Esperanza was second-in-command. The original founder, Félix Campos Guereta, had by this time escaped into the Nationalist zone. Frutos was a soldier with the Etapas Batallion. The group was also connected with a Cuban national called José León Breu whose own organisation had been dismantled in 1937. Members were infiltrated within the General Staff and the Chilean Embassy. The dentist Eduardo Renard Peruch was the liaison agent between Frutos and the leaders of the Counsel of the Falange who remained in asylum at the embassies. Esperanza claimed that she was also a senior liaison agent who was in direct contact with the Counsel.[175]

The leaders met regularly at the *Café Granja del Henar* in the Gran Vía, and their careless talk resulted the dismantlement of the group following its infiltration by three soldiers within the Transmissions Group named Jaime Rosello Rotlán, Fernando Téllez Casquero and Samuel de Lucas Pérez. Rosello reported his suspicions to their superior officer, the CNT leader Manuel Salgado. According to Rosello "various persons of rightist tendencies were organising a group in order to fight the legitimate government and to favour the rebels in every way."[176] In early July 1938, with the approval and consent of the General Commisar Estebán Fernández, Salgado ordered the informants "uncover all the groups' shady dealings." The case was referred up to the War Ministry's Special Services department which provided the necessary funding and manpower to entrap the leaders together with Jesus Hernández Cid. When Frutos discovered that he was going to be posted to Villacanas, Toledo he introduced the informants to Emilio Gómez Amigo whom he introduced as the new leader of the group. However, the informants identified Esperanza as the effective leader, and they testified that she was the person who was in direct communication with the Counsel of the Falange:

> on one occasion in an effort to intimidate them she [Esperanza] threatened that anyone who attempted to desert the organisation would pay for it with their lives because she claimed to have people on the ground everywhere; she also claimed that the leaders [of the Organisation] were senior generals, and she was ready to approach anyone prepared to listen and ask them to fight in good faith and also to collaborate in terrorist actions … she paid a visit to the Sergeant of the Artillery Park, Francisco Cerezo Rivera, in order to ask about the readiness and morale of the Falange squads in the Park, Cerezo replied that the squads were somewhat neglected and then Esperanza declared that he was under her orders because Federico had entrusted her with the leadership before his arrest, and then Cerezo replied that soon everything would be in order. She also told one of the informants that the Cousel of the Falange had intimated that there would be an imminent coup in Madrid and that she had to go to calle Toledo, 70 in order to deliver some plans. She told Captain Lucas (one of the informants) that the leader of the Falange's civil groups was called José María Guerrero Sánchez who was working in one of the Brigades.[177]

Ortega was arrested in late July 1938 during her attempted escape to Murcia together with her family, Gómez Amigo, his mother and sister, a member of the Jesus Cid Hernández's group, two Paraguayan Embassy asylees and a few others. The Paraguayans claimed that they needed to escape Madrid because they could no longer afford to pay their embassy residence fees rather than because they wanted to avoid military service. The escape line was organised by Esperanza with the assistance of Fernando Téllez Casquero who was believed to be a 'trusted friend' of Gómez Amigo. In reality, Téllez was a paid SIM informant who was provided with sufficient funds to provide a convoy of three vehicles the last of which was armed with guns and hand grenades. Esperanza fell readily into this trap, and she may have come to some arrangement with the SIM. Several senior members of her network had already been apprehended, and the net was closing around many others. She aroused the suspicion of one of the Paraguayan Embassy refugees who believed that she was behaving oddly and had deliberately led him into a police trap.[178] The escape plan was convoluted. It involved a pre-arranged pick-up point on a street corner (the asylees were driven to this in an embassy vehicle), followed by a meeting in a bar and a suspiciously long wait at Esperanza's home. Finally, a conspicuous convoy of three vehicles, the last of which was armed with guns and grenades, made its way out of Madrid. It is possible that Ortega agreed to entrap the male fugitives in order to save herself and her family because she never gave evidence in court and her outcomes are unknown.

Candida Círiza

Candida Círiza Zarrandicoechea and fifty-six others (including thirteen women) were indicted on 27 April 1937 on charges of conspiracy and aiding rebellion.[179] Fernández Valentí staged a surveillance operation outside her home in early April 1937 following the arrest of several fugitives, including a priest, during a failed attempt to cross into enemy territory via a section of the front-lines. The surveillance detail reported that many suspicious persons were seen entering and leaving her premises. The group was charged with "creating a relief organisation for the prisoners and their families who lacked financial resources and also for those who sympathised with the 18 July coup and who lacked economic resources or shelter."[180] The group had links with several embassies and organised escape-lines. The men were held in Porlier and the women in Ventas, but on 16 July 1937 the defendants were placed under house arrest.[181] The women were Gila Círiza Zarrandicoechea, Miranda Procopio de la Fuente Martínez, Matilde Alcalá Prieto, Adela González Rodríguez, Cecilia Castro Mansilla, Josefa Martínez Goyanarte, Magdalena Zarrandicoechea, Concepción Martínez Vega, Francisca Samper Corral, Carmen Gabuccio Sánchez Marmol, Ernestina Pages Torner, Manolita Pazos Queijas and María García Herraiz Amilibia (the last three were acquitted). The case was referred to the Valencian High Court in July 1937. Fifty-six defendants were accused of conspiracy to rebel and/or aiding rebellion under the Code of Military Justice Articles 240 and 421 and thirty-two defendants were eventually indicted.[182] Candida had been safe-housing her brother Félix at her home in Carrera San Geronimo, 38, and both were arrested while Félix attempted to destroy compromising documents (including a membership list and a Nationalist SIM code deciphering book). Almost everyone was rounded up and arrested except Félix Campos Guereta and a few other senior leaders.[183]

The men and women discussed above regularly practised the faith in clandestine masses which were organised by the women. The confessional aspects of the Clandestine Falange's resistance are noticeably absent in the legal records. At the time of her arrest in August 1937, Ángeles Orozco was safe-housing two nuns. Like many of the women discussed above, she organised clandestine masses at her home. A 'waiter' (aged forty, resident of calle Francisco Giner, 10) was arrested in connection with the group, but he was immediately released without charge because he confessed that:

> his real profession was that of a priest and he had only ever visited del Riego [Orozco] on this account, in particular, in order to provide spiritual guidance to the two nuns who were being sheltered at the house. He had had absolutely nothing to do with political activities but acknowledged that he practised his ministry in various private homes.[184]

The authorities seldom trespassed into the private religious sphere, and nothing more was reported on this matter. While confessional practice was instrumentalised by the Falange as a badge of resistance identity, the upswell of religious sensibility and fervour during the war was sincere and heart-felt. Orozco survived the war and died of natural causes on 17 May 1951. She "received the blessed sacraments and the benediction of Our Lord … The Papal Nuncio and the Bishop of Salamanca administered indulgences in the prescribed form."[185]

Gender is a primary way of signifying relationships of power,[186] and while women performed the same or similar roles to men, traditional gender prejudices and assumptions meant that they were perceived to be less of a threat than men.[187] The persistence of traditional patriarchal gender norms worked in favour of the Nationalist cause.[188] The Republican authorities routinely underestimated women who were not considered to be as dangerous or as intelligent as men, and it was generally assumed that they could not run or create resistance networks.[189] Therefore, the political and symbolic value attributed to women's resistance was undervalued, and this is reflected in the legal record. Women's interrogations and cross examinations were less detailed, and they routinely escaped the worst punishments and sanctions. The popular tribunals perceived them as being more naïve, gullible and susceptible to undue influence than men.[190] Defence lawyers were able to invoke these negative gender stereotypes to women's advantage. This subaltern or 'negative gender privilege' constituted a form of symbolic compensation for women's lack of power and status in the public realm.

Despite the prevailing masculinist prejudices, when women engaged in clandestine activities they "engaged whole heartedly and at great personal risk."[191] The women of the mixed-gender Falange groups were able to infiltrate the prisons, military barracks, hospitals and the civil and military administration. In addition to providing crucial welfare-aid, these women also performed 'masculine' resistance roles. Some were the leaders of armed 'squads,' and a small number were implicated in acts of attempted terrorism.[192] A close reading of the archives reveals the strategies deployed by women to subvert and contest the Republican regime. Despite their historical invisibility, the women of the mixed groups were just as skilled and effective at liaison and recruitment as their male counter-parts (if not more so), and it is likely that many more were involved in the activities of the mixed-gender groups than is revealed on record. The 'invisibility' of their gender enabled women to circulate more easily within civil and military organisations. Meanwhile, the most senior male leaders were obliged to hide within the safety of the 'feminine' home space or languish in the overflowing prisons and embassies. After the end of the war on 1 April 1939, Clandestine Falange groups continued to gather social intelligence in their capacity "as transmission belts of Francoist ideology" under the aegis of the SIPM."[193] Part 2 below examines women's roles within the 'autonomous' fifth column groups.

Notes

1 *Asesoría Jurídica*, Testimony of Marcelina Mateos Mateos dated 28 September 1939, Document 179, ANA, Carpeta B 12, RAH, Madrid. This activist claimed that she was arrested after 18 July 1936 on account of her alleged involvement in the death of Lt. Castillo; "after her release she worked [for the cause] with even more ardour."
See also *Expte. 497 instruida contra* María Martín Villate *por el delito/s de Desafección al Régimen*, AHN, FC-CAUSA_GENERAL, 224, Exp. 13. A twenty-six-year-old, single student arrested in April 1937 for being a member of the Falange.

2 Bourdieu, Pierre (2007) *Masculine Domination* (Cambridge: Polity), at p. 30.

3 *Expte. 1679 instruido contra varias personas por el delito/s de Adhesión a la Rebelión,* AHN, FC-CAUSA_GENERAL, 373, Exp.1, 1/1733. The group gathered intelligence and organised embassy asylums and escape-lines (primarily with the Cuban Embassy) and provided welfare-aid to the anti-Republican community.

4 She aroused the resentment of neighbours who denounced her for re-selling rationed items at prohibitively high prices. The contraband goods were obtained from socialist and anarchist storage depots.

5 Expte. 1679, Witness statement of Antonio Sanz García, Imagen 9-10/1733.

6 Melchor Rodríguez García (1893–1972) was a leader of the CNT and a founding member of the FAI in 1927 who became secretary of the woodworker's union in Madrid in 1933. His frequent spells in prison during the monarchy and the Second Republic earned him the sobriquet of "dean of Madrid's central prisons." When the anarchist Juan García Oliver became Minister of Justice in November 1936, he made Rodríguez Director General of the prisons. He was bravely and vehemently opposed to the *sacas* in 1936 and resigned from his post on this account on 14 November 1936 but regained this job at end of the month after the lobbying of the foreign diplomatic corps. His speech at the gates of the Alcalá de Henares prison on 8 December 1936 prevented a *saca* and saved the lives of some 1,500 political inmates. By March 1937 when he left his post, he had "restored order to the prison system and saved the lives of thousands of prisoners." See entry in Romero Salvadó, Francisco (2013) *Historical Dictionary of the Spanish Civil War* (Plymouth: Scarecrow), at pp. 283–284.

7 *Expte. no. 1679*, Police interrogation transcript of Falangist Rosina Cornide Alverola (resident of calle General Porlier, 30, aged twenty-three years, born in Burgos) dated 25 August 1937, Imagen 7/1733. This woman planned to travel to Marseille and then return to Burgos in order to volunteer as a Red Cross nurse.

8 Fal Conde, *Gesto Glorioso del Requete en Madrid* (Julio 1936–Marzo 1939), *Archivo General Militar de Ávila,* C2505, Cp.4/43 and C.2498.20, Legajo no. 285, Carpeta 20, Armario 5. at pp. 6–8.

9 The trial bundle contains dozens of letters of preferment, rationed goods and welfare entitlements from the FNTT, socialist and anarchist organisations and various government bodies.

10 Cervera (1998) *Madrid*, p. 171.
11 See *Expte. 1071 instruido contra varias personas por el delito/s de Conspiración a la Rebelión*, AHN, FC-CAUSA_GENERAL, 197, Exp. 1. Imágenes 1/51. See also article, "The Fifth Column Still Exists, The Police discover a vast Fascist organization and arrest its members," *ABC (Madrid)*, 13 March 1937, p. 10. http:// hemeroteca.abc.es [last accessed on 1 November 2017].
12 *Expte. 56 instruido contra Concepción del Rosal López Vinuesa por el delito/s de Desafección*, FC-CAUSA_GENERAL, 305, Exp. 35. Imagen 52/60.
13 *Expte. 56*, 34/60.
14 "Detenciones y registros," in *ABC (Madrid)*, 18 April 1937, p. 11.
15 Translated as "Little [Blue] Shirt."
16 *Expte. no. 1189 instruido contra Félix Cirizon [sic] Zarrandicoechea por el delito/s de conspiración y auxilio a la Rebelión*, AHN, FC-CAUSA_GENERAL, 191, Exp. 4. Imagen 71/85.
17 See "Nace la Quinta Columna," in Tarín Iglesias, Manuel (1985) *Los años rojos. Un testimonio capital sobre la Quinta Columna en la zona republican durante la guerra civil* (Barcelona: Espasa), pp. 56–62 at p. 60.
18 Ruiz (2012) *El Terror*, p. 326.
19 Píris, Carlos "Los servicios de información franquistas en la capital," in Gómez Bravo, Gutmaro (ed), at pp. 139–168.
20 *Sumario no. 4/1927 del Juzgado Especial del Tribunal Central de Espionaje no. contra Javier Fernández Golfín y otros*, AHN, FC-CAUSA_GENERAL, 1539, Exp. 1. Imágenes 26/1134. Declaration of the Falangist Juan Manuel de La Aldea, aged twenty-three years dated 8 May 1937. In relation to the mobilisation of some 22,000 Carlist requeté militias across Spain during the first months of the war (front-line and auxiliary) see González Calleja, Eduardo. and Julio Arostegui "La tradición recuperada. El requeté carlista y la insurrección," *Historia Contemporánea*, 11, 1994 pp. 29–53, http://ehu.eus [last accessed on 5 June 2019].
The authors argue that before the war "it was a real militia, but without arms … in March 1936 the key problem was arms," pp. 42–43.
21 This is the subject of a recent post-war historiography. See for example, Anderson, Peter (2010) *The Francoist Military Trials, Terror and Complicity, 1939–45* (Abingdon: Routledge/ Cañada Blanch), Anderson, Peter (2017) *Friend or Foe? Occupation, Collaboration and Selective Violence in the Spanish Civil War* (Sussex: Sussex/Cañada Blanch), Anderson, Peter and del Arco Blanco, Miguel Ángel (eds) (2015) *Mass Killings and Violence in Spain, 1936–1952: Grappling with the Past* (New York, NY: Routledge), Gómez Bravo, Gutmaro (2017) *Geografía humana de la represión franquista, Del golpe a la guerra de ocupación (1936–1941)* (Madrid: Cátedra), Richards, Michael (2013) *After the Civil War, Making Memory and Re-Making Spain since 1936* (New York, NY: CUP), Rodríguez Barreira, Óscar (2013) *Miserias del poder, Los poderes locales y el nuevo estado franquista, 1936–51* (Valencia: PUV).
22 See Bouthelier, Antonio y José López Mora (1940) *8 días. La revuelta comunista. Madrid, 5–13 March 1939* (Madrid: Editora Nacional). See also Cervera (1998), pp. 333–335.
23 Bahamonde, Ángel (2014) *Madrid, 1939* (Madrid: Catedra) ebook, Loc 572 and 909 of 3765.
24 Oral testimony of communist commissar Julia Manzanal Pérez ("Chico") dated 24 July 1996. This Republican woman was a former PCE militant in the Carabanchel district who was appointed as a political commissar within the 5th Regiment's Comuna Batallion on 3 November 1936, cited in Montoliú, Pedro (1999) *Madrid en la Guerra Civil, Los protagonistas, Vol II* (Madrid: Sílex), at p. 253.
25 See in particular Part III in Anderson, Peter (2010) *The Francoist Military Trials, Terror and Complicity, 1939–45* (Oxford: Routledge/Cañada Blanch), pp. 60–107 at p. 89.
26 Interview given by General Franco on 7 November 1938 to the vice-president of the United Press James Miller in Franco Bahamonde, Francisco (1943) Palabras del Caudillo 19 abril 1937–7 diciembre 1942 (Madrid: Ediciones de la Vicesecretaria de Educación

Popular) at p. 476. Cited in Preston, Paul (2016) *The Last Days of the Spanish Republic* (London: William Collins), Kindle Edition at Loc 750 of 7454.

27 Preston, Paul (2016) *The Last Days of the Spanish Republic* (London: William Collins), Kindle Edition at Loc 750 of 7454.

28 Pastor Petit (1978) *Los Dossiers*, p. 269.

29 See witness evidence against Benedicta Lobo Pérez in *Causa instruida contra Jesusa Arnaiz Sandino, Manuel Muro Vázquez, Soledad Portomarín Serrano, José Soria Ortiz, Benedicta Lobo Pérez por el delito/s de Derrotismo*, AHN, FC-CAUSA_GENERAL,148, Exp.61. Imágenes 2-3/158.

30 *Causa no.21 contra Ángel Villa Fernández por delitos de Desafección por tenencia de hoja clandestina*, AHN, FC-CAUSA_GENERAL, 258, Exp. 19. The defendant was acquitted.

31 Heiberg and Ros Agudo (2006) *La Trama*, p. 257 and p. 262.

32 Oral evidence of an anonymous Valencian fifth-columnist, in Pastor Petit, Domenèc (2013) *Resistencia y Sabotaje en la Guerra Civil, Espias, Agentes y Quinta Columnistas* (Barcelona: Argos), cited at p. 429.

33 *Expte. no. 1189 instruido contra Félix Cirizon* [sic] *Zarrandicoechea por el delito/s de conspiración y auxilio a la Rebelión*, AHN, FC-CAUSA_GENERAL, 191, Exp. 4. Imagen 40-41/85.

34 Fal Conde, *Gesto Glorioso del Requete en Madrid* (Julio 1936–Marzo 1939), *Archivo General Militar de Ávila*, C2505, Cp.4/43 and C.2498.20, Legajo no. 285, Carpeta 20, Armario 5.

35 *Nota incompleta relativa a la declaración de Julián Zugazagoitia Mendieta sobre el canje de Raimundo Fernández Cuesta, el Servicio de Expatriación de Republicanos Españoles y el yate 'Vita'*, AHN, FC-CAUSA_GENERAL, 1564, Exp. 2, Imagen 3/5. The prisoner-exchange negotiations were conducted between Burgos, the International Red Cross and Indalecio Prieto and Julián Zugazagoitia. Prieto believed that Fernández Cuesta might be able to assist in the conclusion of a negotiated peace settlement with the Nationalists.

36 In 1938 Bonel's official title became Jefe de la Sección Destacada del SIPM del primer cuerpo de Ejercito (Madrid).

37 Píris, Carlos "Los servicios de información franquistas en la capital," in Gómez Bravo, Gutmaro (ed), pp. 139–168 at p. 150.

38 Alía Miranda, Francisco (2015) "Negrín ante un enemigo 'invisible' la Quinta Columna y su lucha contra la República durante la guerra civil Española (1937–9)," *História y Política*, 33, Madrid (enero–junio 2015), pp. 183–210 at p. 188.

39 Píris, Carlos "Los servicios de información franquistas en la capital," in Gómez Bravo, Gutmaro (ed), pp. 139–168 at p. 156.

40 *Expte. no. 42 contra Daniel Ismael Fernández García, Ángel Naredo Fabian, Herminio Zapico Liebala, Jaime Abad García por el delito/s de Alta Traición, espionaje y derrotismo*, AHN, FC-CAUSA_GENERAL, 154, Exp. 8. Imagen 7/104.

41 The French intelligence services also ignored the involvement of women, even within the 'spheres of welfare aid.'

42 *Archives de la Bibliothèque de Documentation Internationale Contemporaine, Université Paris X Ouest Nanterre: Espagne-Guerre, 1936–9, F.A, 167.* Cited in Francisco Alía Miranda (2017) *La Guerra Civil en Ciudad-Real, conflicto y revolución en una provincia de la retaguardia Republicana* (Ciudad Real: BAM), at p. 320.

43 See Marcot, François "Pour une sociologie de la Résistance: intentionnalité et fonctionnalité," in Prost, Antoine (ed) (1997) *La Résistance, une histoire sociale* (Paris: Atélier/Ouvrières), pp. 21–29. Resistance groups were also formed and organised in accordance with the practical skill-sets required by the groups as well as by the will of resisters to engage in resistance activities.

44 Alcocer, Santos (1976) *La Quinta Columna* (Madrid: G. del Toro), pp. 151–154. Here the author bumps into his friend Adolfo on the corner of calle Ponzano just after having evacuated his safe-house on Gran Vía on account of the bombings in around June 1937. Adolfo offers to replace his fake CNT card with a more useful Communist one and intimates that he has "an interesting job for him to do" in the fifth column which also reveals the improvisational and functionalist aspects of resistance recruitment.

45 Oral testimony of Manuel Valdés Larrañaga dated between 1995 and 1996 as cited in thesis of Javier Cervera Gil (1996) *Violencia política y acción clandestine: la retaguardia de Madrid en Guerra (1936–39)* (Madrid: Universidad Complutense de Madrid), p. 402.

46 *Sumario, No. 4/1937 del Juzgado Especial del Tribunal Central de Espionaje no.1 contra Javier Fernández Golfín y otros*, AHN, FC-CAUSA_GENERAL, 1539, Exp. 1. Imágenes 1134.

47 Fal Conde, *Gesto Glorioso del Requete en Madrid* (Julio 1936–Marzo 1939), *Archivo General Militar de Ávila,* C2505, Cp.4/43 and C.2498.20, Legajo no. 285, Carpeta 20, Armario 5.

48 See "La Quinta Columna y la Falange Clandestina," in Cervera (1998) *Madrid*, pp. 283–337, Píris, Carlos "Los servicios de información franquistas en la capital," at pp. 139–168.

49 Paz, Armando (1976), p. 139.

50 Bahamonde Magro, Ángel, Cervera Gil, Javier (1999) *Así Terminó la Guerra de España* (Madrid: Marcial Pons), p. 247.

51 *Causa 42 instruida contra varias personas por el delito/s de Alta Traición,* AHN, FC-CAUSA_GENERAL, 159, Exp. 1.

52 See *Expte. Instruido contra María Luisa López Ochoa Motta por el delito/s de Espionaje y Alta Traición,* FC-CAUSE_GENERAL, 77, Exp. 22. Imágenes 1-13.

53 *Causa 42 instruida contra varias personas por el delito/s de Alta Traición*, AHN, FC-CAUSA_GENERAL, 159, Exp. 1. Imagen 1862/2519. A former Civil Guard, Emilio Fonseca became an international Red Cross lorry driver after being 'purged' from the Civil Guard in July 1936. He was also implicated in the *Los 195* network.

54 See *Causa 42 instruida contra varias personas por el delito/s de Alta Traición*, AHN, FC-CAUSA_GENERAL, 159, Exp. 1. The barrister Dolores Muñoz Tuero (discussed in Chapter 2) was accused of coaching witnesses in the *Los 195* trial but the charges against her were reduced to *Desafección.* See also, *Causa 25, instruido contra Ricardo Guerra Blanco por el delito/s de Alta Traición, AHN, FC-CAUSA_GENERAL, 145, Exp. 44.* Imágenes 112. Ricardo Guerra Blanco was the President of the *Tribunales Especiales de Guardia* (the emergency military courts courts) who was also accused of conspiring with the Norwegian business attaché Félix Schlayer to aid the escape of fugitives from Madrid.
Causa 59 instruida contra Rogelio Periquet y Rufilanchas por el delito/s de Alta Traición, AHN, FC-CAUSA_GENERAL, 146, Exp. 2. Imágenes 1-95. Periquet was a defence lawyer in the trial of *Los 195.* Periquet was arrested mid-trial in July 1938 and accused of coaching witnesses and attempting to pervert the course of justice (discussed below).

55 Cervera (1998) *Madrid*, p. 289. According to information gathered by SIFNE in dispatch no. 24501 Commander Antonio Rodríguez Sastre was the leader of a fifth-column group within the *Junta de Compras del Ministerio de Guerra.* This man was also involved in the *Organización Golfín-Corujo.*

56 *Expte. no 1071 instruido contra varias personas por el delito/s de Conspiración a la Rebelión*, AHN, FC-CAUSA_GENERAL,197, Exp. 6. This group was also known as "*España Una*" – the group's radio code name. It was led by Antonio del Rosal y López de Vinuesa, and it managed to infiltrate various CNT groups.

57 Ángel Bahamonde has also identified "an abundance of false medical certificates which were certified by Madrid's military medical tribunals which were presided over by Lt. Colonels Antonio Jiménez Arrieta, Clodoaldo Padilla Casas and Emilio Romero Maldonado who formed part of the Clandestine Falange" in Bahamonde, Ángel (2016) *Madrid, 1939, La conjura del coronel Casado* (Madrid: Cátedra), Kindle ed. at Loc 1510 of 3765.

58 Ellwood, Sheelagh "Entrevista con Dolores Muñoz Tuero "Los tribunales populares fueron buena gente," in *Guerra Civil de Historia 16, "Sociedad y Guerra" vol 14* (1986), pp. 125–129 at p. 126.

59 "Ángel Ferrant en la guerra civil," in *Anales de Historia del Arte* (2008) Volumen Extraordinario, pp. 535–555. This article relates to the sculptor Ángel Ferrant (Madrid, 1890–1961) who was, among other titles, President of the Sección de Tesoro Artístico del Consejo Central de Archivos, Bibliotecas y Tesoro Artístico and President of the Junta Delegada del Tesoro Artístico de Madrid (Artistic Treasures Committee) in September

1936. The article discusses Ferrant's arrest by the Republican SIM in May 1937 alongside his brother Alejandro Ferrant and his secretary Francisca Serra for their involvement in the San Francisco el Grande affair. All three were good friends of Francisco Ordeig Ostembach, the leader of this group, but they were rapidly released thanks to the 'frantic intervention' of members of the Artistic Treasures Committee and their discussions with the anarchist Manuel Salgado Moreiro (then head of the Brigada de Servicios Especiales) and General Miaja, at p. 541.

60 *Expte. 1344*, Imagen 3/12.

61 Proportionally, 30% were infiltrated in the Civil Guards, 43% in the Assault Guards and 27% in the carabineers. Source: Cervera, Javier "Infiltración del quintacolumnismo y espionaje en el orden public y seguridad republicanas," *Diacronie, Studi di Storia Contemporanea: La voce del silenzio: intelligence, spionaggio e conflitto nel XX secolo*, 28 (April, 2016), www.studistorici.com/2016/12/29/cervera_gil_numero_28 [last accessed 1 June 2017], pp. 1–25 at p. 10.

62 Cervera, Javier "Infiltración del quintacolumnismo y espionaje en el orden public y seguridad republicanas," at p. 10.

63 Heiberg and Agudo (2008) *La Trama*, p. 262.

64 Píris (2018), p. 158.

65 For a detailed, 'fine-grained' examination of the uses of selective violence 'from below' in the identification and classification of Franco's defeated 'enemies' in the post-war see Anderson, Peter (2017) *Friend or Foe? Occupation, Collaboration and Selective Violence in the Spanish Civil War* (Sussex: Sussex/Cañada Blanch).

66 Píris (2018), p. 161.

67 See Ruiz, Julius (2005) *Franco's Justice: Repression in Madrid after the Spanish Civil War* (Oxford: OUP). Anderson, Peter (2010) *The Francoist Military Trials, Terror and Complicity, 1939–45* (Abingdon: Routledge/Cañada Blanch).

68 DGS Report dated [June 1937] in *Sumario no 4/1937 del Juzgado Especial del Tribunal Central de Espionaje no. 1 contra Javier Fernández Golfín y otros,* AHN, FC-CAUSA_GENERAL, 1539, Exp. 1 Imagen 880/1134.

69 See Marcot, François "Pour une sociologie de la Résistance: intentionnalité et fonctionnalité," in Prost, Antoine (ed) (1997) *La Résistance, une histoire sociale* (Paris: Atélier/Ouvrières), pp. 21–29.

70 "Detenciones," *ABC (Madrid)*, Sunday, 18 April 1937, p. 10.

71 *Expte. no. 1189 instruido contra Félix Cirizon [sic] Zarrandicoechea por el delito/s de conspiración y auxilio a la Rebelión*, AHN, FC-CAUSA_GENERAL,191, Exp. 4.

72 *Expte. no. 46 intruido contra varias personas por el delitos de Alta traición,* AHN, FC-CAUSA_GENERAL, 156 Exp 53 Imagen 72/668.

73 *Causa 42*, AHN, FC-CAUSA_GENERAL, 159, Exp.1. Trial Testimony of Carlos Alfonso Sanz Imágenes, 1979-80/2519.

74 For example, see *Causa 31 instruida contra Estebán Calleja Verdejo, Eutiquio González Rubio, José Ojeda Gamez por delito/s de Traición*, AHN, FC-CAUSA_GENERAL, 149, Exp. 11. This trial dated 8 June 1938 involved three prison guards who were accused of treason for aiding and abetting the prison escape of Miguel Pereda Pelayo. See also, *Expte. no. 46 contra varias personas por delito/s de Alta Traición*, AHN, FC-CAUSA_GENERAL, 156, Exp. 53. Imágenes 40-3/668.

75 *Causa 30 instruida contra María Juana Escalonilla Peña, Francisca Escalonilla Peña por el delito/s de Alta Traición*, AHN, FC-CAUSA_GENERAL, 155, Exp. 43. Imágenes 6/28 See also, *Causa 46, Imagen 51-52/668*, Declaration of Francisca Escalonilla Peña dated 2 August 1938.

76 *Causa no. 30, Imagen 27/8.*

77 *Expte. 42 instruido contra varias personas por el delito/s de Alta Traición, espionaje y derrotismo*, AHN, FC-CAUSA_GENERAL, 154, Exp.1. SIM report dated March 1938, Imagen 249/250.

78 *Expte. 42*, SIM report dated March 1938, Imagen 249/250.

79 *Causa 42 instruida contra varias personas por el delito/s de Alta Traición, espionaje y derrotismo*, AHN, FC-CAUSA_GENERAL, 159, Exp.1. Witness testimony of Antonio Martínez Peinado (aged thirty-seven years) dated 25 May 1938. Imagen 282/2519.
80 *Causa 42*, AHN, FC-CAUSA_GENERAL, 159, Exp.1. Imagen 282/2519. Witness testimony of Antonio Martínez Peinado dated 25 May 1938. He worked as a CNT security guard.
81 *Causa 42*, Witness statement of Francisca Martínez Ramírez, Imagen 48/2519
82 *Causa 42*, Sentencing report dated 18 July 1938, Imágenes 2215-6/2519.
83 *Causa 42*, Witness statement of Antonio Martínez Peinado, Imagen 282/2519.
84 *Causa 42*, Witness statement of Francisca Martínez Ramírez dated 17 April 1938, Imagen 49/2519
85 *Causa 42*, Trial testimony of Francisca Martínez Ramírez, Imagen, 1944/2519.
86 *Causa 42*, Witness statement of Francisca Martínez Ramírez, Imágen 46/2519
87 *Causa 42*, Trial testimony of Francisca Martínez Ramírez, Imágenes 1945/2519.
88 *Causa 42*, Witness statement of Francisca Martínez Ramírez, Imágen 43/2519.
89 *Causa 42*, Witness statement of Francisca Martínez Ramírez, Imagen 46/2519
90 Juliá, Santos (ed) (1999) *Víctimas de la guerra civil* (Madrid: Temas de Hoy), pp. 361–337
91 *Causa 42*, Witness statement of Manuel Villafranca Muñoz dated 9 May 1938, Imagen 79-81/2519
92 *Causa 42*, Witness statement of Jeronimo López Batanero dated 7 April 1938, Imagen 55-6/2519
93 *Causa 42*, Witness statement of Francisca Martínez Ramírez, Imagen 46/2519
94 *Causa 42*, Trial testimony of Commander Carlos Alfonso Sanz, Imágenes 1979-80/2519.
95 Yusta, Rodrigo, Mercedes (2005) *La guerra de los vencidos, El maquis en el Maestrazgo turolense, 1940–1950* (Zaragoza: IFC). This author makes these observations in relation to the conduct of Francoist trials against female members of the Maquis, see pp. 115–117.
96 *Causa 42*, Testimony of Francisca Martínez Ramírez Imágen 41/2519.
97 *Causa 42*, Letter into Court in Defence of Francisca Martínez Ramírez dated 12 July 1938, 1651/2519.
98 Bahamonde Magro, Ángel, Cervera, Javier (1999) *Así terminó la guerra de España* (Marcial Pons: Barcelona), p. 247.
99 *Causa 42*, Witness statement of Antonia Lario Alonso dated 6 April 1938, Imágen 109-112/2519.
100 *Causa 42*, Witness statement of Jeronimo López Batanero dated 7 April 1938, Imágen 55-6/2519.
101 *Causa 42*, Imagen 1927/2519. Trial testimony of Jeronimo López Batanero, Imagen 1928/2519.
102 *Causa 42*, Witness statement of Antonia Lario Alonso dated 5 April 1938, Imágen 111/2519.
103 *Causa 42*, Witness statement of Dr Lorenzo Méndez Calvo dated 5 April 1938, Imágen 55-6/2519.
104 *Causa 42*, Witness statement of Antonia Lario Alonso dated 5 April 1938, Imagen 111/2519
105 *Sumario no 4/1937 del Juzgado Especial del Tribunal Central e Espionaje no 1 Contra Javier Fernández Golfín y otros*, FC-CAUSA_GENERAL, 1539, Exp. 1.
106 *Causa 42*, Witness statement of Antonia Lario Alonso dated 5 April 1938, Imagen 110/2519
107 See Chapter 4, Espinosa Romero, Jesús "La delegación del estado para la recuperación de documentos en Madrid," in Oviedo Silva, Daniel, Pérez-Olivares García, Alejandro (eds) (2016) *Madrid, una ciudad en guerra (1936–48)* (Madrid: Catarata), p. 140.
108 *Causa 42*, Witness statement of Antonia Lario Alonso dated 5 April 1938, Imagen 111-12/2519.
109 *Causa 42*, Trial testimony of Dolores López Mendizábal, Imágen 1960/2519.

110 *Causa 42*, Witness statement of Dolores López Mendizábal dated 5 April 1938, Imagen 105/2519.

111 *Causa 42*, Witness statement of Dolores López Mendizábal dated 5 April 1938, Imagen 106/2519.

112 *Causa 42*, Trial testimony of Carmen de Blas Aranteguí, Imagen 197-78/2519.

113 Alberto Vargas Laguna in *La Razón de Domingo* dated 10 February 2013 at http.//*Larazon.es* [last accessed 5 May 2017].

114 *Expte. 42, contra Daniel Ismael Fernández* García, *Ángel Naredo Fabian, Herminio Zapico Liebala, Jaime Abad García por el delito/s de Alta Traición, espionaje y derrotismo*, AHN, FC-CAUSA_GENERAL, 154, Exp. 8. Imagen 5/104.

115 *Causa 42*, Witness statement of José Banús Masdeu dated 5 April 1938, Imagen 32/2519.

116 José Banús Masdeu became a wealthy and prominent property developer after the war. His influence and contacts within the Francoist regime ensured that he was granted the necessary licences and permissions to develop the coastal town of Puerto Banús among other significant developments.

117 *Causa 42*, Witness statement of José Banús Masdeu dated 5 April 1938, Imagen 32/2519.

118 *Sumario no 81/1938 del Juzgado Especial por espionaje y otros delitos contra la seguridad exterior del estado contra Antonio Rodríguez Aguado y otros*, FC-CAUSA_GENERAL, 1540, Exp. 1 and 1542, Exp. 1.

119 *Causa 42*, Imagen 1930/2519. Transcript of interrogation of José Banús Masdeu dated May 1938.

120 *Causa 42*, Witness statement of José Moreno Ciges dated 5 April 1938, Imágenes 1934-5/2519.

121 "La causa contra los ciento novento y cinco, veintitres penas de muerte," *ABC (Madrid)*, 3 August 1938, p. 4. http://hemeroteca.abc.es/nav/Navigate.exe/hemeroteca/madrid/abc/1938/08/03/005.html. But see different death penalty figures provided by Ángel Bahamonde and Cervera Gil in (1999) *Así terminó la guerra*, p. 247.

122 *ABC (Madrid)*, 3 August 1938, p. 4.

123 Source: Alberto Vargas Laguna in *La Razón de Domingo* dated 10 February 2013 at http.//*Larazon.es* [last accessed 5 May 2017].

124 Obituary of Pedro Marquina, *ABC (Madrid)*, 29 December 1966 (husband of de Blas).

125 Obituary of Carmen de Blas Aranteguí, *ABC (Madrid)*, 20 November 1986.

126 *Causa 79 instruida contra Pilar del Olmo Sánchez por el delito/s de Espionaje*, AHN, FC-CAUSA_GENERAL, 146, Exp. 42. Imágenes 1-27. The defendant was initially charged on counts of espionage and treason. Del Olmo was absolved of espionage on 19 August 1938 because the court found no evidence that she was "an agent" for the organisation; "she had never donated to it or received funds from it or practiced as an active member or propagandist for the said auxiliary organization." Imagen 25/27. The case was referred by the Judge Francisco Serraller to the lower courts on counts of disaffection.

127 *Expte. no 503 instruido contra Pilar del Olmo Sanchesz por el delito/s de Desafección al Régimen*, AHN, FC-CAUSA_GENERAL, 320, Exp. 24. Imagen 4/25. The trial for disaffection was never concluded. Pilar was released on provisional bail on 20 September 1938.

128 María Felisa Parés, twenty-seven years old, was a shirt maker by profession and the "Group L" Leader within Auxilio Azul; one of the members of her group, Teresa Juanena Ayuso (code name 1-L-3), was also involved in "Los 163" Group in May 1938 but was acquitted and subsequently joined Auxilio Azul (see Chapter 2).

129 *Causa 42*, AHN, FC-CAUSA_GENERAL, 159, Exp. 1. Imagen 2267/2519.

130 *Expte. 145 instruido contra Julia Martí de Tortajada, Josefa Tortajada Ortola por delito/s de desafección al Régimen*, AHN, FC_CAUSA_GENERAL, 179, Exp. 11. Imagen 3/68.

131 *Expte. 42 intruido contra varias personas por el delito/s de Alta Traición, espionaje y derrotismo*, AHN, FC-CAUSA, GENERAL, 154, Exp. 10, Imagen 56/136. See letter to the tribunal dated 11 January 1939 from Doctors Fernando Pérez Rodríguez and Diego González

Bernal (forensic medics for tribunals no. 10 and 4 respectively). Her male co-defendant was diagnosed with a much less obscure medical condition:
"With respect to the defendant Fermín García Ortega, we must disclose that it was not possible to practice a thorough examination of his ear for lack of the necessary equipment although a visual observation would confirm that there is a great deal of wax in his right ear which must be concealing a perforated ear drum."

132 This officer claimed that there were around 100 armed fifth-columnists who were embedded within the War Ministry and prepared to take over this building during a Francoist occupation.

133 *Archivo General Militar de Ávila*, C2505, Cp.4/43 and C.2498.20, Legajo no. 285, Carpeta 20, Armario 5, Imagen 2/20.

134 Oviedo Silva, Daniel and Pérez-Olivares García (eds) (2016) *Madrid, una ciudad en guerra (1936–48)*, p. 142.

135 *Expte. no 39 (bis) instruido contra Pilar Ovejas Ovejas, Alberto Castilla Olavarría por el delito/s de Espionaje*, AHN, FC-CAUSA_GENERAL, 77, Exp. 7.

136 Graham, Helen (2002) *The Spanish Republic at War* (Cambridge: CUP), p. 342.

137 Pastor Petit, Domenèc (2006) *Traidors a Catalunya, La cinquena columna (1936–9)*, p. 69.

138 *Servicios de la Frontera Nordeste de España.*

139 *Sumario no 4/1937 del Juzgado Especial del Tribunal de Espionaje no1. Contra Javier Fernández Golfín y otros*, AHN, FC_CAUSA_GENERAL, 1539, Exp. 104/1134

140 Cervera (1998) *Madrid*, at pp. 300–306. See also Ruiz (2012) *El Terror*, pp. 333–334 and 350, Rieger Max (1937) *Espionaje en España* (Madrid: Espuela de Plata).

141 *Sumario no 4/1937*, Imagen 104/1134. Statement of Ignacio Corujo López-Villaamil dated 19 May 1937.

142 *Sumario no 4/1937*, Imagen 5/1134. Report of the *Comisaria General de Investigación y Vigilancia* report dated 11 July 1937.

143 *Sumario no 4/1937*, Imagen 33/1134. Witness statement of Gerardo Sanz Rubert dated 9 May 1937.

144 Imagen 21/1134. Witness Statement of Augustin Aguirre Enriquez dated 7 May 1937. For an analysis of the activities of Juan Manuel de la Aldea, see Moreno Cantano, Antonio César "Quintacolumnismo y guerra civil en Madrid: La trayectoria del Falangista Juan Manuel de la Aldea," *Aportes*, 83, año XXVIII (3/2013), pp. 53–68. The article uses biographical frames in order to examine Juan Manuel de la Aldea Ruifernández Gracia's activities as a fifth-column spy and saboteur and his subsequent lived experiences of detention, torture and imprisonment in May 1937 using his own unpublished typescript memoire and Causa General archives.

145 Imagen 6/1134.

146 *Asesoría Jurídica*, Testimony of Matilde Casáñ Pablo dated 14 October 1939, *Carpeta* B 12. Source: www.plataforma2003.org [last accessed 21 February 2017]. The full reference for this ANA document was not provided on the website.

147 Imagen 59/1134.

148 Imágenes 793/1134.

149 Imagen 794/1134.

150 Imagen 795/1134.

151 Imagen 6/1134.

152 Imagen 796/1134. Statement of María Teresa Abarzuza y Robles dated July 1937.

153 Imagen 6/1134

154 Imagen 796/1134.

155 Imagen 6/1134. Declaration of Sofía Espeso Luengo, widow aged thirty-eight years dated 8 July 1937.

156 Imagen 101/1134. Declaration of Manuel Espeso Luengo (aged twelve) dated 8 July 1937.

157 Imágenes 89/1134 and 98/1134. Evidence of Sofía Luengo Arras who was 'interviewed at home because she was confined to her bed' and María Teresa Abarzuza respectively.
158 Imagen 797/1134.
159 Imagen 799/1134.
160 Cervera (1998) *Madrid*, p. 290.
161 Paz, Armando (1976) *Los servicios de espionaje en la guerra civil de España (1936–9)* (Madrid: San Martín), p. 143.
162 Antonio Rodríguez Aguados' escape-line network paid these sums in Republican *pesetas* to local peasant guides in 1937, see Laguna Reyes, Alberto and Vargas Márquez, Antonio (2019) *La Quinta Columna, La guerra clandestina tras las líneas republicanas 1936–1939* (Madrid: Laesfera), ebook at p. 161.
163 *Causa no. 24 instruida contra varias personas por el delito/s de Alta Traición*, AHN, FC-CAUSA_GENERAL, 155, Exp. 34.
164 *Causa no. 24*, Imagen 4/163.
165 *Causa no. 24*, Imagen 3/163.
166 *Causa no. 24*, Imagen 4/163.This former Assault Guard was invalided out of service at the start of the war. He escaped from Madrid in late 1936.
167 *Causa no. 24*, Imagen 3/163.
168 Imagen 4/163.
169 Imagen 4/163.
170 *Expte. 46 instruida contra varias personas por el delito/s de Alta Traición*, AHN, FC-CAUSA_GENERAL, 156, Exp. 53, Imágenes 52-55/668. Interrogation report of Esperanza Ortega Cebrían dated 2 August 1938.
171 *Expte. 46*, Imagen 89/668.
172 *Expte. 46*, Imagen 26/668.
173 Expte. 46, Imagen 8/668.
174 *Expte. 46*, Imágenes 33/668 and 40/668.
175 *Expte. 46*, Imagen 27/668. Interrogation report of the informants Jaime Rosello Rotlán, Fernando Téllez Casquero and Samuel de Lucas Pérez dated 27 July 1938.
176 *Expte. 46*, Imágenes 26/668.
177 *Expte. 46*, Imágenes 27-8/668. Testimony of the three informants dated 27 July 1938.
178 *Expte. 46*, Imagen 204/668.
179 *Expte. no. 1189 instruido contra Félix Cirizon [sic] Zarrandicoechea por el delito/s de conspiración y auxilio a la Rebelión*, AHN, FC-CAUSA_GENERAL, 191, Exp. 4.
180 *Expte. 1189*, Imagen 8/85.
181 *Expte. 1189*, Imagen 36/85.
182 *Expte. 1189*, Imagen 67/85.
183 *ABC (Madrid)*, Sunday, 18 April 1937, p. 11.
184 Expte. 1679, Witness statement of Miguel Ichaurrondo Arriaran, Imagen 12/1733.
185 *ABC (Madrid)*, dated 18 May 1951. Obituary of Doña Ángeles Orozco Viuda de del Riego.
186 Scott, Joan W. "Gender a Useful Category of Historical Analysis," *The American Historical Review*, 91 (5) (1986), pp. 1053–1075 at p. 1067.
187 Galíndez, Jesus de (2005) (first ed 1945) *Los Vascos en el Madrid sitiado* (Tafalla, Navarra: Txalaparta), p. 151.
188 Ruiz (2012) *El Terror*, p. 327.
189 Rodríguez López, Sofía and Cazorla Sánchez, Antonio "Blue Angels: Female Fascist Resisters, Spies and Intelligence Officials in the Spanish Civil War, 1936–9," *Journal of Contemporary History*, 53 (4) (2016), pp. 692–713 at p. 712.
190 Ramón y Cajal, Santiago, Nelken, Margarita (1938) *La mujer* (Madrid: M. Águilar). This collection of traditional and bio-medical 'aphorisms' on 'the nature of women' reflects

the entrenched misogyny of this period and women's habitual interiorisation of symbolic violence. The feminist Nelken lends her name to this imprint.

191 Cervera (1998) *Madrid*, p. 171.

192 See *Expte. no. 46 contra varias personas por delito/s de Alta Traición*, AHN, FC-CAUSA_GENERAL, 156, Exp. 53. (discussed above) and *Asesoría Jurídica*, Testimony of María del Carmen Carnicero Espino [1939], Document 239, ANA, Carpeta B 12, RAH, Madrid.

193 Píris (2018), p. 159.

Part 2

The women in Madrid's autonomous fifth-column resistance

4 Traitors and rebels

Part 2 examines Madrid's 'autonomous fifth column' which was composed of dozens of small groups and hundreds of individuals who performed acts of dissidence and subversion in the rear-guard independently from the organised groups and networks. This chapter examines civilian resistance from Republican legal and retributive matrices. Most of the cases discussed below were heard in the *Tribunales Especiales de Guardia* established in 1938. Meanwhile, the lesser tribunals (*Jurados de Urgencia*) operated from 1936 and determined crimes of disaffection of which around 44% were expedited between October 1936 and March 1937.[1] These new tribunals were established in order to identify enemies of the state and classify their crimes in ascending order of severity from disaffection and defeatism to crimes of high treason, military rebellion and espionage.

As indicated in the introduction, the concept of civilian resistance has been transformed by new histories 'from below' that have identified types of informal resistance which fall outside traditional parameters of organised and armed resistance. Such resistance includes types of economic, passive, popular and everyday resistance.[2] The autonomous fifth-column resistance examined here mainly involved individuals and small groups of on average between five to twelve persons. The resisters were united by their ideological opposition to the Republican regime and were prepared to do whatever was in their means to sabotage and impede the war effort. Some of the groups were connected to but not actively involved in the Clandestine Falange networks discussed in Part 1, and they seldom had any direct contact with Franco's nationalist intelligence services. Nevertheless, these fifth-columnists also courted risk and personal danger. Their actions constituted a 'cloud of gestures' that helped to sustain a 'climate of resistance' supportive of the organised resistance efforts.[3] This autonomous resistance may be categorised as '*resistenz*' rather than armed or organised political resistance and is conceptualised in 'shades of grey' for it arose from a variety of complex personal, political, religious motivations that also imbricated forms of accommodation and survivalist practices.[4] It included passive resistance such as practicing the

Catholic rites in private (which was never illegal) or performing the Falangist raised-arm salute in the home space while continuing to use the Republican closed-fist salute in public.[5] Military desertion also falls into this grey area as the actors were often motivated as much by self-preservation as by political impulses.

Forms of spontaneous civilian resistance arose immediately after 18 July 1936 within pre-existing associational, professional, friendship and neighbourhood groups.[6] This type of unarmed civilian resistance should be distinguished from the isolated skirmishes of the '*pacos*' (pro-rebel snipers) during summer and autumn 1936 whose futile resistance gestures represented the final death throes of a failed military coup rather than the beginnings of any organised armed resistance.[7] According to the leaders of Madrid's Defence Junta the *pacos* posed little threat to the Republican regime.[8] There is evidence that women aided and abetted the snipers who fired at the Republican militias from the balconies of private buildings. For example, Dolores Alonzo Zarzuela and her daughter Zoraida Cardenas Alonso were arrested in November 1936 after Zoraida's husband was charged with 'military rebellion' for engaging in '*pacoteo*' from the family home.[9] These isolated acts of terrorism only served to confirm the popular but misplaced fears of a dangerous hidden enemy within "comprised of Falangist *señoritos* and UME officers."[10] The isolated sniper attacks tailed off after December 1936 when it became evident that Franco's troops had failed in their efforts to occupy the capital.

In contrast, the autonomous resistance discussed below was a socially and culturally significant phenomenon that lasted for the duration of the war and embraced a spectrum of Spanish society that was united by its Catholicism and a deep resentment and hostility towards the Republican regime. Because the resisters were most often neighbours, friends and colleagues there was little need for the use of sophisticated security checks, code-names or complex organisational structures. Members were well-known to each other and naturally came across each other on a regular basis. Clandestine meetings took place within the framework of everyday routines and habits, and often without attracting any undue suspicion. Paradoxically, the resisters were self-appointed 'people of order' (*personas de orden*) whose declared aims were to 'subvert, sabotage and disrupt daily life in as many ways as possible.' The key objectives were to avoid conscription, lower civilian morale and generally undermine the Republican war effort.

Forms of active resistance included safe-housing fugitives and draft-dodgers, sabotaging military equipment and falsifying identification documentation, as well as stock-piling controlled or restricted items (*acaparamiento*), diverting goods from official supply depots and the dissemination of false or defeatist rumours (*propalar bulas*) derived from censored Nationalist radio broadcasts.[11] Another aim was to perform acts of everyday sabotage that might impede the routine functioning of Republican institutions.[12] According to the popular tribunal archives examined here, there was scant large-scale commercial, industrial or military sabotage. Frequently, such charges were based on flimsy and unfounded allegations that resulted in acquittals.[13] These findings are in line with the earlier historiography,[14] although there are instances of industrial and military sabotage in the military archives.[15] Out of a total of 14,862 popular tribunal cases some 366 involved the illegal possession of arms including twenty-seven cases which related to the illegal possession of explosives.[16] Small-scale military or industrial sabotage cases included the following: (1) "various acts of sabotage" perpetrated in an armaments factory by four German nationals following a denunciation by the factory director,[17] (2) a small number of firearms were damaged by disaffected soldiers,[18] (3) an alleged attempt to sabotage the National Electricity company,[19] (4) the severing of a communications cable situated between a communications hut and a front-line trench,[20] and (5) the deliberate sabotage of fuel supplies belonging to the 111 Mixed Brigade.[21]

The autonomous resistance provided like-minded friends with safe spaces within which to conserve morale, rally to a common cause and passively resist. Clandestine meetings generally took place in the private domestic space, less frequently in public spaces such as bars and cafés and parks, in contrast with the practices of the organised Falange groups who were often required to liaise with strangers and operate under code-names. Large reunions (whether to celebrate Nationalist victories or clandestine masses) were dangerous because they might attract the suspicion of the roving security militias, neighbourhood invigilation committees and building security committees. The watchful gaze of the concierges and of vigilant members of the local housing committee also represented a substantive threat. The archives indicate that large dissident gatherings and dinner-parties, in particular after Nationalist victories, attracted suspicion, denunciation and criminal sanctions. Gathering in secret to listen to censored Nationalist radio broadcasts also became one of the most powerful forms of passive resistance.[22] *Desafectos* imagined these resistance activities, in particular the clandestine masses celebrating Nationalist victories, as positive symbolic contributions to Franco's holy Catholic crusade. Such practices represented potentially dangerous forms of political contestation in circumstances where prominent anti-Republicans were forced into hiding and denied full citizenship rights including employment, voting and pension rights.

The autonomous resistance involved forms of everyday resistance strategies which have been defined as a "disguised, diffuse and invisible subaltern resistance that constitutes a type of infra politics that is deployed by individuals or groups in order to both survive and undermine repression in circumstances where rebellion is too risky."[23] The legal records revealed a wide range of strategies of evasion and avoidance, draft-dodging and desertion, foot-dragging at work, disloyalty, non-compliance with government orders, ration and identity card fraud and black market activities. The 'body' also constituted a fertile site of resistance. All manner of diseases, feigned and real, mental and physical were adduced, often with the collusion of sympathetic trial lawyers and medics, as evidence in order to suspend popular tribunal trials or to obtain conditional releases.[24] To the great advantage of many of the female defendants, various gender-specific psycho-pathologies and illnesses were presented to the tribunals by skilful lawyers as evidence in mitigation in order to reduce or avoid lengthy prison sentences.

While outside the scope of this work, it is important to contextualise and observe that Madrid's fragmented and polarised civil society often shared similar material hardships and adversities and ideological enemies were obliged to devise strategies for peaceful cohabitation and accommodation within familial and friendship networks and local neighbourhood groups. This is reflected in the memories of a Falangist draft-evader who recalled a peaceable and routine life in Madrid after June 1937 involving the usual round of social engagements, birthday parties and saint's day celebrations where Republican friends were invited to dance and sing together so long as no one brought up the subject of politics or the war.[25] While almost all civilians across the religious, political and ideological spectrum recalled experiences of extreme hunger, material deprivation and endless food queues during the thirty-two months of total war in the capital, there were also opportunities for merriment, dancing and frequent cinema visits.[26] In significant ways daily life continued as normal despite the conflict and a wary accommodation arose between Republican and anti-Republican friends and neighbours. The tribunal cases discussed below reveal the multiple strategies and uses of 'intimate violence,' but also how obligations of kinship and friendship frequently cut across ideological divides.

Treason

Approximately 2.4% of the total 14,862 popular tribunal cases related to crimes of treason. The majority of these cases related to draft-dodgers and military deserters who were charged individually, in pairs or in small groups. Out of some 364 treason cases only twenty-one cases of 'high treason' and three 'treason' cases related exclusively to women. In the majority of cases women were accused of aiding and abetting intimates or family members who were deserters or conscription avoiders. There were around sixty-eight group trials involving five or more persons, and most often these cases related to acts of desertion or conscription avoidance. Of these, some twenty cases also involved female defendants and fourteen of these related to the Clandestine Falange groups discussed in Chapter 3. Consequently, when women were accused of high treason or treason they were most often involved with the Clandestine Falange. The most committed female resisters were ardent Falangists (*Falangistas de Corazón*) and Catholic women who chose to join the Falangist networks discussed in Part 1.

False documentation

False identification documentation and good-character vouchsafes (*avales*) were important for the survival of Madrid's clandestine community.[27] A lucrative black-market in false passports, identification documents, political party and union membership cards and ration cards arose in response to this new demand. In May 1938, a group of eleven individuals aged between forty and fifty-eight years (including four women) were arrested and charged with high treason; only six went on to trial. The case was known in the local media as *El Asunto de los Carnets*. The group generated fake documentation and safe-housed fugitives for payment. One of the leaders, Josefa Miguélez Peña, was a former estate agent and member of Acción Popular. Her husband, Joaquín Latas Folgueira, was also a member of this Catholic party and a landlord who 'had never worked' and was currently in litigation with his bank over a mortgage default relating to tenanted properties. Carlos Viña Campa was a committed Falangist, and another defendant was a nun. The leader, Juan Díez Rodríguez, had been made redundant from the Orbaz Light factory before the war but remained a prominent member of Central Syndicate of the UGT (Varied Works Division) since joining in 1919. The defendants lived centrally in calles Claudio Coello, Ayala and Alcalá. They were arrested on 3 May by SIM agents and accused of high treason for "the falsification of syndical and political documents, hiding disaffected persons and passive resistance to government orders."[28] The men were taken to Porlier and the women to Ventas pending trial on 3 June 1938 in the *Tribunal Especial de Guardia, Juzgado No. 1*.

Juan Díez Rodríguez supplied false character vouchsafes, union cards and passports to "notoriously disaffected persons [in exchange for cash] and such persons were thereby able to avoid the sanctions of the tribunals."[29] Díez also committed acts of perjury by standing as a good-character witness for complete strangers in political trials. He was able to obtain blank, lost or stolen UGT membership cards and other union cards and passports through a variety of (unidentified) Republican contacts. His wife Elvira Rodríguez Borbolla was an accomplice. The former Acción Popular members Josefa Miguélez Peña and her husband Joaquín Latas Folguera sourced the clients. Miguélez' case was aggravated because she had demonstrated "a manifest preference for the government of Order and believed that Generals Goded and Fanjul were technically proficient and knew how to keep everyone in line."[30] This couple worked alongside José Ramón Tarrazo Gómez and a fifty-eight-year-old widow named Serafina Lecaros Salazar who was a free-lance manicurist and a Peruvian national who enjoyed the protection of the Peruvian Embassy. Her job enabled to her to circulate between embassies and private homes. She was also a devout Catholic who had safe-housed nuns in 1936 at great personal risk. The group sourced its clients within embassy, local neighbourhood and prison networks. The clients either wanted to avoid criminal sanctions or needed false credentials for employment reasons. The Falangist Carlos Viña Campa was found in possession of an incriminating hand-written note indicating that he had visited Antonia Lario (a member of Los 195), at the request of her sister, while Antonia was being held at the Naval Office (Ministerio de la Marina).[31] The members also met potential clients at *Bar Retiro*. One of the go-betweens (who passed money and documents) was a forty-year-old nun named Augustina López Prieto who was evacuated from her convent in 1936 and now lived undercover with Lecaros as a domestic. The racket in false documents was a lucrative business, and fees varied depending on the client's financial means or connection with the group; some clients only provided IOUs which would be settled after the conflict.

The group was dismantled by the SIM after it was discovered that a popular tribunal defendant had approached an 'intermediary named Gordizar' who then put him in contact with Lecaros who then passed him on to Díez who ultimately provided him with safe-housing and a false union card for the large sum of 1,700 pesetas (the intermediaries also received introduction fees).[32] During interrogation Díez was unable to recall the number of false documents generated since July 1936. He testified that "Josefina [sic] Miguélez Peña approached me because she knew that I was a longstanding affiliate of the UGT." This testifies to the functionalist aspects of resistance practice.[33] The group had 'helped' many individuals including Enrique Corral Águila, who, according to Josefa Miguélez, was Antonio Goicoechea's former right-hand man, and also many "people who had never worked before":

> she [Josefa] put me in touch with her brother in law who was a doctor and also a friend of Viña Campa … I also obtained a union card for José María López Torres … and received 50 pesetas for this, from Alfonso Múñoz González the ex-marquis of Tarancón 75 pesetas … José María López Torres who was being persecuted for his right-wing ideas was safe-housed in my home and provided with documents for 300 pesetas … I also intervened in the case of Juan Iglesias who was accused of being a priest, he was released without doubt because of my good-character vouchsafe for which I received 150 pesetas … I also provided another vouchsafe for Dr Medina who worked in the Muncipal Benefits Office (Beneficiencia Municipal) who wanted a promotion, and I got 204 pesetas from him which I gave to Josefina Miguélez … when asked about a manuscript note which referred to "the notes in series A and B from 100 pesetas to 2 million pesetas and the 50 peseta and 25 peseta notes of series A,B,C and D" he answered that Josefa Miguélez had told him that these notes would be valid when 'the others' got in.[34]

The prosecution proposed a life-sentence for Díez Rodríguez and lengthy terms for the other five defendants. Díez was eventually sentenced to twenty years in a labour camp on 10 August 1938. Josefa Miguélez Peña, her husband Juan Latas Folgueira, Serafina Lecaros Salazar and Carlos Viña Campos were each sentenced to six years imprisonment. The nun Augustina Prieto López and Díez's wife, Elvira Rodríguez Borbolla, were absolved.[35] Elvira "blamed Josefa Miguélez for getting her husband into trouble … he was a good man who had acted out of necessity … and helped persecuted persons" and claimed that "she had had no idea whatsoever about her husband's business affairs as she always kept herself to the kitchen."[36] Luckily for Elvira 'the kitchen' represented a safe space from the reprisals of the tribunal which accepted her testimony. She was acquitted of all charges. It is hard to comprehend how this defendant might have been entirely ignorant of her husband's treasonous and lucrative business affairs. Nonetheless, the negative privileges and compensations arising from patriarchal domination served Elvira well in this instance. Republican gender prejudices and assumptions regarding women's inferior mental, emotional and intellectual abilities informed judicial attitudes towards the levels of knowledge, understanding, guilt and complicity of female defendants.[37]

El Asunto de los Carnets was an exceptional case because it involved an organised criminal network which operated over a sustained period and managed to distribute hundreds of false documents for profit. The network also safe-housed fugitives and liaised with popular tribunal defence lawyers like Victorino Gómez Jiménez who had success in obtaining the acquittal and release of *desafectos*. However, crimes relating to the distribution or purchase of false documents on the black market most often constituted 'one-off' transactions rather than sustained organised activities. In addition, most civilians were obliged to have recourse to black-market activities at some stage or another whatever their political complexion.

In May 1938 six persons were arrested and accused of high treason in the emergency military court (*Tribunal Especial de Guardia no.1*) for 'aiding military desertion, defeatism and document fraud.'[38] The group included a conscription evader named Joaquín Ortíz Fernández Montes aged thirty-six years who was a member of the Izquierda Republicana (Left Republican party) and former editor of the *Nueva República* newspaper. His father and girlfriend, Felipa Sancho Cano Téllez, were also arrested. Felipa had threatened to break up with him 'unless he legalized his situation' and efforts were made to obtain a false work permit.[39] Felipa lived in a boarding house in calle San Bartolomé, 12 which was owned by an unemployed seamstress named Concepción ("Concha") Martín Buitrago (aged fifty) who had previously worked at Almacenes Félix Gómez. Concha had known Joaquín Ortíz for many years because both had grown up in the small village of Herencia. Ortíz was safe-housed with Concha until May 1937, and it was Concha who asked her friend Arturo Barrios[40] for a false work-permit for Ortíz. With this aim, Barrios contacted his brother in law, Pedro Chamorro Muñoz, who owned a small leather factory in calle Hernán Cortés, 5, and he in turn asked José Jurado Escalona who owned a leather shop in calle del Carmen, 12. According to Barrio 'there was a certain amount of friendship between the families,' and this statement indicates how obligations of friendship and loyalty also informed participation in illegal and risky practices.[41] The defendants were all charged with high treason.[42] Concha was accused of defeatism (she 'often spoke badly of the Republic') and of conducting clandestine meetings with soldiers with the intention of aiding conscription evasion and desertion. On 4 June 1938 Ortíz was found guilty of avoiding his military duties by hiding and falsifying his age, employment and place of birth in collaboration with his father, girlfriend, Concha and the other defendants. Ortíz was sentenced to thirty years, Concha and Barrios to ten years, Chamorro and Jurado to nine years and Felipa to six years hard labour. This case illustrates how anti-Republicans engaged in illegal and black-market activities in their efforts to avoid conscription. Both conscription avoidance and desertion posed significant problems for the Republican regime throughout the war, but particularly after the middle of 1938. The government's concerns were reflected in a new ministerial order that sought to impose sanctions against the relatives of deserters.[43] The sanctions for treason (a capital crime) and defeatism were harsh, especially during 1938 when instances of desertion saw a significant increase and a general war-weariness took hold of the civilian rear-guard.

Black-market activities

Around 2.4% of the popular tribunal cases related to treason in the form of black-market offences often involving illegal stock-piling of controlled items (*acaparamiento*) and ration-card fraud. Dolores Soto Sánchez[44] was an auxiliary nurse (single, aged thirty-seven years) and a resident of calle Sandoval in Chamberí.[45] During the war she was employed in a succession of auxiliary jobs including as a nursing assistant in two venereal clinics which were situated in calle Olavida and calle Sevilla; such clinics operated across Madrid and evidence the perceived problem posed by the spread of venereal disease at this time. Prior to this job she was a medical assistant under the employment of the Madrid Town Council. She was arrested on 14 October 1937 because of evidence of her affiliation with Acción Popular. She had managed to avoid an earlier arrest after receiving a tip-off from her colleagues at the Town Council whereupon 'she failed to come into work despite the terrible staff shortages at this time.' The severe labour shortages provided women like Dolores with new opportunities for work, so long as they concealed their questionable political antecedents. The assiduous DGS subsequently made a home arrest and Dolores was imprisoned in Ventas. During police interrogation she claimed that there must have been some administrative error for 'she was confident that she would soon be released because she was a member of the CNT and had voted for the Popular Front during the February 1936 elections.' However, evidence of her membership in Acción Popular was adduced from records in the Control de Nóminas. Nonetheless, Dolores was absolved and released on 30 November 1937 (Judges Ricardo Guerra, Jesus Alonso and Emilio Ulloa presiding). The judges ruled that although there was evidence of her membership of Acción Popular she had never "practised any conduct which, in conjunction with this political antecedent, demonstrated any disaffection or hostility to the Republican regime."[46] This finding was unusual. Normally, proof of membership within one of the CEDA parties constituted *prima facie* evidence of disaffection and usually resulted in conviction and a fine or imprisonment. However, in this case evidence of good character and conduct was provided. The defendant had donated blood to a socialist town councillor named Arteaga whose good-character reference, together with those of three other Republican men, secured her unconditional discharge.

Dolores was arrested once again in September 1938, but this time in relation to ration card fraud. She was now employed by the Madrid Town Council as a children's nurse in Dispensary No. 18 situated in Plaza Moret. She had fraudulently obtained blank ration cards in order to obtain illegal milk rations from a variety of local dairies and through a female contact at the Cuban Embassy. The contraband was stored with a Republican music teacher, Pedro Hedo Escalera, who lived in calle Cardinal de Císneros 67. His wife was the concierge of this building. The Hedo family received three cans of condensed milk per week in exchange for storage. An administrative assistant named Teresa Moreno Álvarez and a cleaner named Filomena Carretero Durán who also worked at the No. 18 children's dispensary had supplied Dolores with numerous blank ration cards. Dolores confessed under interrogation that "she had been using the false ration cards for a period of around 20–25 days and that she had distributed illegal milk supplies to local residents whose names and addresses were unknown to her."[47] On this occasion the social capital afforded by influential Republican allies at the Town Council was of little use. On 20 September 1938 Dolores was found guilty of selling nine cans of condensed milk daily for the elevated sum of 2 pesetas and 30 centimos. Around sixty-five cans were found in Dolores' home at the time of her arrest, some of which had been allocated to Carmen Vera (a Cuban national) who was supposed to transfer the milk to the Cuban Embassy. Dolores was deemed to be the leader of this black-market group and sentenced to one year's imprisonment and fined 100,000 pesetas. The other defendants received varying prison sentences of two to four months imprisonment and large fines of between 4,000 and 2,000 pesetas.[48] The case is illustrative of the motivations of resisters which frequently combined profit motives with a genuine desire to hamper and impede the Republican war effort. The dire food shortages at this time are reflected in the government's strenuous efforts to crack down on black-market activities by imposing punitive penal and economic sanctions.

Rebellion

Around 9.3% of the total 14,862 popular tribunal cases involved treasonous crimes that were heard in the emergency military courts (Jurados de Guardia). Of these trials 8% related to cases of 'military rebellion' and only 1.3% related to cases of 'desertion.' The popular military courts expedited 197 cases of 'desertion' and 1,198 cases of 'military rebellion' and 'assistance and adhesion to rebellion.'[49] The vast majority of the rebellion cases related to ordinary conscripts who wanted to avoid the rigours of combat for personal reasons rather than because they were political dissidents or conscientious objectors.[50] Defendants frequently testified that the 'food was better and more abundant in the Nationalist zone' or that they wanted to cross the enemy lines in order to join relatives and loved ones. For obvious reasons, few soldiers confessed to feelings of disaffection or indifference, fear, war-weariness or resentment at the conduct of the war or the injustices of *enchufismo* (string-pulling and preferential treatment) within the ranks. However, such feelings, together with the shortages of food, material and equipment, are amply evidenced in soldier's letters and diaries.[51] The sanction for treason, rebellion or desertion was capital punishment; however because of the scarcity of suitable conscripts many deserters were not executed but instead assigned to disciplinary battalions in the capital where defeatism and disaffection found fertile spaces in which to flourish. The vast majority of the women who were accused of crimes of military treason or 'aiding rebellion' were the relatives or intimates of conscript evaders or deserters. Relatives often aided conscription avoidance and desertion by seeking the assistance of escape-line operators.[52]

After 18 July 1936 hundreds of men went into hiding in order to evade compulsory conscription. Dozens of vigilante committees were established during 1936 from within the anti-fascist women's organisations and various local communist groups with the aim of denouncing draft dodgers to the authorities.[53] Catholic and right-wing soldiers wanted to avoid military duty for ideological reasons, and they also feared that their previous involvement in lay Catholic groups such as Acción Católica or their membership of right-wing Catholic parties such as Acción Popular might lead to discrimination and victimisation during military service. The conscript Juan Antonio López Santiago was officially reported to have died as a result of a Nationalist bombardment during the Ebro campaign in 1938. However, his widow testified after the war that her husband had repeatedly written to her expressing his fears of being a victim of repression in the ranks. She believed that he had been "assassinated by members of his battalion … [because he was] a person of 'order,' who was also a member of Acción Católica, and had previously attempted to avoid conscription."[54]

María Luisa Pascual Herrero (aged thirty-one years) was sentenced to ten years hard labour for treason because she had helped her lover to avoid conscription.[55] Her lover Ignacio Crespo, an infantry lieutenant, deserted the Republican army and was safe-housed by María Luisa's aunt who was subsequently sentenced on 12 March 1937 to three years hard labour for this crime.[56] On 29 May 1938 Fernández Tebar a Republican school teacher ('*Maestro Nacional*') aged sixty-one years and his wife Julia aged sixty years (a housewife) were arrested by the Congreso DGS because they had obtained false documents in order to assist their two sons to obtain asylum at an embassy in order to avoid call-up.[57] Anunciación González was the girlfriend of one of the sons. She was able to obtain false documentation on the black-market. The parents were found guilty of high treason. Fernández was sentenced to twenty-five years imprisonment and Julia to twelve years. Anunciación's case was remitted to the *jurados de urgencia* for disaffection.[58]

The case of Dolores Hurtado Callejón illustrates how 'disaffected elements' devised strategies of resistance within a dangerous Republican social field.[59] In late May 1938 Dolores's brother Francisco deserted the 98th Brigade which was stationed at that time on the Levante front. He immediately returned to the capital and sought the help of his sisters Jeronima and Dolores who lived in an attic in calle Goya, 89. On 1 June 1938 the women 'asked for help in a crisis from old Republican friend' named Carlos Alonso Núñez (aged forty-five years) who had been a family-friend for over thirty years and was very probably Dolores's lover. Jeronima and Dolores paid several visits to his flat (as witnessed by the concierge) before finally meeting with him at 9 p.m. Alonso was a prominent member of the General Workers Union (UGT), President of the Syndicate of Lithographers (*carnet no.70 del Sindicato de Litografos* dated 26 August 1924) and a Socialist Party member (*Carnet no.1923* dated 1 January 1922). It was agreed that Francisco would hide with Alonso or with one of his contacts until Dolores obtained the necessary false papers for her brother to obtain a safe non-combatant position in the rear-guard. Francisco made the error of complaining to Alonso about the 'terrible conditions at the front' and claiming that 'he would much rather be shot in Madrid than return to the fronts.' A serious argument ensued. Alonso allegedly argued that "at this critical time everyone should go where they are told and if all the soldiers did the same thing as him the Republic would be lost." During the heated argument tensions were raised and Dolores was said to have stated that she had:

> friends in high places and these friends would provide her brother with false documents in order for him to join the services of an official rear-guard organization, most probably the SIM, because she was certain that one could join that organization with perfect ease given that half of its employees were fascists.[60]

While Dolores set about acquiring false documents the main problem was where to safe-house her brother. The conspirators feared that Alonso's concierge or his neighbours might become suspicious if an extra bed were moved into his home or if the Hurtado's domestic were to be seen bringing food on a daily basis. Therefore, it was agreed that Francisco would hide with Alonso's friend, a man named Landeira who owned a guest-house somewhere near Plaza de la Cebada. Through his contacts in the Eastern Socialist Club, Alonso was 'easily' able to obtain a stolen safe-conduct pass (property of the Republican SIM IVth Army Division) from a man named Gaspar Esteva. The false pass had originally belonged to a military liaison agent who moved between the Republican High Command and the government in Madrid. Alonso gave Dolores the false pass for 'safe-keeping,' and the original name was carefully erased and replaced with a false name and photograph of Francisco.[61] Dolores trusted Alonso and gave him Francisco's address. During his SIM interrogation Alonso was persuaded to denounce the family. He testified that he had 'only pretended to go along with the plan so that he might discover Francisco's hiding place and denounce him to the

SIM.' Subsequent to Alonso's confession, the SIM visited Landeira's guest-house in calle Oriente, 6 in order to arrest Francisco who unwittingly fled to Alonso's house and was arrested shortly afterwards. After her brother's arrest Dolores contacted a woman named Ofélia de Aragón who had contacts in the SIM (IVth Army Division) and might be able to organise the destruction of the false SIM pass which constituted the key evidence in this case. Dolores' efforts were unsuccessful. Francisco was sentenced to death for treason, and the records do not indicate whether the sentence was commuted. Dolores was sentenced to six years hard labour and Gaspar Esteva Sánchez was condemned to twenty-five years in a labour camp. Alonso was not prosecuted for his involvement in the affair. Dolores failed in her efforts to use her social connections to save her brother. However, she had perfectly good reason to believe that many '*rabanos*' were infiltrated within the Republican SIM and that by 'pulling strings' and using influential contacts (*enchufes*) it might be possible to infiltrate her brother within the Madrid SIM and thereby save his life.

While survivalist impulses determined the majority of the cases of rebellion and desertion, a significant number of young men (often Falangists) wanted to avoid conscription in order to enlist in the Nationalist ranks. Many such cases also involved acts of minor sabotage including the theft of personal issue rifles and munitions or "jamming rifles and tampering with munitions material."[62] In one case a group of young Falangist conscripts managed to escape from Madrid under the protection of an embassy vehicle. The fugitives escaped to Marseille by boat from Barcelona and then made their way by car to Burgos in order to enlist in the Nationalist columns.[63]

In April 1938 a group of eight men and two women were arrested on suspicion of high treason. They were found guilty of having formed a clandestine 'cell' (*nucleo*) whose purpose was to 'aid and abet soldiers who wanted to avoid front line duties.' Pedro Muela Fernández (a bank clerk with Banco Hispano Americano) and his sister Francisca Muela Fernández used her flat in calle Leganitos, 53 as a safe-house for "those who wanted to avoid fulfilling their military obligations by going into hiding."[64] Pedro went into hiding and pretended to be performing his military service in Valencia. He continued to draw his monthly salary from the Banco Hispano Americano and wrote a series of colourful letters to his sister and other relatives in order support this fiction. The letters vividly depicted an imagined life in Valencia and contained amusing accounts of flirtations with young Valencian ladies. In fact, he remained in hiding at his sister's flat for the entire duration. After several weeks of police surveillance, Francisca's property was raided and items of military and naval apparel were confiscated. These included a naval cap, an old Assault Guard's uniform and Argentinian Embassy armbands which were used by the draft evaders in order to circulate in public without attracting suspicion. Some items were supplied by one of the defendant's girlfriends, Dorotea Gómez López. The police also confiscated 'a large tubular lantern' which was 'ready for use in order to transmit signals in Morse code,' some silver coins, around

1,000 pesetas in bills and coins, various maps that 'described the Nationalist troop movements,' copies of war reports and a transistor radio which was procured in order to receive daily news reports from the fascist radio stations. The prosecution claimed that the defendants had worn the uniforms in order to circulate defeatist news amongst soldiers at the various fronts. Pedro, the ring leader, testified that he and his male friends were prominent Falangists who wanted to avoid the draft because they feared arrest on account of their former political affiliations.[65] The defendants were old school friends and committed Catholics. One was the son of a minor civil servant who had received a full bursary at the prestigious Cardinal Císneros school. Pedro was found in possession of a manuscript copy of the Falangist Hymn '*Cara al Sol*.' Another defendant, a graphic illustrator, designed the cover illustration for Julián Cortés Cavanilla's "*San Antón, Prisión Roja*."[66] The cover illustration bore an imprint of the defendant's palm in red ink.[67] Cavanillas was an old school-friend.

There were a few instances of organised conscription evasion. Josefina Gisbert Poveda and her husband were found guilty of treason and defeatism for aiding and abetting the desertion of a new conscript.[68] Josefina was a Falangist who does not appear to have had any direct contact with the Clandestine Falange. She was twenty years old, married and her occupation was recorded as unpaid labour in the home (*sus labores*). Her young husband, Manuel Entrena Ruiz, was a former bank clerk who had earlier been posted on the front-lines within a signals and communications division. At some time in early April 1937, Gisbert arranged to meet a new conscript, Luis González, at a pre-arranged location in the Retiro Park. González was also a Falangist who was due to be posted to a position in the Sierras but was keen to join the enemy. The trial evidence suggests that both she and her husband may have had previous experience of aiding desertion. Gisbert had been actively on the look-out for 'Falangist friends' within the army. Upon first meeting González she invited him to her house and wrote a letter of recommendation on his behalf to her husband at the fronts:

> this matter relates to a Falangist friend, and you know how much I like to help these types of friends.

The court found that Manuel Entrena had:

> welcomed [González] with great affection and interest … and informed him of other trustworthy people upon whom he could rely … although he advised González to wait [before crossing over into enemy lines] because he believed that Franco would be sure to triumph in only a few days.[69]

There is no evidence that money was exchanged in respect of the 'services' that were offered by the couple. González successfully escaped into Nationalist territory at some time after April 1937 and was never apprehended. The defendants were originally charged with 'intention to assist an act of military desertion,' and they revealed the names of any accomplices. On 14 May 1938 the couple were sentenced to twenty years (Gisbert) and twenty-five years (Entrena) hard labour. The court found that they were both liable in their capacity as accomplices in a treasonous act that involved "the evasion into the enemy camp of the army recruit Luiz González under articles 7 and 8 of the Decree of 22 June 1938."[70]

Escape-lines

Those who wanted to escape into enemy territory were most often required to navigate the wild and dangerous Castilian Sierras with the assistance of local escape-line guides. The eventual aim being to reach the ports of Barcelona or Valencia which provided access by boat into France. The fugitives and military deserters were then able to re-enter Spain via San Sebastián. Another common escape route was by car to Valencia then on to Barcelona and from there to Port Bou and into France.[71] In addition, several escape-lines were routed via Barcelona to Andorra and then over the Pyrenees on foot into France.

Trinidad de la Sanz Herraz (aged fifty-two years) was a devout Catholic peasant small-holder who lived with her husband Natalio (a labourer, aged sixty-six years) in the small village of Alameda del Valle (near Rascafrios) in the outskirts of Madrid. This village was where the Montaña Battalion had been stationed. The SIM detachment assigned to this battalion had been tasked with investigating the possible existence of fifth-column organisations in the villages of the Alameda Valley. It was believed that local fifth-column groups were passing information to the enemy and aiding and abetting desertion.[72] In March 1937 the couple were denounced to the SIM by neighbours. It was alleged that their anti-Republican activities included encouraging desertion and organising escape-lines. Two soldiers (Geronimo Martínez and Juan Santos) received orders from the SIM to "entrap the couple by pretending that they were seriously disillusioned with life at the front. They expressed a desire to pass into the fascist camp."[73] It is not clear whether any money was exchanged for assisting the soldiers. The couple asked their neighbour, Lozoya Aniceto San González, to act as a mountain guide into the enemy territory. The evidence against Trinidad included a manuscript document which was submitted as evidence of anti-Republican propaganda. It was signed and dated "The Year of 1937, Alameda del Valle, in the Province of Madrid." The document was illustrated with a hand-drawn gothic crucifix and was written in the rhythmic and incantatory style of a prayer:

> In the name of God, may he be with us here now and with all of us. I ask, in his name, for Peace throughout all of Spain and, God willing, peace will come soon, and we will never see such events again.

> I also want the Church to be united with the State as it always has been and I ask that we be governed by people of faith, good conscience and charity. I want the rich and the poor, the middling classes, the good and the bad to live together, I forgive them all from the bottom of my heart and I also wish that the present day blasphemy be punished from henceforth and I want the catechism to be restored in all schools and churches … And if any one should doubt the existence of God, he really does exist, I have seen him with my own eyes … I am doing everything in his name and out of love for everyone in general, I don't want to harm anyone, what I really want is more respect and obedience for the laws of our departed redeemer, Jesus Christ.[74]

The document was cited by the defence in an 'expert psychiatric evaluation' which sought to demonstrate that Trinidad was suffering from 'a type of paranoid dementia,' more specifically identified as a form of 'invasive paraphrenia of a mystical type which rendered her criminally incapable.' Trinidad was also said to have experienced 'holy visions' that evidenced the 'miraculous and prophetic anti-Republican discourses which circulated in Spain at this time.'[75] Trinidad was acquitted of all charges of 'adhesion to rebellion and dissemination of right-wing propaganda' on the grounds of diminished responsibility. In contrast, her husband was found guilty of an attempted adhesion to rebellion (under Article 240 of the Military Justice Code) and sentenced to three years internment in a labour camp. There was no evidence to indicate that the couple had been working in association with any organised networks. The 'blasphemy' alluded to in Trinidad's letter referred to Republican secularising measures and the violent extra-judicial repression which had taken place after 18 July 1936.

On 2 July 1937, some fifteen family members and friends were indicted on counts of treason and espionage. The defendants included a minor and two women, Escolástica Ramírez y Ramírez and Baldomera Heras Salmerón.[76] The main defendant Marcelo Ramírez y Ramírez was a resident of Aldeanueva de Barbarroya (Toledo), a small village situated outside Madrid which was separated from the enemy zone by an easily navigable river. Marcelo worked as a militia within an anti-aircraft defence group in the capital. He was accused of being in regular contact with his father and other relatives in the 'fascist zone.' He had sent them photographs of the position of anti-aircraft batteries. He was assisted by his brother-in-law, Doroteo García Rivas, and two siblings Benito and Escolástica. Another defendant, Saturnino Rivas Bodas, was accused of having been instructed by the enemy forces (*fuerzas enemigas*) to leave all the village doors open upon the arrival of the Moors. Two other defendants, Mariano Bodas Ramírez and Inocente García y García, worked at a mill situated in the 'loyal zone' (Republican zone). These men passed letters and information into the enemy zone using a concealed wire cable and a box. It was alleged that the defendants had encouraged the villagers of Aldeanueva to defect to the enemy zone. Large quantities of animal feed were regularly smuggled across the river into the enemy zone using a boat which had been supplied by the Nationalists. Several members of the group attempted to escape into the Nationalist zone, but they were intercepted by Republican militias who had placed the group under surveillance. The remainder of the defendants including Baldomera Heras Salmerón were in regular communication with the enemy and had organised escape-lines which allowed locals to pass back and forth over into the Nationalist zone in order to visit friends and family. In this way intelligence was easily passed across the lines. Madrid's tribunals passed the case on to the courts of espionage and high treason in Valencia, and the outcome is unknown.[77]

Those who managed to escape Madrid often made their way to Barcelona and used overland mountain escape routes through Andorra into France. On 6 October 1937 a group of frontier guards (*carabineros*) posted in Seo de Urgell apprehended as many as "350–400 individuals who were attempting to cross the border clandestinely via Andorra, they were accompanied by various guides who fired at the security forces."[78] The majority of the fugitives were deserters and draft dodgers of 'conscription age' and between seventeen and thirty-three years. However, the party also included a man aged sixty-nine years and María Claustra Subira Serra, a devout Catholic who wanted to join her brother who was a priest who had escaped into France. The escape-line organisers were a married couple named Francisco Boix Betriu and his wife Anita Fuster and several others. The couple were based in Barcelona where they actively sought contact with fugitives and deserters. They worked in concert with Carmen Cendros Ibáñez and her husband Jaime Grau Batet, two male religious, two tax clerks, a broker named José Suné Benet and several women who ran safe-houses on the border between Spain and Andorra. This couple would routinely accompany fugitives who had recently arrived in Barcelona to a pre-determined location near the village of Calaf where a woman named María Burgues, with the aid of her domestic Dolores Vendrell Vives and her partner Juan Fuster, would hide the fugitives at her farmhouse, Masiá Valcebre, pending their escape into France. Other safe-houses were located at Can Llere, Can Casanovas, Can Salanet and Can Barres, San Lllei in Valdera and Casa Blanch. This last house was located in the municipality of Clariena and owned by María Ferrer Tristany who had risked her life at the start of the war by hiding the priest Subira Serra. From here liaison agents and mountain guides co-ordinated by Francisco Calvo would accompany small groups of on average eight persons to Puente de Foltats in private cars and a taxi belonging to a man named Tonet de Berga. From here, guides would accompany the fugitives on the final leg of their journey to the French border. María Burgues charged an arrangement fee of 1,000 pesetas which was shared between herself and other safe-house providers. In addition, separate fees of between 500, 700 and 900 pesetas were paid to the guides Carlos Rufi Nieto, Luis Sales, Masferrer and three others and to various local liaison agents including a bodega owner in Solana. On average each fugitive was charged a total of 2,300 pesetas to include housing, travel and living expenses. Around fifty-five persons, including several fugitives, were arrested. The court of espionage and high treason found all of the defendants guilty of high treason. The frontier guards had uncovered:

> an organisation whose aims were to facilitate the escape into France of fugitives, deserters and enemies of the Republic who wanted join the Fascist side (*bando fascista*), the evasions were organised on a large scale and included recruitment agents, liaison agents and guides, all of whom received a fixed fee, all these activities constituted High Treason … in light of the grave harm perpetrated against the Republic and the serious damage to the normal functioning of military services, the war effort and social discipline in the rearguard.[79]

Upon entry into the Nationalist zone, Spanish civilians and military deserters were routinely interviewed by the Nationalist SIPM. They were able to provide valuable military and political intelligence. Soon after the front-lines were consolidated in the Nationalist zone observation posts were established and a 'declaration system' was devised (*sistema de declaración*) in order to record the statements of fugitives and deserters from the Republican-held zones so as to supplement official intelligence reports and to make better use of air reconnaissance operations.[80]

Defeatism

The maintenance of civilian morale was of primordial importance to the war effort because circumstances of 'total war' required the entire mobilisation of civilian society.[81] Madrid's situation was unique because it was besieged by rebel forces for the duration of the war. Communication and supply lines were permanently compromised, and a key issue for the authorities was how to maintain morale despite circumstances of increasing material scarcity and deprivation. Rationing was implemented in November 1936. The capital also experienced an infrastructural crisis at the start of the war following the influx of refugees from the rebel-held zones. Instances of planned and co-ordinated defeatism, including the dissemination of Nationalist war reports, helped to sow discontent and disaffection in the rear-guard.[82]

On 22 June 1937 a new crime of treason known as 'defeatism' was created which criminalised any expressions of criticism or dissent (whether public or private) against the Republican regime, the war effort and all activities that might tend to lower public or military morale or affect public order. Defeatism included the dissemination of inaccurate or demoralising information in relation to the progress of the war (*propagar bulas*), the circulation of anti-Republican propaganda, criticism of the Republican government or its policies or personnel, and allegations of governmental or military incompetence or corruption.[83] Around 3.6% of the popular tribunal cases (some 545 cases) related to this crime. Around 25.5% of cases (i.e. some

139 cases) involved women of all classes and political backgrounds. Most cases involved complaints about the rationing or criticisms against the Republican conduct of the war. Some of the most serious cases related to allegations of local or high-level governmental corruption regarding the administration and distribution of provisions. In such cases the sanctions tended to be more severe, frequently as much as six years imprisonment in a labour camp, although the sentencing procedures were fairly arbitrary and did not follow any particular rationale.[84] When analysed from gendered frames, the government was also sensitive to issues surrounding masculinity, and in particular allegations of cowardice among rear-guard security personnel. The crime fell under category of treason and had the potential to attract long terms of imprisonment together with fines and the loss of civil and legal rights. In a few instances it attracted the death penalty, most often in cases of pre-meditated desertion involving groups or serious financial corruption or rationing infractions.

The government adopted a variety of different approaches in order to address the problem of maintaining civilian morale with little success.[85] It implemented censorship regulations and ran numerous propaganda campaigns, mostly directed at women who were responsible for family provisioning and survival. The censors intercepted hundreds of private letters which contained evidence of defeatist views and opinions. Even when expressed in private correspondence, instances of defeatism might result in arrest. There was no clear rationale as to sentencing procedure, and those found guilty of crimes of defeatism were liable to harsh punishments. Defeatism was a crime of treason, and in the most serious cases it attracted terms of imprisonment of up to thirty years, but the most usual sentence was a term of 'six years and one day.' Defeatism among the ranks regularly attracted much harsher punishments.

After the Battle of Madrid, the capital was isolated for the remainder of the war and cut off from vital food, clothing and fuel supplies. Even loyal Republican citizens were obliged to resort to everyday resistance strategies including participation in the illegal black-market.[86] By as early as June 1937 defeatism was rife. Despite the discourses in the press and propaganda which identified it as a 'middle-class' phenomenon which was orchestrated by the fifth column, in reality defeatist sentiments straddled social and ideological divides, and a good number of working-class women were caught within the nets of this new repressive legislation. María Martín Baeza (married, aged thirty-seven years) was the concierge of a building situated in calle del Oso, 7. On the morning of 6 April 1938 she was denounced by two of her neighbours and by 3 p.m. she was being interrogated by officers at the Inclusa police station for having openly stated:

> in a defiant (*descarada*) and fairly insistent way … and in a manner injurious to the Republican government … that the Government was shameless (*el Gobierno era sin verguenza*) … it takes 15-year-old boys right up to

> the front-lines and similar comments … that her husband went to work but the Government workers were the ones who ate all the food and took everything meanwhile her own children had consumption.[87]

Felisa Manuel Rabanal was a sixty-three-year-old widow from Valladolid who lived in a run-down tenement in Tejar de Frascuelo, Choza numero, 6. She was denounced by three female clients on 9 November 1938 for "abusing the credulity of the public for profit, for insulting the esteemed President of the Republic and other prominent government leaders and for disseminating lies and defeatist news."[88] By 1938 this former seamstress and civil administrative assistant was reduced to begging and tarot reading in order to make ends meet. She was denounced by her disgruntled clients for saying that 'the Republicans had deliberately orchestrated the bombings so that houses could be looted.' Her case was dismissed, and she was freed on 15 November 1938.

Benedicta Lobo Pérez's fifth-column group was comprised of five neighbours (three of whom were women). The defendants lived in calle Claudio Coello in the Salamanca district (also the venue of *El asunto de los carnets* above). They met on the roof terrace of their building in order to discuss the progress of the war and listened to illegal 'fascist' broadcasts at home. They were denounced to the police on 9 May 1938 by three female neighbours and accused of 'treason, defeatism and of attending secret meetings in order to conspire against the Republic.' While they had no previous political affiliations, the case was aggravated by the fact that they had compiled detailed lists of local left-wing sympathisers 'which they intended to hand-over after the Nationalist occupation of Madrid.' The defendants were denounced for being disloyal and critical of the Republican war effort and found guilty of defeatism. Benedicta claimed that "the Republican soldiers are a bunch of idiots" and "who knows how many crimes they [the Republicans] are committing against our people in Teruel."[89] In addition, José Soria Ortíz was a driver for the French Red Cross Hospital situated at Claudio Coello, 92 who might have obtained military intelligence from the front-lines, but no evidence was adduced in this regard.

Defeatism and accusatory practices

Most cases of defeatism involved ordinary war-weary civilians who had spoken or behaved unduly against the government and were subsequently denounced by neighbours, work colleagues, acquaintances or intimates.[90] "Every denunciation resulted in some kind of drama played at the level of the family, neighbourhood, work place or other centres of assembly and gossip."[91] Often denunciations arose from purely personal rather than religious or ideological motives. This type of 'intimate violence' is a central feature of civil war and may be viewed as 'the dark face of social capital.'[92] Positions of power were often abused pursuant to personal jealousies and rivalries and in order to exact revenge.[93] Esperanza González López, aged twenty-nine years and resident in Carabanchel, was a variety hall artist who was arrested for defeatism on 16 September 1938.[94] She had been drinking with a male companion and other female friends at the Bar Alhambra, calle de Sevilla, 6 at around 2 p.m. in the afternoon when she was overheard by a group of soldiers from the rear-guard health security group (Grupo de Sanidad) of the 111th Mixed Brigade 'complaining bitterly and loudly' about the state of the capital's rationing. She was asked 'to lower her voice and change the subject of her defeatist conversation.' During interrogation Esperanza testified as follows:

> This morning I went to the shops to buy some wool to knit a jersey for my son and I was somewhat upset at not being able to find any, I related these events to a male friend at the Bar Alhambra and I told him that I wished I could fly to America in order to bring back wool and everything else that I wanted.[95]

Her male co-defendant Luis Martínez Galiano and other witnesses corroborated this testimony. Luis Martínez also explained that the soldiers had been "continually firing underhand and insinuating comments at Esperanza and her girl-friends."[96] The situation had escalated into a heated argument and Esperanza had taunted and provoked the soldiers by telling them that "instead of butting into in her conversation they would be better off marching to the fronts."[97] This defiant retort struck at the heart of masculine insecurities relating to discourses impugning the heroism of military service behind the lines. The angry soldiers retaliated by denouncing her to a passing police officer. Both were acquitted after friends gave evidence at trial that the principal complainant (an army commissar) had sexually propositioned Esperanza five days earlier and met with rejection:

> his advances had been politely rejected whereupon the commissar had insulted her and called her a shameless woman and then he had stated that he could not understand why she was out in the street at that time … the two women quickly distanced themselves from the commissar who continued to shout-out comments that the women were unable to hear.[98]

This case evidences the role played by historic feuds and petty quotidian squabbles in a great many denunciations; here the quarrel related to issues surrounding masculinity rather than loyalty to the Republican cause. In this case the defendant was fortunate; evidence of sexual impropriety played a key role in her acquittal. Other women were less fortunate; a few weeks earlier, on 27 August 1938, Encarnación Casado Jiménez (single, aged twenty-nine), an illiterate domestic worker (*obrera del hogar*), got into an altercation with a police officer on the corner of calle Goya and Velázquez while she was trying to board a tram with a young infant. Evidence suggests that the officer jostled her in the queue whereupon she stumbled and began to "shout insults and invectives against the Republican government ... saying that we are worse off than ever with this government ... they are a bunch of pimps and hustlers (*chulos y macarras*)."[99] Circumstances were aggravated because she resisted arrest, refused to give her name and sarcastically observed that the war-effort would be better served if the officer were to take himself off to the fronts instead of wasting his efforts on the arrest of a woman who was nearly pushed in front of a moving tram. The *Tribunal Especial de Guardia no. 1* sentenced her to six years imprisonment in a labour camp for defeatism.

Later, in September 1938, an illiterate dairy woman who had been evacuated from the Carabanchel district to a village in the outskirts of Madrid was denounced by her new neighbours for treason and defeatism. She was an anti-Republican, and rumours circulated that her husband had escaped across enemy lines in order to join Franco. Hearsay evidence was adduced which indicated that she had been boasting to people that her husband had been invalided out of the Nationalist army "because they [the Nationalists] are more humanitarian and better than us."[100] She was also accused of having conducted clandestine meetings with manager of the local bank in order to listen to the illegal Nationalist broadcasts at his home. The village community disliked this upstart newcomer and resented her 'unusual' friendship with a local middle-class notable. Her brother-in-law also gave evidence that his brother had most probably deserted in order to escape his bossy wife who was older, wealthier (she owned the dairy) and wore the trousers. Evidence came to light that one of her denouncers was a former friend who had fallen out with her over her refusal to supply black-market milk following a government crack-down. This case is of interest because it demonstrates how the war-time rationing and regulations created dangerous jealousies and festering local resentments. When the neighbours became aware of the treasonous implications of their accusations, they withdrew the formal complaint and the defendant was absolved at some time in late February 1939. While popular justice was harsh, arbitrary and lacking in due process, false accusations usually resulted in acquittals.

Defeatism and adaptation to the new field of power

In order to survive in the rear-guard anti-Republicans were required to adapt and 'play new games,' and the minority who could not or would not were liable to forms of selective violence and political repression. On 2 July 1938 Gonzalo Tomás Soriano, a forty-year-old unmarried accountant who was also the secretary of the new local housing committee appeared at the Buenavista police station in order to denounce a fifth-column conspiracy in his building. The main suspect was Ramona González who lived on the third floor of Tomás' building which was situated in calle de Jorge Juan, 61 in the Salamanca district. She was aged sixty-one years and lived alone. On the previous night at around 10.30 p.m. Tomás had gone to visit her to ask her to join the new housing committee and receive her financial contributions towards the general upkeep of the building. The debate over the membership and the contributions developed into a heated political argument. Tomás testified that Ramona had claimed that the Republicans were 'a shameful bunch' and that the press reports were deceitful:

> she would not join the committee when there was nothing to eat ... and the war would not end because the leaders were a shameless bunch (*unos sin vergüenzas*); and that if Negrín had nothing to eat the war would now be over; that the workers were a bunch of donkeys that were now standing on their hind legs and that in Italy things were very good ... the defendant continued by saying that she had a friend, who despite having lost all her possessions, continues to defend fascism on account of the fact that it is good for the workers ... they [the Republicans] have left corpses abandoned in the roads and this was very bad, and that in response to his [the witness Tomás Soriano's] reminders of the fascist massacres in Seville, the Bull Ring in Badajoz, Zaragoza and in all the fascist dominated zones, she replied that this was not certain and that we can't know anything more than what's happening right here. With reference to the poor state of the German and Italian economies she told him that he, the witness, could have no idea about this as he'd never been to those countries.[101]

The row continued into the early hours. Tomás went on to claim that:

> From the outset of the 'Movement' the defendant always praised General Franco, criticized the [food] queues and *did not want to make any improvements to the property* [author's italics] ... this denunciation could have important ramifications because the denouncer had the impression that the defeatist and fascist comments of the defendant were not her own ideas (*del criterio personal suya*) ... perhaps she's heard of these ideas in certain houses that she frequents and who knows if she's planning to be a defeatist agent (*agente propagador*). The denouncer believes that some of the neighbours, at least, have right wing ideas and that according to some of the other neighbours this woman is against the Republican regime.[102]

González was arrested and taken to the Buenavista police station for questioning. During interrogation she denied all allegations and 'while she did not recall the remarks she had made against Negrín, it was quite possible that she may have made these.' Tomás testified that her 'defeatist and fascist views were rational and coherent albeit hostile to the regime.' However, he added that this opinionated and talkative woman was incapable of forming her own ideas and he intimated that her mind had been influenced by ideas that had originated in other households. González was detained in Ventas women's prison pending trial. On 6 July 1938 she was examined by a forensic medical expert who reported that:

> She is a woman who is extremely exhausted, she is in a physically poor state and at 61 years she expresses herself with an extraordinary loquacity, but, although her ideas appear to be coherent, they lack any real thread and it is really easy for her to jump from one subject to another … she, spontaneously and of her own accord, relates an endless concatenation of facts that bear no relation to each other, nor do they serve as a valid response to questions asked of her. She is, you could say, a 'talking machine' that is automatically and simultaneously playing various records that relate to different ideas, you never reach the end of the discussion unless you break off the conversation.[103]

On the basis of this evidence González was absolved and freed on 13 July 1938. The court found that the defendant was suffering from senile dementia caused by malnutrition, vascular sclerosis and a premature cerebral anaemia. Her illness meant that "her political views could not be attributed as much value as those expressed by more sober minds and consciousnesses."[104] The defendant was acquitted on the basis that because she was suffering from a mental illness, it was impossible to establish *mens rea*. The case illustrates how medical evidence was used to avoid the worst rigours of the new 'popular justice.' The prevailing medico-legal discourses constructed women as irrational, apolitical and gullible. Consequently, 'weak minded and impressionable' women often enjoyed the benefits of more lenient sentencing practices. This case also illustrates how personal rather than political motives frequently informed this form of selective violence.[105] González refused to play the new 'game-rules.' Arguably, her 'defeatist and fascist' ideas and her healthy scepticism of the Republican press reports did not bring her before the courts,[106] rather it was her stubborn refusal to join the housing committee and to pay her share of the building maintenance which had led to her arrest. Personal feuds were resolved within the crucible of the wider ideological conflict. However, this defendant was able to successfully navigate the new legal regime and escape the worst sanctions of the law with the aid of a competent lawyer and a sympathetic tribunal.

Defeatism and war-weariness

By as early as September 1936 food, fuel and other basic commodities were in short supply. Madrid's situation was unique in the context of the conflict because it was virtually surrounded and besieged from October 1936 for the duration of the war. The Valencia Road soon came to provide the only access to the rest of the Republican-held territory. Rationing was implemented in early November 1936, and winter 1936 was particularly bitter. The sustained Nationalist aerial bombings that commenced in August 1936 shattered thousands of windows leaving civilians to freeze during the following winter. Fuel was scarce, and restaurants and bars were only authorised to serve a single menu based on rice-soup or meat and potato stew.[107] Women stood for hours in the food queues and were obliged to devise novel strategies to supplement the increasingly meagre family rations. They made excursions into the surrounding countryside in order to barter clothing and valuables in exchange for eggs, meat and potatoes among the local farmers. Deprivation straddled socio-economic divides, and even privileged women like the monarchist Luca de Tena sisters allegedly had to wait in line for hours for the most basic items:

> My sisters went off to queue to buy things, a baker-woman in calle de Rosario, who was very indebted to my father, would give us bread every day, and my sister who was sick at home for most of the war, got help from the Swiss International Red Cross for the Children of Spain, a few cans of milk and a couple of ounces of chocolate.[108]

Julio Palacios recalled the unstinting bravery of the 'little women' (including his sister) who

> overcame their survival instincts in order to fearlessly traverse the streets and squares, basket in arms, in the midst of the sectarian gunfire [during the Casado Coup], so that homes would not be deprived of a miserable punnet of lentils.[109]

Women controlled consumption and subsistence within the domestic space.[110] By as early as January 1937 severe restrictions were placed on food, tobacco, fuel, clothing, medicines and other basic items, and living conditions rapidly deteriorated. Throughout autumn and winter 1936, and again in January 1937, the government ran a series of campaigns encouraging women, children and men of non-military age to evacuate the capital on account of the devastating air-raids and the alarming shortages. These governmental appeals were largely ignored, particularly among the workers who did not want to abandon their homes for fear of losing their possessions. In February 1937 Dolores Ibárruri and Margarita Nelken appealed directly to 'Madrid's Mothers' to evacuate the city with their children to little effect. Seventy percent of the trials for defeatism were heard during 1938.[111] The generalised low morale was fuelled by a succession of devastating Republican military defeats (22 February, Teruel; 15 April, Viñaroz and 13 June, Castellón). The Munich Agreement in September 1938 and the disastrous Republican defeat at Ebro during winter 1938 made it evident that, without the active intervention of France and England or additional aid from Russia, the Republicans would most probably lose the war. The loss of Barcelona in January 1939 extinguished the popular will to 'resist at all costs.' A general war-weariness took hold in Madrid and defeatism became wide-spread.[112]

Over the course of 1938 supplies of food and fuel reached dangerously low levels, and the threat of epidemic disease loomed despite the Red Cross vaccination initiatives.[113] A young, single working-class woman was sentenced to six years in a labour camp in June 1938 on account of her refusal to perform voluntary harvest work. She demanded fair compensation and complained that the female volunteers had been 'given too little to eat for so much work ... work that the men should be doing.' She encouraged some fifty women to down tools and return to the capital and was imprisoned for defeatism and incitement to rebellion.[114] By late 1938, the civilian population was suffering from severe malnutrition due to a near-starvation diet of "Negrín's pills" (lentils). On 26 December 1938 two working-class women were denounced for complaining about the milk rations on the Canillejas tram. They were immediately imprisoned in Ventas. One was a mother of two young children who was married to a wounded soldier who had been invalided out of the army due to combat-related epilepsy. The other was a thirty-two-year-old mother of three young children. On the day of their arrest they had just returned from a foraging expedition to a farm near Barajas in order to buy cabbages. They endured several days in prison before their case was dismissed on 9 January 1939.[115] Gloria Ruiz Bravo was imprisoned on 27 December 1938 for complaining about the "meagre rations."[116] This forty-seven-year-old, single, working-class woman was arrested by a policeman after she was overheard telling her friend (who was a concierge) and another acquaintance that her Christmas eve celebrations "hadn't been much fun because all the family had to eat were lentils without oil."[117] The three women were immediately arrested and taken to Cuatro Caminos police station. Ruiz stayed in Ventas until 14 January 1939 when her case was suspended and she was released. Men were often less fortunate because what they 'said' was deemed to carry more political force and import. In January 1939, a printer aged sixty-three years was sentenced to an exemplary six years of hard labour because he was overheard to say that:

> the rebels were certain to win the war and that the Republican authorities were starving the civilians.[118]

As evidenced by the cases above, it was most often the poorest and most vulnerable members of society who suffered the worst treatment at the hands of the police and the tribunals. The wealthy and well-connected are less visible in the records.

Disaffection

Around 73% of the popular tribunal cases related to the new crime of 'disaffection against the Regime' which was created by government order on October 1936 during a state of national emergency.[119] This new crime was drafted in a purposely wide and vague manner in order to encompass a variety of dispositions and practices that 'while being legal in accordance with laws enacted prior to 18 July 1936, might in the present circumstances be deemed to be disaffected or hostile to the regime.' The new legislation was created at the same time as the emergency popular courts (*Jurados de Urgencia*) in order to adjudicate actions that "by their nature are hostile or contrary to the Regime but which do not possess the attributes of a crime."[120] As indicated in the introduction, this new 'popular justice' broke with the provisions of the Republican Constitution of 1931, Section VII (Justice) and marked a singular departure from the established democratic and judicial norms.[121] Those actions that might be considered 'as acts of hostility or disaffection' were listed in Article 2. They included: (1) impeding orders issued by public authorities in relation to defence, general provisioning, public health and/or the consumption of light, gas and water, (2) disseminating false news and rumours in relation to the progress of the war, the government or the economy, (3) any conduct that, while not being illegal, demonstrates disaffection towards the regime and (4) all other activities deemed damaging to the Government, People (*pueblo*) or Republic.

The punishment for the crime of disaffection was the suspension of civil and political rights for a period of one to five years and fines of anywhere between 250 and 100,000 pesetas. After 31 December 1936, the popular tribunal adopted a harder stance on sentencing practices and many sentences involved a period of imprisonment in Ventas women's prison or in new labour camps such as Cehegín (Murcia), Muchamiel (Alicante) and Alacuas (Valencia).[122]

A former subscription to the monarchist *ABC* newspaper, membership of the right-wing CEDA parties, the possession of religious artefacts, Falangist or CEDA propaganda or monarchist memorabilia were considered *prima facie evidence* of disaffection. All symbolic resistance performances were proscribed. Housemaids were arrested for making the fascist raised-arm salute on balconies in solidarity with the rebel fly-overs.[123] The failed coup and the ensuing breakdown of the Republican levers of power in 1936 meant that the capital's rear-guard was turned into a dangerous and hostile environment for those who were perceived to hold anti-Republican beliefs. Personal enmities, envy and the desire to settle personal scores played a significant factor in many denunciations evidencing the privatisation of the political at this time.

Public order offences also fell under the categories of disaffection and rebellion. In December 1937 María Gómez León and around twenty other dairy owners were summarily arrested and imprisoned for disaffection and 'aiding rebellion' because of their failure/refusal comply with new orders issued by the JDM's Ministry of Supplies in regard to the timely delivery of milk to a new central government depot.[124] The authorities believed that the fifth column deliberately incited acts of public protest and disorder, and the distribution of pamphlets encouraging 'mothers' and ordinary workers to protest against the shortages was widespread.

The new legislation explicitly criminalised spreading false rumours or news relating to the movement of troops or war operations, Government actions or the economic situation, or whatsoever other information tending to create opinions adverse to the Republic or to create an adverse state of opinion or alarm.

Consequently, any casual or inadvertent criticism of Republican policies or military operations might fall under the scope of this provision including observations in private correspondence which was subject censorship. Despite the censors, Madrid's press and radio often contained sensitive intelligence relating to front-line activities and the positions of troops. The new legislation sought to address this potential security risk. Traditional gender prejudices meant that women were unfairly targeted for repression on account of their 'loose tongues,' and the fears of women's talk were evidenced in the visual propaganda of this period.[125] Misogyny and the fear of right-wing monarchist and Catholic women is reflected in a famous CNT/FAI poster depicting a grotesque gorilla wearing a crown and a rosary under the heading *¡Cuidado Al Hablar! : La Bestia Acecha.* (Watch your words: The Beast is stalking!). Similarly, another poster issued by communist Radio 5 was entitled *¡No hablar, El enemigo os escucha!* It depicted three stern-looking middle-aged Catholic women, traditionally dressed in black and wearing headscarves, chatting animatedly in public; below them appears the contorted face of an *Africanista* soldier which is attached to a large white ear. The soldier transforms the women's 'loose-talk' into Morse-code. The posters reflected deep-seated anxieties surrounding anti-Republican women and also culturally embedded racism and colonialism.[126] The tribunal records indicate that women were arrested because they had publicly criticised the regime, often while they waited for hours in the long food queues which became sites of grievance and protest against the government and also sites of petty squabble and denunciation. The authorities believed that the fifth column circulated within the food queues disseminating false and defeatist news. The dissemination of anti-Republican propaganda routinely attracted custodial sentences. María Fernández López was arrested for having a secret printing press and making propaganda for the Falange and Acción Popular.[127] This woman was accused of disaffection and adhesion to rebellion for making right-wing propaganda in her house and for threatening to burn down the concierge's lodge in her building. She was sentenced to two years hard labour in 1936 and released from Cehegín labour camp in August 1938.[128]

Disaffection straddled wide social and cultural divides. María Álvarez de Toledo (married, aged thirty-five, ex-Duchess of Santa Cristina and Alba)[129] was arrested and detained by the DGS for being a senior activist within the monarchist Renovación Española. Magdalena Pla Riquelme (fifty-three years, single) was a worker at the 'Osram factory.' She was arrested for being an activist within Acción Popular.[130] Both the ex-Duchess and the factory worker were respectively sentenced to five years and three years imprisonment in a labour camp. Pla Riquelme was transferred to the Cehegín (Murcia) until her release on 28 November 1938. The 'ex-Duchess of Santa Cristina' had 'substantial financial means' and was fined 100,000 pesetas and received the maximum sentence for disaffection, i.e. five years imprisonment in Alacuás (Valencia). It was found that she had sought to mislead the tribunal by claiming that she was the wife of a simple farmer and ignorant of politics. Her country estate was searched and monarchist memorabilia was confiscated including a signed photograph of Alfonso XIII. Most incriminatingly, she was a Falangist activist. She was the close friend of a female cousin of José Antonio Primo de Rivera with whom she had 'driven around Madrid rallying fascist support after 18 July.'

Approximately 1% of those charged with disaffection were professionals (teachers and one pharmacist). Seven percent were nurses. Another 7% were nuns, and 5% were employed in clerical and administrative jobs. A significant proportion came from working-class backgrounds: domestic workers (7%), factory workers (9%), seamstresses (4%) and persons employed in commerce, e.g. shop assistants (3%). Around 57% were employed in '*sus labores*' (unpaid domestic work at home). Most women (around 72%) had no prior record of affiliation with any of the outlawed political parties. Instead, they were accused of being '*fascistas*,' '*notoriamente desafectas*,' '*manifiestamente derechistas*' or simply '*enemigas del Régimen*.' Around 28% were arrested because they were affiliated to proscribed right-wing Catholic and monarchist parties and their names were listed in the Control de Nóminas and their political affiliations were as follows: Acción Popular (approx. 45%), Renovación Española (approx. 35%), FE/FE de las Jons (11%), Tradicionalistas (3%) and other Nationalist parties (6%).[131]

The majority were Catholics and a significant number were devout Catholics who had been involved in lay Catholic groups before the war or they were right-wing party activists who had participated in propaganda activities during the February 1936 general elections. Esperanza Ponce de León (fifty-eight years, single) was a member of the monarchist party Renovación Española and also "extremely religious."[132] Aurelia Osorio Rivas had worked at the Ministry of Public Instruction for fourteen years. On 25 December 1936, the tribunal Secretary Ricardo Calderon certified that "she has made propaganda on behalf of Gil Robles and his friends. She is a Catholic person."[133] Some had worked in right-wing party offices as archivists or telephone operators.[134] Dolores Molini Burriel (and her four sisters) were imprisoned for making propaganda during the February elections on behalf of Acción Popular (AP) and sentenced to six months in prison in December 1936.[135] Similarly, Carmen Carrascal de Espinosa was sentenced to one year in a labour camp having been found to be an active member of the JAP[136] and also the secretary of AP in Azuaga (Badajos). The court sentenced her on the basis that "she has come to Madrid with the intention of conspiring in the fascist movement."[137] Mercedes Urtasan Díaz was arrested on 16 April 1937 by the DGS.[138] During the February 1936 elections she dedicated herself to right-wing propaganda and appeared on the membership lists of Renovación Española, the Falange and Acción Popular. Devout Catholic working-class women like Magdalena Pla Riquelme were also activists in Acción Popular before the war.[139] In particular, any association with the Falange party constituted *a priori* incriminating evidence of disaffection and potential fifth-column involvement. María Paz Alonso Cueto gave herself up the Comisario Palacio at some time in late December 1936 because she had received repeated death threats. She had been walking along the Gran Vía when she was apprehended by militias who drove her to the Radio Comunista in calle Atocha. There she was interrogated for seven hours and subsequently released having been treated "very well." A DGS police report dated 7 January 1937 stated that Alonso Cueto was "a woman of great courage and strong character, who had wanted to hide the reasons for her stay in prison but that after repeated questioning she had finally admitted to being a member of the Falange Española and to been associated with Primo de Rivera's family. The DGS believed that she was a very dangerous woman."[140] On 30 May 1937 the Jurado de Urgencia 8 sentenced her to four years, eleven months and twenty-nine days imprisonment for disaffection on account of her association with FE and her intimate links with right-wing elements.[141] Similarly, two female students (aged twenty-two and twenty-four years respectively) were apprehended while hiding in the attic of a building situated in calle de Embajadores, 47, Inclusa District. They were denounced in November 1936 by the concierge of the building and by various members of a recently established neighbourhood 'security committee.' The sisters were convicted and imprisoned for being members of the Falange Party. Before 18 July they "had visited the sister and cousin of Primo de Rivera on a daily basis … Isabel Andrade Martín was frequently seen to have been driven about in a car which was owned by the Primo de Riveras."[142] Victoria López Jimeno was a teenage factory worker who had visibly fraternised with the management and "came to work an hour late every day."[143] She was denounced by a co-worker for being a member of the Falange Española, and it was claimed that she had worn her fascist pin and made the Falangist salute in the lunch canteen before the war. López Jimeno was found to be 'manifestly sympathetic towards fascism.' Aged seventeen years, she was sentenced to two years and seven months in a labour camp.

The importance of Republican networks of influence

In order to survive in the rear-guard Republican allies were essential. On 16 April 1937 Mercedes Urtasan Díaz (aged seventeen years)[144] was accused of being a member of Acción Popular, Renovación Española and the Falange Española. In normal circumstances such allegations, if proven, would result in a fine and/or imprisonment and the suspension of political and civil rights for a period of years. The DGS provided evidence of aggravating circumstances; she had conducted right-wing propaganda before the February 1936 elections and had danced with Gil Robles at an election party. Urtasan's father had also been imprisoned for disaffection. However, various influential Republican character witnesses appeared on her behalf during her trial on 18 May 1937. These included the concierge of her building, her husband (who was a Republican soldier fighting on the Teruel front) and a nephew of Largo Caballero. Urtasan was acquitted and released. The case was expedited in four weeks. María Vázquez Paris (aged thirty-two, single)[145] was arrested together with her colleague Isabel Benito Bajo (aged thirty-seven, single) on 8 May 1937 for working as typists and archivists at the offices of Acción Popular before the war. Evidence of such employment would normally have resulted in a prison sentence. However, Vázquez was acquitted because Julián Besteiro was a family friend and could vouch for both Vázquez and Bajo's pro-Republican beliefs. Besteiro testified that, prior to working for Acción Popular, the women had sought employment at his office in the Congreso de Diputados. They found employment with Acción Popular as a last resort and in desperation of finding paid employment.[146] The case was expedited, and both women were acquitted and immediately released on 22 June 1937. Such accounts reflect the partial and arbitrary nature of the new popular justice. Bajo's name was also recorded (possibly erroneously) in Rafael Casas de la Vegas' list of persons who were extrajudicially killed during the Terror.[147]

In October 1936 a group of Catholic women, some of whom were members of the Falange and Acción Popular, established a clandestine printing press that disseminated propaganda leaflets exhorting Madrid's citizens to join the rebel cause.[148] The leader of this group, María Redondo Piquenque, had no political affiliations prior to the war, but she was accused of 'being a fascist element.' The other women were members of the Falange and Acción Popular. Redondo was a devout Catholic and the co-owner (with a brother) of a small printing press. The case was expedited, and she was released from prison on 1 December 1936. The popular tribunal was lenient in this case. Redondo received a non-custodial sentence, a suspension of civil and political rights for a period of years and a modest 1,500 *peseta* fine. The bulk of the case-file documentation relates to tracing funds with respect to the payment of the fine. The sentencing judges, Vicente Manzanares, Daniel Segura and Andres Rueda, frequently dispensed custodial sentences for less serious crimes. These judges presided over the women's tribunals (*Jurados de Urgencia* numbers 7 and 8) which at first were heard in the women's prisons. It may be that 'useful connections' within the police or the judiciary may have helped to secure the defendant's release.

The above outcomes may be compared with those of Socorro Usero Fojos, aged twenty-three years, single and a servant who 'had no-one to vouchsafe her good conduct.' Usero was arrested by CPIP militias on 24 November 1936 for "expressing joy at the sight of enemy planes flying over Madrid."[149] She was also found to have moved home without duly notifying the town hall in accordance with new security legislation, listening to fascist radio emissions and 'awaiting the entry of Nationalist troops in Madrid with satisfaction.' Usero's case took months to process. She remained in prison until her trial on 24 June 1937 when she was sentenced to 'one year and one days forced labour,' scheduled for release on 9 May 1938. Similarly, Aurea Solano Sánchez (unmarried, thirty-two years old) was arrested in the presence of her parents at the Atocha station on 27 July 1937 for attempting to resist an 'on the spot security search.' It was believed that she might be a fifth-column spy. She had no prior political affiliations. She was not a resident of Madrid and had been living in temporary accommodation in a hostel with her sister. The building concierge and other neighbours gave evidence that the defendant was not known to them. However, a neighbour gave evidence that the defendant "was out until late every day only returning to her room to sleep ... she was a woman of fairly extremist religious views (*mujer de tendencias religiosas bastante arriesgadas*)."[150] During her trial the prosecution could not produce substantive evidence of fifth-column practices. However, Solano Sánchez angrily declared in open court that "it was all the same to her whether Franco and his followers won the war whether the legitimate Popular Front government won the war."[151] This defiant and disloyal speech act constituted an act of disaffection which led on 28 August 1937 to a custodial sentence of four years detention in Cehegín labour camp together with a suspension of all civil and political rights for a period of ten years. Solano was a stranger in the capital and lacked the necessary contacts to vouchsafe her good character.

Madrid's autonomous fifth column was an imagined community that facilitated the construction of a new political and religious national Catholic identity within a context of repression and devastating material deprivation. Active resistance practices and forms of everyday sabotage served to boost collective morale among Madrid's beleaguered anti-Republican community. The autonomous fifth column was made up of dozens of small groups and hundreds of individuals who were united by their anti-liberal and anti-democratic beliefs and their desire to sabotage, hamper or disrupt the Republican war effort in as many ways as possible. The autonomous resistance mainly involved acts of passive and everyday resistance and sabotage which included listening to censored Nationalist radio broadcasts, conducting clandestine masses, organising secret celebrations to mark Nationalist victories or engaging in small-scale ration-card fraud and black-market activities. Very few of the groups examined above were charged with high treason, and these cases involved large-scale organised documentation fraud and escape-line operations. It was the 'idea of resistance' over and above significant acts of sabotage or armed resistance that enabled 'Clandestine Madrid' to preserve its collective identity and morale. Those who were keenest to embrace more active and politically engaged forms of resistance joined organised Clandestine Falange groups. This was relatively easy to do because Clandestine Madrid was a tight-knit and interconnected community. The vast majority of treason and rebellion cases involved survivalist acts of desertion or conscription evasion, mainly concerning individuals who wanted to avoid the rigours and deprivations of Republican army life rather than join the Nationalist ranks.

Women formed an integral part of the autonomous resistance and were often responsible for the spiritual, material and affective well-being of the family and the wider community during a moment of extreme danger and uncertainty when anti-Republican men were obliged to withdraw from the public space. Women's fifth-column practices imbricated survivalist and everyday resistance strategies in a context of political repression and devastating material deprivation. They used Republican kinship networks in order to obtain false documentation, suborn character witnesses or destroy incriminating evidence. They also safe-housed relatives who were fugitives, draft-dodgers or deserters and took steps to obtain the necessary documentation to ensure their survival. Well-connected women used their influence within intimate and informal Republican power networks in order to safely navigate the new social field, provide for their families and where necessary circumvent the worst sanctions of the popular justice. Middle- and upper-class women frequently escaped harsh prison sentences, while working-class women lacked the necessary social and cultural capital or the economic resources to successfully navigate the disciplinary regimes of the police and the courts. There were significant continuities between the new revolutionary Madrid and the old regime. The vast majority of fifth-column women were charged with the lesser crime of disaffection despite the fact that by 1938 defeatism had become widespread. However, both disaffection and defeatism were viewed seriously by the authorities and attracted custodial sentences often involving hard labour and harsh (means-tested) fines.

Selective violence in the form of civilian denunciations constituted a key feature of the new popular justice. The emergency popular tribunals were created on 23 August 1936 in response to the urgent need to defend the Republic from its internal enemies and to channel the violent extra-judicial 'popular justice' within new legal frames. This new 'people's justice' transformed pre-war Republican legal and judicial meanings and represented a dramatic departure from the democratic ideals and legal protections enshrined in the 1931 Constitution.[152] The summary trials were expedited, and due legal process was seldom observed. The lay judges (who represented the various Republican political parties) had the power to determine sentences and appeals. In many cases arrests were arbitrary and often based on flimsy and unfounded denunciations which were prompted by personal rather than ideological motivations including jealousy, revenge or the settling of old scores. In particular, the evidential and sentencing practices relating to crimes of defeatism and disaffection were arbitrary, and it was difficult to discern any consistent sentencing rationale from the records.[153] However, with the exception of military deserters, only those involved in wide-scale, systematic documentation fraud, serious rationing infractions or organised desertion and fugitive escape-lines were charged with rebellion or high treason which attracted life-terms. Most were accused of lesser crimes of disaffection or defeatism. However, in the context of total war, the preservation of civilian morale and the urgent need to defend the Republic from its internal enemies were perceived as vital to the war effort. Consequently, the government used propaganda, new legal measures and encouraged forms of selective and intimate violence in order to combat the 'enemy within.' Care was taken to prosecute even the most minor political crimes which often resulted in custodial sentences, substantial financial penalties and property confiscation. However, on 25 December 1938 pursuant to Negrín's Thirteen Points, the government issued a decree pardoning (but not reinstating) all employees who had lost their jobs subsequent to emergency tribunal sanctions, including all public and private sector employees and all those who had worked in the military or civil administration. No compensation or restoration of property was offered to those whose property was confiscated pursuant to the new Civil Responsibilities Reparations Legislation.[154]

When examined through gendered frames, the new tribunals routinely attributed less political significance to women's resistance actions and women received lighter sentences for similar crimes. Masculinist gender prejudices were embedded in presumptions that women were unable to form their own political views and in beliefs that their minds were more easily 'poisoned' against the Republic by the 'ideas of others.' By the same token, women were able to invoke these negative stereotypes in order to avoid the worst sanctions of the court, and to this extent they were often successful in their strategies to contest and subvert the authorities. Elvira Rodríguez was acquitted of treason because she testified to a 'complete ignorance' of her husband's fraudulent and treasonous activities which often took place in the homespace. She alleged that she had always confined and restricted her activities to the kitchen and this defence was accepted by the tribunal. Others exploited the symbolic 'compensations' afforded by their subaltern gender status in order to subvert and contest the Republican regime by exploiting gendered and pathologising medico-legal discourses to their own advantage in order to negotiate trial suspensions and acquittals.

Notes

1 Cervera (1998) *Madrid*, at pp. 196–197. See also CDMH, Fondos Contemporáneos, Causa General, Tribunales Populares y Jurados de Urgencia y de Guardia de Madrid, ES.28079. AHN/2.2.6. The PARES portal has a useful filtering engine, and cases of defeatism constitute around 73% of the total popular tribunal trials.

2 Yusta, Mercedes "The Early Years of Franco's Regime As 'Seen from the Bottom,' Armed Resistance and Everyday Resistances (1939–1952)," *Vingtième Siécle, Revue d'Histoire*, 27 (3) (2015), pp. 231–244[full text in French] at p. 231. See also, Prada Rodríguez, Julio and Raúl Soutelo Vázquez "La resistencia económica en el primer franquismo. Una aproximación al estraperlo desde la memoria oral: Ourense, 1939–1952," in Trujillano Sánchez, José Manuel, and Díaz, Pilar (eds) *Testimonios orales y escritos. España 1936–1996. Actas V Jornadas Historia y Fuentes Orales: Ávila, Octubre 1996* (Ávila: Fundación cultural Santa-Teresa), pp. 77–94, Bernal Rodríguez, Antonio Miguel "Resignación de los campesinos andaluces: la resistencia pasiva durante el franquismo," in Ortiz Heras, Manuel, Ruiz González, David and Sánchez Sánchez, Isidro (eds) (1993) *España franquista: causa general y actitudes sociales ante la dictadura* (Albacete: Universidad de Castilla-La Mancha), pp. 145–159.

3 See the sociological arguments on the significance of widespread civilian resistance discussed in Nord Philip (2015) *France 1940, Defending the Republic* (New Haven: YUP), ebook Loc 183-6/209.

4 Ian Kershaw, a member of the Bavaria Project, conceptualised resistance from below in Nazi Germany and argued that it "embraced all forms of limited and partial rejection, whatever the motives, of specific aspects of Nazi rule. Instead of dealing in images of black and white, resistance was portrayed in shades of grey" in Kershaw, Ian (2002) *Popular Opinion and Political Dissent in the Third Reich 1933–1945* (Oxford: Clarendon), p. 193. See also Eley, Geoff "Hitler's silent majority? Conformity and Resistance Under the Third Reich (Part I)," *Michigan Quarterly Review*, XLII (2) (Spring, 2003).

5 'Grey' resistance is conceptualised in Broszat, Martin "Resistenz und Widerstand," in Broszat et al. (ed) (1981) *Bayern in der NS-Zeit* (Munich: Oldenbourg). An example of passive and symbolic resistance is illustrated by a defendant who trained his five-year-old daughter to use the fascist raised arm salute at home and the closed fist salute in public, see *Causa instruida contra Jesusa Arnaíz Sandino, Manuel Muro Vázquez, Soledad Portomarín Serrano, José Soria Ortíz, Benedicta Lobo Pérez por el delito/s de Derrotismo*, AHN, FC-CAUSA_GENERAL, 148, Exp. 61. Imágenes 2-3/158.

6 See for example, *Expte. 1344 instruido contra varias personas por el delito/s de Adhesión y Auxilio a la Rebelión*, AHN, FC-CAUSA_GENERAL, 50, Exp. 45. The Iglesia de San Francisco el Grande group comprised around a dozen devout Catholic men and women who looked after the artwork and the church buildings; this group had links with the Clandestine Falange through their leader, the Falangist architect Francisco Ordeig and the group came to form part of the Clandestine Falange (see Chapter 3).

7 The colloquial term '*paco*' to denote rebel snipers is derived from the conflation of the traditional Catholic *señorito* Christian name 'Paco' and the onomatopoeic 'pac-pac' sound of rifle-fire.

8 Oral Testimony Santiago Carillo dated 10 June 1996, Montoliú, Pedro (1999) *Madrid en la guerra civil, Los protagonisatas Vol. II* (Madrid: Sílex), pp. 78 and 83.

9 *Expte. 22 contra Dolores Alonsa Zarzuela, por delito/s de Desafección*, AHN, FC-CAUSA_GENERAL, 219, Exp. 29.

10 De Guzmán, Eduardo (2004) *Madrid rojo y negro* (Madrid: Oberón), p. 54. The author of this memory text describes the anarchist's efforts in July 1936 to "crush the fascist redoubts in the heart of the city including the Montaña barracks … and other fascist strongholds."

11 *Expte. no. 1743 instruido contra varias personas por el delito de Espionaje*, ES.28079. AHN/2.2.6/FC-CAUSA_GENERAL, 4, Exp. 13. See also *Expte. 672, contra* Matilde Serrano Mannara *por delitos de Desafección y Adhesion a la Rebelión*, AHN, FC-CAUSA_GENERAL, 231, Exp. 38.

12 Cervera (1998) *Madrid*, p. 283.

13 See for example, *Expte 134 instruido contra Francisco Aguirre Roiloba, Rogelio López Llaser, Andres Martín Bengoechea, Teresa Mayoural Corrales, Donato López LLaser pore el delito/s de Alta Traición*, FC-CAUSA_GENERAL, 152, Exp. 32. The defendants were mechanics who worked in a rivet factory. These three men and a woman were denounced by co-workers for sabotage but were eventually acquitted.

14 Pastor Petit, Domenèc (2013) *Resistencia y sabotaje en la Guerra Civil* (Barcelona: Enigma), p. 426. Pastor Petit concludes that, in general, sabotage was not practised by fifth-columnists.

15 López García, Alfonso "Bombas que nunca mataron: el sabotaje pacífico durante la Guerra Civil Española," *Aportes*, 95, año XXXII (3/2017), pp. 201–246 at p. 236. This article examines military sabotage in both zones, military sabotage more prevalent in the Nationalist zone.

16 Most of these cases involved firearms and ceremonial weapons (e.g. military swords) which were discovered subsequent to routine house searches of suspected fifth-columnists. Many of these cases were remitted to the lower courts on charges of disaffection.

17 *Causa 1655 instruida contra Otto Joost, Egon Wiedwal, Reinhold Hoffman por el delito/s de Sabotaje*, AHN, FC-CAUSA_GENERAL, 198, Exp. 24. Imágenes 1-3. It is not known whether these four German factory workers were connected with German or Nationalist intel-

ligence services because the case was referred to the 'High Court of Espionage and High Treason' in Valencia on 27 August 1937 and there are no further records.

18 *Causa no 29 instruida contra Joaquín Riu Puyuelo por el delito/s de Espionaje y Sabotaje*, AHN, FC-CAUSA_GENERAL, 258, Exp. 40. This case is interesting because the defendant had made a written pledge to donate 10 pesetas montly to Socorro Blanco in furtherance of the Nationalist cause. The case also evidences the existence of a secret Socorro Blanco bank account.

19 *Causa no 22 contra Carlos Andreu Peracho, Celestino García Rojas, Francisco Sánchez Dorado, Vicente Palancar Pérez por el delito/s de Sabotaje*, AHN, FC-CAUSA_GENERAL, 258, Exp. 29. Imágenes 1-22. The defendants were acquitted on 16 February 1939. Dorado, a carpenter, testified that he and his friends had been scavenging for wood for fuel amongst the detritus on the banks of Manzanares river when they were arrested by a soldier. Imagen 11/22.

20 *Expte. no 101 instruido contra Antonio Baringo Sopeña por el delito/s de Sabotaje*, AHN, FC-CAUSA_GENERAL, 5, Exp. 49. Baringo was a twenty-year-old soldier within the 1st Company of the 597th Battalion of the 150th Mixed brigade. He alleged that he "accidentally stumbled over and severed a communications cable linked to the headquarters of the 597th Battalion on the Ruinas front line whilst rushing to the lavatory." Imagen 6/33. There was no evidence that Baringo had actually severed the cable, and he was absolved on 17 November 1938. Imagen 28/33.

21 *Expte. no 5 instruido contra Francisco Sánchez Struch por el delito/s de Sabotaje*, AHN, FC-CAUSA_GENERAL, 79, Exp. 12. The case related to an eighteen-year-old soldier who was denounced for allegedly adding water to the gasoline supplies of the 111th Mixed Brigade in September 1938.

22 See Cervera, Javier "La Radio: un arma mas de la Guerra Civil en Madrid," *Historia y comunicacion social*, 3 (1998), pp. 263–293 at p. 275. Listening to illegal radio broadcasts fell under the definition of 'clandestine gathering in order to commit the crime of Defeatism.'

23 Vinthagen, Stella and Johansson, Anna "Every day Resistance: Exploration of a Concept and its Theories," *Resistance Studies Magazine*, 1 (2013), pp. 1–46 at p. 4.

24 See oral testimony of Dolores Muñoz Tuero in an undated interview with Borrás (1965), pp. 201–208 at pp. 202–204.

25 Oral testimony Marcial González Bonet dated 10 June 1996, Montoliú, Pedro (1999) *Madrid en la guerra civil, Los protagonisatas Vol. II* (Madrid: Silex), pp. 193–205 at pp. 199–201.

26 Montoliú, Pedro (1999) *Madrid en la guerra civil, Los protagonisas, Volumen II* (Madrid: Silex). See also, Duyagües, Pilar, Balló, Tania and Berger, Gonzalo (eds) (2003) *Querido Diario: Hoy ha empezado la guerra* (Barcelona: Espasa). This rare testimonial of a fifteen-year-old Republican girl in Barcelona reflects the importance of cinema in the daily lives, routines and imaginations of many ordinary citizens during the war.

27 See Chapter X "La importancia de un carnet," in Alfaya, José Luis (1998) *Como un río de fuego, Madrid, 1936* (Barcelona: EUI), pp. 155–158.

28 *Causa no. 43 instruida contra varias personas poer el delito/s de Alta Traición*, AHN, FC-CAUSA_GENERAL, 146, Exp. 27. Imagen 3/227.

29 *Causa no. 43*, Imagen 159/227.

30 *Causa 43*, Imagen 9/227. Witness statement of Juan Díez Rodríguez dated 17 May 1938.

31 *Causa 43*, Imagen 16/227. Witness statement of Carlos Viña Campa dated 22 May 1938.

32 *Causa no. 43*, Imagen 159/227.

33 See Marcot, François "Pour une sociologie de la Résistance: intentionnalité et fonctionnalité," in Prost, Antoine (ed) (1997) *La Résistance, une histoire sociale* (Paris: Atélier/Ouvrières), pp. 21–29.

34 *Causa 43*, Imágenes 4-8/227. Witness statement of Juan Díez Rodríguez dated 17 May 1938.

35 *Causa 43*, Imagen 203/227.

36 *Causa 43*, Imágenes 17-18/227. Witness statement of Elvira Rodríguez dated 18 May 1938.

37 Rodríguez López, Sofía and Cazorla Sánchez, Antonio "Blue Angels: Female Fascist Resisters, Spies and Intelligence Officials in the Spanish Civil War, 1936–9," *Journal of Contemporary History*, 53 (4) (2016), pp. 692–713 at p. 702.

38 *Causa 41 instruida contra varias personas por el delito/s de Alta Traición*, AHN, FC-CAUSA_GENERAL, 146, Exp. 28.

39 *Causa 41*, Testimony of Felipa Sancho dated 4 June 1938, Imagen 86/134.

40 Barrios had conveniently managed to get himself invalided out of active service on account of unspecified 'nephritic attacks.'

41 Witness statement of Arturo Barios Ortega dated 22 May 1938 *Causa 41 instruida contra varias personas por el delito/s de Alta Traición*, AHN, FC-CAUSA_GENERAL, 146, Exp. 28, 18/134.

42 *Causa 41*, Imagen 7/134.

43 Bahamonde Magro, Ángel, Cervera Gil, Javier (1999) *Así Terminó la Guerra de España* (Madrid: Marcial Pons), p. 253.

44 *Expte. no. 882 instruido contra Dolores Soto Sánchez por el delito/s de Desafección al Régimen*, AHN, FC-CAUSA_GENERAL, 234, Exp. 34.

45 Where she had been resident for two years having previously lived in calle del Cardenal Císneros. She lived a peripatetic existence moving from house to house which was also evidence of disaffection.

46 *Expte. no. 882*, Imagen 38/47.

47 *Expte. no. 69 instruido contra Filomena Carretero Durán, Pedro Hedo Escalera, Visitación Hedo Miguel, Teresa Moreno Álvarez, Dolores Soto Sánchez por el delito/s de infracción en material de substencias*, AHN, FC-CAUSA_GENERAL, 146, Exp. 34. Imagen 4/93.

48 *Expte. no. 69*, Imágenes 60-63/93.

49 These military crimes were variously designated as 'rebellion,' 'assistance and adhesion to rebellion' or 'aiding rebellion' and simple 'treason.'

50 Corral, Pedro (2017) *Desertores, Los españoles que no quisieron la Guerra Civil* (Madrid: Almuzara).

51 Matthews, James (2012) *Reluctant Warriors, Republican Popular Army and Nationalist Army Conscripts in the Spanish Civil War, 1936–1939* (Oxford: OUP).

52 *Causa no. 24 instruida contra varias personas por el delito/s de Alta Traición*, AHN, FC-CAUSA_GENERAL, 155, Exp. 34.

53 Nash, Mary (1995) *Defying Male Civilization: Women in the Spanish Civil War* (Denver, Colorado: Arden), p. 102.

54 *Expte. sobre el Ejercito republicano*, AHN, FC-CAUSA_GENERAL, 1562, Exp. 3. Imagen 3/22. The motivations behind this widow's testimony are unclear.

55 *Causa no.38 instruida contra Aurelia Sánchez Soria por el delito/s de Alta Traición*, AHN, FC-CAUSA_GENERAL, 145, Exp. 19.

56 *Expte. 4401*, FC-CAUSA_GENERAL, 20, EXP. 2, and *Expte. 254*, FC-CAUSA_GENERAL, 114, Exp. 8.

57 *Causa no.36 instruida contra Anunciación* González *Bustamente, Julia Tamargo San Martín, Manuel Fernández Tebar por el delito/s de Alta traición*, AHN, FC-CAUSA_GENERAL, 145, Exp. 26. This type of case was frequently expedited. On 1 June 1938 the husband (Fernández Tebar) was sentenced to twenty-five years in a labour camp, his wife (Tamargo San Martín) to twelve years, and the girlfriend of one of the draft dodgers (González Bustamente) was referred to popular tribunals on charges of handling and using a false certificate (*cedula falsa*).

58 *Causa no. 36*, AHN, FC-CAUSA_GENERAL, 145, Exp. 26.

59 *Expte. no. 5 instruido contra Gaspar Esteva Sánchez, Dolores Hurtado Callejón, Francisco Hurtado Callejón por el delito/s de Alta Traición*, AHN, FC-CAUSA_GENERAL, 59, Exp. 41, Imágenes 1-54.

60 *Expte. no. 5*, Witness statement of Carlos Alonso Núñez dated 4 July 1938, Imagen 4/54.

61 *Expte. no. 5*, Imagen 8/54. Witness statement of Carlos Alonso Núñez dated 4 July 1938 and photograph of forged military identity card (a very basic forgery) which was submitted as evidence. The card stated as follows: "SOLDIER, YOUR DUTY IS TO WIN … BE DISCIPLINED … POSSESS A GENUINE SPIRIT OF SACRIFICE … YOU BELONG TO A RACE OF HEROES THAT ONCE AGAIN ARE FIGHTING FOR THE INDEPENDANCE OF YOUR COUNTRY … UPHOLD THE FLAG OF JUSTICE AND LIBERTY AND PROGRESS, THAT OF OUR CAUSE, BE BRAVE AND ABNEGATED, CHOOSE DEATH ABOVE DEFEAT, YOUR DUTY IS TO WIN, AND THOSE WHO WIN ARE THOSE WHO KNOW HOW TO FACE DANGER WITHOUT THE FEAR OF DYING." Such discourses regarding discipline, duty, sacrifice and self-abnegation reveal cultural affinities between the 'emotional regimes' of the Republican army and the Clandestine Falange at this time.

62 *Causa 26 instruida contra varias personas por el delito/s de Alta traición.* AHN, FC-CAUSA_GENERAL,148, Exp.62, Imágenes 1-238.

63 *Expte.1679 instruido contra varias personas por el delito/s de Adhesion y auxilio a la Rebelion*, AHN, FC-CAUSA_GENERAL, 373, Exp. 1. Imágenes 1-1733.

64 *Causa no.26 instruida contra varias personas por el delito/s de Alta Traición*, AHN, FC-CAUSA_GENERAL, 148, Exp. 62, Imagen 237/239.

65 *Causa no.26*, Imagen 3/239.

66 *ABC* Seville, obituary dated 16 October 1991. Julián Cortés Cavanillas (b. 1908 d. 1991) was a Spanish monarchist writer and journalist who worked for the right-wing *ABC* newspaper. He was also involved in Ángel Herrera Oria's early *El Debate* publications. In 1931 he wrote a book on the fall of Alfonso XIII which was a 'best-seller' between 1931 and 1932 and which ran to eight editions and sold 50,000 copies. Together with Ramiro Maeztú, Quintanar, Pemán, Vegas Latapié and Sainz Rodríguez he established the monarchist Catholic Acción Española publication in December 1931. He was imprisoned at the start of the war because of his polemic military publication '*Pajaritos de Papel*.' He was the *ABC*'s Rome correspondent between 1945 and 1962 and 1967 and 1971. He also appeared briefly as himself 'the Spanish correspondent for *ABC*' in the famous Hollywood "Roman Holiday" film with Audrey Hepburn and Gregory Peck.

67 *Causa no.26*, Imágenes 27-29/239.

68 *Causa no. 13 instruida contra Josefina Gisbert Poveda y Manuel Entrena Ruiz por el delito de Alta Traición y Derrotismo*, AHN, FC-CAUSA_GENERAL, 147, Exp. 50, Imágenes 1-68.

69 *Causa no. 13*, Imagen 38/68.

70 *Causa no. 13*, Imagen 38/68.

71 Mother María Luisa Fernández and Mother María Leturia (1939) *Catorce meses de aventuras bajo el dominio rojo* (Rome: ACI).

72 *Causa No. 1672 instruida contra Trinidad Heras Sanz and Natalio Heras Sanz el delito/s de Adhesion y auxilio a la Rebelion*, AHN, FC-CAUSA_GENERAL, 148, Exp. 40, Imagen 6/120.

73 *Causa No. 1672*, Imágenes 108-120/120.

74 *Causa No. 1672*, Imagen 35/120.

75 See Ramón Solans, Francisco, "Persecución, Milagros y profecias en el discurso Católico Zaragozano durante la Segunda República," *Historia Social*, 78 (2014), pp. 81–98. See also, Christian, William (1996) *Visionaries: The Spanish Republic and the Reign of Christ* (California: UCP).

76 *Expte. no. 96 instruido contra varias personas por delito/s de espionaje*, AHN, FC-CAUSA_GENERAL,51, Exp. 23. Imágenes 1-15.

77 The PARES website does not contain records of the Valencian proceedings.

78 Source: "Autos de procesamiento y prisión incondicional, dictados por el Juez del Juzgado Especial no. 3 del Tribunal Especial de Espionaje y Alta Traícion de Catalunya, contra varios individuos que formaban parte de un grupo que fué sorprendido cuando trataban de pasar clandestinament la frontera por Andorra" FC-CAUSA_GENERAL, 1636, Exp. 138. Imagen 2/23.

79 *Autos de procesamiento y prisión incondicional*, AHN, FC-CAUSA_GENERAL, 1636, Exp. 138. Imagen 22/23
80 Paz, Armando (1976) *Los Servicios de Espionaje en la Guerra Civil de España 1936–9* (Madrid: San Martín), p. 82.
81 Campos Posada, Ainhoa "Resistir es fácil con la tripa llena. Escasez y derrotismo en el Madrid de la Guerra Civil," in Oviedo Silva, Daniel and Pérez-Olivares García (eds) (2016) *Madrid, una ciudad en guerra (1936–48)* (Madrid: Catarata), pp. 97–132 at p. 97.
82 Cervera (1998) *Madrid*, p. 283.
83 e.g. *Expte. no 100 instruido contra Ángela Rodríguez Amado por el delito/s de Desafección al Régimen*, AHN, FC-CAUSA_GENERAL, 237, Exp. 4. This woman was arrested for 'behaving in a hostile manner towards the Republic.' She was denounced for declaring that "the government was supported by a bunch of criminals [and that] fascists were also human-beings and they are committing atrocities against them." Imagen 4/84.
84 Campos Posada, Ainhoa "Resistir es fácil con la tripa llena..." The author reviewed 136 cases of defeatism of which ninety-six related to men, p. 116.
85 Campos Posada (2016) "Resistir...," at pp. 111–115.
86 See Rodríguez Barreira, Oscar "Cambalaches: Hambre, moralidad y mercados negros de Guerra y post-Guerra," *Historia Social*, 77 (2013), pp. 1–21, at p. 2. This author compares black-market practices in various European countries during the Second World War and the 1940s using conceptual frames derived from Scott, C. James (1998) *Seeing Like a State. How Certain Schemes to Improve the Human Condition Have Failed* (New Haven: Yale University Press).
87 *Causa instruida contra María Martín Baeza por el delito/s de Derrotismo*, AHN, FC-CAUSA_GENERAL, 146. Exp.17, Imagen 5/79.
88 *Causa no 124 instruida contra Felisa Manuel Rabanal por el delito/s de Derrotismo*, AHN, FC-CAUSA_GENERAL, 147, Exp. 6, Imágenes 6/37 and 35-36/37
89 *Causa instruida contra Jesusa Arnaiz Sandino, Manuel Muro Vázquez, Soledad Portomarín Serrano, José Soria Ortiz, Benedicta Lobo Pérez por el delito/s de Derrotismo*, AHN, FC-CAUSA_GENERAL,148, Exp.61. Imágenes 2-3/158.
90 The phenomenon of denunciation in modern European history is examined in Fitzpatrick, Sheila and Gellately, Robert (eds) (1996) *Accusatory Practices, Denunciation in Modern European History, 1789–1989* (Chicago: UCP). Here denunciations are defined at p. 1 as "spontaneous communications from individual citizens to the state (or to another authority such as the church) containing accusations of wrongdoing by other citizens or officials and implicitly or explicitly calling for punishment."
91 Joshi, Vandana (2003) *Gender and Power in the Third Reich, Female Denouncers and the Gestapo (1933–45)* (London: Palgrave Macmillan), p.19.
92 Kalyvas, Stathis (2006) *The Logic of Violence in Civil War* (New York, NY: CUP), pp. 332–333.
93 Zugazagoitia, Julián (2001) *Guerra y vicisitudes de los Espanoles* (Barcelona: Tusquets), pp. 90–91, here the author observes 'that selfish and vengeful motivations' often resulted in the 'most strange and arbitrary outcomes' where committed militants were denounced despite their proven left-wing credentials.
94 *Causa no.113 contra Luis, Martínez Galiano y Esperanza González López por el delito/s de Derrotismo*, AHN, FC-CAUSA_GENERAL, 147, Exp. 47.
95 *Causa no.113*, Statement of Esperanza González López dated 16 September 1936, Imagen 6/39.
96 *Causa no.113*, Statement of Luis Martínez Galiano, tobacco factory worker dated 16 September 1936, Imagen 12/39.
97 *Causa no.113*, Imagen 5/39.
98 *Causa no.113*, Statement of Carmen Castilla Gianini, aged thirty-two years, 'profesión vice-tiple' [sic] dated 17 September 1936, Imagen 17/39.
99 *Causa no. 110 contra* Encarnación, Casado Jiménez, AHN, FC-CAUSA_GENERAL, 147, Exp. 44, Imagen 3/36.

100 *Causa no. 50 contra* María Martínez Gutiérrez, AHN, FC-CAUSA_GENERAL, 156, Exp.32, Imagen 9/49. The case is particularly interesting because this illiterate woman wrote an affectionate and detailed letter to her husband (the letter was written on her behalf by her sister-in-law) that touchingly describes the daily routines in a rural village where food was seemingly less scarce and life continued along its habitual routines; "the doves and the cows are doing well." See Imagen 8/49.

101 *Causa no.46 instruida contra Ramona González González por el delito/s de Derrotismo*, AHN, FC-CAUSA_GENERAL, 149, Exp. 5. Witness statement of Tomás Soriano dated 2 July 1938 made at the Comisaria Buenavista, Imagen Num 3/39

102 *Causa no. 46*, Imagen, 6/39.

103 *Causa no, 46*, Imagen 28/39. Witness statement of Forensic Psychiatrist Dr. David Querol Pérez dated 6 July 1938.

104 *Causa no, 46*, Imagen 28-29/39.

105 See "Chapter 7, A Theory of Selective Violence," in Kalyvas, Stathis (2006) *The Logic of Violence in Civil War*, Section 7.2 "Denunciation," at pp. 176–181. The author argues at p. 173 that "selective violence entails the personalization of violence and requires information that is asymmetrically distributed between political actors and individual citizens." He also observes that "denunciation constitutes a key micro-foundation of intimate violence" at p. 332.

106 According to foreign correspondent Lester Ziffren "Defeats were never admitted in the Loyalist press which was engaged principally in publishing material intended to strengthen the public morale" in Preston, Paul (2008) *We Saw Spain Die, Foreign Correspondents in the Spanish Civil War* (London: Constable), [ebook] Loc 673 of 12145.

107 Abella, Rafael (2004) *La vida cotidiana durante la Guerra Civil. La España Republicana* (Barcelona: Planeta), p. 152.

108 Oral testimony Marcial Gónzalez Bonet dated 10 June 1996, Montoliú, Pedro (1999) *Madrid en la guerra civil, Los protagonisatas Vol. II* (Madrid: Silex), pp. 193–205 at p. 198.

109 Palacios, Julio (April 1939) *En la España Roja: Memorias de un agente del SIPM*, AHM (Madrid), Cuartel General del Generalísimo, Armario 5, Legajo 277, Carpeta 18 (Rollo 29). Text transcribed in full in article by Manuel Aguilera "La Quinta Columna durante el Golpe de Casado," *Aportes 69*, XXIV (1/2009), pp. 99–111 at p. 109.

110 See also, "Physical Survival" in Diamond Hannah (1999) *Women and the Second World War in France, 1939–48, Choices and Contraints* (London: Longman), pp. 50–69.

111 Cervera (1998) *Madrid*, p. 377.

112 Preston, Paul (2016) *The Last Days of the Spanish Republic* (London: William Collins), [ebook] Loc. 664.

113 By 1939 the standard ration was 55 grams of lentils, beans or rice with occasional sugar or salted cod. According to the Quaker International Commission for the Assistance of Child Refugees these rations were insufficient to maintain life. It was claimed that 400 people died in Madrid from lack of food each week. Source: Chapter 3 "The Power of Exhaustion," in Preston, Paul (2016) *The Last Days of the Spanish Republic* (London: William Collins), [ebook] Loc. 676.

114 *Causa no. 43 contra* Ángela Jiménez Ríos *por el delito/s de Derrotismo*, AHN, FC-CAUSA_GENERAL, 146, Exp. 26.

115 *Causa no. 3 instruida contra Concepción Benitez Flores, María Juana Sánchez*, AHN, FC-CAUSA_GENERAL, 258, Exp. 25.

116 *Causa 11, instruida contra Gloria Ruiz Bravo, por el delito/s de Derrotis*mo, AHN, FC-CAUSA_GENERAL, 155, Exp. 16.

117 *Causa 11*, Imagen 11/19.

118 *Expte. 1764 instruido contra Félix Moliner Pons por el delito/s de Derrotismo.* ES.28079.AHN/2.2.26/FC-CAUSA_GENERAL,258, Exp.16, Imagen 9/47.

119 See MPhil Dissertation of Flynn, Angela (2013) *Las Desafectas al Régimen: Anti-Republican Women and Republican Justice (1936–9)* (Oxford: Unpublished MPhil). Chapter 2 explores the legislation on disaffection in greater detail.

120 See *Gaceta de Madrid*, Num. 285, 11 October 1936, p. 289, www.boe.es/datos/pdfs/BOE/1936/285/B00289-00289.pdf.

121 See "Los Jurados de Urgencia," in Sánchez Recio, Glicerio (1991) *Justicia y Guerra en España. Los Tribunales Populares (1936–1939)* (Alicante: Instituto de Cultura Juan Gil-Albert), pp. 64–71.

122 See Ruiz, Julius "'Work and Don't Lose Hope': Republican Forced Labour Camps during the Spanish Civil War," *Contemporary European History*, 18 (4) (November 2009), pp. 419–441. The article examines the use of forced labour in Republican Spain during the civil war. It argues that labour camps were an integral part of Republican 'popular justice.' Enforced labour would rehabilitate 'fascists' and enable them to contribute to the economic reconstruction and transformation of Spain.

123 *Expte. 240, contra Gervasia Alonso Álvarez por delito/s de Desafección*, AHN, FC-CAUSA_GENERAL, 227, Exp. 1.

124 *Expte. 64, contra varias personas por el delito/s de auxilio a la Rebelión*, FC-CAUSA_GENERAL,10, Exp. 24, Imágenes 1-715.

125 See *Carteles de Propaganda, Archivo Fotográfico de la Delegación de Propaganda de Madrid durante la Guerra Civil*, PARES. Centro documental de la Memoria Histórica. Ministerio de Cultura. http://pares.mcu.es.

126 Lithograph, Hinsberger, Alexis (1907–1996) CNT/FAI [date 1937?] SOURCE: Spanish Civil War, Bibliotecadigitalhispanica.bne.es. *Carteles de Propaganda, Archivo Fotográfico de la Delegación de Propaganda de Madrid durante la Guerra Civil*, anon., AGA,33, F, 04061,55241,001.

127 *Expte. 290*, AHN, FC-CAUSA_GENERAL,12, Exp. 95. See also *Expte. 123, contra Adriana Vizcaino Gines por delito/s de Desafección*, AHN, FC-CAUSA_GENERAL, 12, Exp. 19. This defendant made propaganda for AP, but very few details are provided in this case.

128 *Expte. 672, contra Matilde Serrano Mannara por delitos de Desafección y adhesión a la rebelión*, AHN, FC-CAUSA_GENERAL, 231, Exp. 38.

129 *Expte. 2451*, AHN, FC-CAUSA_GENERAL, 15 EXP. 36 and *Expte. 222*, AHN, FC-CAUSA_GENERAL, 359, EXP. 37.

130 *Expte. 149, contra* Pla Riquelme, Magdalena *por el delito/s de Desafección al Régimen*, AHN, FC-CAUSA_GENERAL, 110, EXP. 12.

131 MPhil Dissertation of Flynn, Angela (2013) *Las Desafectas al Régimen: Anti-Republican Women and Republican Justice (1936–9)* (Oxford: Unpublished MPhil), p. 61.

132 *Expte. 628, contra* Esperanza Ponce de León *por delito/s de Desafección* FC-CAUSA_GENERAL, 225, Exp. 16, Imagen 5/28.

133 *Expte. 1764, contra* Aurelia Osorio Rivas, *por delito/s de Desafección*, AHN, FC-CAUSA_GENERAL, 363, Exp. 19.

134 *Expte, contra* María Vázquez Paris and Isabel Benito Bajo, *por delito/s de Desafección*, AHN, FC-CAUSA_GENERAL, 126, Exp. 36. Both worked for Acción Popular, Vázquez as secretary and archivist for four years, Bajo as telephone operator.

135 *Expte. No.76, instruido contra* Molini Burriel, Concepción Molini Burriel, Dolores Molini Burriel, Francisca Molini Burriel, Luisa Molini Burriel *por delito/s de Desafección al Régimen*, AHN, FC-CAUSA_GENERAL, 130, EXP. 1. These women also appear in a list of female victims of the extra-judicial repression, see Rafael Casas de la Vega (1994) *El Terror: Madrid 1936, Investigación Histórica y Catalogo de Víctimas Identificadas* (Madrid: Fénix), Appendix II, *Relación de Asesinados en Madrid y Provincia*, pp. 399–407.

136 *Juventudes de Acción Popular.*

137 *Expte. 2698*, AHN, FC-CAUSA_GENERAL, 13, Exp. 123. Imagen 2/4.

138 *Expte. 496, contra* Urtasan Díaz, Mercedes *por delito/s de Desafección*, AHN, FC-CAUSA_GENERAL, 359. Exp. 39, Imagen 3/37.

139 *Expte. 3691*, AHN, FC-CAUSA_GENERAL, 26, EXP. 146, *por delito/s de Desafección.* This woman was sentenced to three years in a labour camp.

140 *Expte. 184*, AHN, FC-CAUSA_GENERAL, 112, Exp. 3.

141 *Expte. 352, contra varios por delito/s de Desafección* (including María Paz Alonso Cueto), AHN, FC-CAUSA_GENERAL, 113, Exp. 38, Imagen 106/288. She also lost civil and

political rights for ten years. This woman also appears on the *Casas de la Vegas* list of victims of the Terror, but court records indicate that she remained in prison during the war.

142 *Expte. no. 304 instruido contra Isabel Andrada Martín, Eugenia Andrada Martín por el delito/s de Desafección al Régimen*, AHN, FC-CAUSA_GENERAL, 263, Exp. 24, Imágenes 21/61.

143 *See case of Victoria López Jimeno por delito/s de Desafección* in *Expte. 21*, FC-CAUSA_GENERAL, 112, Exp. 31 and *Expte. 263*, FC-CAUSA_GENERAL, 237, Exp. 22.

144 *Expte. 496, contra Mercedes Urtasan Díaz por el delito/s de Desafección*, AHN, FC-CAUSA_GENERAL, 39, 6, Imágenes 30-37/37.

145 *Expte.359, contra María Vázquez Paris por el delito/s de Desafección*, AHN, FC-CAUSA_GENERAL, 129, Exp. 36.

146 *Expte. 359, contra* Vázquez Paris, María, FC-CAUSA_GENERAL, *por el delito/s de Desafección*, 129, Exp. 36, Imagen, 24/35.

147 Casas de La Vega, Rafael (1994) *El Terror Madrid, 1936, Investigación Histórica y Catálogo de Víctimas Identificadas* (Madrid: Editorial Fénix), Appendix II, *Relación de Asesinados en Madrid y Provincia*, at p. 400.

148 These women were María Redondo Piquenque, María (thirty-five years old and unmarried with no prior political affiliations) Rosa Moreno Rodríguez, Navidad Carrasco Viretti and María Fernández López. See *Expte. 23 instruida contra María Redondo Piquenque por el delito de Desafección al Régimen*, AHN, FC-CAUSA_GENERAL, 235, Exp. 4. Imagen 10-21/73. The case was heard on 4 November 1936 in the *Jurado de Urgencia no.8*.

149 *Expte. 538, contra* Socorro Usero Fojo *por delito/s Desafección*, AHN, FC-CAUSA_GENERAL, 222, Exp. 29. Imágenes 21-26/33.
Expte. 538, Imágenes 21-26/33.

150 *See Expte. 524 instruida contra Aurea Solano Sánchez por delitos de Desafección al Régimen*, FC-CAUSA_GENERAL, 231, Exp. 19. Imagen 29/40.

151 *Expte. 524*, Imagen 34/40. The presiding magistrate in this case was Judge Ricardo Guerra who was accused of treason and of membership of the Socorro Blanco group in 1938.

152 See Sánchez Recio, Glicerio (1991) *Justicia y Guerra en España. Los Tribunales Populares (1936–1939)* (Alicante: Instituto de Cultura Juan Gil-Albert).

153 See also observations of Campos Posada, Ainhoa "Resistir es fácil con la tripa llena," at p. 118

154 Fernández, Raúl C. Cancio (2007) *Guerra Civil y Tribunales: De los Jurados Populares a la Justicia Franquista (1936–1939)* (Cáceres: Universidad de Extremadura), p. 98.

5 Female spies

This chapter considers female spies who acted independently from the organised groups and the spaces in which they operated. Around 2.4% of the popular tribunal cases related to crimes of espionage (i.e. some 359 cases). Aside from the female spies who formed part of the Clandestine Falange groups discussed in Chapter 3, only around forty-six women were indicted for espionage in Madrid. Eight of these cases were referred up to the courts of espionage and high treason in Valencia and Barcelona, and another four were referred to the 'special military courts' for rebellion. The remaining indictments were reduced to charges of disaffection (twelve cases), dismissed for lack of evidence (seven), suspended on health or other grounds (six) or acquitted (nine). The vast majority of the trials involved male conscripts and officers who acted individually or in small groups. These men sent intelligence from the front-lines to the fifth column in the capital or directly over the lines to the SIPM; in particular the disciplinary battalions were hot-beds of dissent and subversion.[1] The popular tribunal records only contain eleven cases of espionage involving foreign nationals (German, Italian and one Chinese street-vendor).[2] Foreign undercover agents were rare in Madrid, many more were in circulation in Barcelona, although before the war in May 1936 spies associated with Colonel François de la Rocque's Parti Social Français (PSF) and the '*Cagoule*' operated in the central cafés and bars of Madrid.[3] Most of the autonomous spies were males infiltrated within the civil and military administration, including the battalions, barracks, embassies, Home Office, Naval Office, law courts and military hospitals.

Those accused of espionage came from a variety of social backgrounds. However, there is an over-representation of working-class women, sex-workers and barrack auxiliaries. Disadvantaged female groups often bore the brunt of the new Republican justice because they had little recourse to financial or social networks of support. Very often such women were falsely accused from a variety of motives including petty quarrels or revenge and often spent some considerable time in prison before acquittal and release. Others worked as administrative assistants, typists in the barracks or as voluntary and unskilled auxiliary nurses. Others were single mothers or variety club actresses, women of "indeterminate profession and dubious morality" and brothel workers. Social class is an important way of signifying relationships of power and notions of difference embedded in inequality.[4] The socially disadvantaged often received poorer treatment at the hands of Republican justice.

A dozen or so aristocratic and upper-middle-class women were arrested for espionage in the capital. It was suspected that these women had access to sensitive information through their connections with senior Republican political or military figures. These cases were viewed seriously by the authorities and referred to the courts of espionage and high treason in Valencia and Barcelona. By summer 1938, a small and visible coterie of well-connected, upper-middle-class women were perceived to pose a real threat to Republican security. The silences and gaps in the witness evidence mean that, in most of the cases examined below, it is difficult to tell who these women reported to or whether they operated on their own initiative. However, even in circumstances where women worked alone, they still formed part of an 'imagined political community' because they shared the same ideals and interests and identified as part of the same nation as those who belonged to the groups and networks of the Clandestine Falange.

Republican spaces

Military units and barracks

Most cases related to women who were employed as auxiliaries within Republican civil and military institutions including the War Ministry, military hospitals and barracks. María del Pilar Martín Bascarán worked as a typist at the General Headquarters of the Colonel Mangada Battalion which was posted in Navalperal de Pineda in September 1936.[5] She was infiltrated within the battalion by Commander Urbano González Ribera who gave her 1,000 pesetas and her accomplice Carlos del Castillo 'probably more money' in order to take classified documents to rebel contacts across the front-lines. The pair were arrested near the Republican front-lines in Villacastín and returned to Navalperal during which time they were, rather surprisingly, able to return the classified documents into the custody of González Ribera. They were charged with espionage under sub-sections 1 and 2 of Article 228 of the Military Code of Justice. González was also charged with rebellion alongside another individual named 'Rivera' who managed to avoid arrest.

Women who fraternised with soldiers and those who were actively involved in the war effort were regularly suspected of espionage or treason.[6] These women were most often the intimates of soldiers and officers, and the authorities feared that "confidences exchanged in the bedroom posed a grave risk to security."[7] In 1937 the Republican government issued a poster campaign warning soldiers of the dangers of inadvertently passing intelligence to the enemy via intimate relationships. Balbina Ledesma Paz was a semi-literate militia-woman who worked as a cleaner in several military barracks. She was arrested for espionage in June 1938 following a denunciation by one of her officer lovers who was the Commander-in-Chief of a battalion in the 150th Brigade. The denunciation set in motion a lengthy investigation which involved numerous military and civilian witnesses. Balbina was married to a Falangist civil guard who was imprisoned for disaffection at the start of the war, and it was alleged that she formed part of a fifth-column group. Balbina had maintained links with other Falangists who included friends and colleagues of her husband who was associated with the former monarchist leader Calvo Sotelo. It was also alleged that at the time of her arrest she had been planning to escape into the Nationalist zone.

After her husband's escape from prison into the Nationalist zone, she was 'bereft of financial support' and volunteered her cleaning services at various barracks with the expectation of eventually obtaining paid remuneration. She also entered into a succession of intimate relationships with military officers. It was suspected that she had been communicating military intelligence to the fifth column as a result of her auxiliary work in the barracks, although no concrete evidence was ever adduced in this regard. During her SIM interrogations Balbina claimed that she was now a member of the Socialist Youth (JSU)[8] and that she was working for Republican officers as a 'mole' and 'counter-spy.'[9] She claimed to have infiltrated various military barracks in order to flush out 'disaffected elements' and alleged that Ángel Dieguez Duenas, who was a commissar with Fortifications Division, was her liaison agent. Balbina had allegedly approached him in December 1937 and "requested access to General Miaja because she wanted to expose a conspiracy that involved numerous officials whom she had already denounced to the police, but they had not taken any action."[10]

Economic necessity may, in part, have motivated Balbina's actions. It was alleged that she had no financial means 'other than that which she obtained by cohabiting with several men.' Mariano Grande (the chief commissar) produced evidence from various military witnesses that Balbina had:

> dedicated herself to an extra-marital life with various individuals, but mostly with the Commander in Chief of the 199 Battalion of the 150th Brigade who had denounced her as being a loose-living (*mujer de vida alegre*), interfering, argumentative and undesirable person on account of which he had ceased all relations with this woman … she also had developed contacts in the 36th Brigade … but she was denied access to this company on account of the fact that she may have been a dangerous element and that her amorous activities may have constituted a form of espionage … she is an openly dissolute woman (*mujer de vida publica*) who actively seeks to make important liaisons for unknown ends … her shady and dubious practices are highly suspicious … as are her claims that she is actively working to denounce disaffected military elements amongst those with whom she consorts … she does not have any means of economic subsistence other than that which she procures by cohabiting with several men.[11]

Her low status and her inability to successfully cultivate networks of influence and protection ensured that she was unable to negotiate any concessions using back-channels. Juan Saiz Orozco was a married infantry Major at the Pablo Iglesias barracks (aged thirty-one years). He testified on 24 June 1938 that he had first made the acquaintance of the defendant after his return from the front-lines in January 1937. She was working as a cleaner in the Pablo Iglesias barracks and he offered her a job as his personal laundress. From August 1937 onwards, he began to 'notice something strange in Balbina's attitude because she met with elements who were not very loyal to the cause (*no muy afectos a la causa*) for which reason she was arrested.' 'This Balbina woman' wrote directly to him and informed him that he might obtain her release if he provided a good-character reference:

> something which the witness took no notice of because he had no concrete proof of her loyalty, which had raised some suspicion on account of the friendships that she kept, although she told him that she had befriended some fascists in order to obtain information from them in order to denounce them.[12]

Without the necessary social capital or influence Balbina languished in prison. It was only on 3 March 1939 that she was released from Ventas and acquitted on the basis of a "lack of evidence of any disaffection against the Regime."[13] Popular Justice was arbitrary and trial outcomes were dependant on the particular tribunal, personal networks of influence and the historical moment. In December 1937 the security authorities were alarmed by the fact that the Clandestine Falange groups were rapidly co-ordinating and consolidating their efforts, and new emergency courts were established (*Tribunales Especiales de Guardia*) in order to swiftly process crimes of treason and espionage. These new expedited courts (presided by one qualified judge and two lay judges) dispensed with the most basic legal and juridical safeguards and standards, and their creation by decree on 1 December prompted the immediate resignation of Manuel Irujo the Minister of Justice.[14] Sentencing became more severe in 1938 in step with a succession of serious Republican military defeats and with the rise of the fifth column, and this may explain how Balbina came to be held in Ventas pending trial without any substantive evidence against her for nearly one year.

In July 1937 Ángeles Eizmendi Téllez Girón, aged twenty-nine years (the divorced ex-Countess de la Puebla de Montalbán), was arrested by Comisaria de Chamberí police officers on suspicion of espionage.[15] Eizmendi had been an activist with Acción Popular before the war. She was arrested during a raid on an apartment in calle General Arranda, 8 which belonged to Jacinta Sánchez where she and her mother were lodging. After 18 July Eizmendi and her mother Bernadina had been obliged to flee their home in Claudio Coello, 28. They eventually secured safe lodgings with Jacinta on the recommendation of Pastora Imperio. The arresting officers testified that Eizmendi had behaved suspiciously during the property search and had attempted to 'physically resist arrest.' The search of her landlady's[16] premises lasted from 3 p.m. until 11 p.m. and dozens of valuable items were confiscated including jewellery, cash (which had been illegally hoarded in contravention of the new legislation), identity documents and good-character vouchsafes. Eizmendi was caught *in flagrante* in the bathroom while she was attempting to hide her jewellery within various bars of soap. During the lengthy police search she made efforts to ingratiate herself with the police and offered one of the men a glass of cognac. She maintained that she had been arrested by the Chief of the Chamberí police station pursuant to 'a malicious denunciation' by a domestic following the theft of an item of jewellery which had been reported to the police. However, during trial one of the arresting police officers testified that her surveillance and arrest were effected under the orders of the Director of the DGS in Valencia.[17]

Eizmendi was accused of espionage because she had regularly frequented the military barracks in Chamberí during summer 1937, in particular the Regimento Motorizado de Ametralladoras (the Motorised Machine Gun Regiment). She had also entertained "at her own considerable expense"[18] military personnel and CNT members in local bars and cafés. It was believed that she communicated intelligence which was obtained from these soldiers to Socorro Blanco. Ángeles claimed that she was a loyal Republican and that she had donated her home and her two cars to the anarchists at the start of the war. She cultivated contacts with Republican groups and "in particular with the communist organisations" and "donated many valuable gifts in aid of the cause" including a valuable pearl necklace.[19] She claimed that she had always been in sympathy with the 'people' and that even before the war both she and her employees had regularly eaten "the same food, at the same table, in the same space."[20] Two of her former employees (a chauffeur and a carpenter) provided good-character vouchsafes to this effect. They claimed that she was a "great friend of the working classes … and she often got into rows with her family on account … of her democratic beliefs."[21] Las Águilas de la Libertad (the Eagles of Liberty) had invited her to join their militia group, but her mother had dissuaded her from this course of action.

Eizmendi's defence claimed that she had only frequented the barracks in order to obtain rationed goods in exchange for cash and that she was able to demonstrate her gratitude to the soldiers by inviting them out for drinks. She sought to represent herself as a loyal *miliciana* and made concerted efforts to maintain her social position and status within the newly established Republican elite. During the first months, she decided to "follow the fashion" and dressed in a boiler suit (*mono*). According to her landlady this was evidence of her "eccentric character."[22] However, the new dress code conferred power and status and enabled her to be mistaken for an official militia woman.[23] She subscribed to the "*La Traca*" periodical, and also fraternised with military and security elements in cafés and bars.[24] She also retained significant amounts of economic capital which aroused suspicion. Dozens of valuable pieces of jewellery in Toledan gold, platinum, diamonds, pearls and precious stones were confiscated from her residence as potential reparations. Both prior to and after her arrest she made efforts to use her social capital and wealth in order to cultivate powerful and influential Republican allies within the military and the anarchist groups in order to survive within an hostile 'enemy rear-guard.' Her wallet was confiscated, and it was found to contain dozens of safe-conduct passes and good-character vouchsafes (*avales*) which were all carefully itemised and included:

> A certificate [of good character] from La Maternidad, another certificate from Las Águilas de la Libertad, a photograph dedicated signed and dedicated to her by Assault Guard Fermín García, a certificate from the Joint Defence Committee (Junta Delegada de la Defensa), a character reference from Mr Tato y Amat ... a certificate from Mr Vicento Villa in order to obtain provisions from the Argentine Embassy, a pass signed by the DGS to gain access to the Hotel Paris Madrid ... another certificate from Las Águilas de la Libertad stating that Ángela [sic] is a person who is loyal to the Regime.[25]

The legal record reflects the everyday constraints imposed upon civil liberties in the rear-guard. The state of emergency placed severe restrictions on the free circulation of people and goods in the capital. Citizens were subjected to routine 'stop and searches' and required to carry valid identification, vouchsafes and travel passes at all times. They ran the risk of immediate arrest if such documentation was not to hand.[26] This made daily existence extremely difficult for those *desafectos* who lacked the necessary Republican contacts or were unable to obtain expensive fake documentation. Eizmendi's wallet contained new and important material cultural symbols which evidenced the hardships and complexities encountered in the navigation of everyday life at this time. Signed photographs and the letters of recommendation from important figures within the new regime like 'Mr Tato y Amat' provided protection for those who were fortunate enough to acquire them, whether legitimately or on the black-market. Eizmendi's desire to amass so many vouchsafes evidences the precariousness of her social situation and the quasi-talismanic importance ascribed to these valuable objects. The CNT membership card replaced the rosary and the crucifix as material symbols of succour and protection.

In fact, Ángeles was linked to a small fifth-column resistance group which was linked to a Valencian fifth-column organisation. She frequented the 'La Española Bar' in the Glorieta de Bilbao and was associated with disaffected elements including Anna María Becker, Berta Björsen Bethgen, Pedro Gallo Rodríguez and José Domínguez Arévalo. The group established links in various ministerial departments had was entrusted with 400 pesetas by Ángeles and her mother.[27] It also "cultivated connections within the Left Republican party (Izquierda Republicana), the Communist Party, the FAI and the UGT."[28] Together with her mother, Bernardina Téllez Girón, Ángeles travelled to Valencia and handed over a diamond-encrusted crucifix together with other jewels to Concepción Lozano Montalvo, the widow of Gamboa, the Marquis of Cerralbo, for safe-keeping or for funding the fifth column.[29] It was suspected that the group had links with Socorro Blanco in Valencia and they had sent considerable funds abroad to France.

In November 1937, Ángeles was found guilty of disaffection because the courts could find no substantive evidence of espionage. The fact that she and her mother had transferred large sums of money and valuables into France despite the stringent currency export restrictions represented a seriously aggravating factor. Also, it was established that she was a former member of Acción Popular who had also supported the monarchist Renovación Española and attended a royal gala which had been held in honour of Don Juan de Borbón before the war. The numerous safe-conduct passes and good-character certificates in her possession were also aggravating factors. The presiding magistrate Ricardo Guerra (discussed in Chapter 2 above) absolved Ángeles of the capital crime of treason but found her guilty of the lesser crime of disaffection. She was sentenced on 25 November 1937 to a term of eight years imprisonment in a labour camp, fined 100,000 pesetas and also lost all civil and political rights for a period of ten years.[30] On 5 November her mother made efforts to intercede on her behalf by writing to the Interior Minister Julián Zugazagoitia with the intercession of a close female friend, Concepción Lozano. She also donated 150,000 pesetas into the Republican war chest:

> Dear Minister …While making this donation, I should like to clarify a few issues in order to shed a more perfect light on this extremely difficult matter … grave and unfortunate circumstances have resulted in the arrest of my daughter for disaffection last July on erroneous grounds, my only and much adored child (Ángeles Eizmendi) on whose behalf, as is appropriate in my capacity as a mother, I have been trying to manage this whole affair [sic], we declared our adhesion to the Cause in December 1936 and we did this via our friend Concepción Lozano, the widow of Gamboa (an Left Republican politician), who kindly agreed to intercede on our behalf.[31]

The letter goes on to describe in great detail the byzantine efforts made by Bernardina and her Republican sponsor to transfer monies and valuables from *Credit Lyonais* in Bayonne (France) back into Spain. This case illustrates the strategies used by anti-Republicans to consolidate and maintain their privileged social positions. It demonstrates how women made use of their capital and networks of influence in their attempts to circumvent the law. A receipt from the Home Office dated 7 November 1937 was produced in court as evidence of Bernardina's reparation payments.[32] Despite the social revolution there was continuity in certain Spanish cultural practices; wealth, nepotism and *enchufismo* continued to operate within the Republican rear-guard. Although the term of imprisonment was lengthy and the financial reparations substantial, Ángeles managed to avoid a sentence of life imprisonment for a capital crime. The case also provides evidence of how the principle of equality before the law was compromised. Friends in high places were of vital importance. Influential Republicans such as the anarchist Melchor Rodríguez and the Interior Minister Julián Zugazagoitia interceded in favour of friends and acquaintances so that they might avoid the worst rigours of the new Republican justice. In practice, personal loyalties and obligations often cut across religious and ideological enmities. For example, In the Golfín-Corujo case (discussed in Chapter 3 above) Zugazagoitia became personally involved on behalf of one of the defendants to whom he wrote:

> I assume that given your antecedents and the present circumstances of your case, the tribunal which will hear your case will ensure that justice is done by absolving you; but what I need to tell you is that the matter that you are implicated in has passed up to the Tribunal [Special Military Tribunal] whose intention is to expedite this matter with maximum speed. Luckily, it appears that you won't be spending much more time in prison, as I believe that the Tribunal will transfer your case here [to Valencia] and issue a speedy deliberation, whereupon your situation will be clarified.[33]

Bars, cafés and food queues

During the war "the female *Mata Hari* was not a strange or exotic concept in the social imaginary."[34] The published exploits of the notorious French spy and *femme fatale* Marthe Richard who operated in Spain during World War I (between June 1916 and December 1917) may also have retained some currency.[35] Negative gender stereotypes of the female spy largely fell under two main categories: the dangerous seductress and the vacuous and indiscrete right-wing chatter-box. According to Josep Bertrán i Musitu "attractive and immoral women made the most effective spies, although female agents were generally less intelligent or reliable and needed to be carefully handled."[36] The English journalist Geoffrey Cox dismissively described a French spy who was arrested outside a bar as a "drunk and dangerously loquacious little blond."[37]

Intimate extra-marital relationships with military personnel flouted prevailing patriarchal gender norms surrounding female chastity and modest comportment. Demi-mondaines, actresses and sex-workers were *prima facie* objects of suspicion and discrimination. In particular, the authorities believed that the fifth-columnists paid prostitutes to obtain information from their military clients. There was an assumption that 'immoral' women might easily be suborned by fifth-column elements as spies and disseminators of defeatist information, and 'anti-fascist' propaganda was circulated to this effect. Such women moved freely and 'shamelessly' within (male) public spaces such as bars and cafés. These women's relationships with officers and soldiers were believed to be wholly transactional in nature and based on the mutual exchange of money or gifts for sexual services. In addition, the perceived threat to the integrity and the physical and moral health of the military posed by anti-Republican women cut across class boundaries. Working-class, middle-class and upper-class women might all be potential *mata haris*.

The outcomes of the case of Balbina, who had no 'good character' references may be contrasted with those of the 'ex-Marquise of Valparaiso' Enriqueta Mariateguí Rollán who had money, social status and influence.[38] Following a lengthy surveillance operation conducted by three Buenavista police officers who were also attached to the Censor's Office (Oficina Gabinete de Censura), Mariateguí was arrested for 'suspected espionage.' According to a lengthy surveillance detail:

> She left her house at 18.00 hours on [x] July 1937 heading towards the Retiro Park and on Claudio Coello where she met up with an aviator acquaintance whose name she only remembered as Manolo, he was accompanied by another gentleman who followed them from a distance until they reached Teatro Barral where they carefully surveyed their surroundings … then they surveyed the surroundings at another junction … and afterwards joined a queue which ended at calle Goya and Claudio Coello. She made a plan to meet Manolo on the following day at 7 pm in the foyer of Cine Carretas [but] Manolo agreed they should meet at the Príncipe Vergara Café on the corner of calle Goya, when he didn't show up she wandered around until she arrived at the corner of Torrijos, where she met a young man named Joaquín, whom she had been introduced to by a man who she previously met in Molineros [café], and Joaquín bought her a bottle of champagne, or sparkling wine, and they went off to Café Pelayo but the waiter took some time to serve them so they moved off to the Moka, where they remained until closing time, after which they said good bye and agreed to meet again on the following day.[39]

The defendant's behaviour was highly suspicious, not least because of its impropriety and failure to conform to the prescribed traditional gender norms and expectations. She was found to have been drinking alcohol in bars and cafés in the company of soldiers until the early hours. After her arrest on 27 July 1937 she admitted to having been arrested on three previous occasions. The first time was at home in 1936 following an anonymous denunciation, but she and other family members were released after the intercession of a Republican friend, agent Antonio Mazas, who worked with the University District police. She was arrested again, in April 1937 by the (Rearguard Vigilance Militias) MVR Third Group situated in Paseo del Cisne, 15 after being denounced as a spy, but she was immediately released following the intervention of the duty inspector, Jorge Enríquez, who provided her with a good-character reference.

> When asked why all her acquaintances were military men, she said it was a pure coincidence and nothing more. When asked if she ever saw the

> Inspector of the Third Group of the MVR (Jorge Enríquez) she replied yes, she had gone to see him at his home several times, and said Inspector suggested that she should repay him for her release and for the good character reference by demanding [sic] sexual relations. When asked if Mazas had suggested something similar, she said that Mazas had accompanied her sister to their house, performed a thorough search of the premises (*levantar los precintos*) … and afterwards they sacked the cook because Mazas denounced her as the anonymous informant. If Mazas had made any inappropriate overtures, then her sister might provide evidence in this regard.[40]

Mariateguí was imprisoned in Ventas on 27 July 1937 pending trial in the Special Court of Military Rebellion (*Juzgado Especial de la Rebelión Militar*) on charges of 'suspected espionage.' Her husband was a noble-man named Alfonso Barrosso Villanova[41] who was also a lawyer and an artillery captain. He had taken early retirement pursuant to the 'Azaña laws.' He was arrested as a 'notorious *desafecto*' on 20 July 1936 while holidaying with the family in Torrelodones.[42] He was the victim of *saca* from the Model Prison on either 6,7 or 8 November 1936 ("*detenido y desaparecido*").[43] According to the General Commissary of Investigation he was "evacuated from the Model Prison to Chinchilla in November [1936] and his whereabouts have been unknown since this date."[44] Mariateguí claimed that he had disappeared and that she had heard nothing more from him.[45] The family were all *desafectos*. Mariateguí, aged thirty-seven years, lived with her sister and her mother in the wealthy calle Claudio Coello, 38. When Universidad district officers searched her premises, under the direction of Antonio Mazas, "Monarchist flags and tendentious monarchist propaganda were discovered and our loyal agent [Mazas] referred the evidence to the Comisaria de Investigación Pública (CPIP) in calle Fomento, but the women were released."[46] Mariateguí claimed that her brother-in-law had moved to Palma, Mallorca days before the 18 July coup ("Movement") in order to look after his mother's estate, and they had not heard from him since. There was no evidence that he was in communication with Mariateguí.

The prosecution alleged that Mariateguí frequented the bars and cafés of central Madrid in order to meet with soldiers and to obtain military intelligence for the fifth column. However, no concrete evidence of espionage was submitted. Both Mazas and Enríquez were called to give evidence at trial but failed to appear before the special military tribunal and were never *subpoenaed* to do so. Mariateguí defended her reputation and claimed that she had no control over the subject of the conversations with her military acquaintances:

> in order to forget her recent sufferings, she decided to frequent the bars and cafés of central Madrid, and she acquiesced in whatever conversation was on offer but she never went beyond the limits of polite conversation … her father was a diplomat who had died a long time ago.[47]

The evidence of the Buenavista police officers, together with the earlier arrests and her meetings with military officers, was extremely incriminating. However, Mariateguí used back-channels with the CPIP and had access to important legal contacts (her husband had been a military lawyer). The 'forensic opinions' of both medical experts were promptly accepted by the tribunal. On 9 September 1937, the Presidents of the Military Tribunal (Denla Concha and García Huerta) found that:

> the Defendant has not committed any act which might be considered criminal or hostile or disaffected towards the regime, because there is evidence that, in fact, the case relates to a woman who is highly (*notoriamente*) attracted to the opposite sex in an undisguised way (*que no sabe disimular*) … certainly, upon the evidence of medical experts, the case relates to A PERSON WHO SHOWS SIGNS OF A HYSTERICAL PERSONALITY WITH AN UNDERLYING EROTIC PREDISPOSITION TOGETHER WITH THE RELEVANT RELATED DISORDERS (*TRASTORNOS*) WHICH ARE DERIVED FROM SAID PERSONALITY TYPE, even the General Commissariat of Investigation and Vigilance of Madrid has reported that she is MENTALLY ILL AND THAT THIS MOTIVATED HER EXTRAVAGANT ACTIONS AND LED TO HER BEING SUSPECTED OF ESPIONAGE [written in upper case] … the trial should BE DISMISSED WITH IMMEDIATE EFFECT, the records archived and the Defendant released with immediate effect.[48]

Mariateguí's personal connections and her financial resources enabled her to pull the right strings (*enchufismo*). Her in-laws had appeared in the pre-war high society pages of *Ecos Diversos* and her father was a diplomat. Useful Republican friends and contacts at all levels permitted her to skilfully navigate the disciplinary regimes of the police and the judiciary. She had already successfully avoided the consequences of two earlier denunciations (with the aid of insiders in the police, the CPIP and the MVR) and the current charges of espionage and disaffection were also summarily dismissed.[49] It is unclear from the records whether she was a fifth-column spy, but her actions indicate that this was the case. Certainly, she had the necessary motivation for she was a monarchist whose husband was killed in one of the winter 1936 *sacas*. The case illustrates the arbitrariness of the Republican popular justice and the vital importance of 'friends in high places,' back-channels and financial resources.

Brothels

In February 1937 Dolores Ibárruri observed that the fifth column was composed of 'card sharps, thieves and prostitutes' who polluted Madrid's bars and cafés with "careless and imprudent comments that were subsequently circulated by hidden enemies."[50] Governmental and press discourses surrounding the negative impact of 'immoral' anti-Republican women and their defeatist attitudes on army and civilian morale prevailed at this time. Such women also transgressed traditional standards of acceptable female comportment and behaviour.[51] The government was particularly keen to protect 'the moral and physical health' of its military personnel. The spread of venereal disease among the troops had been a pressing issue since as early as summer 1936. The authorities believed that 'brothel owners and prostitutes were secretly sympathetic to the fascist cause' and posed a security risk. It was believed that before the war their most important and wealthy clients were middle-class and conservative men. Despite the progressive and gender egalitarian platform of the anarchists in government and the activism of Mujeres Libres,[52] there is no evidence in the tribunal records to suggest that the anarchists held substantively different views in relation to this perceived security issue. The popular press fuelled the flames of this paranoia.[53] Militia-men were routinely warned against the perils of 'bedroom confidences':

> In the bed chambers where love is sold the statue of San José which usually resides above the bedhead should be replaced with a red figure whose index figure is pressed to its lips demanding silence.[54]

In March 1937, the prosecution lawyers who acted on behalf of the Ministerio Publico argued that:

> houses of prostitution are centres of espionage, [and] hiding places for fascists which cause moral and material harm to our combatants, a request should be made for the public authorities to close them down … it is also evident that publicly appointed police agents are also conducting [intimate] relationships with brothel ladies (*las damas de las casas de prostitución*) … and this also poses a grave and evident danger.[55]

Carmen Montes Cachero (aged thirty-four years) worked as a brothel-keeper in calle de Silva, no. 7 in the Hospicio district. The Defendant was arrested by agents of the Comisaria Hospicio on 20 March 1937 and accused of being "a woman who had taken steps to acquire a pistol and hand grenades in order to use these … for terrorist purposes."[56] The defendant was in a long-term relationship with a Falangist civil guard named Francisco González López who lost his job during the professional purges and was later imprisoned for disaffection at some time in 1936. González disappeared from prison, and the defendant had no further contact with him. She believed that he was the victim of a *saca*. Between 4 and 6 May 1937 the defendant was found in possession of a military-issue hand grenade following the denunciation of her female employer (the brothel owner). Montes had threatened to blow up the brothel after a heated argument with her employer who had berated Montes for disclosing the whereabouts of her teenage son who was a Falangist draft-dodger. The police searched Montes' premises and a live hand grenade was discovered in her bedroom wardrobe in calle Imperial. She obtained the grenade from a conscript named Augusto Núñez Ramírez who was attached to the Mangada Battalion and who was a regular client. This represented a serious security breach, especially as Montes had received instructions on the use of grenade. Núñez unconvincingly claimed that he had only given the grenade to Montes for safe-keeping because his "escort was afraid of the grenade and would not have it in her room." Most probably Montes paid for the grenade. The gravity of this case meant that it was immediately referred from the popular courts (Jurados de Urgencia) to the military courts on 20 March 1937.

Aggravating circumstances also included the fact that two 'publicly appointed police men' were involved in 'intimate relationships' with the brothel owner and Montes. This was also perceived as a serious public security risk as brothel keepers and their workers were routinely suspected of collaboration with the fifth column. The Home Office prosecutors alleged that Montes acquired the bomb in order to use it in a terrorist attack against the Hospicio police station in revenge for the disappearance of her Falangist civil guard lover. The case was expedited. Although the Home Office sought a sentence of life imprisonment, on 13 May 1938 the defendant was sentenced to twelve years hard labour and transferred from Ventas to Alacuás labour camp (popularly known as the *Carcel de Damas*) for good behaviour. Alacuás was established in a former convent, "a beautiful building surrounded by a leafy park."[57] This was an extraordinary destination for a brothel keeper and indicates that Montes may have had some contact with influential fifth-columnists.

Republican soldiers who were billeted in the capital were relatively well-paid and provisioned in comparison with the rest of the civilian population. 'Loose-women' who deliberately sought the company of soldiers in barracks, bars and cafés were viewed with suspicion and resentment. In May 1937, a 'taxi girl'[58] at the Shanghai Dance Academy was arrested for 'espionage and for taking advantage of her intimate relationships with various military personnel.' This unmarried variety club dancer (aged twenty) had a baby daughter who was looked after by a nanny while she was at work, and this fact was viewed dimly by her neighbours and the tribunal. Her habits were deemed to be 'irregular and predominantly nocturnal.'

The defendant lived in rented accommodation in calle Montera, 44. She was denounced by two Assault Guards (Antonio Martínez and Ángel Jiménez) who lived on the landing above. She claimed that these men had denounced her merely because they had each made unwanted sexual advances which she had rejected. She had also quarrelled with her former landlords over an outstanding rental arrears of between 800 and 1,000 pesetas, and her former landlady accused her of military espionage and defeatism. It was alleged that she had drawn detailed sketches of air fields, artillery emplacements and fortifications from intelligence provided by her lovers and she repeatedly "boasted about her opposition to the Republican cause, attacked Republican institutions and authorities and asserted that if the fascists triumphed everyone would be better off."[59]

One of her lovers was a fighter-pilot named Lt. Augusto Lecha Villasuso who was posted to various air-bases including Getafe, Madrid, Bararán, Álcala de Henares, Teruel and Barcelona. The other was a military doctor named Antonio Gallo whom she met on a daily basis. Gallo raised suspicions because he was untraceable and had been unable to join the CNT and the medical unions for the lack of good-character vouchsafes. Her close association with military men meant that she may have been privy to sensitive military intelligence but she also enjoyed privileged access to luxury items and rationed goods. Her rent was paid by Lecha.

The defendant was accused of drawing sketches of secret military and artillery positions and of relaying this information to the Nationalists. The nanny claimed that she had never seen any drawings and a search of the defendant's premises revealed nothing incriminating. Nonetheless, the case was transferred to the Courts of High Treason and Espionage in Valencia in summer 1938 and then on to Barcelona in January 1939. However, the key male witnesses (cited above) never provided evidence in court because they could not be called away from active service. Lecha ruthlessly swore an affidavit to the effect that he had "never divulged any sensitive intelligence and his relationship with the defendant was purely physical and arose from the male urge to obtain carnal access to any woman."[60] The case rumbled on until late March 1939 when it was suspended on account of the Nationalist occupation. It is uncertain whether this woman was a spy, no convincing evidence was produced during the Madrid trial, but her bail was posted at the punitive sum of 25,000 pesetas and she remained in prison with no one to vouch for her good character until March 1939. Her outcomes are unknown.

Spies within the civil administration, police and judiciary

The case of the socialite Sara Giralt Gómez illustrates how well-connected anti-Republican women used back-channels within the Republican administration in their efforts to navigate a highly conflictive social field.[61] Such women were influencers who could invoke the aid of informal Republican power networks. Giralt's experiences also provide a partial insight into the complex web of personal and political rivalries within Madrid's judiciary. The fifth column was imbricated within the fabric of Republican civil society.

By 1938 the damaging effects of influential fifth column women on Republican Justice was circulated in the popular press:

> various sectors of public opinion and the Madrid press have insinuated in several articles and opinion leaders that there are a group of women who have sufficient influence among the relevant authorities to commence criminal proceedings and imprison people.[62]

Giralt was an upper-middle-class socialite who had claimed diplomatic immunity as a Cuban national (her parents were Cuban). She was known among her glamorous social circle as "Baby."[63] She was aged twenty-seven years and lived in calle Goya, 83 together with her mother, father and brother. The family members were accused of being "fascists who frequently hosted celebratory gatherings and small meetings, and … assisted the Panamanian embassy in its crimes of disaffection."[64] Her apartment was situated above the Panamanian Legation but did not form part of it.

In summer 1938 Giralt and her sister, María Teresa, became embroiled in a very public power struggle between two senior officials in Madrid's Regional High Court. The feuding notables were the socialist President of the Regional High Court, Luis Zubillaga Olalde (a former local politician), and the communist Chief Prosecutor, Feliciano López y López de Uribe (former Dean of the College of Lawyers). Zubillaga was a close friend of the *desafecto* attorney Rogelio Rufilanchas Periquet and his secretary (and lover) María Teresa (who also happened to be Sara's sister). Meanwhile, the Chief Prosecutor was a close friend of Sara who, in turn, was "a close friend of Madrid's Chief of Police, Commissar Teodoro Illera Martín."[65] The Chief Prosecutor and the President of the Regional High Court were also known to have forged links with the anarchist Melchor Rodríguez in October 1936 in their efforts to save rightists from the prison *sacas* during winter 1936.[66]

Sara Giralt was arrested on charges of espionage during one of her frequent visits to the Regional High Court in late June 1938. She moved with ease and confidence in the court space and aroused the keen irritation of senior court officials who resented and feared the presence of anti-Republican women in the High Court:

> it was ordered that the Sub Commissar of the Chamberí Police Station, Sr. Bermejo, would provide his services in order to search every person entering the building and, above all women … so imagine my shock and surprise when … I caught sight of a young lady, who is a well-known for her fascist activism and who visits the Palace of Justice with excessive frequency, rapidly mounting the stairs from the lower-ground floor in an arrogant and flagrant manner (*aire jaque y destocado [sic]*) without the least hindrance or impediment from anyone … I immediately called for Sr. Bermejo.[67]

New police security measures had recently been implemented in order to address the problem of the fifth column in the courts. The new regulations meant that everyone, including the wives of lawyers, barristers and court personnel, would be subject to routine body searches. On the day of her arrest Giralt had sought the urgent aid of the Chief Prosecutor López de Uribe. Her sister María Teresa, on the good authority of General Miaja's wife, had warned her that President Zubillaga was planning to arrest her in a tit-for-tat reprisal. Zubillaga was angry that his dear friend Rufilanchas and María Teresa had been arrested on 22 June at the behest of the Chief Prosecutor for coaching witnesses in the *Los 195* case. One of the defendants, Manuel Villafranca (who was later executed), gave evidence, on Rufilanchas' advice, that he had been tortured while in SIM custody. He also accused the trial prosecutor Peinador Porrua of being in league with the Republican SIM. Meanwhile, María Teresa was arrested for disaffection for losing her temper and shouting out *¡Arriba España!* during a prison visit to Rufilanchas who by this time was imprisoned in Porlier. In light of these arrests, President Zubillaga arrested Sara in an effort to obtain the release of his friends in a prisoner exchange. We should recall that Sara was intimate with the Chief Prosecutor. Nonetheless, the Chief Prosecutor held firm with his prosecution of Rufilanchas and the exchange never materialised. Sara's case also went on to trial, to the acute embarrassment of the government and the court officials.

There was plenty of circumstantial evidence against Sara. In the months leading up to the coup she had entertained the leader of Renovación Española Antonio Goicoechea at her home. She claimed that Goicoechea was merely a distant relative rather than a co-conspirator.[68] In addition, her husband was an Italian national and an artillery captain named José Corsino who promptly sought asylum at the Panamanian Embassy after 18 July "in order to avoid military service … given that his loyalties were completely fascist."[69] He was later arrested for disaffection, and Sara used her connections with the Chief Police Commissioner and Feliciano López y López de Uribe in order to secure her husband's release in November 1936. In mid-December 1936 Sara also obtained the release of her brother-in-law, Carlos Corsini, once again with the aid of López de Uribe and the permission of the Special Delegate of Prisons Melchor Rodríguez García.[70] Finally, Sara obtained the release of José Bielza (her husband's brother-in-law) in the autumn of 1936; however, Bielza was subsequently arrested by the SIM whilst attempting to board a plane in Alicante. Sara had organised the flight. Bielza was found guilty of treason and executed.

After her arrest Sara sought the aid of her close friend the Republican MP Albino Lasso Conde.[71] Chief Prosecutor Zubillaga declared in his witness statement that:

> Sara Giralt … constantly boasted about her influence (*se hace gala de esas influencias*) and offered her protection to whomever she pleased … in both word and deed she implied that 'we [the fifth column] are more powerful than you' with reference to the most powerful authorities in Madrid [the Regional High Court] … most recently her arrogance and imprudence have reached unprecedented levels because she has had the audacity to ask her lover, the Republican MP Albino Lasso Conde, to intercede on her behalf at the offices of the President of the Regional court [i.e. Zubillaga].[72]

The war was progressing in the Nationalists' favour at this time, and Sara's trial became the focus of a very bitter and public power struggle between the socialist and communist factions within the high court. Both Zubillaga and López de Uribe accused each other of treason and of being 'fifth column collaborators working at the behest of high-society *desafectas*.' López de Uribe compromised the standing and authority of the Regional High Court by openly declaring during cross-examination that he 'was prepared to throw any judge who dared to accuse him of abetting the fifth column out of the window.' The dispute between the President and the Chief Prosecutor quickly came to the attention of a scandalised popular press and the Ministry of Justice. It was referred to the Supreme Tribunal (No. 2) in Barcelona on 7 September 1938.[73] The ensuing public furore brought Republican Justice into disrepute and prompted an urgent special investigation of the Supreme Tribunal.[74] Zubillaga and López de Uribe were suspended from their posts on 10 September 1938.[75]

Although there was no concrete evidence that Sara Giralt had ever passed intelligence to the Nationalists, her husband José Corsino escaped into the Nationalist zone in 1936 and she was in regular contact with him. Sara used her influence within the police and the judiciary in her attempts to pervert the course of justice and obtain the release of her sister. Sara was also released upon the intercession Albino Lasso Conde who was a political ally of López de Uribe. Lasso Conde gave the court a personal guarantee that Sara, who was imprisoned in Ventas pending trial, would remain under house arrest until her appearance before the Supreme Court in Barcelona. The court granted her special leave to transfer from prison to house arrest at Lasso Conde's home in Madrid during the summer of 1938. During the proceedings Lasso Conde obtained a travel visa for Sara and arranged for her and her family to escape to France via Barcelona. However, Sara was intercepted in Alicante by the SIM on 16 September 1938 (together with her parents, her brother and her daughter Lydia) while attempting to board an Air France Alicante–Barcelona flight. Sara falsely claimed that she was flying to Barcelona in order to give evidence in the Supreme Tribunal case.[76] In January 1939 the Supreme Court found that, while there was no evidence that Sara was a spy, she was a dangerous disaffected element and she was exiled from Spain.[77] She emigrated to South America with Lasso Conde and her husband.

The case demonstrates how the well-connected and influential were better equipped to navigate the court system and avoid the worst sanctions. Sara's relationships with senior members of the Republican police, judiciary and administration ensured that she was granted house arrest and later exiled rather than imprisoned for treason. Her sister María Teresa and Rufilanchas were also released. However, they were once again arrested on 28 August 1938 for 'seeking refuge at Panamanian Legation,' but this new case was also provisionally dismissed.[78] It appears that 'friends in high places' had a material effect on trial outcomes and fifth-column women were mindful of cultivating powerful Republican networks. The fortunate and well-connected were more equal before the law at this time.

Embassy spies

As indicated in Chapter 2 diplomatic corps played an important role in the provision of political asylum for anti-Republicans. There were between 10,000 and 12,000 asylum seekers in Madrid's embassies and consulates in November 1936. By early 1937 this number was reduced to just over 6,000 asylum seekers.[79] Madrid's embassies and consulates provided safe spaces for the co-ordination and operation of the Clandestine Falange networks.[80] The networks maintained regular contact with "a sympathetic diplomatic corps that provided it with safe houses, facilities and an assured means of radio communication with the rebels."[81]

Joséfina Jiménez Sotillo[82] was twenty years old, single and a resident at calle Castello, 20. She was unemployed at the time of her arrest by police officers of the Centro District on 6 August 1937, but it was believed that she was a spy and a go-between for members of the Falange at the Panamanian Consulate. She was arrested Café Gran Via while meeting her lover José Ordoñez Díez (aka "Hilario") who was a member of Acción Popular. Hilario was a military academy student who was "a subversive element prior to the outbreak of the movement."[83] After his release from prison in March 1937, Hilario sought refuge at the Panamanian Consulate. Jiménez met this individual two or three times per week. She regularly received correspondence 'from a Panamanian subject' at a regular drop-off point in the calle de Goya metro station. The surveillance detail indicated that she would quickly read the correspondence and then immediately destroyed it. A young boy of twelve years had regularly brought letters from Hilario to her lodgings,[84] but this method of communication ceased after the boy was knocked down by a car. A key aspect of the incriminating evidence against Josefina was that she regularly met with soldiers of various categories and grades which led the police to believe that she was a liaison agent ('*enlace en la calle*') for various elements who have sought asylum at the Panamanian Consulate.[85]

Josefina "had no father and her entire family consisted of a mother and a very young brother who were evacuated to Albacete and she had no visible means of support except those which she managed to obtain on her own account."[86] She had also been arrested in the Café Jauja at an earlier date, on 8 February 1937, together with Hilario and three others, by the Hospicio district police because they were 'not carrying the necessary documentation as proof of their living circumstances.' According to the Control de Nóminas, Josefina had been a propagandist for Acción Popular prior to the war and she had also paid a 5 pesetas membership subscription.[87] This reflected both her political and social aspirations. While the Falange's pre-war discourses attracted lower-middle-class women, membership within Acción Popular tended to attract members of the local upper middle-classes.[88] After her release from prison on 11 February 1937 Josefina was evacuated to Alicante where she spent some fifteen days, and then a further fifteen days in Valencia where, with the intercession of a Jefe de la Comandancia de Valencia, she managed to obtain a military safe-conduct pass for Madrid to which she returned on or around 15 March 1937.[89]

Upon her return to Madrid Josefina lived an 'irregular life,' moving from a succession of guest houses and lodgings, perhaps in order to elude the Republican security. One of her former landladies testified that she believed her to be a prostitute.[90] It was also shown that she received regular financial support from a man named Martínez.[91] Carlos Martínez Soriano was a tall, white haired gentlemen of a certain age who worked as a civil servant at the Home Office in Valencia.[92] Martínez provided financial support and supplied her with a good-character reference (*aval*) from the Valencia tax offices, the "*Consejo de Dirección del Ministerio de Hacienda, Secretaria Especial de la Inspección de los Tributos*," along with the contact details and telephone numbers of various military and police personnel who could 'protect her' – these were Manuel Tarrazo and Juan Santamaría, police inspectors with the Hospicio District police, a man named Pedro Alarcón and an agent with the Criminal Investigation Brigade who were introduced to the defendant by Soriano who accompanied Josefina on her return journey to Madrid.[93]

In March 1937, Josefina joined the International Red Cross (IRC), Western Division as a propaganda co-ordinator. The division was led by Carlos Cuesta. The IRC liaison agent was Enrique Gutiérrez (who was attached to the IRC's Pérez Carballo Group), and regular meetings took place in *Bar Molí*. Josefina was promptly dismissed for dereliction of duties by Eduardo Dato but continued to make use of her IRC membership card. Her defence argued that the defendant had sought to 'redeem her irregular life by marrying [José Ordoñez]' and that the letters received from him were purely personal. A former landlady, África Llaberga Llesca, testified that:

> [She] had only known Josefina for two months, after which she let go of her room, for reasons unknown: She never received any men and, given her shy nature, she had never heard her say anything against the government … she didn't have a great amount of money and, according to the witness, she was fairly ill-educated (*su cultura es bastante deficiente*) and she hardly knows how to write.[94]

Nonetheless, she was literate enough to make a careful note of her weekly expenses which were paid by Soriano and which included sums paid for 'lipsticks, pedicures, sweets, *turrón* and bonbons.' Another witness gave evidence that Josefina had been her lodger for only fifteen to twenty days and that during this time she only saw the defendant with a young man [Eduardo Dato] who was wearing an IRC arm band. The witness also gave evidence that she had asked Josefina to vacate her room because of 'the payment situation.'

The defence argued that her 'deficient education' rendered her incapable of 'aiding rebellion.' Meanwhile, the prosecution requested that she be sentenced to twelve years in a labour camp on the basis that 'she was a spy and that had the correspondence from the Panamanian consulate been purely personal it would have been sent via the normal postal services and there would have been no need to destroy it.' The case was transferred from the military tribunal to the Jurados de Urgencia on charges of disaffection where the prosecution submitted photographic evidence which indicated that she 'had frequented bars and cafés together with a French national named Marcela.'[95] The women met with military men like the American brigadier Alfredo Rippz at various locations in the capital including the New York Hotel. Josefina only "used her lodgings for sleep, she always ate away from home and spent the whole day out and about."[96]

The presiding judge of the Jurado de Urgencia no. 7 was Ricardo Guerra Blanco. He was tried for high treason in 1938 for aiding Félix Schlayer to organise asylum and escape-lines. The treason charges against Josefina were dropped, and on 11 November 1937 she was found guilty of disaffection "for conducting a relationship with an individual who is in asylum in an embassy and is a member of Acción Popular and for whom she acts as a liaison agent (*enlace*)."[97] She was sentenced to one year and one day hard labour at Muchamiel (Alicante) labour camp. She was released on 11 November 1938. This case is illustrative of the security fears surrounding 'immoral women.' Jiménez lacked family connections, money and education. Despite her socially disadvantaged background, she became a socially aspirational propagandist for Acción Popular before the war. She was a committed activist who chose to return to Madrid within weeks of her arrest and evacuation in February 1937 despite the manifest risks. Using a variety of strategies including guile, initiative and seduction, she managed to obtain the necessary documentation and financial support from Soriano in order to fund her return and living expenses in the capital. It is reasonable to assume that she was engaged as a liaison agent within a larger network and was treated leniently by Ricardo Guerra who was himself involved in fifth-column activities.

Presumed spies

Certain sectors of female Spanish society attracted more suspicion than others. Among the most suspect were the relatives of soldiers at the fronts (especially if the family was known to have right-wing sympathies), devout Catholics, nuns, nurses who worked in the military or prison hospitals and those who had relatives in the Nationalist zone or who were associated with members of the Falange. Finally, those who did not conform, for whatever reason, to conventional standards of dress, comportment or behaviour also attracted suspicion.

The relatives of conscripts and officers

Intimate relations between soldiers and female civilians constituted a potential security threat. Written communications between soldiers and civilians were subject to censorship. In April 1938 the conscript Cervero Bosch was posted to an observation position with the 108th Mixed Brigade. He sent his girlfriend a copy of an army publication entitled "The Voice of The Trenches." Inserted between the pages were pencil sketches of buildings and locations that had been the subject of artillery bombardments and, therefore, constituted weak and undefended zones close to the front-lines. There were also various maps and plans setting out the position of material and troops. The censors alerted the SIM and both Cervero and his girlfriend fell under surveillance for several weeks. The SIM alleged that:

> the sole and exclusive objective [of the sketches] was to provide vital information in relation to the geographical location and position of military targets such as cables, trenches, batteries, reference point buildings, territorial boundaries, all information that was essential to the successful identification of potential targets for enemy air-strikes.[98]

It was feared that his girlfriend Ana Arce Folgara was a spy who was passing this military intelligence on to the fifth column. The defence claimed that the plans merely related to designs and drawings of the couple's future marital farm-house. In January 1939, the courts were still deliberating as to whether "the plans and sketches detailed in the prosecution documents related to important information regarding the [Republican fronts] which may have fallen into the possession of the enemy."[99] The case never came to trial because of the Nationalist occupation of Madrid in on 28 March 1939.

Devout Catholics ('Beatas')

During the 1920s the social Catholic movement provided women with new opportunities for agency in the public space through lay confessional groups like Acción Católica. The Catholic church supported the social and political mobilisation of women as part of a modern crusade to re-Christianise society.[100] This new political citizenship confirmed negative gender stereotypes regarding pious and conservative women (*beatas*) and encouraged discourses against women's suffrage prior to 1931 among the Left and anticlerical parties.[101]

During the war the authorities feared that pious Catholic women had mobilised in order to demoralise soldiers billeted among the civilian population. It was believed that such women circulated defeatist news broadcast via Nationalist Radio Burgos and Seville. The case of the rebel and spy Eugenia García Arteaga is illustrative of how confessional motivations played an important role in the mobilisation of anti-Republican resistance.[102] It also demonstrates how resistance communities were united by the Catholic faith and their imaginings of a Nationalist victory. On 18 October 1937, a group of neighbours who lived in the Colonia de los Rosales, a lower-middle-class housing estate in Charmartín de la Rosa, were arrested by Buenavista police officers. Around fifteen members of this Catholic group were imprisoned and charged with 'espionage and aiding rebellion.' The group regularly gathered in a local bar which was owned by a member. They also met privately in order to discuss the progress of the war, profess the faith and to listen to illegal Nationalist broadcasts which, in and of itself, *prima facie* constituted the crime of defeatism.[103] The defendant's homes were searched and a transistor radio was confiscated. It was believed that the group comprised "various people of a right-wing disposition who had dedicated themselves to espionage and to assisting rebellion."[104] The leader was Eugenia García Arteaga. She was a single woman aged twenty-seven years who worked at home (*sus labores*). Her home provided a safe space for clandestine gatherings which aroused suspicion among her Republican neighbours. She was accused of having "dedicated herself to forming relationships with Republican military officials in order to obtain information and pass it to the enemy."[105]

García was intimate with an air-force captain, and it was suspected that she was able to access classified military intelligence. She also fraternised with soldiers of the 11th Brigade and the 68th Brigade. In early October 1937, the 68th Brigade was billeted at the Nebrija Institute and within private residences in Chamartín. García's father had volunteered to billet four officers at their home on the Colonia de los Rosales estate where he was employed as a caretaker. One of the officers, Alfredo Boigues Serrano (a Lieutenant Carabineer), came to suspect that García was a *desafecta* "on account of her conversation and conduct, she had secretly confessed that she was looking forward to the entry of the Nationalist troops in the capital." He also alleged that she had offered to "help him escape into the Nationalist zone with the assistance of contacts who were infiltrated within the Republican army."[106] Boigues denounced her to the Buenavista police. He claimed that he had instigated romantic relations in order to ascertain the nature and extent of her subversive activities. The DGS took these allegations seriously and launched an intensive surveillance operation in order to establish the 'right-wing and religious antecedents of the group' and whether it had performed acts of espionage or disseminated defeatist propaganda.

García Arteaga had two brothers who were presumed to be in the rebel zone. She alleged that she had no idea of their whereabouts but they 'may have been affiliated to the Falange.' The Republican authorities also suspected that she was in contact with agents in the Nationalist zone and had organised escape-lines for military deserters. One of García's brothers, Mariano, had fled Rosales after 18 July on the advice of his girlfriend Rosario Polo. He had gone to live in a small hotel 'for fear of personal rather than political reprisals.' The hotel was run by a 'notorious *desafecta*' who had been fined for pouring boiling water onto an anti-fascist rally from her balcony. Mariano, a former member of both Acción Popular and the Falange, had been working as a militia prison guard in Ventas. He and García had also been accused of having illegally smuggled letters and packages to the political prisoners.[107] At the time of García's arrest on 18 October 1937, Mariano had deserted his duties and managed to evade arrest.

On 27 October 1937 fifteen individuals, including six women, were charged by the Special Tribunal of Military Rebellion No 4 of being "rebel elements and inciting Rebellion."[108] The women in the group were accused of conspiring to demoralise Republican soldiers and to incite desertion. García (and fourteen others) were also accused of espionage and military rebellion.[109] The group had created detailed plans of various classified military positions in Madrid and gathered intelligence regarding the movements of Republican troops in and around the capital. García was also accused of being 'an accessory to the murder of the brother of the Mayor of Chamartín de La Rosa during the period of revolutionary violence.' She was also charged with disseminating false and defeatist information. Such actions fell within the definition of the military crime of 'conspiracy to aid rebellion.' Both the civil and military courts were involved in this case.[110]

The other defendants included García's father, her brother Mariano and various Catholic neighbours. A number of soldiers and officers were also implicated. García confessed that her neighbour, a postal worker and a topographer named José Dorda (married, aged thirty-nine), had assisted her in the compilation of maps and plans which formed part of a dossier of classified information relating to the movement of troops and current troop positions around Madrid. García was accused of passing this information on to contacts in the Nationalist zone. The defendants were members of Acción Popular or belonged to lay confessional organisations such as Acción Católica, Mujeres de Acción Católica and the Juventudes de Acción Católica.[111] They were also associated with the Instituto de Las Damas Catequistas. García was accused of being associated with Acción Popular, Acción Católica and Las Damas Catequistas. These organisations were mainly organised and administered by upper-class and middle-class women. The Damas Catequistas was a charitable religious congregation which taught the catechism to thousands of young girls in underprivileged working-class suburbs such as Cuatro Caminos and Puente de Vallecas.[112] It attracted the patronage of upper-class women and afforded working- and lower-middle-class women like García opportunities for acquiring a measure of social prestige, social mobility and networking opportunities. It also provided a space for pious and highly visible forms of confessional practice.[113] While social Catholic organisations provided women with opportunities for employment and preferment, they also perpetrated forms of symbolic violence against working-class women which frequently inspired popular resentment. According to María de Echarri, a key spokeswoman and leader of Acción Católica, a key aim of this organisation was to construct young working-class girls as pious and compliant workers:

> as future workers, to acculturate them in Catholic discourses and to construct them as pious Catholic women who would be protected against immorality within the sheltering vale of religion, culture and good example.[114]

The female members of this clandestine group were devout Catholics. They were popularly and disparagingly known as *beatas* and, therefore, subject to all the negative associations and prejudices aroused by this anticlerical stereotype. According to Rosario Polo (also a member of the Damas Catequistas), García's visible piety and her involvement in Catholic groups before the war inspired resentment within members of the local Republican community. Several witnesses also testified that the socially aspirational García was 'imprudent, talkative and had an opinionated character.' The motivations behind many denunciations were personal as much as political or anti-Catholic.

García's father was a former member of Acción Popular and had served a short prison sentence for disaffection. The Central Post Office employee José Dorda was accused of being García's principal co-conspirator and of having created maps and plans and interfering with postal communications. He supported Acción Católica and had also been arrested for disaffection and fined 250 pesetas. He had also been a member of the Real Archicofradia de la Corte de María since childhood. "He had religious beliefs and had paid a monthly subscription of 5 pesetas to the Culto y Clero de Santa Teresa y Santa Isabel of Chamberí during 1932 and 1933." According to his testimony, "he stopped paying the monthly subscription in 1934 when the 80 million peseta fund was utilised to vote in the '*bienio negro*.'"[115] Another co-defendant, Leonor Maliche, had been the President of the Chamartín section of the Damas Catequistas and was accused of disseminating defeatist propaganda. The group included the female relatives of Nationalist soldiers and of local right-wing families. For example, Lázaro Arellano managed small, family-owned, fabric and shoe shops. He "wished he were in the rebel zone with his relatives but was unable to leave on account of a lack of funds and he looked forward to Franco's entry into Madrid."[116]

During the interrogations at the Buenavista police station, García denied being a member of any political group or organisation and self-represented as a devout Catholic who "had regularly attended several Churches, in particular, the Church of San Miguel in Chamartín in her capacity as a pious parishioner *(feligresa)*."[117]

Despite her visible piety, García also stayed out until late at night and fraternised with soldiers and officers in various bars and cafés. Her father amended his original witness statement in order to emphasise that she normally returned home by 9 p.m. García's behaviour manifestly flouted the injunctions of Acción Católica which supported a war-time campaign of austerity and modesty in order "to counteract the rebellion of Spanish women, and in particular pious women, against the Church in accordance with the sermons of the Bishop of Palencia."[118] The bishop exhorted women to dress and behave modestly and to avoid make-up as part of a war-time national regeneration. The Nationalist zone was undergoing a traditionalist gender backlash at this time. Catholic female self-abnegation and self-restraint represented forms of symbolic collective expiation for the social collapse and ensuing violence, attributed by many Catholics to the Republic's modernising and laicising measures before the war. Therefore, women in the rebel-held zones were required to practice modesty as part of the war effort.[119]

These gender normative discourses also circulated amongst Catholics in Madrid's rear-guard. Traditional models of 'respectable femininity' also prevailed in the secular Republican gender discourses of this time and were reflected in the findings of the popular tribunals.[120] According to various testimonies, the 'pious' García was morally suspect because she had frequented the barracks, bars and cafés of Chamartín without a chaperone. The daily habits and practices of Catholic women like García often balanced constraint and agency in ways that implicitly contested the prevailing discursive gender norms. Her nocturnal meetings transgressed the prescribed feminine scripts which were available to her at this time.[121] Her comportment challenged traditional gender stereotypes and notions of acceptable feminine behaviour. Practices of amusement, entertainment and desire also informed García's fraternisations with soldiers in addition to religious motivations.

In December 1937, the High Court acquitted her of espionage and aiding rebellion. Instead, she was found guilty of 'inciting Rebellion' and sentenced to twelve months hard labour. The charges against the other co-defendants were reduced to disaffection. The court found that García had been:

> performing suspicious activities and that she had encouraged Alfredo Boigues Serrano to escape to the enemy side and offered to the provide the necessary assistance with the help of her friends on the other side.[122]

This case demonstrates how informants were used by the Republican SIM and the police to successfully infiltrate fifth-column groups.[123] The finding of guilt in this case rested almost exclusively on the hostile witness evidence of Boigues. His initial denunciation at Buenavista police station set in train a lengthy surveillance operation. His methods represented an inversion of stereotypically female 'honey-trap' espionage practices.[124] Boigues was eventually posted to active service at the fronts and therefore was never called to provide evidence at trial. The case demonstrates how the popular tribunals endorsed traditional Catholic and masculinist conceptions of acceptable female behaviour. Questions of chastity, modesty and propriety were relevant with regard to the actions and behaviours of women, whereas the morality and sexual probity of male defendants were rarely interrogated by popular tribunals.

Nuns

During the early months of the conflict in the capital hundreds of religious (male and female) were evacuated from their houses and obliged to live as fugitives within the Catholic community. They were also required to adopt secular dress.[125] In particular, those who had belonged to the enclosed orders sometimes adopted unusual civilian clothes and hairstyles (many wore wigs in order to disguise their close-cropped hair), and their use of antiquated idioms and expressions often aroused suspicion. Very few nuns were denounced as spies but around 7% of women charged with disaffection were nuns.[126] In a few cases nuns were found guilty of espionage for passing sensitive social and military intelligence to the Nationalists. In this way Ginestra Manzano (aged seventy-three) was absolved of disaffection but found guilty of espionage and treason.[127] Manzano was forced to abandon her convent and go into hiding following the 11 August 1936 Decree. She was arrested and imprisoned together with three other nuns from the same community in November 1936. She had spent over thirty years teaching young girls. In a witness statement dated 23 November 1936 she declared that she had never been affiliated to any political party, never listened to fascist radio stations nor passed any written information to Ramón Miquel Gonzalea. Gonzalea was the brother of one of her co-defendants. He had decided to remain in rebel territory (Santander) after the outbreak of war during his summer vacation. He owned the apartment in Claudio Coello, 14 where all four nuns had been hiding. Ginestra Manzano testified that 'she was ignorant of the political events leading up to and after 18 July.' She also professed to have no idea why she was sent away from her convent on or around 11 August. Manzano's evidence was rejected by Jurado de Urgencia no. 8, the popular tribunal of first instance. She and her three co-defendants were sentenced to imprisonment in Ventas on 10 March 1937 on charges of espionage and treason (as defined under sub-section 4, Article 125 of the Penal Code). Manzano was found guilty for forwarding news that "favoured the progress of the enemy army."

Catalina Colón Rodríguez[128] was a Puerto Rican national and a novice nun who, together with the rest of her community, had been evacuated from the Convent of the Daughters of Charity in November 1936. At first the community sought refuge in a flat situated in Paseo de la Ronda, 36, but they were obliged to move into a succession of safe-houses. Colón was arrested on 6 March 1937 on charges of espionage and possession of false documentation. She was initially denounced to the Buenavista police station for behaving suspiciously in the food queues.[129] Colón and eight other nuns were arrested by two communist militia at an apartment situated in Paseo del Doctor Esquerdá. It later transpired that nuns were denounced by the owner of the apartment who was a relative of one of the nuns; he was afraid of reprisals and wanted to be rid of his unwelcome guests. The nuns had attracted the unfortunate attention and suspicion of neighbours. Colón was accused of attempting to gather intelligence in the food queues. In a witness statement dated 11 March 1937 she denied all charges and claimed that she had no knowledge of or contact with the rebel movement. Her suspicious behaviour was due to her religious vocation and to the fact that she was a foreign national. Catalina claimed that she had merely been queuing for food in unfamiliar surroundings. She was acquitted and released in April 1937.

Nurses and nursing auxiliaries

Around 7% of the women accused of disaffection between July 1936 and March 1937 worked as nurses or auxiliaries in Madrid's military and civilian hospitals or at the fronts.[130] Those who harboured 'hostile ideological beliefs' were often suspected of being spies and saboteurs who passed intelligence to the Nationalists and deliberately injured their patients. Many were initially accused of treason or espionage, but the charges were reduced to disaffection because of a lack of evidence. Nurses performed a vital welfare role and 'disloyal' nurses posed a serious security risk. The fears of an invisible fifth column also led to false accusations against those who held rightist ('*derechista*') beliefs. In one case a nurse was arrested and charged with disaffection for "organizing fascist meetings with other nurses in order to conspire against the Republic."[131]

Magdalena Noin Ormachea was a Spanish national (b. 1914) of Cuban parentage who worked as a nurse at Hospital Militar No. 14.[132] She operated as a go-between for the Falangist leader Juan del Amo (who was in prison in Valencia awaiting execution) and his nineteen-year-old lover María Luisa López Ochoa who was a patient in the military hospital. López Ochoa was charged with espionage and conspiracy in the 18 July military coup. Her father General López Ochoa, who was dubbed the "Butcher of Asturias" by the Left, was extra-judicially killed at the start of the war whereupon she and her mother were obliged to go into hiding. Her trial for espionage was suspended due to a pulmonary illness (haematosis) contracted as a result of the deprivations of living on the run and hiding in damp basements.[133] Noin Ormachea's case came to the attention of Ángel Pedrero who suspected her of being a Socorro Blanco agent.[134] It was believed that the poetic love letters between del Amo and López Ochoa contained secret coded messages. Noin was arrested while attempting to smuggle a letter out of the hospital on behalf of another patient. This letter was not submitted as evidence because she was able to destroy it. She had also been disciplined by the hospital authorities for various misdemeanours including passing contraband (a bottle of cologne to a prison patient), providing relatives with the address and contact details of the hospital director and passing information between a lawyer and one of her patients. After several months in Ventas, Magdalena's case was referred to the popular tribunals on lesser counts of disaffection.

'Othering' in the rear-guard

The records indicate that foreigners, newcomers (there were hundreds of refugees at this time) and those who behaved in unusual or eccentric ways were more liable to become the targets of unfounded accusations of espionage. Such denunciations must be understood as forms of 'selective violence' within a context of a virulent fifth-column paranoia, total war and acute material scarcity. They provided a measure of civilian 'self-policing' and evidence how the Republic at war was constructed from below as well as from above and often arose from personal and private motivations, rivalries and disputes. Most denunciations were anonymous.[135] The influx of refugees from the rebel-held zones and the evacuees from the capital's bombed zones also heightened feelings of 'stranger-danger' in the rear-guard and placed severe demands on the capital's overburdened and strained infrastructure, thereby engendering rivalries and resentments.

The vulnerable, intellectually challenged or mentally ill

Those who failed to conform to conventional cultural norms and expectations often aroused fear and suspicion. The fear of spies and hidden enemies lasted for the duration of the war. Consequently, the mad, eccentric, vulnerable and homeless sometimes fell victim to unfounded and 'othering' allegations. The vast majority of these accusations eventually resulted in acquittals, but the hapless defendants were imprisoned (often for several weeks) pending trial. Jacinta Fernández Lobo was arrested by a patrol officer in early March 1937 for having wandered into the evacuated war zone around the Princesa Bridge and Usera districts without the requisite passes.[136] She was arrested and prosecuted by the Ministry of War, Propaganda and Press for suspected espionage and held in prison without formal cause for over a month until she was acquitted and released on grounds of mental incapacity. It was established that she was an illiterate person of 'limited intelligence' who had wandered inadvertently into a bombed and evacuated zone. Similarly, Rosario Ballos Fernández was an illiterate domestic who was obliged to sign her witness statement with a thumb-print after her interrogation at the Cuatro Caminos police station.[137] She had raised the suspicion of the local community because 'she was behaving oddly' and appeared to be unfamiliar with the surroundings. In fact, she had been sent to scavenge for coal by her employers on the evening of 22 June 1937 and had strayed into the evacuated zone. At the time of her arrest she was "barefooted and seemingly lost and confused." She approached three local women and allegedly "insistently asked them about the use of the trenches, the situation at the fronts and the troop positions."[138] She was denounced and immediately arrested. The case was dismissed on 26 July 1937 on account of a lack of incriminating evidence.

The majority of the espionage cases against individual women were based on misunderstandings or false allegations that resulted in lesser sentences for disaffection or acquittals. Such cases evidence the heightened levels of fear and suspicion against fifth-columnists in the rear-guard at this time. Frequently, unfounded allegations of espionage arose as a result of altercations in food queues or because of petty neighbourhood jealousies and resentments. An 'argumentative and highly critical' working-class widow was the victim of an unfounded denunciation by her neighbours in calle Argumosa 13 with whom she had previously quarrelled. The tribunals most often treated these malicious and false allegations of espionage as simple acts of disaffection and the women were acquitted.[139]

Those with relatives in the Nationalist zones or belonging to anti-Republican associations

Those who were associated by blood, marriage or acquaintance with 'notorious' anti-Republicans or whose relatives lived in the Nationalist zone also became liable to suspicion and denunciation. It was feared that relatives and intimates might pass vital social and military information to the enemy intelligence despite the censors. This sometimes occurred. However, most often the denunciations were unsubstantiated and resulted in acquittals. María Riesgo Vázquez was accused of espionage and imprisoned in Ventas in May 1937 for making signals to enemy aircraft with her spectacles whilst saying good night to a male friend at the entrance of her house.[140] She was denounced by her neighbours because she was intimate with a Falangist. It was commonly known that her male friend had sustained injuries during the Republican assault on the Montaña Barracks on 19 July 1936, and the couple became objects of suspicion. Riesgo remained in custody for several months, and her case was referred to the popular tribunals on charges of disaffection in December 1937. María Luisa Moralles Manrique was suspected of espionage and arrested in November 1937 because she had wealthy parents who lived on the Canary Islands and she was married to a 'fascist captain.' The courts could find no substantive evidence against her, and she was acquitted.[141] Carmen Rodríguez Urba was a former insurance worker who was dismissed because of her right-wing associations. She had previously been married to a nephew of General Queipo de Llano between 1931 and 1936 and was accused of espionage by the concierge of her building who alleged that had been recruited into the fifth column by her dress-maker (*modista*). She was arrested in January 1937 and imprisoned in San Rafael. The defendant obtained a good-character vouchsafe from her former employer at the *Plus Ultra* insurance company who claimed that she had been an 'exemplary worker and a member of the UGT since 1931.' The case was dismissed after it was discovered that the defendant had been falsely accused by the concierge because of a personal feud. Nonetheless, Rodríguez spent nearly three months imprisoned pending judgement.[142]

Despite the Republican fears to the contrary, the trial records indicate that extremely few 'professional' high-level female spies operated in Madrid at this time outside the Clandestine Falange groups. Most cases of autonomous espionage involved denunciations against ordinary women who were the intimates or kin of soldiers or officers. Many were cleaners and auxiliaries or sex-workers who consorted with military personnel. A few cases related to women who worked in civil and military administration or in the military hospitals. Very few cases resulted in convictions for espionage; the vast majority were dismissed or referred to the lower tribunals on charges of disaffection. None of the cases reviewed above involved Nationalist agents or foreign spies, although Falangist women like Carmen de Blas Aranteguí operated as agents for the SIPM (See Chapter 3 above). Consequently, aside from the female spies within the Clandestine Falange, only a handful of women were actively involved in professional espionage. The most serious cases related to well-connected upper- and middle-class women. The security threat posed by such women was acknowledged by the Republican authorities and popular press in 1938. Such cases were referred from Madrid's 'special military tribunals' to the Valencian and Barcelona high courts of treason and espionage and the outcomes are unknown. The professional and deadly foreign *mata hari* stereotype was, to a great extent, a discursive construction – a figment of the febrile popular Republican imaginary at this time. Nevertheless, the military and social intelligence gathering operations of the men and women of the Clandestine Falange posed a substantial threat to Republican security, and these individuals were prosecuted in the group trials for treason and espionage discussed in Chapter 3 above. The war politicised the private, and personal rivalries, jealousy, revenge and neighbourhood feuds informed many false allegations. Poor and working-class women often spent weeks or months in prison on the basis of unfounded and often malicious denunciations. At least 20% of the cases examined above arose as a result of paranoid 'othering' practices based on unfounded suspicions, and around 46% of the espionage cases examined above resulted in eventual acquittals, suspensions or dismissals.

This chapter illustrates how class and gender represented important matrices for the signification of relationships of power. Patriarchal symbolic violence against women was reflected in legal discourses that associated women's political actions with their private habits and morality; such discourses were rarely evidenced in the discourses surrounding male defendants.[143] Women were judged and disciplined according to perceptions of their moral conduct and sexual propriety as well as for their political actions and beliefs. In particular, women's sexuality was a matter for judicial scrutiny and judgement, whereas men were most often spared from the withering and humiliating legal and public gaze. Wealthy and well-connected women used forms of micro-power and useful Republican connections in an effort to survive the revolutionary power-shift in Madrid and circumvent the sanctions of the new popular justice. Middle- and upper-class women often escaped long-term prison sentences, while the poor and less well-connected lacked the necessary social capital or the economic resources to successfully navigate the new legal system. While the most serious cases of espionage related to middle- and upper-class women, most of those who had the misfortune to appear before the tribunals belonged to the most vulnerable sectors of society. Paradoxically, the 'people's justice' served the poor and ill-educated with less consideration than the wealthier sorts. The new popular justice frequently delivered harsher and more arbitrary forms of justice to the most economically and culturally disadvantaged. 'Bourgeois' social and cultural capital still held a currency and value within Republican society and the tribunals. Middle-class women frequently continued to enjoy the influence and privileges pertaining to their class and status despite the revolutionary atmosphere of the first months of the conflict.

Notes

1 Cervera (1998).

2 (1) *Causa no. 1315 instruida contra Adolfo Hyva Konnsckegg*, AHN, FC-CAUSA_GENERAL, 192, Exp. 33. (2) *Exp. 33, Exp no.1023 instruido contra Bernhard Funck por el delito/s de espionaje*, AHN, FC-CAUSA_GENERAL, 92, Exp. 22. (3) *Expte. 1198 contra Anna María Becker, José Domínguez Arévalo, Pedro Gallo Rodríguez, Berta Björsen Bethgen por delito/s de espionaje*, AHN, FC- CAUSA_GENERAL, 53, Exp. 32. (4) *Expte. no. 95 instruido contra Alberto Von Filek*, AHN, FC-CAUSA_GENERAL, 90, Exp. 30. (5) *Expte. no. 973 instruido contra León Bruyne por el delito/s de espionaje*, AHN, FC-CAUSA_GENERAL, 91, Exp. 12. (6) *Expte. no. 596 contra Margarita (Greta) Robertson por el delito/s de espionaje*, AHN, FC-CAUSA_GENERAL, 34, Exp. 115. (7) *Expte. instruido contra Max Germias Schneider, Luís Linartz Voltz por el delito/s de espionaje*, AHN, FC-CAUSA_GENERAL, 9, Exp. 7. (8) *Expte. no. 602 contra Ana María Becker por delito/s de espionaje*, AHN, FC-CAUSA_GENERAL, 34, Exp. 1. (10) *Expte. no. 229 contra Alejandro Pistoleci Manzoni por el delito/s de Adhesión y auxilio a la Rebelión y espionaje*, AHN, FC-CAUSA_GENERAL, 25, Exp. 71. (11) *Expte. no 1312 instruido contra Llu (Luís) Sen Cheng por el delito/s de espionaje*, AHH, FC-CAUSA_GENERAL, 50, Exp. 14. The cases were referred to the Valencian Courts of Treason and Espionage whose records are unavailable in PARES, and their final outcomes are unknown.

3 I came across very few references to the presence of far-right spies in Madrid but see *Sumario no.4/1937 del Juzgado Especial del Tribunal Central de espionaje no. 1 contra Javier Fernández Golfín y otros*, AHN, FC-CAUSA_GENERAL, 1539, Exp. 1, Imagen 16/1134. Witness evidence of Julio Benavides Ortega dated 3 July 1937. The witness testified that at some time in May 1936 he liaised with a Traditionalist Captain who introduced him to a French man [named Dubois?], a Spaniard aged fifty years living in Madrid and a woman named Pepita in the *Granja de Henar*. The Spaniard "personally knew La Rocque [sic] (head of fascism in France) and travelled a lot to Berlin and French Morocco … in effect the young woman belonged to an espionage service which was active in Madrid and in other places in Spain regarding a 'movement' that was expected to break out in the capital in August [1936] … the head of this espionage service was the Spaniard … and the movement would probably have repercussions in all the barracks of Spain." There is extremely little historiography in relation to French far-right spies in Republican Spain at this time but see Dewaele Vaderrábano, Hélène "La extrema derecha francesa en España: mitos y realidades de la Bandera Jeanne d'Arc (1936–1939)," *Historia y política: Ideas, procesos y movimientos sociales*, 8 (2002), pp. 273–302.

4 *Causa 1247 instruida contra Encarnación Garrido Montiel por el delito/s de Espionaje*, AHN, FC-CAUSA_GENERAL, 192, Exp. 7. This case relates to a single, and unemployed hairdresser who volunteered as an auxiliary nurse with the Líster Brigade and who was arrested under suspicion of espionage but was found to be soliciting in an evacuated and prohibited zone (the tribunal found that she had prior form with regard to the solicitation of soldiers).

5 *Expte.no. 255 contra María del Pilar Martín Bascarán, Carlos del Castillo and Urbano González Ribera por el delito/s de Espionaje*, AHN, FC-CAUSA_GENERAL, 81, Exp. 6. Imágenes 1-55. On 28 January María del Pilar was found to be in her eighth month of gestation and suffering from 'acute bartolinitis' which required surgery. She was transferred from San Rafael to the Red Cross hospital in calle O'Donnell, 44 and from there to another hospital. The case was eventually transferred to the Valencian High Court of Treason and Espionage on 13 September 1937 and the outcome is unknown.

6 Seidman, Michael (2002) *Republic of Egos, A Social History of the Spanish Civil War* (London: University of Wisconsin Press), p. 88.

7 e.g. *Expte. no 1336 instruido contra María Ángeles Miralles Conte por el delito/s de espionaje*, AHN, FC-CAUSA_GENERAL, 50, Exp. 36. See also *Expte. contra Eugenia García Arteaga (y otros) por el delito/s de espionaje y auxilio a la Rebelión*, AHN, FC-CAUSA_GENERAL, 9, Exp. 16 (discussed below).

8 *Juventudes Socialistas Unificadas.*
9 *Expte. 432 instruido contra Balbina Ledesma de Paz por el delito/s de Espionaje,* AHN, FC-CAUSA_GENERAL, 293, Exp. 2, Imagen 154/160.
10 *Expte. 432*, Imagen 48/160.
11 *Expte. 432*, Imagen 10/160.
12 *Expte. 432*, 56/160.
13 *Expte. 432*, 158/160.
14 Cancio, Fernández, Raúl C. (2007) *Guerra Civil y Tribunales: De los Jurados Populares a la Justicia Franquista (1936–39)* (Cáceres: Universidad de Extremadura), p. 87. See *Los Tribunales Especiales de Guardia*, at pp. 86–93.
15 *Expte. 847 instruido contra Paulo Calvo Enrique y Ángeles Eizmendi Téllez Girón por el delito/s de Espionaje*, AHN, FC-CAUSA_GENERAL, 234, Exp. 55.
16 Jacinta Sánchez Vilches' flat was protected by the Panamanian Embassy even though she was not a Panamanian subject. She gave evidence at the trial that she first made the acquaintance of Eizmendi after 18 July and that she "appeared at her house dressed in a boiler suit and she believed that she was a Republican official." Imagen 89/122.
17 *Expte. 847*, Imagen 89/122. Trial testimony of Rafael González Urria dated 23 November 1937.
18 *Expte. 847*, Imagen 12-13/122.
19 The arresting officers confiscated many valuables at her friend Rosario Sánchez Vilchez's flat including three small boxes containing dozens of jewels and precious items that were painstakingly itemised in a two-page inventory that included "a cameo gold broach, a ladies watch and chain, a pair of earrings, a silver signet ring, a pair of pearl earrings, a diamond solitaire ring, a pair of gold and black pearl earrings, two ladies broaches mounted with seemingly fine stones … a platinum and diamond broach." Imagen 15/122.
20 *Expte. no 847*, Imagen 21/122. Interrogation transcript of Ángeles Eizmendi dated 5 July 1937.
21 *Expte. no 847*, Imagen 98/122. Letter from Felipe Sainz Martínez dated 23 November 1937. This carpenter had known the defendant for more than twelve years.
22 *Expte. no 847*, Imagen 27/122. Testimony of Jacinta Sánchez Vilches dated 5 July 1937.
23 *Expte. no. 847*, Imagen 89/122. Trial evidence of Jacinta Sánchez Vilches dated 23 November 1937.
24 *Expte. no. 847*, Imagen 86/122.
25 *Expte. no. 847*, Imagen 16/122.
26 See the case of Josefina Sotillo Jiménez who was arrested on suspicion of espionage for failing to show proof of 'financial means' while meeting a male friend in Bar Jauja. This case is discussed below.
27 *Expte. 1198 contra Anna María Becker, José Domínguez Arévalo, Pedro Gallo Rodríguez, Berta Björsen Bethgen por delito/s de espionaje*, AHN, FC- CAUSA_GENERAL, 53, Exp. 32. Imagen 8/29. Concepción Lozano "the widow of Gamboa" was also implicated in this case and accused of espionage/adhesion to Rebellion. The case was provisionally suspended in September 1937.
28 *Expte. 1198*, Imagen 9/29.
29 *Expte. 1198 contra Anna María Becker, José Domínguez Arévalo, Pedro Gallo Rodríguez, Berta Björsen Bethgen por delito/s de espionaje*, AHN, FC- CAUSA_GENERAL, 53, Exp. 32. Imagen 8/29.
30 *Expte. no 847*, Imagen 106/122.
31 *Expte. no 847*, Imagen 93/122. Letter dated 5 November 1937 from Bernardina Téllez Girón (resident at Hotel Victoria, Valencia) to Julián Zugazagoitia at the Home Office.
32 *Expte. no 847*, Imagen 87/122.
33 *Sumario no 4/1937*, FC-CAUSA_GENERAL, 1539, Exp. 1. Imagen 983/1134. Letter dated 25 July 1937 from Julián Zugazagoitia (on Home Office letterhead) to Emilio Fernández Peña.

34 Rodríguez López, Sofía (2008) *Quintacolumnistas, Las mujeres del 36 en la clandestinidad almeriense* (Almería: IAE), p. 58.

35 In 1932 Commander G. Ladoux published a non-fictional work entitled *Marthe Richard, Espionne au Service de La France* (Paris: Librarie Champs Elysees) which was subsequently translated into Spanish. This former director of the French Intelligence Services between August 1914 and October 1917 also published an earlier work under the same imprint entitled *Le Chasseur d'Espions (Comment J'ai fait arreter Mata Hari).*

36 Bertrán i Musitu, Josep (1940) *Experiencias de los Servicios de Información del Nordeste de España (SIFNE) durante la guerra* (Madrid: Espasa-Calpe), p. 115.

37 Cox, Geoffrey (1937) *Defence of Madrid, An Eyewitness Account from the Spanish Civil War* (Dunedin NZ: Otago), p. 156. There were very few 'real' French spies in Madrid, and if they had been so indiscrete their names may have appeared more frequently in the legal record.

38 *Causa 1615 instruida contra Enriqueta Mariateguí Rollán por el delito/s de Espionaje*, AHN, FC-CAUSA_GENERAL,198, Exp. 14. Imágenes 1/52

39 *Causa 1615*, Imágenes 16-17/52. Police report by Agents José Lage, Manuel Alfageme and Blas Araque dated 24 July 1937.

40 *Causa 1615*, 17/52.

41 The oldest son of Baron de Pallaruelo who entered the Cavalry Academy on 16 November 1922. See *Ecos Diversos*, *ABC (Madrid)* dated 16 November 1922, p. 12.

42 *Causa 1615*, 47/52. Letter of the *Comisaria General de Investigación y Vigilancia, Madrid* dated 31 August 1937.

43 *Causa 1615*, 16/52.

44 *Causa 1615*, 47/52.

45 *Expte. 494 instruido contra Enriqueta Mariateguí Rollán por el delito/s de Desafección al Régimen*, AHN, FC-CAUSA_GENERAL, 116, Exp. 18, Imágenes 8/32. Witness interrogation report of Enriqueta Mariateguí dated 11 August 1937.

46 *Causa 1615*, Imagen 41/52.

47 *Expte. 494*, Imagen 8/32.

48 *Causa 1615 instruida contra Enriqueta Mariateguí Rollán por el delito/s de Espionaje*, AHN, FC-CAUSA_GENERAL, 198, Exp. 14. Imágenes 8/52. *Auto* dated 9 September 1937.

49 *Expte. 494 instruido contra Enriqueta Mariateguí Rollán por el delito/s de Desafección al Régimen*, AHN, FC-CAUSA_GENERAL, 116, Exp. 18, Imágenes 1-32.

50 "'Pasionaria' aboga por la limpieza de la retaguardia, la depuración de los mandos y la movilización general," *ABC (Madrid)*, 20 February 1937, p.

51 Bourdieu (2007) *Masculine Domination*, p. 16 and pp. 100–101.

52 "Although the war conditions prevented the project of libertorios de prostitución from getting off the ground ... Mujeres libres appealed to prostitutes to abandon their occupation and join the movement," see "Education for Empowerment" and section on "Sexuality" in Ackelsberg, Martha (1985) *Free Women of Spain, Anarchism and the Struggle for the emancipation of women* (Indiana: IUP), pp. 133–140 at p. 136.

53 See for example, Leoncio Pérez "La prostitución el arma principal de la quinta columna," in *Claridad* dated 4 March 1937, at pp. 4–5. See also *ABC (Madrid)* dated 2 August 1936, and also *ABC (Madrid)* dated 31 July 1936 and *Claridad* dated 31 October 1936.

54 Ovidio Gónzalez Díaz (1938) *Guerra Civil en Asturias: Nuestros enemigos entre nosotros. (Vida, Crítica y exterminio de una quinta columna)* (Barcelona: Antifascistas), at p. 6. Cited in Gemma Mana, Rafael García, Luis Monferrer and Luis A. Esteve (eds) (1997) *La Voz de los Naufragos, La Narrativa Republicana entre 1936 y 1939* (Madrid: Ediciones de la Torre), at p. 100.

55 *Expte. 296 contra Augusto Núñez Ramírez y Carmen Montes Cachero por delito/s de tenencia ilicita de explosivos*, AHN, FC-CAUSA_GENERAL, 36, Exp. 45 and *Expte. no. 70 instruido contra Carmen Montes Cachero por el delito/s de Tenencia Ilicita de explosivos*, AHN, FC-CAUSA_GENERAL, 167, Exp. 32. Imagen 54/89. Excerpt from sentence of the military *Tribunal de Guardia, no. 3* dated 13 May 1937.

56 *Expte. 296*, 3/89.
57 Queipo de Llano, Rosario (1939) *De La Cheka de Atadell a la Prision de Alacuas* (Valladolid: Santaren).
58 A girl or woman employed by a dance hall to dance with patrons for a fee.
59 *Expte. 24 instruido contra María Higinia Miralles Conte por el delito/s de Espionaje*, AHN, FC-CAUSA_GENERAL, 10, Exp. 17, Imagen 8/175. The case was commenced under her false name in an earlier trial: *Expte. 1336 contra María Ángeles por el delito/s de Espionaje*, AHN, FC-CAUSA_GENERAL, 50, Exp. 36.
60 *Expte. 24*, Declaration of Augusto Lecha Villasuso dated 29 January 1938. Imagen 147/175.
61 *Expte. 20 contra Sara Giralt Gómez por el delito/s de Espionaje*, AHN, FC-CAUSA-GENERAL, 151, Exp. 16. Imágenes 1/122.
62 *Expte. 20*, Imagen 66/122. Declaration of Luis Zubillaga Olalde, President of the Regional Court of Madrid dated 28 July 1938.
63 See "De sociedad. Ecos Diversos," *ABC (Madrid)*, 16 February 1932, at p. 44. Cited in Campanario, Juan Miguel *La aventura política de Albino Lasso Conde, un ingeniero de caminos que fue diputado del Frente Popular y acabó siendo condecorado por Franco*, Paper given at the XI Congreso de Historia Contemporánea, Granada (September 2012) [last accessed on 8 May 2017] at www 3.uah.es/jmc/lasso7ago12.pdf.
64 *Expte. 20*, Imagen 18/122. Prosecution summary.
65 *Expte. 20*, Witness statement of Rogelio Periquet, Imagen 122
66 Preston, Paul (2012) *El Holocausto*, p. 343.
67 *Expte. 20*, Statement of Don Nicolás Cortés García, Secretary of the Court, dated 30 June 1938, Imagen 36/122.
68 *Expte. no. 20*, Imagen 65/122. Declaration of Sara Giralt Gómez dated 25 July 1938.
69 *Expte. no. 20*, Imagen 18/122.
70 *Expte. no. 20*, Imagen 57/122. Declaration of Don Melchor Rodríguez García dated 22 July 1938. The anarchist leader and Delegate of Prisons, Melchor Rodríguez, was popularly known as 'the Red Angel' on account of the thousands of anti-Republican lives he saved during the war. He was appointed as Special Delegate of Prisons in December 1936, and he played an important role in preventing the prison *sacas*. Rodríguez gave evidence in July 1938 that López de Uribe had gone to visit him at his office after midnight and addressed him using the familiar diminutive "Melchete." He asked him 'in complete confidence' to 'officially endorse' the night-time release of Carlos Corsini although the release of prisoners was strictly prohibited after 6 p.m. in order to prevent illegal prison '*sacas*.'
71 In 1936 Albino Lasso Conde was elected as the Left Republican MP for Cuenca. The outbreak of the war found him on holiday in San Sebastián where he joined with the civil governor's forces in their efforts to quash the Rebellion. In July 1938 Lasso Conde continued as a Republican MP but was also a commander in the Engineers Régiment. See *Expte. no. 20*, Imagen 18/122. See also the conference paper by Campanario, Juan Miguel *La aventura política de Albino Lasso Conde, un ingeniero de caminos que fue diputado del Frente Popular y acabo siendo condecorado por Franco*, given at the XI Congreso de Historia Contemporanea, Granada dated September 2012 [last accessed on 8 May 2017] at www 3.uah.es/jmc/lasso7ago12.pdf.
72 *Expte. no. 20*, Declaration of Luis Zubillaga Olalde, President of the Regional Court of Madrid dated 28 July 1933, Imagen 66/122.
73 *Causa no.8/1938 contra Sara Giralt y otros por Espionaje y Desafección al Régimen*, AHN, FC_TRIBUNAL_SUPREMO_RECURSOS, 150, Exp. 8, Imagen 2/31.
74 *Sumario no. 8/1938 instruido por el Juzgado Especial del Tribunal Supremo contra Luis Zubillaga Olalde y Feliciano López López de Uribe, presidente y fiscal respectivamente de la Audiencia de Madrid, el diputado a Cortes Albino Lasso Conde y Teodoro Illera Martín, Comisario de Seguridad por su participacion y declaraciones en los hechos que se atribuyen a Sara Giralt ó en otra Causa instruido contra ella por delito/s de espionaje y desafección al Régimen*, AHN, FC_TRIBUNAL_SUPREMO_RESERVADO, Exp. 8.

75 "Orden declarando en situacion de disponible gubernativo al Presidente de la Auciencia territorial de Madrid, don Luis Zubillaga y Olalde," *Gaceta de la República: Diario Official, num. 253*, 10 September 1938, p. 1172 and *Orden declarando en situacion de disponible gubernativo a don Feliciano López y López de Uribe, Fiscal Jefe de la Audiencia de Madrid, Gaceta de la República: Diario Official num.* 253, 10 September 1938, p. 1172. Also cited in Campanario, Juan Miguel *La aventura política de Albino Lasso Conde* [last accessed on 8 May 2017] at www3.uah.es/jmc/lasso7ago12.pdf.

76 *Expte. 20*, Imagen 19/122. Declaration of Sara Giralt Gómez dated 22 September 1938. Lasso Conde was waiting for her at the Hotel Majestic in Barcelona.

77 *Causa no. 8/1938 contra Sara Giralt Gómez y otros por espionaje y Desafección al Régimen*, AHN, FC_TRIBUNAL_SUPREMO_RECURSOS, 150, Exp. 8, Imagen 28/31.

78 *Expte. instruido contra María Teresa Giralt, Consuelo Gómez Suelto, Santiago Martínez de la Riva, Rogelio Periquet Rufilanchas, Manuel Rogelio Ledesma Adan, por delito/s de Desafección al Régimen* FC-CAUSA_GENERAL, 71 Exp. 16. Imágenes 1/6.

79 Cervera (1998) *Madrid*, p. 350.

80 *Sumario no 81/1938 del Juzgado Especial por espionaje y otros delitos contra la seguridad exterior del estado contra Antonio Rodríguez Aguado y otros*, FC-CAUSA_GENERAL, 1540, Exp. 1 and 1542, Exp. 1. This organisation was led by the Falangists Antonio Rodríguez Aguado and Joaquín Jiménez de Anta, and its headquarters were based in the Turkish Embassy after Rodríguez Aguado sought refuge there in early 1937. See also, Cervera, Chapter 11 "En busca de un refugio seguro," pp. 339–374. A list of all the embassies and consulates in Madrid that were prepared to receive political asylum seekers together with the number of refugees in various diplomatic buildings is provided at pp. 369–374.

81 Graham, Helen (2002) *The Spanish Republic at War* (Cambridge: CUP), p. 342.

82 *Expte no 882 contra Josefina Jiménez Sotillo por el delito/s de Desafección al Régimen*, AHN, FC-CAUSA_GENERAL, 233, Exp. 35. Imágenes 1-207, Imagen 15.

83 *Expte no 882*, Imagen 107/207. Witness evidence of Felisa Martínez Ezcurra dated 17 August 1937. This woman was Hilario's landlady.

84 *Expte no 882*, Imagen 111/207. Witness evidence of Africa Labarge Viese dated 17 August 1937.

85 *Causa no 1602 instruida contra Josefina Jiménez Sotillo por el delito/s de Adhesión y auxilio a la Rebelión*, AHN, FC-CAUSA_GENERAL, 173, Exp. 54. Imagen 5/23.

86 *Expte no 882 contra Josefina Jiménez Sotillo por el delito/s de Desafección al Régimen*, AHN, FC-CAUSA_GENERAL, 233, Exp. 35. Imagen 187/207. Plea in mitigation after sentence dated 11 November 1937.

87 *Expte no 882*, Imagen 121/207.

88 Blasco Herranz, Inmaculada (1997) *Armas femeninas para la contrarevolución: La Sección Femenina en Aragón (1936–50)* (Málaga: IAM), p. 75.

89 *Expte no 882*, Imagen 103/207.

90 During the trial for disaffection *Expte. 882* (see above) evidence was also submitted into court that she regularly attended a venereal disease clinic.

91 *Causa no. 1602*, Imagen 11/23.

92 *Expte no 882*, Imagen 109/207. Soriano arranged the accommodation for Jiménez upon her return to Madrid.

93 *Expte no 882*, Imagen 101/207. These men gave evidence (in their own defence) that they only knew Jiménez in her capacity as the girlfriend of Soriano: Imágenes 130-135.

94 *Causa 1602*, Imagen 12/23.

95 *Expte no 882 contra Josefina Jiménez Sotillo por el delito/s de Desafección al Régimen*, AHN, FC-CAUSA_GENERAL, 233, Exp. 35. Imagen 100/207.

96 *Expte no 882*, Imagen 109/207. Witness evidence of landlady Esperanza Villa Toca dated 17 August 1937.

97 *Expte. 882*, Imagen 181/207.

98 *Causa 26 instruida contra Vicente Cervero Bosch y Ana Arce Folgara por el delito/s de Espionaje*, AHN, FC-CAUSA_GENERAL, 155, Exp. 37. Imagen 39/94.

99 *Causa 26*, Imagen 82/94.

100 Thomas, María (2013) *The Faith and the Fury, Popular Anticlerical Violence and Iconocasm in Spain, 1931–36* (Brighton: Sussex), pp. 49–57. Vincent Mary "The politicization of Catholic women in Salamanca, 1931–1936," in Frances Lannon and Paul Preston (eds) (1990) *Élites and Power in Twentieth Century Spain: Essays in Honour of Sir Raymond Carr* (Oxford: OUP), pp. 107–126. See also, Blasco, Inmaculada (2003) *Paradojas de la ortodoxia, política de masas y militancia católica femenina en España (1919–1939)* (Zaragoza: PUZ).

101 Salomón Chéliz, Ma Pilar "Beatas sojuzgadas por el clero: la imagen de las mujeres en el discurso anticlerical en la España del primero tercio del siglo XX," *Feminismo/s*, 2 (2003), pp. 41–58.

102 *Expte. 1764 instruido contra Eugenia García Arteaga (y otros) por el delito/s de Espionaje y auxilio a la Rebelión.* ES.28079.AHN/2.2.26/FC-CAUSA_GENERAL, 9, Exp. 16, Imágenes 306.

103 Cervera, Javier "La Radio: un arma mas de la guerra civil en Madrid," *Historia y comunicación social*, 3 (1998), pp. 263–293 at p. 275. Gathering together for the purpose of listening to Radio Salamanca, Sevilla or Burgos constituted *prima facie* 'a criminal clandestine gathering in order to commit the crime of Defeatism.'

104 *Expte. 1764 instruido contra Eugenia García Arteaga (y otros) por el delito/s de Espionaje y auxilio a la Rebelión.* ES.28079.AHN/2.2.26/FC-CAUSA_GENERAL, 9, Exp. 16, Imágenes 2/306.

105 *Expte. 1764*, Imágenes 2/306.

106 *Expte. no 1764, Expte. 1764 instruido contra Eugenia García Arteaga (y otros) por el delito/s de Espionaje y auxilio a la Rebelión*, FC-CAUSA_GENERAL, 9, Exp. 16, 299/306.

107 Ventas was Madrid's model women's prison which was constructed under the supervision of Victoria Kent Siano who was a Republican lawyer and Radical Socialist politician and MP who was appointed Director General of prisons between 1931 and 1934. She later joined the Left Republican party and ran in the February 1936 elections. Ventas opened in 1935. During the first year of the war it was used as a male prison.

108 *Causa 1764 instruida contra Eugenia García Arteaga por el delito/s de Incitación a la Rebelión*, FC-CAUSA_GENERAL, 174, Exp. 28. Imagen 11/104.

109 *Expte. 1764 instruido contra Eugenia García Arteaga (y otros) por el delito/s de Espionaje y auxilio a la Rebelión*, FC-CAUSA_GENERAL, 9, Exp. 16, Imágenes 1/306.

110 *Expte. 1764*, Imagen 102/306.

111 The Youth Section of Acción Católica de la Mujer established in 1919.

112 The Institute of Ladies of the Catechism was a charitable social Catholic religious congregation that was established in 1901 by María Dolores Rodríguez Sopeña (beatified in 2003). Its aims were to teach piety and the catechism to the poor and underprivileged. It was composed of predominantly upper-class women who were dedicated to the "protection, acculturation and moral teaching of the working classes. By 1929 it had 1469 teachers and 127 honorary '*señoritas*' across Spain." Source: Blasco, Inmaculada (2003) "Movilización en tiempos de Guerra," in *Paradojas de la Ortodoxia* (Zaragoza: Prensas Universitarias de Zaragoza), p. 58. See also www.catequistasopena.org [sic].

113 Blasco (2003) "Movilización en tiempos de Guerra," p. 58.

114 Echarri, María de "Ninas hoy…mujeres manana," *El Universo. Revista de Acción Católica, y de Cultura General*, 10 (9 July 1929). Cited in Arce Pinedo, Rebecca (2008) *Dios, Patria y Hogar, La Construcción Social de la mujer española por el católicismo y las derechas en el primer tercio del siglo XX* (Santander: Universidad de Cantabria), p. 104.

115 *Expte. 1764*, Imagen 7/306.

116 *Expte. 1764*, Imagen 5/306.

117 *Expte. 1764 instruido contra Eugenia García Arteaga (y otros) por el delito/s de Espionaje y auxilio a la Rebelión.* ES.28079.AHN/2.2.26/FC-CAUSA_GENERAL, 9, Exp. 16, Imagen 2/306.

118 Blasco (2003) "Movilización en tiempos de Guerra," p. 302.

119 Blasco (2003), p. 301.

120 "Gender appropriate behaviour which subscribes to expected social norms of respectable femininity, embodies patterns of belief, customs values and rules of conduct.

Male defined social conventions are embedded in social structures and cultural norms." Nash, Mary (1995) *Defying Male Civilisation: Women in the Spanish Civil War* (Denver: Arden), at p. 53.

121 Enders, Victoria Lee and Radcliff, Pamela Beth (eds) (1999) *Constructing Spanish Womanhood* (New York, NY: State University of New York Press), p. 3.

122 *Expte. 1764 instruido contra Eugenia García Arteaga por el delito/s de Incitación a la Rebelión*, ES.28079.AHN/2.2.26/FC-CAUSA_GENERAL, 174, Exp. 28, Imágenes 66/102.

123 See also the case of *Alberto Castilla Olavarría and Pilar Ovejas Ovejas, Expte. no. 39 (bis) instruido por el delito/s de Espionaje*, AHN, FC-CAUSA_GENERAL, 77, Exp. 7.

124 The classic 'honey trap' espionage tactic involves seduction in order to extract secrets. A precedent already existed in the Spanish social imaginary in the form of the Dutch exotic dancer and spy, Mata Hari, who was executed in France in 1917 for passing confidential information to the Germans.

125 Primo de Rivera, Pilar (1983) *Recuerdos de una vida* (Madrid: Dyrsa). The author recalled helping to disguise a nun using a wig that had previously adorned the statue of a saint; the nun was made uncomfortable by this 'sacrilege' but the dangerous circumstances required it.

126 MPhil Dissertation of Flynn, Angela (2013) *Las Desafectas al Régimen: Anti-Republican Women and Republican Justice in Madrid 1936–9* (Oxford: Unpublished MPhil), p. 70.

127 *Expte. 319, contra Manzanos, Ginestra por delito/s de Desafección al Régimen*, AHN, FC-CAUSA, GENERAL, 158, EXP. 10, See also, *Expte. 592, por delitos de Alta Traición*, AHN, FC-CAUSA_GENERAL. 9, EXP. 1.

128 *Expte. 1041 instruido contra Catalina Colón Rodríguez por el delito/s de Espionaje*, AHN, FC-CAUSA_GENERAL, 92, Exp. 17, Imágenes 1/28.

129 *Expte. 1041*, Imágenes 16/28 and 25/25.

130 MPhil Dissertation of Flynn, Angela (2013) *Las Desafectas al Régimen: Anti-Republican Women and Republican Justice in Madrid 1936–9* (Oxford: Unpublished MPhil), p. 70.

131 *Expte. 115 contra* Margarita Álvarez Santiago, *por delito/s de Desafección*, AHN, FC-CAUSA_GENERAL, 231, Exp. 11.

132 *Expte. no 396 instruido contra Magdalena Noin Ormaechea por el delito/s de Espionaje*, AHN, FC-CAUSA_GENERAL, 187, Exp. 50. Imágenes 1-73.

133 *Expte. 11 contra María Luisa López Ochoa Motta por el delito/s de Espionaje y Alta Traición*. FC-CAUSA_GENERAL, 77, Exp. 22. Imágenes 1-13 only.

134 *Expte. no 396*, Imagen 21/73. Letter dated 10 September 1938 from the Head of the SIM, Ángel Pedrero to the Senior Judge of the *Triubnal especial de guardia*.

135 As indicated in the introduction, see Kalyvas (2006) *The Logic of Violence*, at pp. 176–181, "The 'shame' surrounding the social phenomenon of private and anonymous [rather than public] denunciation … is reflected in the pejorative terms used to refer to denouncers … This stigma drives even people who have denounced for 'legitimate' political and ideological reasons to keep it concealed … Thus denunciation is not easily observable, even *ex post*." At p. 177.

136 *Expte. con el Registro 608 tramitado contra Jacinta Fernández Lobo por el delito/s de Espionaje*, AHN, FC-CAUSA_GENERAL, 34, Exp. 4, and *Expte. 1046 instruido contra Jacinta Fernández Lobo por el delito/s de Espionaje*, AHN, FC-CAUSA_GENERAL, 45, Exp. 13, Imágenes 1-47.

137 *Causa no 1491 contra Rosario Ballos Fernández por el delito/s de Espionaje*, AHN, FC-CAUSA_GENERAL, 196, Exp. 38, Imagen 16/34.

138 *Causa no 1491*, Imagen 15/34. Witness statement of denouncer Felipa Pacheco Núñez dated 22 June 1937.

139 *Expte. no 17 instruida contra Amalia Vaquero Puebla por el delito/s de espionaje*, AHN, FC-CAUSA_GENERAL, 5, Exp. 9, Imágenes 1-15.

140 *Expte. no.1320 instruido contra María Riesgo Vázquez por el delito/s de Espionaje*, AHN, FC-CAUSA_GENERAL, 50. Exp. 12, Imágenes 1-25.

141 *Expte. 1781 instruido contra María Luisa Morales Manrique por el delito/s de Espionaje*, AHN, FC-CAUSA_GENERAL, 202, Exp. 32.

142 *Expte. no. 799 instruido contra Carmen Rodríguez Urba por el delito/s de Espionaje*, Archivo Histórico Nacional, FC-CAUSA_GENERAL, 87, Exp. 9, Imagen 30/62.

143 Interestingly, similar patriarchal gender prejudices are also evidenced in the operation of the Francoist military tribunals during the post-war, see "Las mujeres y la guerrilla," in Yusta, Rodrigo, Mercedes (2005) *La guerra de los vencidos, El maquis en el Maestrazgo turolense, 1940–1950* (Zaragoza: IFC), pp. 110–120 at p. 111.

Conclusion

The work constitutes a modest contribution to the gender historiography of the Spanish Civil War. It re-evaluates women's engagement in the Nationalist war effort through an examination of the role played by women in the fifth column. It demonstrates how fifth-column women were more able to mobilise a clandestine resistance than their male counterparts who were physically and symbolically excluded from the public space at this time. Women occupied key liaison and leadership roles, primarily within Auxilio Azul, but also within the Clandestine Falange and dozens of autonomous groups. They held the fragile threads of the clandestine networks together. Hundreds more helped to sustain the spiritual, material and affective life of Clandestine Madrid during a highly conflictive moment. However, while women's subversive activities often involved the symbolic transgression of gender norms, their new-found social and political agency was conceptualised within the objective conditions and precepts of Catholicism and understood within traditional national Catholic discourses of 'holy Crusade.'[1]

The illegal coup unleashed a dramatic and violent change in the Republican social field after 18 July 1936. Anti-Republicans were obliged to change their habits in order to survive, and many were forced into hiding or asylum. Over 8,000 individuals lost their lives in Madrid during the extra-judicial repression which took place at the start of the war. Homes and businesses were impounded, and hundreds of anti-Republicans were imprisoned for political crimes. Many middle-class anti-Republican women entered the workplace for the first time. Formerly legal activities were retrospectively criminalised under the new emergency disaffection legislation. Churches were closed, and religion was forced underground. It was only after the stabilisation of the battle-fronts in mid-1937 that any semblance of normality returned to the rear-guard, although ordinary civilians endured severe material, economic and psychological hardships for the duration of the war. During the war a significant sector of anti-Republican women mobilised against the Republican regime and helped to create a subversive and clandestine national Catholic space in the heart of Republican Madrid.

The chief importance of the fifth column resided in its welfare-aid and auxiliary activities; as the war progressed intelligence gathering also became a key aspect of fifth-column practice. Anti-Republican women saved hundreds of lives. Their resistance initiatives weren't 'merely auxiliary'; they were crucial and resulted in the preservation of life, the support of an underground confessional community and the preservation of Catholic habitus during a period of severe social upheaval. Although a temporary gender-power shift occurred at this time, patriarchal and masculinist values determined the important, dangerous and 'noble tasks.' Women's welfare-aid fell outside the parameters of 'authentic and active' resistance in the eyes of the male resistance leaders, and consequently the political and symbolic value attributed to women's resistance has been routinely overlooked in the histories of this period. In addition, the Republican security services attributed scant importance to the actions of female resisters, and this was reflected in their lack of prominence in the legal and police record. Traditional and enduring gender prejudices resulted in the invisibility of women's significant and effective resistance efforts.

After the outlawing of the Falange Party on 14 March 1936, women became key liaison agents between the imprisoned leaders and the members on the ground. This explains how women were best-positioned to mobilise a 'resistance of the first hour' after 18 July. Auxilio Azul was the largest and most effective fifth-column network in the capital and in the whole of the Republican-held zone. It was formed soon after 18 July 1936 in order to provide safe-housing and escape-lines for fugitives. Its origins lay in the illegal underground activities of the pre-war Sección Femenina. Although Pilar Primo de Rivera was forced into hiding after 18 July, a small number of women formed a clandestine rescue and aid network which was initially led by the young Falangist activist María Paz Martínez Unciti until her death in November 1936. Thereafter, her sister Carina, who was a devout Catholic, became the leader of what came to be known as Auxilio Azul (Blue Aid). The organisation was never dismantled, and by the end of the war it is said to have amassed an estimated 6,000 members and affiliates. However, the paucity of original source materials, the self-censorship of the protagonists and their gender-specific resistance practices meant that their considerable efforts have been forgotten.

Falangist and national Catholic women were political agents in their own right, and their gender 'invisibility' was recognised as a useful asset by the party cadres who encouraged them to 'conceal guns in their coats and inside their boots.' Many of Auxilio Azul's most senior leaders (with the notable exception of Carina) were 'old shirts.' However, by as early as November 1936 the organisation began to attract a wider constituency of disaffected Catholics including members of Acción Católica and former members of the outlawed monarchist, CEDA and Traditionalist parties. Auxilio Azul's distinctive emotional regime combined the fascist ideology of the Falange with traditional Catholic discourses of 'crusade and martyrdom.' Women's routine domestic and affective labour was politicised within a subversive anti-Republican resistance space, and many of those who self-identified as dutiful supporters of the national Catholic cause were in fact highly politicised activists who often engaged in extremely dangerous and illegal activities.

While the women in the mixed-gender Clandestine Falange groups often performed the same or similar roles as men, traditional gender prejudices and assumptions meant that they were perceived to be less of a threat by the Republican authorities. The persistence of patriarchal gender norms in the Republican social field worked in favour of the Nationalist cause. The Republican security did not perceive women to be as dangerous or intelligent as men, and it was assumed that they could not organise and lead resistance networks.[2] The women of the mixed-gender Falange groups were able to successfully infiltrate the prisons, military barracks, hospitals and the civil and military administration. In addition to providing crucial welfare-aid, these women also performed 'masculine' resistance roles. Some were the leaders of armed 'squads,' and a small number were implicated in acts of terrorism and violence. Many more were involved in the social intelligence gathering operations which continued after the war under the auspices of the SIPM for the purposes of identifying the friends and enemies of the nascent Franco regime.[3]

The autonomous fifth column facilitated imaginings of a new national Catholic nationhood in the Republican-held zones. It was the 'idea of resistance' over and above any large-scale acts of sabotage or armed resistance that helped Clandestine Madrid to maintain its collective identity and preserve morale while awaiting the occupation of the capital by Franco's troops. The autonomous resistance sprang into life at the start of the war within dozens of small groups and hundreds of individuals who were united by their politico-religious beliefs and their desire to sabotage, hamper or disrupt the Republican war effort in as many small ways as possible. Minor acts of sabotage and everyday resistance served to boost morale and instil a sense of agency. Those who dared to embrace more active and organised forms of resistance joined the organised Clandestine Falange which was relatively easy to do, for within the tight-knit circles of Clandestine Madrid almost everyone knew someone who might be trusted as '*una persona de confianza*.' Women formed an integral part of the autonomous resistance and were often responsible for the spiritual, material and affective well-being of the family and the wider community during moments of extreme danger and uncertainty when anti-Republican men's freedom in the public space was restricted. The extra-judicial violence of the earliest months and the legal repression generated feelings of persecution and resentment among the anti-Republican community which played a significant role in the 'structurally revanchist and repressive policies of the post-war.'[4] Forms of intimate and selective violence assisted in the consolidation of Francoism 'from below.'[5]

After the arrival of the Nationalist troops, the imperative to preserve bourgeois Catholic habitus was fulfilled and 'order' was restored. Public worship was immediately reinstated, and *Te Deums* rang from the churches for the first time in thirty-two months. Religion re-occupied the public space and tradition came out of the shadows.[6] Many of the women who mobilised to protect the Fatherland and the faith during the war chose to return to the private domestic space in accordance with the values and durable dispositions of their gendered class and Catholic habitus. Prominent fifth-columnists enjoyed privileged ex-combatant status and the material, financial and symbolic rewards that accompanied this distinction.[7] Former male leaders were rewarded for their contributions to the Nationalist war effort with military decorations, financial compensation and positions in government and bureaucracy. Senior female leaders were rewarded with military decorations, financial compensations and positions within the Sección Femenina. Although peace was declared on 1 April 1939, the fifth column continued its practices of selective violence in the form of social intelligence gathering. 'Franco's Justice' and conditions of extreme poverty during the 1940s gave rise to new forms of organised and everyday civilian resistance.[8]

With the arrival of Auxilio Social on 28 March 1939, the official Sección Femenina hierarchy was established in the capital. It was tasked with the provision of health, education and welfare services and women's political impulses were channelled into gender-appropriate initiatives. This afforded a minority of elite Falangist women possibilities for political agency despite the general exclusion of women from power.[9] To the traditional Catholic and conservative ideology of female domesticity, the Franco regime added new duties to the state. As with other authoritarian regimes at this time, it held that "women should serve the state and the nation, as well as God and society, by raising children in the virtues and values of national Catholicism."[10] The Nationalist victory settled the position of women in Spanish society for decades. The egalitarian legislation passed by the Second Republic during the Azaña Premiership was dismantled including the legislation on women's voting rights, labour reforms, the family, divorce and civil marriage which had provided new and considerable opportunities for women.[11] As early as 1936 a decree was issued in the rebel-held zones that banned co-education in secondary schools, and primary school teachers were instructed to orientate young girls towards their 'elevated function' in the family by developing their domestic skills.[12] Women's freedom to work was restricted when the Nationalist Labour Charter (*Fuero de Trabajo*) dated 9 March 1938 was implemented throughout the whole of Spain. Franco's Charter sought to return women to the private space.[13] Both during the Second Republic, and more so during the conflict, the women examined here experienced a temporary gender-power shift while consciously participating in a violent political struggle to 'turn back the clock' in order to re-instate traditional patriarchal norms and values. They were mobilised by Catholic and class habitus and the real and perceived threats to their established way of life, class interests and religious beliefs.[14] After Auxilio Azul was demobilised, the majority of these national Catholic women withdrew into anonymity and relinquished the public space.

Notes

1 Mother María Luisa Fernández and Mother María Leturia (1939) *Catorce meses de aventuras bajo el dominio rojo* (Rome: ACI), p. 30.

2 Rodríguez López, Sofía and Cazorla Sánchez, Antonio "Blue Angels: Female Fascist Resisters, Spies and Intelligence Officials in the Spanish Civil War, 1936–9," *Journal of Contemporary History*, 53 (4) (2016), pp. 692–713.

3 Píris (2018) "Los servicios de información Franquistas…" p. 161. Anderson, Peter (2017) *Friend or Foe? Occupation, Collaboration and Selective Violence in the Spanish Civil War* (Sussex: Sussex/Cañada Blanch).

4 Saz Campos, Ismael (2004) *Fascismo y Franquismo* (València: Universitat de València), [ebook] pp. 168–170. The author argues that "Although the forces of democracy and socialism had been vanquished, it might only be a matter of time before the 'hydra' was reawakened from within its old social bases//Consequently, the desire for revenge, vengeance and extermination of political enemies, together with the complete absence of any coherent policy together with insecurities surrounding a purely reactionary project, combined to make repression a structural feature of the dictatorship" at p. 169. See also Juliá Díaz, Santos (ed) (1999) *Víctimas de la Guerra Civil* (Madrid: Planeta de Agostini), Mir, Conchita "Violencia política, coacción legal y oposición interior," *Ayer*, 33 (1999), pp. 115–145.

5 Anderson, Peter (2017) *Friend or Foe?*

6 Vincent, Mary "Expiation as Perfromative Rhetoric in National-Catholicism: The Politics of Gesture in Post-Civil War Spain, *Past and Present,* Volume 203, Issue supplement 4, 2009, pp. 235–256 at p. 250.

7 Píris (2018) "Los servicios de información Franquistas," p. 161. Heiberg and Ros Agudo (2006) *La Trama*, p. 194. See also Alcalde, Ángel (2014) *Los excombatientes Franquistas (1936–1965)* (Zaragoza: PUZ), p. 354.

8 For analyses of Franco's justice see Anderson, Peter (2010) *The Francoist Military Trials, Terror and Complicity, 1939–45* (Abingdon: Routledge/Cañada Blanch) and Ruiz, Julius (2005) *Franco's Justice: Repression in Madrid after the Spanish Civil War* (Oxford: OUP). For conceptualisations of post-war civilian resistance see Yusta, Rodrigo, Mercedes (2003) *Guerrilla y resistencia campesina, La resistencia armada contra el franquismo en Aragón (1939–1952)* (Zaragoza: PUZ), Yusta, Rodrigo, Mercedes (2005) *La guerra de los vencidos, El maquis en el Maestrazgo turolense, 1940–1950* (Zaragoza: IFC), also Di Febo, Giuliana (1979) *Resistencia y movimiento de mujeres en España* (Barcelona: Icaria). According to Mercedes Yusta, di Febo's remains a seminal contribution to the historiography of women's anti-Francoist resistance, see Yusta Rodrigo, "Las mujeres en la resistencia antifranquista, un estado de la cuestión," *Arenal, Revista de historia de las mujeres*, Editorial Universidad de Granada, 2005. ⟨hal-01493607⟩. Submitted to HAL open access archives in 2017. Last viewed 5 June 2019. For the Republican and subsequent Francoist repression against women see Holgado, Fernando Hernández (2003) *Mujeres Encarceladas, La Prisión de Ventas: De la República al Franquismo, 1931–1941* (Madrid: Marcial Pons Historia). For an analysis of 'everyday resistance' and black-market economies see Rodríguez Barreira, Óscar "Cambalaches: Hambre, moralidad popular y mercados negros de Guerra y post-Guerra," *Historia Social*, 77 (2013), pp. 1–21.

9 Ofer, Inbal (2010) *Señoritas in Blue, the making of a female political elite in Franco's Spain, The National Leadership of the Sección Femenina de la Falange 1936–1977* (Padstow: Sussex Academic Press). Ordinary women were excluded from this 'empowerment,' and Auxilio Social's coercive social welfare efforts have been called to account in Cenarro, Ángela (2006) *La Sonrisa de Falange, Auxilio Social en la Guerra Civil y en la posguerra* (Madrid: Crítica).

10 Morcillo, Aurora (2008) *True Catholic Womanhood, Gender Ideology in Franco's Spain* (Illinois: Northern Illinois University Press). For an analysis of patriotic and authoritarian constructions of womanhood in Vichy France see Pollard, Miranda (1998) *Reign of Virtue, Mobilizing Gender in Vichy France* (Chicago: UCP). For Nazi constructions see Koonz, Claudia (2013) *Mothers in the Fatherland, Women, the Family and Nazi Politics* (London: Routledge). See also, Lannon, Frances "True Catholic Womanhood, Gender Ideology in Franco's Spain (Review)," *The Catholic Historical Review*, 89 (2) (2003), pp. 320–321. "The national Catholic state reduced the status of women to their biological reproductive functions and made them inferior to men" in Joly, Maud "Las violencias sexuadas de la Guerra Civil Española: paradigma para una lectura cultural del conflicto," *Historia social*, 61 (2008), pp. 89–107.

11 Bussy Genevois "Citoyennes de la Seconde République," in Barrachina, Marie Aline, Bussy Genevois, Daniele, Yusta, Mercedes (eds) (2007) *Femmes et Democratie, Les Espagnoles*

dans l'espace public (1868–1978) (Paris: Edition du Temps), p. 142. See also, Yusta Rodrigo, Mercedes "Du familial au politique. Engagements fémenins dans la guerrilla antifranquiste en Espagne (1936–1952)," in Bergès, Karine, Burgos-Vigna, Diana, Yusta Rodrigo, Mercedes, Ludec, Nathalie (eds) (2015) *Résistantes, Militantes, Citoyennes. L'Engagement Politique des Femmes aux XXe et XXIe Siècles* (Rennes: PUV), p. 89.

12 Romero Salvadó, Francisco (2013) *Historical Dictionary of the Spanish Civil War* (Plymouth: Scarecrow Press), pp. 358–359.

13 See Cobo Romero, Francisco and Ortega López, Teresa María "Francoist Anti-feminism and the Violent Reversal of Women's Liberation, 1936–1951," in Anderson, Peter and del Arco Blanco, Miguel Ángel (eds) (2015) *Mass Killings and Violence in Spain, 1936–1952: Grappling with the Past* (New York, NY: Routledge), pp. 59–71.

14 See Pierre Bourdieu (2013) *Outline of a Theory of Practice* (Cambridge: CUP), p. 76.

Bibliography

DIGITAL ARCHIVAL SOURCES

Portal Digital de Archivos Españoles (PARES)
CENTRO DOCUMENTAL DE LA MEMORIA HISTÓRICA:

CDMH, Fondos Contemporáneos, Fiscalía del Tribunal Supremo, Causa General. ES.28079. AHN/2.2.2

CDMH, Fondos Contemporáneos, Causa General, Tribunales Populares y Jurados de Urgencia y de Guardia de Madrid, ES.28079.AHN/2.2.6.

CDMH, Fondos Cruz Roja Internacional, ACICR, C_ESCI,1,2,3,4,15,78,180,186,187,190, 196,200,238.

Boletín Oficial del Estado (www.boe.es):

- *Gaceta de Madrid*
- *Gaceta de la República*

NON-DIGITAL ARCHIVAL SOURCES

Archivo Documental de 'Nueva Andadura' (ANA) held in Real Academia de la Historia (RAH):

FET y de Las JON: *La Sección Femenina, Historia y Organización,* ANA, Carpeta 1-B.

Historia de la Sección Femenina escrita por Pilar Primo de Rivera, undated typescript, ANA, Carpeta 1-B.

Sección Femenina 'Blue Series' legal archives, Carptetas B-12 and B-18.

Archivo General Militar de Ávila (AGMAV):

AGMAV, C. 2505, Cp.4/42 1 1

AGMAV, C. 2505, Cp.4/43 1 1

AGMAV, C. 2498,20 1 18

Archivo de la Universidad Pontificia de Salamanca (UPSA):

Acción Católica de España (ACE), Mujeres de Acción Católica, MAC, Inventario (1934-68), Memorias Diocesanas.

Las Jóvenes de Acción Católica, (JFAC), Inventario (1926-1961), Memorias Diocesanas, 1-7. Estadísticas Diocesanas (1936-45), 8-9.

NEWSPAPERS AND MAGAZINES

ABC (Madrid), http://hemeroteca.abc.es

El Sol, El Heraldo de Madrid-Biblioteca Nacional de España, Hemeroteca Digital de España. Ministerio de Cultura, http://hemerotecadigital.bne.es

La Razón de Domingo at http://*Larazon.es*

Marxists Internet Archive at http://marxists.org

PROPAGANDA AND ARTWORK

Carteles de Propaganda, Archivo Fotográfico de la Delegación de Propaganda de Madrid durante la Guerra Civil, PARES. Centro documental de la Memoria Histórica. Ministerio de Cultura. http://pares.mcu.es

PRIMARY SOURCES

Alcalá -Zamora, Niceto (1944) "Justicia penal de guerra civil" in (*Ensayos de derecho procesal civil, penal, constitucional*), Buenos Aires,

Alcocer, Santos. *La Quinta Columna*. Madrid: G. del Toro, 1976.

Arévalo, Carlos. *Rojo y Negro* [Film]. CEPISCA, 1942.

Azaña, Manuel. *Causas de la guerra de España*. Madrid: Biblioteca de la República, 2011.

Barceló, José Luis. *Madrid 1938, Diario de un niño en guerra*. Málaga: Sepha, 2012.

Bergès, Karine, Burgos-Vigna, Diana, Yusta Rodrigo, Mercedes, and Ludec, Nathalie. *Résistantes, Militantes, Citoyennes. L'Engagement Politique des Femmes aux XXe et XXIe Siècles*. Rennes: PUV, 2015.

Bertrán í Musitu, Josep. *Experiencias de los Servicios de Información del Nordeste de España (SIFNE) durante la guerra*. Madrid: Espasa-Calpe, 1940.

Björsen de Wedel, Herta. *La Carcel de Ventas*. Madrid: Águilar, 1941.

Borkenau, Franz. *The Spanish Cockpit, An Eyewitness Account of the Spanish Civil War*. London: Phoenix Press, 2000.

Bouthelier, Antonio, and López Mora, José. *8 días, La revuelta comunista, Madrid, 5–13 Marzo 1939*. Madrid: Editora Nacional, 1950.

Campoamor, Clara. *La revolución Española vista por una Republicana*. Madrid: Espuela de Plata, 2007.

Carretero, José María. *(El Caballero Audaz). La Quinta Columna*. Madrid: Saez, 1940.

Carrillo, Santiago. *Memorias- El Testimonio Polémico de un protagonista relevante de nuestra Transición*. Barcelona: Editorial Planeta, 2008.

Casado, Coronel Segismundo. *Así cayo Madrid, Ultimo episodio de la guerra civil Española*. Madrid: Guadiana, 1968.

Cora, María Manuela de. *Retaguardia Enemiga*. Madrid: Altalena Editores, 1984.

Cox, Geoffrey. *Defence of Madrid, An Eyewitness Account from the Spanish Civil War*. Dunedin, New Zealand: Otago, 1937.

de la Mora, Constancia. *In Place of Splendor*. New York: Harcourt Brace, 1939

Díaz Plaja, F. *La Guerra de España en sus documentos*. Barcelona: Plaza y Janés, 1975.

Duyagües, Pilar. *Querido Diario: Hoy ha empezado la guerra*. Balló, Tania and Berger, Gonzalo (eds.). Barcelona: Espasa, 2003.

Etchébehere, Mitcha. *Mi Guerra de España: Las apasionantes vivencias de una mujer que llego a ser Capitán de fuerzas Republicanas [POUM]*. Madrid: Plaza y Janés, 1987.

Falcón, Cesar. *Madrid.* Madrid: Hacer Editorial, 2010.

Fernández, María Luisa (Mother), and Leturia, María (Mother). *Catorce meses de aventuras bajo el dominio rojo.* Rome: ACI, 1939.

Fórmica, Mercedes. *Memorias, visto y vivido, escucho el silencio (1931–1947).* Seville: Renacimiento, 2013.

Foxá, Agustín de. *Madrid, de corte a checa.* Madrid: Bibliotex, 2001 (first ed. 1938).

Galíndez, Jesus de. *Los vascos en el Madrid sitiado; memorias del Partido Nacionalista Vasco y de la Delegación de Euzkadi en Madrid desde septiembre de 1936 a mayo de 1937.* Tafalla, Navarra: Txalaparta, 2005 (first ed. 1945).

Guzmán, Eduardo de. *Madrid rojo y negro.* Madrid: Oberon, 2004.

Hemingway, Ernest. *The Fifth Column.* London: Penguin, 1966.

Ibárruri, Dolores. *They Shall Not Pass, The Autobiography of La Pasionaria.* USA: International, 2005.

Iturralde, Juan. *Dias de llamas.* Barcelona: DeBolsillo, 2006.

Jato, David. *La rebelión de los estudiantes.* Madrid: Cies, 1953.

Koltsov, Mijail. *Diario de la guerra de España.* Madrid: Ruedo Ibérico, 1963.

Koonz, Claudia. *Mothers in the Fatherland, Women, the Family and Nazi Politics.* London: Routledge, 2013.

Martínez Sierra, María. *Una mujer por campos de España.* Madrid: Castalia, 1989.

Nelken, Margarita. *La condición social de la mujer en España.* Madrid: CVS Ediciones, 1975.

Primo de Rivera, José Antonio. *Textos de doctrina política.* Madrid: Delegación de la Sección Femenina, 1971.

Primo de Rivera, Pilar *Discurso de Pilar Primo de Rivera, XII Consejo Nacional [pamphlet]*, Sevilla-Huelva, n.p. SF de FET y de las JONS, 1948.

Primo de Rivera, Pilar. *Recuerdos de una vida.* Madrid: Dyrsa, 1983.

Queipo de Llano, Rosario. *De la cheka de Atadell a la prisión de Alacuas.* Madrid: Castellana, 1939.

Ramón y Cajal, Santiago, and Nelken, Margarita. *La Mujer.* Madrid: M. Águilar, 1938.

Rieger, Max. *Espionaje en España.* Madrid: Espuela de Plata, 1937.

Rivera, Pilar Primo de. *Escritos, Discursos Circulares.* Madrid: Graficas Afrodisio Aguado S.A., 1937–1942.

Santillán, Diego Abad de. *Estrategia y táctica, ayer, hoy y mañana.* Madrid: Biblioteca Júcar, 1976.

Schlayer, Félix. *Diplomático en Madrid.* Madrid: Ediciones Espuela de Plata, 2008.

Schlayer, Félix. *Matanzas en el Madrid republicano: paseo, checas, Paracuellos, testimonio del diplomático que descubrió la masacre de Paracuellos.* Barcelona: Ediciones Altera, 2006.

Tarín Iglesias, Manuel. *Los años rojos, Un testimonio capital sobre la Quinta Columna en zona republican durante la guerra civil.* Barcelona: Planeta, 1985.

Uribarri, Manuel. *La Quinta Columna Española. Verdad y Justicia.* La Habana: La Universal, 1943.

Zugazagoitia, Julián. *Guerra y vicisitudes de los Españoles.* Barcelona: Tusquets, 2001.

SECONDARY TEXTS

Abella, Rafael. *La España republicana en la vida cotidiana durante la Guerra Civil.* Barcelona: Planeta, 2004.

Abella, Rafael. *La España nacional en la vida cotidiana durante la Guerra Civil.* Barcelona: Planeta, 2004.

Ackelsberg, Martha. *Free Women of Spain, Anarchism and the Struggle for the Emancipation of Women.* Indiana: IUP, 1985.

Adkins, Lisa, and Skeggs, Beverley. *Feminism After Bourdieu.* Oxford: Blackwell, 2006.

Aguado, Ana, and Ortega, Teresa María (eds.). *Feminismos y antifeminismos. Culturas políticas e identidades de genero en la España del siglo XX.* Valencia: PUV, 2011.

Aguilar Fernández, Paloma. *Memoria y olvido de la Guerra Civil Española.* Madrid: Alianza, 1996.

Alcalá, Cesar. *Las Checas del Terror, Los métodos de represión de la 'justicia roja' y las cárceles clandestinas en Barcelona, Madrid, Valencia y Bilbao.* Madrid: Libroslibres, 2007.

Alfaya, José Luis. *Como un río de fuego, Madrid 1936.* Barcelona: EIU, 1998.

Alía Miranda, Francisco. *La agonía de la República: el final de la Guerra Civil española (1938–1939).* Barcelona: Crítica, 2015.

Alía Miranda, Francisco. *La Guerra Civil en Ciudad-Real, conflicto y revolución en una provincia de la retaguardia Republicana.* Ciudad Real: BAM, 2017.

Alpert, Michael. *A New International History of the Spanish Civil War.* London: Macmillan Press Ltd, 1994.

Álvarez Junco, José. *Spanish Identity in the Age of Nations.* Manchester: MUP, 2011.

Anderson, Peter. *Friend or Foe? Occupation, Collaboration and Selective Violence in the Spanish Civil War.* Sussex: Sussex/Cañada Blanch, 2017.

Anderson, Peter. *The Francoist Military Trials, Terror and Complicity, 1939–45.* Abingdon: Routledge/Cañada Blanch, 2010.

Anderson, Peter, and del Arco Blanco, Miguel Ángel (eds.). *Mass Killings and Violence in Spain, 1936–1952: Grappling with the Past.* New York: Routledge, 2015.

Arce Pinedo, Rebeca. *Dios, Patria y Hogar. La construcción social de la "mujer española" por el catolicismo y las derechas en el primer tercio del siglo XX.* Santander: Universidad de Cantabria, 2008.

Bahamonde, Ángel. *Madrid, 1939. La conjura del coronel Casado.* Madrid: Cátedra, 2014.

Bahamonde Magro, Ángel, and Cervera Gil, Javier. *Así Terminó la Guerra de España.* Madrid: Marcial Pons, 1999.

Balfour, Sebastian. *Spain and the Great Powers in the Twentieth Century.* London: Routledge, 1999.

Barrachina, Marie Aline, Bussy Genevois, Daniele, and Yusta, Mercedes (eds.). *Femmes et Democratie, Les Espagnoles dans l'espace public (1868–1978).* Paris: Edition du Temps, 2007.

Baumeister Martin, Schuler-Springorum (eds.). *"If You Tolerate This"…The Spanish Civil War in the Age of Total War.* New York: Campus Verlag, 2008.

Beevor, Antony. *The Battle for Spain, The Spanish Civil War, 1936–1939.* London: Phoenix Press, 2006.

Blanning, Tim (ed.). *The Oxford Illustrated History of Modern Europe.* Oxford: OUP, 1996.

Blasco, Inmaculada. *Paradojas de la ortodoxia, Política de masas y militancia católica femenina en España (1919–1939).* Zaragoza: PUZ, 2003.

Blasco Herranz, Inmaculada. *Armas femeninas para la contrarevolución: La Sección Femenina en Aragón (1936–50).* Málaga: IAM, 1997.

Blinkhorn, Martin. *Democracy and Civil War in Spain, 1931–1939.* London: Routledge, 1988.

Bloxham, Donald, and Gerwarth, Robert (eds.). *Political Violence in Twentieth Century Europe.* Oxford: OUP, 2001.

Bolloten, Burnett. *La guerra civil española, Revolución y contrarrevolución.* Madrid: Alianza Editorial, 1989.

Borderias, Cristina (ed.). *La Historia de Las Mujeres: Perspectivas Actuales.* Barcelona: Icaria, 2009.

Borrás, Tomás. *Seis Mil Mujeres.* Madrid: Editora Nacional, 1965.

Botti, Alfonso, Montero, Feliciano, and Quiroga, Alejandro (eds.). *Católicos y patriotas, Religion y nación en la Europa de entreguerras.* Madrid: Sílex, 2013.

Bourdieu, Pierre. *La dominación masculina.* Barcelona: Anagrama, 2000.

Bourdieu, Pierre. *Masculine Domination.* Stanford: SUP, 2001.

Bourdieu, Pierre. *Practical Reason.* Oxford: Polity, 2001.

Bravo, Anna, and Bruzonne, Anna María. *In guerra senza armi. Storie di donne, 1940–45*. Rome: Laterza, 1995.

Broszat, Martin. "Resistenz und Widerstand." In *Bayern in der NS-Zeit*, edited by Broszat, Martin, and Frölich, Eike, et al. Munich: Oldenbourg, 1981.

Buchanan, Tom. *Britain and the Spanish Civil War*. Cambridge: CUP, 1997.

Buchanan, Tom. *The Impact of the Spanish Civil War on Britain: War, Loss and Memory*. Brighton: Sussex Academic Press, 2007.

Buchanan, Tom, and Conway, Martin. *Political Catholicism in Europe, 1918–1965*. Oxford: Clarendon Press, 1996.

Butler, Judith. *Gender Trouble, Feminism and the Subversion of Identity*. London: Routledge, 1990.

Carr, Raymond. *Spain: A History*. Oxford: Oxford University Press, 2000.

Casanova, Julián. *De la calle al frente, El anarcosindicalismo en España (1931–1939)*. Barcelona: Crítica, 2010.

Cenarro, Ángela. *La Sonrisa de Falange, Auxilio Social en la Guerra Civil y en la posguerra*. Madrid: Crítica, 2006.

Cervera Gil, Javier. *Contra el enemigo de la República…desde la Ley, Detener, juzgar y encarcelar en guerra*. Madrid: Biblioteca Nueva, 2015.

Cervera Gil, Javier. *Madrid en guerra, La ciudad clandestina 1936–9*. Madrid: Alianza, 1998.

Cervera Gil, Javier. *Madrid en guerra, La ciudad clandestina 1936–9*. 2nd ed. Madrid: Alianza, 2006.

Charnon-Deutsch, Lou, and Labanyi, Jo. *Culture and Gender in Nineteenth-Century Spain*. Oxford: Clarendon Press, 1995.

Christian, William. *Visionaries: The Spanish Republic and the Reign of Christ*. California: UCP, 1996.

Collins Weitz, Margaret. *Sisters in the Resistance, How Women Fought to Free France, 1940–45*. New York, NY: John Wiley, 1995.

Corral, Pedro. *Desertores, Los españoles que no quisieron la Guerra Civil*. Madrid: Almuzara, 2017.

Dawes, Helena. *Catholic Women's Movements in Liberal and Fascist Italy*. Basingstoke: Palgrave Macmillan, 2014.

De Febo, Giuliana. *Resistencia y movimiento de mujeres en España (1936–1976)*. Barcelona: Icaria, 1979.

de La Cueva, Julio, and Montero, Feliciano (eds.). *La secularización conflictiva, España (1898–1931)*. Madrid: Biblioteca Nueva, 2007.

de Prado, Núñez, and Clavell, Sara. *Servicios de información y propaganda en la Guerra Civil española, 1936–1939*. Madrid: UCM, 1992.

de Ros, Xon, and Hazbun, Geraldine (eds.). *Companion to Spanish Women's Studies*. London: Boydell and Brewer/Tamesis, 2011.

Di Febo, Giuliana. *Resistencia y movimiento de mujeres en España*. Barcelona: Icaria, 1979.

Díaz-Plaja, Fernando. *La Vida Cotidiana en la España de la Guerra Civil*. Madrid: Editorial Edaf, 1994.

Douzou, Laurent, and Yusta, Mercedes (eds.). *La Résistance à l'épreuve du genre. Hommes et Femmes dans la Résistance antifasciste en Europe du Sud (1936–1949)*. Rennes: Pur, 2018.

Ealham, Chris, and Richards, Michael (eds.). *The Splintering of Spain, Cultural History and the Spanish Civil War, 1936–1939*. Cambridge: CUP, 2005.

Ellwood, Sheelagh. *Prieta las filas, Historia de la Falange Española, 1933–1983*. Barcelona: Crítica, 1984.

Enders, Victoria Lee, and Radcliff, Pamela Beth. *Constructing Spanish Womanhood, Female Identity in Modern Spain* [online text]. New York: State University Press of New York, 1999.

Fagoaga, Concha, and Saavedra, Paloma. *Clara Campoamor, La sufragista Española*. Madrid: Gráficas Oggi, 1981.

Fernández, Raúl C. Cancio. *Guerra Civil y Tribunales: De los Jurados Populares a la Justicia Franquista (1936–1939)*. Cáceres: Universidad de Extremadura, 2007.

Fernández, Rodríguez. *El Hábito y la Cruz, Religiosas asesinadas en la guerra civil Española*. Madrid: Edibesa, 2006.

Fraser, Ronald. *Blood of Spain: An Oral History of the Spanish Civil War*. New York: Pantheon Books, 1979.

Freeman, Thomas, and Mayer, Thomas (ed.). *Martyrs and Martyrdom in England c.1400–1700*. New York: Boydell, 2007.

Fitzpatrick, Sheila and Gellately, Robert (eds.). *Accusatory Practices, Denunciation in Modern European History, 1789–1989*. Chicago: UCP, 1996.

Gallego Méndez, María Teresa. *Mujer, Falange y Franquismo*. Madrid: Taurus, 1983.

García, Hugo, and Yustta, Mercedes, et al. (eds.). *Rethinking Antifascism, History, Memory and Politics, 1922 to Present*. Oxford: Berghahn, 2016.

Gil Pecharromán, Julio. *José Antonio Primo de Rivera: retrato de un visionario*. Madrid: Temas de Hoy, 1996.

Gómez Bravo, Gutmaro (ed.). *Asedio. Historia de Madrid en la guerra civil (1936–9)*. Madrid: UCM, 2018.

Gómez Bravo, Gutmaro. *Geografía humana de la represión franquista, Del golpe a la guerra de ocupación (1936–1941)*. Madrid: Cátedra, 2017.

Gibson, Ian. *Paracuellos, como fué*. Barcelona: Argos Vergara, 1983.

Gies, David Thatcher. *The Cambridge Companion to Modern Spanish Culture*. Cambridge: CUP, 1999.

Graham, Helen (ed.). *Interrogating Fascism*. London: Bloomsbury, 2016.

Graham, Helen. *The Spanish Civil War: A Very Short Introduction*. Oxford: OUP, 2005.

Graham, Helen. *The Spanish Republic at War*. Cambridge: CUP, 2002.

Graham, Helen, and Labanyi, Jo. *Spanish Cultural Studies: An Introduction*. Oxford: OUP, 1995.

Guixà, Josep. *Espias de Franco, Josep Pla y Francesc Cambó*. Madrid: Fórcola, 2014.

Heiberg, Morten, and Ros Agudo, Manuel *La trama oculta de la guerra civil. Los servicios secretos de Franco*. Barcelona: Crítica, 2006.

Higgonet, Margaret, Jenson, Jane, Michel, Sonya, Collins Weitz, Margaret (eds). *Behind the Lines: Gender and the Two World Wars*. London: YUP, 1987.

Holgado, Fernando Hernández. *Mujeres Encarceladas, La Prisión de Ventas: De la República al Franquismo, 1931–1941*. Madrid: Marcial Pons Historia, 2003.

Jackson, Gabriel. *A Concise History of the Spanish Civil War*. London: Thames and Hudson, 1976.

Jenkins, Richard. *Key Sociologists: Pierre Bourdieu*. London: Routledge, 1992.

Joshi, Vandana. *Gender and Power in the Third Reich, Female Denouncers and the Gestapo (1933–45)*. London: Palgrave Macmillan, 2003.

Juliá Díaz, Santos. *Madrid 1931–34, De la fiesta popular a la lucha de clases*. Madrid: Siglo veintiuno, 1984.

Juliá Díaz, Santos (ed.). *Víctimas de la Guerra Civil*. Madrid: Planeta de Agostini, 1999.

Juliá Díaz, Santos. *Violencia política en la España del siglo XX*. Madrid: Taurus, 2000.

Kalyvas, Stathis. *The Logic of Violence in Civil War*. New York: CUP, 2006.

Kershaw, Ian. *Popular Opinion and Political Dissent in the Third Reich 1933–1945*. Oxford: Clarendon, 2002.

Kershaw, Ian. *The Nazi Dictatorship Problems and Perspectives of Interpretation* (4th ed.). London: Bloomsbury, 2015.

Kowalsky, Daniel. *La Union Sovietica y la Guerra Civil Española*. Barcelona: Crítica, 2003.

Labanyi, Jo (ed.). *Constructing Identity in Contemporary Spain, Theoretical Debates and Cultural Practice*. Oxford: Oxford University Press, 2002.

Laguna Reyes, Alberto, and Vargas Márquez, Antonio. *La Quinta Columna, La guerra clandestina tras las líneas republicanas 1936–1939*. Madrid: Laesfera, 2019.

Lannon, Frances. *Privilege, Persecution, and Prophecy: The Catholic Church in Spain, 1875–1975*. Oxford: Clarendon Press, 1987.

Lannon, Frances. *The Spanish Civil War*. Oxford: Osprey Publishing, 2002.

Lannon, Frances, and Preston, Paul (eds.). *Élites and Power in Twentieth Century Spain: Essays in Honour of Sir Raymond Carr*. Oxford: OUP, 1990.

Ledesma, José Luis. *Los días de llamas de la revolución*. Zaragoza: IFC, 2003.

Lines, Lisa. *Milicianas, Women in Combat in the Spanish Civil War*. Lanham: Lexington, 2011.

López, Rosario Sánchez. *Entre la Importancia y la Irrelevancia, Sección Femenina: de la República a la Transición*. Murcia: Editora Regional Ensayo, 2007.

Maestre, Espinosa (ed.). *Violencia Roja y Azul, España, 1936–1950*. Barcelona: Crítica., 2010

Mahmood, Saba. *The Politics of Piety: The Islamic Revival and the Feminist Subject*. Princeton: PUP, 2005.

Mana Delgado, Gemma, García Heredero, Rafael, Monferrer Catalán, Luis, and Juárez, Esteve. *La voz de los naufragos: La narrativa republicana entre 1936 y 1939*. Madrid: Ediciones de la Torre, 1997.

Marqués, Pierre. *La Croix-Rouge pendant la guerre d'Espagne (1936–9)*. Paris: L'Harmattan, 2000, p. 241.

Matthews, James. *Reluctant Warriors, Republican Popular Army and Nationalist Army Conscripts in the Spanish Civil War, 1936–1939*. Oxford: OUP, 2012.

McNay, Lois. *Gender and Agency: Reconfiguring the Subject in Feminist and Social Theory*. Oxford: Polity Press, 2000.

Montero, Feliciano (ed.). *La Acción Católica en la II República*. Alcalá: UAH, 2008.

Montero García, Feliciano, Moreno Cantano, Antonio, Tezanos, Gandarillas (eds.). *Otra Iglesia. Clero disidente durante la Segunda República y la guerra civil*. Gijón: Trea, 2013.

Montoliú, Pedro. *Madrid en la guerra civil, Volumen I*. Madrid: Silex, 1999.

Montoliú, Pedro. *Madrid en la guerra civil, Los protagonisas, Volumen II*. Madrid: Silex, 1999.

Moradiellos, Enrique. *Francisco Franco, Crónica de un caudillo casí olvidado*. Madrid: Editorial Biblioteca Nueva, 2002.

Moradiellos, Enrique. *Mitos de la Guerra Civil Española*. Barcelona: Península, 2004.

Moral Roncal, Antonio. *Diplomacia, humanitarismo y espionaje en la Guerra Civil Española*. Madrid: Biblioteca Nueva, 2008.

Moral Roncal, Antonio. *El asilo diplomático en la Guerra Civil Española*. Madrid: Actas, 2001.

Morcillo, Aurora. *True Catholic Womanhood, Gender Ideology in Franco's Spain*. Illinois: Northern Illinois University Press, 2008.

Nash, Mary. *Defying Male Civilization, Women in the Spanish Civil War*. Denver: Arden, 1995.

Nogales, Manuel Chaves. *La defensa de Madrid*. Seville: Espuela de Plata, 2011.

Nord, Philip. *France 1940: Defending the Republic*. New Haven: YUP, 2015.

Núñez Seixas, José Manoel. *La sombra del césar, Santiago Montero Díaz, una biografía entre la nación y la revolución*. Granada: Comares, 2012.

Ofer, Inbal. *Señoritas in Blue, the Making of a Female Political Elite in Franco's Spain, The National Leadership of the Sección Femenina de la Falange 1936–1977*. Padstow: Sussex Academic Press, 2010.

Orduña Prada, Monica. *El Auxilio Social, (1936–40) La Etapa Fundacional y los Primeros Anos*. Madrid: Escuela Libre Editorial, 1996.

Ortiz Heras, Manuel, Ruiz González, David, and Sánchez Sánchez, Isidro (eds.). *España franquista: causa general y actitudes sociales ante la dictadura*. Albacete: Universidad de Castilla-La Mancha, 1993.

Oviedo Silva, Daniel, and Pérez-Olivares García, Alejandro (eds.). *Madrid, una ciudad en guerra (1936–48)*. Madrid: Catarata, 2016.

Paniagua, Javier, and Lajo Cosido, Benjamín. *Sombras en la retaguardia testimonios sobre la 5a columna en la retaguardia en Valencia*. Valencia: Centro Francisco Tomás y Valiente, 2002.

Passmore, Kevin. *Fascism: A Very Short Introduction*. Oxford: Oxford University Press, 2002.

Passmore, Kevin (ed.). *Women, Gender and Fascism in Europe*. Manchester: MUP, 2003.

Pastor Petit, Domènec. *Los dossiers secretos de la Guerra Civil*. Barcelona: Argos, 1978.

Pastor Petit, Domènec. *Resistencia y sabotaje en la Guerra Civil*. Barcelona: Enigma, 2013.

Pastor Petit, Domènec. *Traidors a Catalunya, La cinquena columna (1936–9)*. Barcelona: Base, 2006.

Payne, Stanley. *Fascism in Spain, 1923–77*. London: University of Wisconsin Press, 1999.

Pérez, Janet, and Ihirie, Maureen (eds.). *The Feminist Encyclopedia of Spanish Literature*. Westport, CT: Greenwood Publishing Group, 2002.

Pollard, Miranda. *Reign of Virtue, Mobilizing Gender in Vichy France*. Chicago: UCP, 1998.

Preston, Paul. *Comrades, Portraits from the Spanish Civil War*. London: Harper Perennial, 1999.

Preston, Paul. *Doves of War, Four Women of Spain*. London: Harper Collins, 2002.

Preston, Paul. *Las Tres Españas del 1936*. Barcelona: Delbolsillo, 2011.

Preston, Paul (ed.). *Revolution and War in Spain, 1931–1939*. London: Methuen, 1984.

Preston, Paul. *The Last Days of the Spanish Republic*. London: Harper Collins, 2016.

Preston, Paul. *The Spanish Civil War, 1936–1939*. London: Weidenfeld and Nicholson, 1986.

Preston, Paul. *The Spanish Civil War, Reaction, Revolution and Revenge*. London: Harper Perennial, 2006.

Preston, Paul. *The Spanish Holocaust, Inquisition and Extermination in Twentieth Century Spain*. London: Harper Press, 2012.

Preston, Paul. *We Saw Spain Die, Foreign Correspondents in the Spanish Civil War*. London: Constable, 2008.

Prieto Borrego, Lucia. *Los dias de la ira. Entre Mijas y el Guadiaro, de la República a la Sierra*. Málaga: UCM, 2013.

Prost, Antoine (ed.). *La Résistance, une histoire sociale*. Paris: Atélier/Ouvrières, 1997.

Puzzo, Dante A. *Spain and the Great Powers*. New York: Columbia University Press, 1962.

Ráguer, Hilarí. *La pólvora y el incienso, La Iglesia y la Guerra Civil Española (1936–39)*. Barcelona: Península, 2001.

Reddy, William. *The Navigation of Feeling: A Framework for the History of Emotions*. Cambridge: CUP, 2001.

Reverte, Jorge. *La Batalla de Madrid*. Madrid: Crítica, 2004.

Richards, Michael. *A Time of Silence, Civil War and the Culture of Repression in Franco's Spain, 1936–45*. Cambridge: CUP, 1998.

Richards, Michael. *After the Civil War, Making Memory and Re-Making Spain Since 1936*. New York: CUP, 2013.

Richmond, Kathleen. *Las Mujeres en el Fascismo Español, La Sección Femenina de la Falange, 1934–1959, [trans. José Luis Gil Aristú]*. Madrid: Alianza, 2003.

Rodríguez Barreira, Óscar. *Miserias del poder, Los poderes locales y el nuevo estado franquista, 1936–51*. Valencia: PUV, 2013.

Rodríguez López, Sofía. *Quintacolumnistas, Las mujeres del 36 en la clandestinidad almeriense*. Almería: IEA, 2008.

Rodríguez López, Sofía. *El patio de la cárcel, La Sección Femenina de FET-JONS en Almería (1937–77)*. Seville: Centro de Estudios Andaluces, 2010.

Romero Salvadó, Francisco. *The Spanish Civil War, Origins Course and Outcomes*. Hampshire: Palgrave, 2005.

Romero Salvadó, Francisco. *Historical Dictionary of the Spanish Civil War*. Plymouth: Scarecrow Press, 2013.

Ruiz, Julius. *El Terror Rojo, Madrid 1936* transl. Jesus de La Torre. Barcelona: Espasa, 2012.

Ruiz, Julius. *Franco's Justice: Repression in Madrid After the Spanish Civil War*. Oxford: OUP, 2005.

Sánchez Blanco, Laura. *Rosas y Margaritas, Mujeres falangistas, tradicionalistas y de Acción Católica asesinadas en la Guerra Civil*. Madrid: Actas, 2016.

Sánchez Recio, Glicerio. *Justicia y Guerra en España. Los Tribunales Populares (1936–1939)*. Alicante: Instituto de Cultura Juan Gil-Albert, 1991.

Sánchez Recio, Glicerio. *La República contra los Rebeldes y los Desafectos, La Represión Económica durante la Guerra Civil*. Madrid: Universidad de Alicante, 1991.

Savage, Mike. *Social Class in the 21st Century*. London: Pelican, 2016.

Saz Campos, Ismael. *Fascismo y Franquismo*. València: Universitat de València, 2004.

Scott, James C. *Weapons of the Weak: Everyday Forms of Peasant Resistance*. New Haven: Yale University Press, 1985.

Seidman, Michael. *Republic of Egos: A Social History of the Spanish Civil War*. London: University of Wisconsin Press, 2002.

Sémelin, Jacques. *Purify and Destroy: The Political Uses of Massacre and Genocide*. London: Hurst & Co., 2013.

Sémelin, Jacques. *Sans armes face à Hitler, 1939–45, La résistance civile en Europe*. Paris: Les Arènes, 2013.

Shubert, Adrian, and Álvarez Junco, José. *The History of Modern Spain, Chronologies, Themes, Individuals*. London: Bloomsbury, 2018.

Sevillano Calero, Francisco. *Rojos, La representación del enemigo en la guerra civil*. Madrid: Alianza, 2014.

Suárez Fernández, Luis. *Crónica de la Sección Femenina y su tiempo*. Madrid: Asociación Nueva Andadura, 1992.

Súñer, Ramón Serrano. *Entre el silencio y la propaganda, la Historia como fué. Memorias*. Barcelona: Planeta, 1977.

Tapia, Alberto Reig. *La Cruzada de 1936, Mito y Memoria*. Madrid: Alianza Editorial, 2006.

Thatcher, Jenny, Ingram, Nicola, Burke, Ciaran, and Abrahams, Jessie (eds.). *Bourdieu – The Next Generation: The Development of Bourdieu's Intellectual Heritage in Contemporary UK Sociology*. Abingdon: Routledge, 2016.

Thomas, Hugh. *The Spanish Civil War*. London: Penguin, 2003.

Thomàs, Joan María. *Lo que fué la Falange*. Barcelona: Plaza y Janés, 1999.

Thomàs, María. *The Faith and the Fury, Popular Anticlerical Violence and Iconocasm in Spain, 1931–36*. Brighton: Sussex, 2013.

Thompson, Edward, P. *Tradición, reveulta y consciencia de clase, Estudios sobre la crisis de la sociedad preindustrial*. Barcelona: Crítica, [transl. Eva Rodríguez], 1979.

Tumblety, Joan (ed.). *Memory and History, Understanding Memory as Source and Subject*. London: Routledge, 2013.

Tusell, Javier. *La Segunda República en Madrid: elecciones y partidos políticos*. Madrid: Tecnos, 1970.

Tusell, Javier. *Sociologia electoral de Madrid: 1903–1931*. Madrid: Editorial Cuadernos para el dialogo, 1969.

Tusell, Javier. *Vivir en Guerra, Historia ilustrada, España, 1936–1939*. Madrid: Ediciones Sílex, 2003.

Vega, Rafael Casas de la. *El Terror: Madrid 1936, Investigación histórica y catalogo de victimas identificadas*. Madrid: Editorial Fénix, 1994.

Vincent, Mary. *Catholicism in the Second Spanish Republic, Religion and Politics in Salamanca, 1930–1936*. Oxford: OUP, 1996.

Vincent, Mary. *Modern Spain (1833–2002) People and State.* Oxford: OUP, 2007.

Vincent, Mary, and Shoemaker, Robert Brink. *Gender and History in Western Europe.* London: Arnold, 1998.

Von List, Corinna (French ed.). *Résistantes.* Paris: Alma, 2012.

Yusta Rodrigo, Mercedes. *Guerrilla y resistencia campesina, La resistencia armada contra el franquismo en Aragón (1939–1952).* Zaragoza: PUZ, 2003.

Yusta Rodrigo, Mercedes. *La guerra de los vencidos, El maquis en el Maestrazgo turolense, 1940–1950.* Zaragoza: IFC, 2005.

ARTICLES

Aguilera Povedano, Manuel. "La Quinta Columna durante el Golpe de Casado." *APORTES* 69, no. XXIV (2009): 99–111.

Alejandre, Juan Antonio. "La Justicia Penal durante la Guerra Civil." *Revista de Historia* 16, *Guerra Civil* 14 (1986): 6–14.

Álvarez Lopera, José. "Ángel Ferrant en la guerra civil." *Anales de Historia del Arte*, Volumen Extraordinario, (2008): 535–555.

Anderson, Peter. "Singling Out Victims: Denunciation and Collusion in the Post-Civil War Francoist Repression in Spain, 1939–45." *European History Quarterly* 39, no. 1 (2009): 7–26.

Andrieu, Claire. "Women in the French Resistance: Revisiting the Historical Record." *French Politics, Culture and Society* 18, no. 1 (2000): 13–27.

Aróstegui, Julio. "'Conspiración contra la República' en la guerra civil." *Historia* 16, no. 3 (1986): 6–40.

Asociación de Historia Contemporánea. *Comunicado-Situación Actual de los Archivos en España.* Murcia: Asociación de Historia Contemporánea, 2004.

Biganne, Julia. "The Rewards of Female Fascism in Franco's New State: The Recompensas Y of the Sección Femenina de la Falange, 1939–45." *Bulletin of Spanish Studies* XC, no. 8 (2013): 1313–37.

Blasco Herranz, Inmaculada (Translated from Spanish by Jeremy Roe). "Citizenship and Female Catholic Militancy in 1920's Spain." *Gender and History* 19, no. 3 (2007): 441–66.

Box, Zira. "Presentación: Más que un programa, un modo de ser." *Historia y Política: Ideas Procesos y Movimientos Sociales* 27 (2012): 13–25.

Box, Zira, and Saz, Ismael. "Spanish Fascism as a Political Religion (1931–1941)." *Politics, Religion and Ideology* 12, no. 4 (2011): 371–89.

Boyd, Carolyn P. "The Politics of History and Memory in Democratic Spain." *Annals of the American Academy of Political and Social Science* 617 (The Politics of History in Comparative Perspective) (2008): 133–48.

Cantano, Moreno, and César, Antonio. "Quintacolumnismo y guerra civil en Madrid: La trayectoria del Falangista Juan Manuel de la Aldea." *Aportes* 83, no. XXVIII (2013): 53–68.

Castillo, José Romero. "La memoria histórica de algunas mujeres antifranquistas." *Anales* 21 (2009): 175–88.

Cenarro, Ángela. "Movilización femenina para la guerra total (1936–9)." *Historia y política: Ideas, procesos y movimientos sociales* 16 (2006): 159–82.

Cervera, Javier. "Violencia política y acción clandestina: La retaguardia de Madrid en Guerra 1936–9." *Doctoral Thesis.* Universidad Complutense de Madrid, 1996. http://eprints.ucm.es/2456/1/T21383.pdf

Cobo Romero, Francisco, del Arco Blanco, Miguel Ángel, and Ortega López, Teresa Maria. "The Stability and Consolidation of the Francoist Regime. The Case of Eastern Andalusia, 1936–1950." *Contemporary European History* 20, no. I (2011): 37–59.

De Groot, Joanna, and Sue, Morgan. "Beyond the 'Religious Turn'? Past, Present and Future Perspectives in Gender History." *Gender and History* 25 (2013): 395–442.

De la Cueva, Julio. "Religious Persecution, Anticlerical Tradition and Revolution: On Atrocities Against the Clergy During the Spanish Civil War." *Journal of Contemporary History* 33, no. 3 (1998): 355–369.

Dewaele Vaderrábano, Hélène. "La extrema derecha francesa en España: mitos y realidades de la Bandera Jeanne d'Arc (1936–1939)." *Historia y política: Ideas, procesos y movimientos sociales*, 8 (2002): 273–302.

Eley, Geoff. "Hitler's Silent Majority? Conformity and Resistance Under the Third Reich (Part I)." *Michigan Quarterly Review* XLII, no. 2 (2003).

Eley, Geoff. "Hitler's Silent Majority? Conformity and Resistance Under the Third Reich (Part II)." *Michigan Quarterly Review* XLII, no. 3 (2003)

Ellwood, Sheelagh. "Entrevista con Dolores Muñoz Tuero - Los tribunales populares fueron buena gente." *Guerra Civil de Historia* 16, *Sociedad y Guerra* 14 (1986): 125–29.

Gahete Muñoz, Soraya. "La Sección Femenina de Falange. Discursos y Practicas en Madrid." *Arenal* 22, no. 2 (2015): 389–411.

García, Hugo. "La historiografía de la Guerra Civil en el nuevo siglo." *Ayer, revista histórica contemporánea* 62, no. 2 (2006): 285–305.

García, Hugo. "War and Culture in Nationalist Spain, 1936–9: Testimony and Fiction in the Narrative of the 'Red Terror'." (transl. Neil Harman)." *Journal of War and Culture Studies* 2, no. 3 (2009).

Gellately, Robert, and Fiztpatrick, Sheila. "Introduction to the Practices of Denunciation in Modern European History." *Journal of Modern History* 68 (1996): 931–67.

González Calleja, Eduardo "La violencia política en la España del siglo xx: un balance historiográfico." *Mélanges de la Casa de Velázquez, Tranferts culturels dans le monde hispanique* 38, no. 2 (2008):213–240.

González Calleja, Eduardo, and Arosteguí, Julio. "La tradición recuperada. El requeté carlista y la insurrección." *Historia Contemporánea* 11: 29–53, Last accessed on http://ehu.eus on 5 June 2019.

Graham, Helen. "Casado's Ghosts: Demythologizing the End of the Spanish Republic." *Bulletin of Spanish Studies* 89, no. 7–8 (2012): 255–78.

Graham, Helen. "The Spanish Civil War." *The Historical Journal* 30, no. 4 (1987): 989–93.

Holgado, Fernando Hernández. "Carceleras Encarceladas." *Cuadernos de Historia Contemporanea* 27 (2005): 271–90.

Jackson, Ángela. "Review of: Hugo García's "The Truth About Spain: Mobilizing British Public Opinion, 1936–39"." *Bulletin for Spanish and Portuguese Historical Studies* 37, no. 1 (2012): 211–15.

Joly, Maud. "Las violencias sexuadas de la Guerra Civil Española: paradigma para una lectura cultural del conflicto." *Historia Social* 61 (2008): 89–107.

Julía, Santos. "La Historia social y la historiografía española." *Ayer, revista histórica contemporánea* 10 (1993): 28–46.

Kebadze, Ninno. "The Right to be Selfless and Other Prerogatives of the Weak in the Rhetoric of the *Sección Femenina.*" *Romance Quarterly* 55, no. 2 (2008): 109–27.

Lannon, Frances. "Women and Images of Women in the Spanish Civil War." *Transactions of the Royal Historical Society 6th Series* 1 (1991): 213–28.

Lannon, Frances. "True Catholic Womanhood, Gender Ideology in Franco's Spain (Review)." *The Catholic Historical Review* 89, no. 2 (2003): 320–21.

López García, Alfonso. "Bombas que nunca mataron: el sabotaje pacífico durante la Guerra Civil Española." *Aportes* 95, no. XXXII (2017): 201–46.

Lüdkte, Alf. "De los heroes de la resistencia a los coautores. "Alltagsgeschichte" en Alemania." *Ayer* 19, Historia de la vida cotidiana (1995): 46–69.

Maestre, Gonzalo. "El tema religioso-católico en Falange Española durante la Segunda República." *Aportes* 90, no. XXXI (2016): 65–100.

Marco Sola, Luisa. "El factor Cristiano. Católicos y sacerdotes antifranquistas en los medios republicanos." *El Argonauta español, Janvier, La presse espagnole et la guerre civile. Entre rupture et propaganda (1936–1939)* 7 (2010): 1–24. https://journals.openedition.org/argonauta/421. Last accessed 11 July 2019.

Martínez Rus, Ana María. "Mujeres y guerra civil: Un balance historiográfico." *Studio Histórico de la Historia Contemporánea* 32 (2014): 333–43.

Mir, Conchita. "Violencia política, coacción legal y oposición interior." *Ayer* 33 (1999): 115–145.

Montero, Julio, and Cervera, Javier. "Madrid en los años treinta. Ambiente social, político, cultural y religioso." *Studia et Documenta: Rivista dell Istituto Storico San Josemaría Escrivá* 3 (2009): 13–39.

Moral Roncal, Antonio Manuel. "An Analysis of Foreign Diplomatic Aid to the Catholic Clergy During the Spanish Civil War (1936–1939)." *Religions* 4, no. 1 (2013): 96–115.

Moral Roncal, Antonio Manuel. "María Rosa Urraca Pastor: de la militancia en Acción Católica a la palestra política carlista (1900–1936)." *Historia y Política* 26 (2011): 199–226.

Morant, Toni. "'Para influir en la vida de del estado futuro': Discurso y práctica Falangista sobre el papel de la mujer y la feminidad, 1933–45." *Historia y Política* 27 (2012): 113–141.

Moreno Cantano, Antonio César. "Quintacolumnismo y Guerra Civil en Madrid: la trayectoria del falangista Juan Manuel de la Aldea." *Aportes* 83, no. 3 (2013): 53–68.

Ofer, Inbal. "Fragmented Autobiographies: A Style of Writing or Self-Perception? The Case of Pilar Primo de Rivera." *Iberoamericana* III, no. 9 (2003): 37–51.

Ofer, Inbal. "Historical Models. Contemporary Identities: The Sección Femenina of the Spanish Falange and its Redefinition of the Term 'Femininity." *Journal of Contemporary History* 40, no. 4 (2005).

Pérez-Reverte, A. "La Película Maldita," in *XL Semanal*, dated 19 April, 2010.

Plamper, Jan. "The History of Emotions: An Interview with William Reddy, Barbara Rosenwein and Peter Stearns." *History and Theory* 49 (2010): 237–65.

Portelli, Alessandro. "On the Peculiarities of Oral History." *History Workshop Journal* 12 (1981): 96–107.

Prada Rodríguez, Julio. "Mujeres contra la revolución. La movilización femenina conservadora durante la Segunda República Espanola y la Guerra Civil." *Femmes et Militantisme* 8, no. 20 (2008). Accessible via *Amnis* [on line] http://journals.openedition.org/amnis/599; DOI: 10.4000/amnis.599

Prada Rodríguez, Julio, and Vázquez, Raúl Soutelo. "La resistencia económica en el primer franquismo. Una aproximación al estraperlo desde la mermoria oral: Ourense, 1939–1952." In *Testimonios orales y escritos. España 1936–1996. Actas V Jornadas Historia y Fuentes Orales:Ávila, Octubre 1996*, edited by Trujillano Sánchez, José Manuel, and Díaz, Pilar. Ávila: Fundación cultural Santa-Teresa, 1996.

Prieto Borrego, Lucía. "El terror rojo en la Causa General de Casares." *Baetica* 22 (2000): 525–45.

Prieto Borrego, Lucia. "Justicia Popular y Justicia Militar en Málaga." 2007. *Historia y Memoria, Todos los nombres, Mapa de Fosas y Actuaciones de los Tribunales de Responsabilidad Políticas en Andalucía*, Gómez Oliver and Martínez López (eds) (Almería: EUA): 1–15 Last accessed on 7 January 2020 on www.todoslosnombres.org

Prieto Borrego, Lucía. "Los comités frentepopulistas: otra visión de la retaguardia republicana." *Ayer* 102 (2016): 287–320.

Reddy, William. "Historical Research on Self and Emotions." *Emotions Review* 1, no. 4 (2009): 302–15.

Rodríguez Barreira, Óscar. "Cambalaches: Hambre, moralidad popular y mercados negros de Guerra y post-Guerra." *Historia Social*, 77 (2013): 1–21.

Rodríguez López, Sofía. "La Sección Femenina, La imagen del poder y el discurso de la diferencia." *Feminismo/s 16* (December 2010): 233–257.

Rodríguez López, Sofía, and Barreira, Oscar Rodríguez. "La Quinta Columna y la Guerra Civil en Andalucía. El Socorro Blanco, el Sindicato Católico de la Aguja y Falange" *Andalucía en la Historia* ,46 (October–December 2014): 72–77.

Rodríguez López, Sofía, and Cazorla Sánchez, Antonio. "Blue Angels: Female Fascist Resisters, Spies and Intelligence Officials in the Spanish Civil War, 1936–9." *Journal of Contemporary History* 53, no. 4 (2016): 692–713.

Ros Agudo, Manuel. "El espionaje en España en la guerra civil y la segunda guerra mundial: una vision general." *Diacronie, Studi di Storia Contemporanea* 28, no. 4 (2016): 2–18.

Rosenwein, Barbara. "Worrying About Emotions in History." *The American Historical Review* 107, no. 3 (2002): 821–45.

Ruiz, Julius. "A Spanish Genocide? Reflections on the Francoist Repression After the Spanish Civil War." *Contemporary European History* 14, no. 2 (2005): 171–91.

Ruiz, Julius. "Defending the Republic: The García Atadell Brigade in Madrid, 1936." *Journal of Contemporary History* 42, no. 3 (2007): 449–72.

Ruiz, Julius. "'Incontrolados' en la España republicana durante la guerra civil: el caso de Luis Bonilla Echevarría." *Historia y Política* 21 (2009).

Ruiz, Julius. "Seventy Years on: Historians and Repression During and After the Spanish Civil War." *Journal of Contemporary History* 44, no. 3 (2009): 449–72.

Ruiz, Julius. "'Work and Don't Lose Hope': Republican Forced Labour Camps During the Spanish Civil War." *Contemporary European History* 18, no. 4 (2009): 419–41.

Salomón Chéliz, Ma Pilar. "Beatas sojuzgadas por el clero: la imagen de las mujeres en el discurso anticlerical en la España del primero tercio del siglo XX." *Feminismo/s* 2 (2003): 41–58.

Sánchez Recio, Glicerio. "De Genocidios, Holocaustos, Exterminios, sobre los procesos represivos en España durante la Guerra Civil y la Dictadura. Debate sobre la naturaleza de la represión en España." *Hispania Nova, Revista de Historia Contemporánea* 10 (2012).

Sánchez Recio, Glicerio. "El control político de la retaguardia republicana durante la Guerra Civil. Los tribunales populares de justicia." *Espacio, Tiempo y Forma, Serie V, Historia Contemporánea* 7 (1994): 585–98.

Scott, Joan. "Gender: A Useful Category of Historical Analysis?" *American Historical Review* 91, no. 5 (1986).

Scott, Joan W. "Gender: Still a Useful Category of Analysis?" *Diogenes* 57, no. 1 (2010): 7–14.

Sena, Laura. "La Cárcel de las 'Damas de España'." (27 September 2009). http://Levante.emv.com. 15 February 2013 [Press Article].

Solans, Francisco Ramón. "Persecución, milagros y profecias en el discurso Católico Zaragozano durante la Segunda República." *Historia Social*, no. 78 (2014): 81–98.

Stearns, C., and Stearns, P. "Emotionology: Clarifying the History of Emotions and Emotional Standards." *The American Historical Review* 90 (1985).

Viñas, Ángel. "Playing with History and Hiding Treason: Colonel Casado's Untrustworthy Memoirs and the End of the Spanish Civil War." *Bulletin of Spanish Studies* 91, no. 1 1-2 (2014): 295–323.

Vincent, Mary. "*Camisas Nuevas*: Style and Uniformity in the Falange Española 1933–43." In *Fashioning the Body Politic, Dress, Gender, Citizenship*, edited by Wendy Parkins. Oxford: Berg, 2002.

Vincent, Mary. "Expiation as Performative Rhetoric: The Politics of Gesture in Post-Civil War Spain." In *Past and Present*, supplement 4, edited by M. J. Braddick, 2009.

Vincent, Mary. "Made Flesh? Gender and Doctrine in Religious Violence in Twentieth Century Spain." *Gender and History* 25, no. 3 (2013): 668–80.

Vincent, Mary. "The Martyrs and the Saints: Masculinity and the Construction of the Francoist Crusade." *History Workshop Journal* 47, no. 1 (1999): 68–98.

Vincent, Mary. "Ungodly Subjects: Protestants in National-Catholic Spain, 1939–53." *European History Quarterly* 45, no. 1 (2015): 108–31.

Von Greyerz, Kaspar. "Ego-Documents: The Last Word?" *German History* 28, no. 3 (2010): 273–82.

Yusta, Mercedes. "Rebeldía familiar, compromiso individual, acción colectiva. Las mujeres en la resistencia al franquismo durante los años cuarenta." *Historia del Presente* 4 (2004): 31–46.

Yusta, Mercedes. "The Early Years of Franco's Regime As "Seen from the Bottom," Armed Resistance and Everyday Resistances (1939–1952)." *Vingtième Siécle, Revue d'Histoire* 27, no. 3 (2015): 231–244.

Yusta Rodrigo, Mercedes. "Las mujeres en la resistencia antifranquista, un estado de la cuestión." *Arenal, Revista de historia de las mujeres*, Granada: Editorial Universidad de Granada, 2005. hal-01493607.

Appendix A – sources

Primary sources

The main sources consulted here were (1) Republican popular tribunal records (1936–9) which form part of the Causa General documentation which is digitally available on PARES (Portal de Archivos Españoles), the Spanish Ministry of Culture's open-access web archives, (2) the Falange's Sección Femenina Blue Series in the Asociación de la Nueva Andadura (ANA) Archives which are held in the Real Academia de la Historia, Madrid (RAH) and (3) various memory texts. The trial testimonies, legal depositions and memory texts discussed below constitute 'ego-documents,' namely, documents in which an ego intentionally or unintentionally discloses or hides itself.[1] Such personal narratives reproduce and create collective discourses and serve to document and construct social relationships.[2]

Republican popular tribunal records (1936–9)[3]

The Causa General documentation was gathered pursuant to a legal enquiry instigated by decree on 26 April 1940 with the aim of "providing a definitive and complete account of the criminality that existed under the Marxist rule."[4] The enquiry was central to Franco's *post facto* justification for the coup. Serrano Súñer described the Causa's findings as 'back-to-front justice' (*justicia al revés*) that served the interests of Franco's nascent dictatorship.[5] The main problem in using judicial evidence lies in its inherent biases,[6] and the Causa General's findings constituted a "complex web of truths and falsehoods."[7] A manifest conviction bias underpinned its compilation, the quality of the evidence varies from region to region and due standards of legal proof were seldom observed.[8] The testimonies of individuals such as Ángel Pedrero, the head of Madrid's Republican military intelligence services, were obtained under torture and interrogation and with the certain expectation of execution or life imprisonment.[9]

The sources examined here relate to the Republican popular tribunal trials which were heard in the capital between 1936 and 1939 and gathered after the war into the Causa General. No such complete trial records exist in relation to Barcelona and Valencia, and the activities of the fifth column in Madrid are representative of those in other Republican-held towns and cities.[10] The originals are now held in the Centro Documental de la Memoria Histórica in Salamanca, but from 2007 digitalised records were made available on the Spanish Ministry of Culture's PARES website. These trial documents provide a valuable insight into Republican justice during the war and the lived experiences of those caught within the disciplinary webs of the courts and the police. The inherent biases of the new Republican 'popular justice' mean that these sources should be approached with caution. Similarly, the witness testimonies should be analysed against the grain, not least because members of the fifth column were trained to memorise pre-rehearsed scripts in the event of arrest and interrogation.[11] Nonetheless, the archives offer a wealth of detail on Madrid's fifth column and everyday life in the capital at this time. The trial bundles include thousands of pages of police reports, interrogation and witness statements, legal and medical reports, interlocutory and asset-tracing documents and trial transcripts. The easiest way to search the digitalised documents is to input individual names into the primary search engine. A secondary filtering engine facilitates searches by reference to criminal categories (e.g. treason, espionage, rebellion, defeatism, disaffection). This made it possible to compile the statistics set out in the main body of this work.[12]

A total of 14,862 cases were heard in Madrid's emergency popular tribunals between 1936 and 1939.[13] This figure reflects the extent of the Republican government's desire to repress anti-Republican activities. During the first months of the conflict the popular courts operated daily and around the clock within the prisons. Approximately 2.4% of the total 14,862 popular tribunal cases related to crimes of treason, another 2.4% related to espionage, 3.6% related to defeatism, 8% related to military rebellion, 1.3% related to military desertion and 73% related to disaffection.[14] Around 2.5% of the trials related to the illegal use or possession of weapons, 2.4% to black-market crimes and 1.6% to 'public enquiries into unlawful deaths' including deaths caused by explosions, the unauthorised use of machine guns and hand grenades or death by drowning. 'Accidental death' accounted for 0.04% of cases. Still fewer cases related to common crimes of rape (0.04%), homicide (0.22%), bodily harm or assault (2.1%) and robbery (0.6%). These common crimes were heard in the conventional courts which operated alongside the popular tribunals.

Unsurprisingly, men dominated the legal record, and it was necessary to read the trial bundles closely and 'against the grain' for evidence of women's resistance. The evidence against men for serious capital crimes often comprised lengthy interrogation reports and detailed trial transcripts, whereas women's interrogation reports were often only one page in length and female defendants were seldom accorded detailed cross-examination at trial. These observations are made in relation to the Clandestine Falange trials of treason and espionage where women made up between 10 and 15% of the defendants. Women were more equally represented in the summary trials for 'disaffection' of which around 44% were expedited between October 1936 and

March 1937.[15] The cases were based on local and intimate denunciations or a recorded history of membership in one of the proscribed right wing CEDA parties; little evidence was adduced and the interrogation reports are short, and in most cases there are no full trial transcripts, only interlocutory documents, asset tracing documents and sentencing documents.

Subsequent to my review of thousands of pages of documentation, I discovered that the diseased body and the infirm mind also constituted fertile sites of resistance within the regimes of the prison and the court. All manner of illnesses, feigned or real, mental and physical were invoked in order to suspend trials and obtain conditional releases.[16] The archives contain thousands of medical reports, doctor's letters, psychiatric evaluations and invalidity certificates. The pathologising gendered medico-legal discourses included 'female psychosis' and 'sexual hysteria' and are worthy of their own separate study.[17] More frequently, the records contained hundreds of instances of malnutrition, tuberculosis, chronic bronchitis or pulmonary emphysema evidencing the severe food shortages and material deprivations at this time.[18] Sympathetic medical, administrative and judicial experts were also important fifth-column collaborators who sought delay or suspend trials on fabricated medical grounds in order to wait out the war.[19]

The legal archives under-represent the confessional aspects of the resistance. The majority of the proceedings examined here were commenced between 1937 and 1939. At this time private religious practice was cautiously tolerated by the authorities, although clandestine religious gatherings were regarded as potential hot-beds of fifth-column subversion and were subject to denunciation by suspicious neighbours. The Republic was keen to repair the damage to international relations caused by the religious persecution of the earliest months. Religion belonged in the private sphere, and the secular authorities were careful not to encroach on this private space during interrogation and cross examination.[20] Perhaps more significantly, very few defendants were willing to further incriminate themselves or their relatives and associates by openly avowing to Catholic beliefs and practices. Consequently, we must look to the Blue Series archives (described below) and to the memory texts for evidence of the religious motivations which often underpinned the political resistance.

The Sección Femenina Blue Series archive

The Sección Femenina (SF) Blue Series forms part of the Asociación de la Nueva Andadura (ANA) archives held in the Real Academia de la Historia (RAH), Madrid.[21] There are few early records because in 1938 most of the documents held in its Salamanca offices were destroyed in a fire.[22] In addition, during the Transition Period (1975–8) many important records relating to the Falange and its Women's Section were transferred into private archives or deliberately destroyed because of fears that the transition to democracy might revive old conflicts and encourage reprisals.[23]

The ANA archives contain a typescript by Pilar Primo de Rivera entitled *Historia de la Sección Femenina.*[24] It was created during or soon after the events, and a serialised version was published in *Revista Y* in fifteen separate instalments between March 1938 and May 1939.[25] It reveals the manifest partisan bias of a political activist who was deeply involved in the politics of the Falange and the Franco regime and who continued to lead the Sección Femenina until its dissolution in April 1977. The typescript evidences women's complicity in dangerous and illegal political activities both prior to and after 18 July 1936.[26] The text contests the official Falangist discourses relating to women's 'natural' predisposition towards 'self-abnegation and submission' and traditional portrayals of Falangist women as meek, submissive, pious and dutiful.[27] Here, Pilar fashions herself and her comrades as committed grassroots activists who were prepared to condone violence and break the law in furtherance of their ideological aims.

The ANA, Serie Azul, Asesoría Jurídica, Carpetas (Files) B-12 and B-18 contain hundreds of legal depositions made pursuant to applications for the prestigious Catholic Queen Isabel "Y" Awards which were bestowed to women in recognition of their 'significant services in aid of Franco's Glorious Movement.' There were three categories of "Y" award (Gold, Silver and Red). Gold was almost exclusively reserved for those who 'died in active service' including María Paz Martínez Unciti and Carmen Tronchoni.[28] The quasi-sacralisation of the Falange's heroic '59 Fallen Women' reinforced new constructions of an elite, committed and and self-sacrificing Falangist female identity.[29] The awards constituted important forms of symbolic and political capital as they conferred official recognition of women's services to the Francoist war effort. The award took material form in a modest "Y" shaped lapel-pin, but its symbolic value was much greater and facilitated positions and preferment in the new regime. In total around 6,000 "Y" awards were bestowed between 1939 and 1945, over 3,000 between 1939 and 1940.[30] This number was high because collective awards were conferred to members of the Regional Divisions, laundry services and nursing units.[31]

The ANA files examined here contain 153 depositions from former members of Auxilio Azul. These women had applied for Silver "Y" Awards and their depositions were sworn at the Sección Femenina's Legal Department (Asesoría Jurídica) between September 1939 and February 1940. Each deposition consisted of an individual hand-written or typed testimony of a few brief and frequently formulaic paragraphs which was signed in the presence of lawyers and ratified by Carina Martínez Unciti, the leader of Auxilio Azul. The awards formed part of an effort to construct a body of ceremonial practice that would reflect the Sección Femenina's new status as an instrument of the state.[32] The testimonies include those of Rafaela de Castro Gutiérrez who was General Secretary of Auxilio Azul,[33] and Carina Martínez Unciti Saiz who was leader until the group's demobilisation in April–May 1939.[34] Another senior member, María del Carmen López Mancisidor, testified that she had helped to compile a comprehensive membership list at the request of her

Group Leader Emilia Martí Melguizo.[35] I was unable to locate these records in the public archives, but they may still be held in a private family archive.[36]

The testimonies constitute the partisan recollections of a self-selected group of politically committed Sección Femenina women. The majority were between eighteen and fifty-five years of age and from middle- or upper-middle-class backgrounds and educated as Catholics.[37] The Y insignia represented useful assets during the repressive and economically catastrophic early 1940s.[38] They bestowed political capital and possibilities for professional preferment within the Sección Femenina and constituted supporting evidence in applications for pensions or compensation from the state.[39] These prestigious awards were distinguished by publication in the *Boletín Oficial del Movimiento* (BOM).[40] After the war former members enjoyed ex-combatant status and its associated privileges including military and civil honours such as the White Cross of Military Merit, the Medal of Suffering for the Nation and pensions.[41] Widows of ex-combatants were also eligible to receive pensions and financial compensation. The symbolic and material rewards afforded by association with the fifth column were significant. However, Clandestine Madrid was a small community, and it was possible to verify who had been active in the fifth column.[42] It would have been a 'high-risk' strategy to volunteer false evidence under oath during the repressive post-war regime, not least because Carina was counter-signatory to every Y application. While it is possible that a minority provided false testimonies, perhaps from motives of fear, peer pressure or the desire for prestige or economic rewards, it may be safe to assume that most of these guarded testimonials retain a measure of truth-value.

The testimonies also represent a site of construction of a new female politico-religious resistance identity. Most are short, impersonal and formulaic and therefore difficult to 'read against the grain.' They do, however, provide ample evidence of a complex hierarchy of Groups, Sub-Groups, code-names and a wide-range of resistance activities.[43] The women deployed a distinctive subaltern gendered rhetoric that simultaneously performed and contested traditional Catholic normative gender discourses surrounding female modesty, self-abnegation and self-sacrifice.[44] These testimonies support the post-war discourses surrounding a national Catholic 'community of suffering' that helped to consolidate and unite the warring factions within the Francoist regime. However, while the Silver Y testimonies examined here form part of a specific Francoist discourse of martyrdom and crusade that came to dominate the official war memory, they are not, in and of themselves. accusatory documents because, while the Republican regime was generally condemned, individual perpetrators were not identified and named.[45]

Memory texts

Little has been written on Catholic and Falangist women's activism either prior to or during the war. Patriarchally determined dispositions of 'self-censorship and self-effacement' informed the memories and self-representations of most Spanish women during this period and reveal the unconscious interiorisation of sexism at this time.[46] The scarcity is also due to a lack of mainstream publishing interest in Catholic and right-wing women in the histories of this period.[47]

Personal testimonies are often dismissed as partisan and unrepresentative: "such documents generally require caution since they can be highly biased; the great majority of the authors are self-serving and motivated by partisan concerns. These authors tend to forget 'non-conformist truths' and substitute rhetoric for reality."[48] Their manifest conviction bias makes them problematic and difficult to work with and through. Consequently, I made less use of these sources than originally anticipated, not least because the scope of this work did not permit a detailed 'multi-voiced' analysis of group memory scripts across the ideological spectrum.[49] Also, there are few works written by ordinary individuals, especially women and young people.[50] Most importantly, a detailed and 'fine-grained' analysis of the collective 'voices' of the 'Red Terror' may have undermined my efforts to achieve a balanced narrative, in particular because these memory texts almost exclusively dwelt on persecution and suffering rather than illegal fifth-column activism.[51]

Pilar Primo de Rivera's official autobiography reflects the distortions of politics on group memory and says very little about the pre-war activism or war-time resistance practices of the Sección Femenina.[52] Similarly, Mercedes Formica's autobiography refers to her membership in the SEU almost in passing, perhaps indicating a desire to underplay an involvement in political subversion.[53] The texts evidence the creation of immutable group memory scripts which exclusively focus on the 'red terror' and the redemptive aspects of 'Crusade' and 'Liberation,' with little regard to the underlying structural and political problems that gave rise to the 'fratricidal' conflict. Rosario Queipo de Llano's narrative dwells on experiences of imprisonment in García Atadell's Checa and in the Alacuas labour camp in Valencia.[54] Herta Björnsen de Wedel (a German Catholic) was arrested for espionage and imprisoned in Ventas between April 1937 and March 1938. She organised asylum and escape-lines for anti-Republicans prior to her arrest in December 1936. However, her narrative dwells on discourses of Republican oppression and memories of imprisonment in Atocha and Ventas prisons rather than on her active role in the fifth column.[55] Mother María Luisa Fernández provides valuable insights into the religious repression of the early months and recalls the spiritual assistance provided by fifth-column women in the prisons.[56] All these works "contribute to a distinctive eschatological discourse relating to the 'Red Terror.'"[57] Comparisons were drawn between Madrid's terror and the Russian revolution in 1917.[58] Rosario Queipo de Llano wrote of the "ferocity of the Spanish *bolcheviques* during a period of massacres and martyrdoms. Humanity will be in awe of such evil and savagery."[59] Even decades after the events, Pilar Primo de Rivera's own unchanging memory scripts continued to represent the extra-judicial repression as the "domination of ideas and practices imported from Russia."[60]

These narratives of victimhood, suffering, martyrdom and redemption formed part of a new Catholic anti-Republican social imaginary which denied the victims of repression any personal or collective agency.[61] The suffering was represented as part of a pre-destined Divine Plan whereby 'Catholic martyrdom' would be redeemed by the 'Nationalist Liberation.' However, despite their manifest ideological bias, historical inaccuracy, class prejudices and hatreds, the memory texts constitute useful source materials because they provide an insight into the disruption of Catholic habitus and the fashioning of (temporary) war-time resistance identities. These formulaic and stylised narratives have been likened to a 'new melodramatic literary genre' which came to constitute a post-war Francoist publishing phenomenon and served to strengthen and consolidate the Franco regime.[62] These memory texts should be considered against more recent and nuanced oral histories that balance narratives of repression during the early months with recollections of peaceful co-existence and accommodation between ideological enemies during thirty-two months of total war in the capital.[63]

In an effort to nuance and contest these Francoist discourses of suffering and abjection, the work demonstrates how Madrid's anti-Republicans were not wholly passive victims and martyrs. Instead, many of the women examined above were effective influencers who exercised forms of informal micro-power and agency. The work also demonstrates how private loyalties and kinship networks frequently cut across the bitter religious and socio-political divisions that were unleashed as a result of the failed military coup.

Secondary sources

While a good deal has now been written on Republican, Catholic and Falangist women, as yet there is still scant historiography on the role played by Nationalist women in the Republican-held zones during the civil conflict.[64] There is also a paucity of general literature on the fifth column,[65] and almost nothing on the women whose efforts facilitated the rise of the fifth column in 1937.[66] A recent collection of articles entitled *Madrid, Una ciudad en guerra* (2016) has highlighted the general lack of historiography on the capital and on the fifth column in particular.[67] Most histories of Madrid focus on repression,[68] or on the Battle of Madrid (November 1936 until March 1937).[69] Much less has been written on the material, social and political conditions in the capital with the exception of Javier Cervera's thesis on political violence in Madrid,[70] which was subsequently published under the title *Madrid en Guerra, La Ciudad Clandestina, 1936–9*.[71] This author argues that Madrid's Clandestine Falange networks were co-ordinated in around spring 1937.[72] The author has also written numerous articles on society, politics and culture in Madrid both prior to and during the war.[73] Francisco Alía Miranda has recently written an informative chapter on the Clandestine Falange in Ciudad Real which contains a good synthetic overview of the operations of the Clandestine Falange in Madrid.[74] Meanwhile, Morten Heiberg and Ros Agudo have written a significant monograph on the Nationalist intelligence services during the Spanish Civil War entitled *La trauma oculta de la guerra civil.*[75] Javier Paniagua and Benjamín Lajo (2002) considered the personal testimonies of the civil servants in Valencia's Town Council who claimed to have been involved in the fifth column.[76] José Luis Alfaya (1998) provides a valuable insight into the operations of the 'Clandestine Church' within the Madrid-Alcalá diocese during the war.[77] The Antonio Luna Group's involvement in the Casado Coup has been examined in recent works by Paul Preston (2016) and Ángel Bahamonde (2014) that focus on the end of the war.[78] See also the article by Manuel Aguilera entitled "La Quinta Columna durante el Golpe de Casado."[79] Most recently Gutmaro Gómez Bravo's new edition entitled *Asedio. Historia de Madrid en la Guerra Civil (1936–1939)* contains a chapter by Carlos Píris on the Francoist intelligence services which highlights continuities between the pre-war underground Traditionalist and Falangist groups and the fifth column during the war.[80]

Very little has been written on fifth-column women, although their resistance efforts facilitated the rise of the fifth column in 1937.[81] *Seis Mil Mujeres* (1965) by the Nationalist author Tomás Borrás offers a hagiographical account of Auxilio Azul using interviews and oral testimonies.[82] The work was commissioned by a Francoist imprint to commemorate Madrid's 'brave and forgotten' women, and the work has sometimes been dismissed by academics on account of its Falangist rhetoric and conviction bias.[83] Nonetheless, established historians such as Javier Cervera and Julius Ruiz have cited it as a valid source. The author's interviews with former Auxilio Azul members constitute valuable albeit highly mediated oral testimony reflecting the collective memory scripts of the participants. An appendix to the work contains photographic evidence of the organisation's Demobilisation Records dated April 1939. *Seis Mil Mujeres* is corroborated by the ANA testimonies and the popular tribunal records discussed above. Much more recently, Sofía López Rodríguez has written a monograph on the Socorro Blanco network in Almería and an article on women, religion and the fifth column in Andalucía.[84] See also her authoritative monograph on the Sección Femenina in Almería between 1937 and 1977.[85] Rodríguez highlights the need to re-evaluate Nationalist women's role in the war effort generally and in particular within the Republican-held rear-guard.[86] Finally, Alberto Laguna and Antonio Vargas have devoted a chapter to Auxilio Azul, also citing Borrás, in a recent general publication on Madrid's fifth column.[87]

Notes

1 Presser, Jacob (1958) *Memoires als gescheidbron* (Winkler Prins Encyclopedie, VIII, Amsterdam and Brussels) pp. 208–210. The English translation cited here is taken from Dekker, R. (ed) (2002) *Ego documents and History: Autobiographical Writing in its Context since the Middle Ages* (Amsterdam: Hilversum), at p. 7 as cited in von Greyerz, Kaspar "Ego-documents: The Last Word?," *German History*, 28 (3) (2010), pp. 273–282 at p. 277. This author provides a concise and accessible summary of the shifts in the research field on ego documents

(including diaries, autobiographies, family, chronicles, travel accounts, letters and legal testimonies) since the 1980s. He summarises the conceptual trajectory from social history to cultural history and 'discourse analysis' during the 1980s, to feminist theories on the possibilities of accessing historical subjective experience as developed by Joan Scott and Judith Butler in the 1990s, to more recent frames by Lois McNay and Lyndal Roper among others that "while trying to avoid the damning reproach of essentialism, have occupied or re-occupied a middle ground between pure constructivism and the evidence of experience offered by their sources," p. 276.

2 Von Geyerz (2010) "Ego-Documents," at pp. 276–277.

3 CDMH, Fondos Contemporáneos, Causa General, Tribunales Populares y Jurados de Urgencia y de Guardia de Madrid, ES.28079.AHN/2.2.6.

4 *Boletín Oficial de España*, 4 May 1940.

5 Serrano Súñer, Ramón (1977) *Entre el silencio y la propaganda, la Historia como fué. Memorias* (Barcelona: Planeta) pp. 244–245, cited in Ruiz, Julius "Seventy Years On: Historians and Repression During and After the Spanish Civil War," *Journal of Contemporary History*, 44 (3) (2009),p. 454.

6 Kalyvas, Stathis (2006) *The Logic of Violence*, p. 393.

7 Gibson, Ian (1983) *Paracuellos: Como fué* (Madrid: Argos), pp. 20–22.

8 Ruiz, Julius (2005) *Franco's Justice, Repression in Madrid after the Spanish Civil War* (Oxford: OUP), pp. 3–5, Vincent, Mary "Religious Violence in the Spanish Civil War," in Ealham, Chris and Richards, Michael (eds) (2005) *The Splintering of Spain, Cultural History and the Spanish Civil War, 1936–1939* (Cambridge: CUP), p. 74.

9 e.g. *Testimonio del Fiscal Secretario de la pieza segunda de particulares del procedimiento sumarismo de urgencia no. 1549 seguido por la Jurisdicción Militar Nacional contra Ángel Pedrero García, jefe del Servicio de Investigación Militar* (SIM), FC-CAUSA_GENERAL, 1520 Exps. 2 y 3 dated 12 May 1942.

10 See for example Pastor Petit, Domènec (2006) *Traidors a Catalunya, La cinquena columna (1936–9)* (Barcelona: Base).
Pastor Petit, Domènec (2013) *Resistencia y sabotaje en la Guerra Civil* (Barcelona: Enigma).

11 See "Enseñar a mentir," in Tarín Iglesias, Manuel (1985) *Los años rojos, Un testimonio capital sobre la Quinta Columna en zona republican durante la guerra civil* (Barcelona: Planeta), pp. 63–66.

12 PARES, CDMH, Archivo Historico Nacional, Instituciones Contemporaneas, 2.2, Poder Judicial "*Tribunales Populares y Jurados de Urgencia y de Guardia de Madrid*," ES.28079. AHN/2.2.6.

13 CDMH, Fondos Contemporáneos, Causa General, Tribunales Populares y Jurados de Urgencia y de Guardia de Madrid, ES.28079.AHN/2.2.6.

14 ES.28079.AHN/2.2.6. Sources: The percentages in relation to treason, espionage and defeatism are approximated because the website filter engine duplicates findings, so that, for example, cases of espionage are also retrieved as cases of treason. The crime of defeatism is included as a form of treason.

15 Cervera, Javier (1998) *Madrid en Guerra la Ciudad Clandestina, 1936-1939* (Madrid; Alianza) at pp. 196–197.

16 See oral testimony of Dolores Muñoz Tuero in an undated interview with Borrás (1965), pp. 201–208 at pp. 202–204.

17 *Causa 1615 instruida contra Enriqueta Mariateguí Rollán por el delito/s de Espionaje*, AHN, FC-CAUSA_GENERAL,198, Exp. 14. Imágenes 8/52. *Auto* dated 9 September 1937.

18 See for example Medical Letter into Court dated 2 May 1938 requesting a transfer for Manuel Albarán Ordoñez aged fifty-three years to 'a place in the countryside with space and air to convalesce,' *Sumario no 81/1938 del Juzgado Especial por espionaje y otros delitos contra la seguridad exterior del Estado contra Antonio Rodríguez Aguado y otros*, AHN, FC-CAUSA_GENERAL, 1540, Exp. 1, Imagen 1727/1805.

19 Ángel Bahamonde has identified "an abundance of false medical certificates which were certified by Madrid's military medical tribunals which were presided over by Lt. Colonels Antonio Jiménez Arrieta, Clodoaldo Padilla Casas and Emilio Romero Maldonado who

formed part of the Clandestine Falange" in Bahamonde, Ángel (2016) *Madrid, 1939, La conjura del coronel Casado* (Madrid: Cátedra), Kindle ed. at Loc 1510 of 3765. See also Ellwood, Sheelagh "Entrevista con Dolores Muñoz Tuero "Los tribunales populares fueron buena gente," in *Guerra Civil de Historia 16, "Sociedad y Guerra" vol 14* (1986), pp. 125–129 at p. 126.

20 I am grateful to Professor Mary Vincent for these observations.

21 ANA was an official association of veterans of the Sección Femenina created after the dissolution of the organisation in 1977. The ANA association was dissolved in 2006 and its offices were closed. The ANA Archives were transferred to RAH in 2007.

22 Gallego (1983) *Mujer, Falange y Franquismo*, p. 53.

23 Blasca (1997) *Armas Femeninas*, p. 18.

24 *Historia de la Sección Femenina por Pilar Primo de Rivera, Libro Primero, Primera Parte* (undated typescript), ANA, Carpeta 1-B, RAH, Madrid.

25 Sections of the typescript were reproduced in *Y, Revista de la mujer nacional –sindicalista*, between January 1938 and May 1939. See Vincent, Mary "Chapter 12, Spain," in Passmore, Kevin (ed) (2003) *Women Gender and Fascism in Europe* (Manchester: MUP), p. 209.

26 *Historia de la Sección Femenina por Pilar Primo de Rivera, Libro Primero, Primera Parte* (typescript), ANA, Carpeta 1-B, RAH, Madrid.

27 Gallego (1983) *Mujer*, p. 34.

28 *Asesoría Jurídica*, Report on Carmen Tronchoni, Document 7, ANA, Carpeta B 18, RAH, Madrid.

29 A recent commemorative work identifies sixty-three female victims of Republican repression. See Sánchez Blanco, Laura (2016) *Rosas y Margaritas, Mujeres falangistas, tradicionalistas y de Acción Católica asesinadas en la Guerra Civil.* See also Ofer, Inbal, "Historical Models. Contemporary Identities: The Sección Femenina of the Spanish Falange and its Redefinition of the Term 'Femininity,'" *Journal of Contemporary History*, 40 (4) (2005), at p. 666.

30 Biganne "The Rewards of Female Fascism," at p. 1315.

31 e.g. the Sección Femenina of Medina del Campo was granted a collective Silver "Y" on 16 November 1939. See Declaration dated 16 November 1939, Document RSA:1095, ANA, Carpeta B 12, RAH, Madrid.

32 Richmond, Kathleen (2003) *Women and Spanish Fascism: The Women's Section of the Falange 1934–1959* (London: Routledge), p. 40.

33 *Asesoría Jurídica*, Testimony of Rafaela de Castro Gutiérrez dated 6 November 1939, Document 143, ANA, Carpeta B 12, RAH, Madrid. She joined the Falange in June 1936.

34 *Asesoría Jurídica*, Testimony of Carina Martínez Unciti dated 1 February 1940, Document 95, ANA, Carpeta B 12, RAH, Madrid.

35 *Asesoría Jurídica*, Testimony of María del Carmen López Mancisidor Solano dated 6 October 1939, Document 201, ANA, Carpeta B 12, RAH, Madrid.

36 Barrachina, Marie Aline "La section féminine et ses paradoxes (1934–1977)," in Marie Aline Barrachina, Danièle Bussy Genevois and Mercedes Yusta (eds) (2007) *Femmes et Democratie, les Espagnoles dans l'éspace public (1868–1978)* (Paris: Éditions du Temps), at p. 147.

37 See Chapter I "Childhood in Old Spain (1906–1923)," in de la Mora, Constancia (1939) *In Place of Splendor* (New York, NY: Harcourt Brace & Co), pp. 3–52. This author was the sister of the senior Falangist Marichu de la Mora Maura. Here she recounted her traditional upper-middle-class Catholic upbringing.

38 Biganne, Julia "The Rewards of Female Fascism in Franco's New State: The Recompensas Y of the Sección Femenina de la Falange, 1939–45," *Bulletin of Spanish Studies*, XC (8) (2013), pp. 1313–1337, at p. 1317.

39 *Asesoría Jurídica*, Testimony of Isabel Arroyo Pertasse dated 4 October 1939, Document 202, ANA, Carpeta B 12, RAH, Madrid. This operative was known by the code name 1-K-2 during the war. She began voluntary work for Madrid's Auxilio Social in April 1939 and was one of a few women who were promoted to salaried employee status from May to October 1939.

40 e.g. A collective Silver "Y" award was granted to all the Sección Femenina members of Medina del Campo. A notice of this award was published in BOM. Source: *Asesoría Jurídica*, Declaration, dated 16 November 1939, Document RSA: 1095, ANA, Carpeta B 12, RAH, Madrid.

41 Heiberg and Ros Agudo (2006) *La Trama*, p. 194.

42 e.g. *Asesoría Jurídica*, Certificate dated 1939, Document 294, ANA, Carpeta B 12, RAH, Madrid. The Auxilio Azul Group Leader María Carmen Timmermans made a sworn declaration to the effect that Mercedes Pagés López Guerrero was a member of Auxilio Azul.

43 "Emotional regimes" and "emotives" are conceptualised in Reddy, William (2001) *The Navigation of Feeling, A Framework for the History of Emotions* (Cambridge: CUP). In particular, see Chapter 3 "Emotional Expression as a Type of Speech Act," at pp. 63–111. See also Jan Plamper "The History of Emotions: an interview with William Reddy, Barbara Rosenwein and Peter Stearns," *History and Theory*, 49 (May 2010), pp. 237–265.

44 See Kebadze, Ninno "The Right to be Selfless and Other Prerogatives of the Weak in the Rhetoric of the Sección Femenina," *Romance Quarterly*, 55 (2) (2008), pp. 109–127. See also Gahete Muñoz, Soraya (2015) "La Sección Femenina de Falange. Discursos y Practicas en Madrid," *Arenal*, 22 (2) (July–December 2015), pp. 389–411 at p. 402.

45 Richards, Michael (ed) (2013) *After the Civil War, Making Memory and Re-Making Spain since 1936* (New York, NY: CUP), ebook p. 41. Also, see section on 'Sacred and performative memory' at pp. 103–105. These observations are limited to the Silver Y testimonies, for in some of the more detailed 'Gold Y' testimonies (relating to women 'killed in action') the perpetratros are sometimes identified and named.

46 Similar observations are made about resistance women in France on both the Left and the Right in Andrieu, Claire "Les résistantes, perspectives de récherche," in Prost (ed) (1997) *La Résistance*, pp. 91–93. Similar forms of 'ego-atrophy' have been identified in Italian resistance women, see Richet, Isabelle "Women and Antifascism, Historiographical and Methodological Approaches," in García, Hugo, Yusta, Mercedes et al. (eds) (2016) *Rethinking Antifascism, History, Memory and Politics, 1922 to Present* (Oxford: Berghahn), ebook Loc 3972 of 9519.

47 The scarcity of memory-texts has been noted in Tavera García, Susanna "Las mujeres de la Sección Falange: Una afirmación entre el activismo político y la sumisión patriarcal, 1934–1939," in Ana Aguado and Teresa Ma. Ortega (eds) (2011) *Feminismos y antifeminismos, Culturas, políticas e identitdades de genero en las España del Siglo XX* (Valencia: PUV), pp. 207–228 at pp. 209–210.

48 See "Memoires, Autobiographies, Local Histories," in Kalyvas (2008), pp. 410-411.

49 According to Portelli, it is important to consider bearers of both right-wing and left-wing memory, "especially young people, not just in the name of some abstract notion of pluralism, but because they have information and experiences that I could not have tapped otherwise." See Portelli, Alessandro (2003) *The order has been carried out* (London: Palgrave), at p. 17.

50 There are very few children's memory texts with the notable exception of Barceló, José Luis (2012) *Madrid 1938, Diario de un niño en guerra* (Málaga: Sepha) and Duyagües, Pilar (Balló, Tania and Berger, Gonzalo eds) (2003) *Querido Diario: Hoy ha empezado la guerra* (Barcelona: Espasa).

51 A recent work on the construction and consolidation of power during early Francoism has attempted such an analysis, see Rodríguez Barreira, Óscar (2013) *Miserias del poder, Los poderes locales y el nuevo estado franquista, 1936–51* (Valencia: PUV).

52 Primo de Rivera, Pilar (1983) *Recuerdos de una vida* (Dyrsa: Madrid), at pp. 59–79.

53 Fórmica, Mercedes (2013) *Memorias, visto y vivido, escucho el silencio (1931–1947)* (Seville. Renacimiento), p. 180.

54 Queipo de Llano, Rosario (1939) *De la cheka de Atadell a la prisión de Alacuas* (Valladolid: Santarén).

55 Björnsen de Wedel, Herta (1941) *La Carcel de Ventas* (Madrid: Águilar).

56 Mother María Luisa Fernández and Mother María Leturia (1939) *Catorce meses de aventuras bajo el dominio rojo* (Rome: ACI).

57 This work analyses the prison experiences of anti-Republican and Republican women during the war and in the post-war, see Hernández Holgado, Fernando (2003) *Mujeres encarceladas, La prisión de Ventas: de la república al franquismo, 1931–41* (Madrid: Marcial Pons), p. 93.

58 See also Foxá, Augustín (2001) *Madrid de Corte a Checa* (Madrid: Bibliotex), pp. 275–276, Borrás (1965), pp. 7–8 and Schlayer, Félix (2001) *Diplomático en el Madrid Rojo* (Madrid: Espuela de Plata), pp. 42–43.

59 Queipo de Llano (1939) *De la cheka*, p. 51.

60 Primo de Rivera, Pilar (1983) *Recuerdos*, p. 76. In fact, Stalinist infiltration within Republican governmental, administrative and military structures was highly disorganised and ultimately ineffective, see Kowalsky, Daniel (2004) *Stalin and the Spanish Civil War* (New York: Columbia University Press).

61 Rodríguez López, Sofía and Oscar Rodríguez Barreira "La Quinta Columna y la Guerra Civil en Andalucía," *Andalucía en la Historia*, 46 (October–December 2014), pp. 72–77 at p. 72.

62 García, Hugo "War and culture in Nationalist Spain, 1936–9: Testimony and Fiction in the narrative of the 'Red Terror'" (transl. Neil Harman), *Journal of War and Culture Studies*, 2 (3) (2009), pp. 289–304.

63 Montoliú, Pedro (1999) *Madrid en la guerra civil, Los protagonisas, Volumen II* (Madrid: Silex). See for example Oral Testimony Marcial González Bonet dated 10 June 1996, Montoliú, Pedro (1999) *Madrid en la*. See also, Duyagües, Pilar (Balló, Tania and Berger, Gonzalo eds) (2003) *Querido Diario: Hoy ha empezado la guerra* (Barcelona: Espasa). This rare testimonial of a fifteen-year-old Republican girl in Barcelona reflects the importance of cinema in the daily lives, routines and imaginations of many ordinary citizens during the war.

64 Notable exceptions are Rodríguez López, Sofía and Oscar Rodríguez Barreira "La Quinta Columna y la Guerra Civil en Andalucía," *Andalucía en la Historia*, 46 (October–December 2014), Rodríguez López, Sofía (2010) *El patio de la cárcel, La Sección Femenina de FET-JONS en Almería (1937–77)* (Seville: CEA), Rodríguez López, Sofía (2008) *Quintacolumnistas*.

65 See Chapter 8 "¿Una Quinta Columna?," in Ruiz (2012) *El Terror, Madrid, 1936* (Barcelona: Espasa), pp. 215–229. Also, most recently Laguna Reyes, Alberto and Vargas Márquez, Antonio (2019) *La Quinta Columna, La guerra clandestina tras las líneas republicanas 1936–1939* (Madrid: Laesfera).

66 Ruiz, Julius (2012) *El Terror*, p. 238.

67 Chapter 8, Ruiz (2012), also Oviedo Silva, Daniel, Pérez-Olivares García, Alejandro (eds) (2016) *Madrid, una ciudad en guerra (1936–48)* (Madrid: Catarata).

68 See Ruiz, Julius (2012), Ledesma, José Luis (2003) *Los días de llamas de la revolución* (Zaragoza: IFC) and Espinosa Maestre (ed) (2010) *Violencia Roja y Azul, España, 1936–1950* (Barcelona: Crítica) and Prieto Borrego, Lucía (2013) *Los días de la ira. Entre Mijas y el Guadiaro, de la República a la Sierra* (Málaga: UCM) and Prieto, Borrego "El terror rojo en la Causa General de Casares," *Baetica*, 22 (2000), pp. 525–545. This author has written twenty-six articles and eighteen collaborative papers on the Civil War and early Francoism in Andalucía, see http://dialnet.unirioja.es, Anderson, Peter and del Arco Blanco, Miguel Ángel (eds) (2015) *Mass Killings and Violence in Spain, 1936–1952: Grappling with the Past* (New York, NY: Routledge).

69 Reverte, Jorge (2004) *La Batalla de Madrid* (Madrid: Crítica).

70 Cervera, Javier (1996) *Violencia política y acción clandestina: La retaguardia de Madrid en Guerra 1936–9* (Universidad Complutense de Madrid: Work), pp. 368–398. http://eprints.ucm.es/2456/1/T21383.pdf [last accessed 16 June 2018].

71 Cervera, Javier (1998) *Madrid*, p. 236, pp. 235–222 and pp. 283–294. See also Cervera, Javier (second ed) (2006) *Madrid en Guerra, La Ciudad Clandestina 1936–9* (Madrid: Alianza). The second edition is substantively the same as the first. See also the earlier Núñez de Prado y Clavell, Sara (1992) *Servicios de información y propaganda en la Guerra Civil española, 1936–1939* (Madrid: UCM).

72 Cervera (1998) *Madrid*, p. 290.
73 Cervera, Javier "La Quinta Columna en la retaguardia republicana en Madrid," *Historia, Antropología, Fuentes Orales*, 17, *Tiempos de Transformaciones* (1997), pp. 93–110.
74 See Chapter 9 "La Quinta Columna," in Alía Miranda, Francisco (2017) *La Guerra Civil en Ciudad-Real, conflicto y revolución en una provincia de la retaguardia Republicana* (Ciudad Real: BAM), pp. 319–338.
75 Heiberg and Agudo (2006) *La Trama*, at pp. 183–195.
76 Paniagua, Javier and Lajo Cosido, Benjamín (2002) *Sombras en la retaguardia: Testimonios sobre la 5a Columna en Valencia* (Madrid: Francisco Tomás y Valiente).
77 Alfaya, José Luis (1998) *Como un río de fuego, Madrid, 1936* (Barcelona: EIU).
78 Preston, Paul (2016) *The Last Days of the Spanish Republic* (London: William Collins), Bahamonde, Ángel (2014) *Madrid, 1939* (Madrid: Catedra). See also Bahamonde, Ángel, Cervera, Javier (1999) *Así Terminó la Guerra de España* (Madrid: Marcial Pons) and Alía Miranda, Francisco (2015) *La agonía de la República: el final de la Guerra Civil española (1938–1939)* (Barcelona: Crítica).
79 Aguilera, Manuel "La Quinta Columna durante el Golpe de Casado," *Aportes*, 69 (XXIV) (1/2009), pp. 99–111.
80 See Píris "Los servicios de información Franquistas en la capital," p. 139. Oviedo Silva, Daniel, Pérez-Olivares García, Alejandro (eds) (2016) *Madrid, una ciudad en guerra (1936–48)* (Madrid: Catarata), p. 11. Gómez Bravo, Gutmaro (ed) (2018) *Asedio. Historia de Madrid en la guerra civil (1936–9)* (Madrid: UCM), p. 11.
81 Ruiz (2012), p. 238.
82 Borrás, Tomás (1965) *Seis Mil Mujeres* (Madrid: Editora Nacional). Borrás (1891–1976) was a nationalist journalist and writer who wrote for *Fígaro, La Tribuna, Nuevo Mundo, El Sol, La Voz, ABC, Blanco y Negro.* He also wrote numerous novels, plays and histories including Borrás (2016) *Las Checas de Madrid* (Madrid: Escolar y Mayo).
83 See for example, Gahete Muñoz, Soraya "La Sección Femenina de Falange. Discursos y Prácticas en Madrid," *Arenal*, 22 (2) (July–December 2015), pp. 389–411.
84 Rodríguez López, Sofía (2008) *Quintacolumnistas, Las mujeres del 36 en la clandestinidad almeriense* (Almería: IEA), Rodríguez López, Rodríguez Barreira "La Quinta Columna…", pp. 72–77.
85 Rodríguez López, Sofía (2010) *El patio de la carcel, La Sección Femenina de FET-JONS en Almería* (Seville: CEA).
86 Rodríguez López, Sofía and Cazorla Sánchez, Antonio "Blue Angels: Female Fascist Resisters, Spies and Intelligence Officials in the Spanish Civil War, 1936–9," *Journal of Contemporary History*, 53 (4) (2016), pp. 692–713.
87 Laguna Reyes, Alberto and Vargas Márquez, Antonio (2019) *La Quinta Columna, La guerra clandestina tras las líneas republicanas 1936–1939* (Madrid: Laesfera).

Index

Printed in Great Britain
by Amazon

47524020R00159